THE FLORID

MW00711843

PUBLIC POLICY MANAGEMENT SYSTEM

GROWTH AND REFORM IN AMERICA'S FOURTH LARGEST STATE

SECOND EDITION

Editor

Richard Chackerian

Reubin O'D. Askew School of Public Administration and Policy
Florida State University

Foreword

by

Reubin O'D. Askew

Department of Public Administration
Reubin O'D. Askew School of Public Administration and Policy
Florida State University

Contributors

Reubin O'D. Askew
Robert B. Bradley
Richard Chackerian
Robert E. Crew, Jr.
Richard C. Feiock
David S. Ferguson
Gloria A. Grizzle
Marsha Hosack
William Earle Klay
John B. Phelps

Benjamin E. "Woody" Price
Richard K. Scher
Jack M. Schluckebier
Frank P. Sherwood
Joanne R. Snair
Lance deHaven-Smith
William B. Tankersley
Augustus B. Turnbull, III
Vivian Zaricki

Reubin O'D. Askew School of Public Administration and Policy
and Florida Center for Public Management/Tallahassee

KENDALL/HUNT PUBLISHING COMPANY
4050 Westmark Drive   Dubuque, Iowa 52002

CONTENTS

FIGURES

FIGURES

TABLES

TABLES

FOREWORD
by
Reubin O'D. Askew

As the number, size, and complexity of our governments grow, much greater attention must be given to how policies are implemented. In recent years there has been a flood of legislation in response to our growing social and economic problems. Recognizing the importance of legislative initiatives, it also is important to acknowledge that new policies alone do not solve the public's problems. We must begin to appreciate more fully that policies are not self executing; they do not put themselves into effect. How polices are implemented is an essential part of the effort to make changes in our condition.

Several books written on Florida government have made important contributions to understanding the policy management system in Florida's governments. Manning Dauer's classic, but now dated, *Florida's Politics and Government* is widely read and provides valuable insight into Florida's political system. The more recently published text by Robert J. Huskshorn, *Government and Politics in Florida*, also is a significant contribution.

However, the last serious book on implementing public policy in Florida is the 1954 text, *The Government and Administration of Florida*, written by Wilson K. Doyle, my mentor and former dean, and his colleagues. In the forty-four years between Doyle's book and this one, Florida has been transformed from a modest-sized Southern state to America's fourth largest. An assessment of where we stand and what needs to be done with our systems for implementing public policy is long overdue. It is no secret that the public and many civil servants do not trust the capacity of Florida's governments to be effective and efficient. That the systems for policy management are floundering also is not a secret. This book, of course, will not solve these problems, but it will elevate the debate over what should be done to make Florida's governments better.

FOREWORD

Several features of this book merit particular attention and praise. First, each substantive chapter develops the historical background of the subject. In our rush to change how things are done, we may forget that they have a history and a range of experience that can be the source of insight. Additionally, the historical material is important because Florida is in many respects unique in its social, political, and economic background. The experience of other states can be valuable, but it must be adjusted to account for Florida's pattern of development.

A second feature of the book that merits attention is that a brief discussion of local governments have been included, particularly the relations between local and the state governments. There is no claim that local governments are treated comprehensively, but they are seen as a critical part of the larger policy management system. In the era of decentralization, from the federal to state governments, these relations are particularly important.

Thirdly, a serious attempt is made to present a comprehensive picture of the policy management system which does not shy away from its complexity. At the same time the book provides an understandable and useful framework for making sense out of the complexity. The reasons why it is difficult to achieve results in the Florida system is clarified because of this comprehensive treatment.

I welcome the second edition of this text, particularly perhaps, because I found the first edition very useful in my own Florida Government class. The second edition contains a vast array of updated material which will allow interested parties to develop an understanding of the latest issues in our ever-changing Florida government.

Reubin O'D. Askew
Tallahassee
1998

PREFACE TO THE SECOND EDITION

This book is the product of many discussions with academic colleagues and leaders of Florida's governments. In these conversations there was, nearly to a person, agreement that Floridians need to know more about their governments, particularly what happens after legislation is adopted. Their reluctance to become more involved and to support a reasonable level of taxation is rooted in a variety of factors, but a critical element is that many Floridians have little understanding of government institutions and how these institutions implement policy. It is conceded that government in Florida is not easily understood.

The need to know more extends to many public servants. Some of the same conditions that affect citizens' attitudes and behavior also affect those who run governments in Florida. They may be familiar with the basic elements of the federal government or even those of their "home" state. But, they often are educated in other states and never had the opportunity to acquire an overview of Florida's governmental and administrative systems.

What type of book will best serve these audiences? Part of the answer depends on the state of the research literature. It is extraordinary how little of a scholarly nature has been published on Florida government. The literature in journals is skimpy. This makes it virtually impossible to write a text in the normal sense of the term. Textbooks are codifications of the existing research literature. If that literature is scarce, there is an inadequate basis for a fully developed, fully integrated text. On the other hand, there is a need, as suggested above, for a general treatment of Florida's governments. The compromise that this book represents is original essays by authors who are familiar with the available literature, but who also are directly knowledgeable of specialized aspects of Florida government and administration.

PREFACE

The seventeen chapters cover a wide range of topics, but there is an emphasis that carries on a tradition initiated over forty years ago at the School of Public Administration, Florida State University. The last Florida government text which placed an emphasis on policy management was written by Wilson K. Doyle and his colleagues. Doyle was the dean of the School of Public Administration. The current book also is authored, primarily but not exclusively, by people associated with Florida State University's Askew School of Public Administration and Policy, the descendant of the school where Doyle served as dean.

Many helped in making this book possible. For the first edition thanks are due to Diana Reynolds and Barbara Judd for editorial assistance. Ms. Reynolds was also responsible for putting the manuscript into production and was responsive beyond any reasonable expectation to requests for changes in the manuscript. Ann Moseley Shuford typed with competence and good humor though the multiple drafts and floppy disks misplaced by the editor. Jay Hakes made valuable suggestions for revisions in the manuscript's overall structure and content. Various graduate assistants knowingly and unknowingly help with the project, but the efforts of Jill Tao merit special recognition. The idea for such a book came originally from Frank Sherwood who subsequently contributed to its content as well as financial support from the Jerry Collins Endowed Scholar Chair which he is now retired. For the second edition, Clint Fuhrman was very helpful in putting materials together. In addition, the second edition of the book would not have been possible without the financial support of the Florida Institute of Government, its Director, Scott Daley and its Associate Director, Lance deHaven-Smith. Their support is deeply appreciated.

Richard Chackerian
Tallahassee
1998

CONTRIBUTORS

REUBIN O'D. ASKEW

Reubin Askew is Professor of Public Administration at Florida State University, and Senior Fellow at the Florida Institute of Government. In addition, he is a fellow of the National Academy of Public Administration and Chairman of the Board of Trustees of the Collins Center for Public Policy. He was governor of Florida from 1971–79.

ROBERT B. BRADLEY

Dr. Bradley is currently the Director of the Institute of Science and Public Affairs at Florida State University. He was Director of the Governor's Office of Planning and Budgeting. He has served as Associate Professor of Political Economy at the University of Texas at Dallas, Executive Director of the Florida Advisory Council on Intergovernmental Relations and Executive Director of Florida's Constitutional Commission on Taxation and Budget Reform. He has published studies on a range of topics including contemporary political economy, urban politics, state and local government fiscal affairs, and planning.

RICHARD CHACKERIAN

Richard Chackerian is Professor of Public Administration and Policy at Florida State University and Director of the Ph.D. program in the Askew School of Public Administration and Policy. His primary interest is organization change in the States.

ROBERT E. CREW, JR.

Bob Crew is Associate Dean of the College of Social Sciences and a member of the faculty in the Askew School of Public Administration and Policy at Florida State University. His academic interests are American state politics, public management, political leadership, and criminal justice policy.

RICHARD C. FEIOCK

Richard Feiock is a political scientist specializing in state and local political economy, and presently is a Professor of Public Administration and Policy at Florida State University. His work on local growth policy has appeared in leading journals including *American Journal of Political Science, Political Research Quarterly, Journal of Politics,* and *Social Science Quarterly.* He is co-editor, with Jerry Mitchell, of *Policy Tools for Local Economic Development* from Greenwood Press.

DAVID S. FERGUSON

David Ferguson graduated from Roanoke College in Salem, Virginia, in 1957. He has more than 30 years of personnel experience with private enterprise, state and local governments. Presently, he is Personnel Resource Management Officer for the Florida Department of Transportation.

GLORIA A. GRIZZLE

Gloria Grizzle is Professor in the Askew School of Public Administration and Policy at Florida State University. She does research and teaches in public financial management, policy analysis, and program evaluation.

MARSHA HOSACK

Marsha Hosack is the Executive Director of the Legislative Committee on Intergovernmental Relations, previously known as the Florida Advisory Council on Intergovernmental Relations. Formerly, she was Chief Analyst with the Florida Senate Committee on Governmental Reform and Oversight and Staff Director of the Senate Committee on Governmental Operations. She received her B.A. in 1973 and her M.S. in 1978 from Florida State University.

WILLIAM EARLE KLAY

Earle Klay is Professor and Director of the Askew School of Public Administration and Policy at Florida State University. He was a Senior Governmental Associate in Florida's Executive Office of the Governor and has been an advisor on futures thinking, strategic planning, and policy development for Florida's Legislature and Supreme Court.

John B. Phelps

John Phelps has served as Clerk of the Florida House of Representatives since 1986. He has been the House Deputy Clerk, Staff Director of the Committee on Rules and Calendar, Executive Assistant to the Speaker, and Legislative Policy Analyst. He also has been President of the American Society of Legislative Clerks and Secretaries as well as Chairman of the International Task Force of the National Conference of State Legislatures.

Benjamin E. "Woody" Price

Woody Price is Associate Director of the Florida Center for Public Management at Florida State University. As a member of the American Institute of Certified Planners, he has managed development for more than 16 years as Division Director for the Florida Department of Community Affairs, Deputy County Administrator and Planning Director for Seminole County (Florida), and Director of Research for the East Central Florida Regional Planning Council.

Richard K. Scher

Richard Scher is Professor of Political Science at the University of Florida. He is a recognized specialist in Florida and southern politics, and has published extensively on governors. His most recent book is *Politics in the New South*. Scher's forthcoming books include works on voting rights and modern political campaigns.

Jack M. Schluckebier

Jack Schluckebier serves as City Manager of Casselberry, Florida. He has served as City Manager for more than 10 years in cities in Michigan and Florida. He holds an M.A. degree and a Ph.D. in Public Administration from Florida State University. His interests include local government leadership and public budgeting/finance.

Frank P. Sherwood

Frank Sherwood is an emeritus professor of Public Administration at Florida State University, where he had been on the faculty since 1982. He is a Fellow of the National Academy of Public Administration, elected in 1969, and a former president of the American Society for Public Administration. He has had special interests in human resources management and development in Florida.

JOANNE R. SNAIR

Joanne R. Snair is a management consultant specializing in organization change and budget issues.

LANCE deHAVEN-SMITH

Lance deHaven-Smith is Professor in the Reubin O'D. Askew School of Public Administration and Policy at Florida State University, and Associate Director of the Florida Institute of Government. He received his Ph.D. from Ohio State University in 1980. Dr. deHaven-Smith is the author of six books, one of which won the Manning Dauer Prize for scholarship from the University of Florida. He has written widely on Florida politics and has conducted extensive research at every level of Florida government. In 1995, he served as Staff Director of the Citizens' Commission on Cabinet Reform, which evaluated the decision-making structure of Florida's executive branch.

WILLIAM B. TANKERSLEY

Bill Tankersley is Associate Professor of Public Administration at the University of West Florida. His professional experience includes practice as a certified public accountant, staff analyst for a consulting engineering firm, and regulatory analyst for the Florida Public Service Commission.

AUGUSTUS B. TURNBULL, III

Gus Turnbull, deceased, was Professor of Public Administration and Policy and Vice President for Academic Affairs at Florida State University. His scholarly interests included public budgeting and legislative processes.

VIVIAN ZARICKI

Vivian Zaricki is Executive Director of the Florida Association of Counties. She also is a policy council member of the Florida Institute of Government; member of the International City and County Managers Association; member of the interim steering committee of the Florida State Rural Development Council; and a member of the Rural Economic Development Initiative.

INTRODUCTION

The contributors to this book share a common interest in public policy and how it is managed after it has been formally adopted by the legislature. The organization of the book and its title reflect these interests: *The Florida Public Policy Management System: Growth and Reform in America's Fourth Largest State.* The title also reflects several assumptions that guided the organization of the book. The first, with which many may take issue, is that indeed there is a system. The assumption is not, of course, that there is a rational system, but only that there are a large number of interrelated institutions and processes, and that sense can be made of these elements. The political and social environment and state and local government institutions form a complex web of interests, actions, and cultures that have an influence on one another and produce important consequences for citizens. The second major assumption is that the policy management system is best understood in historical context. Social and political environments evolve and have important consequences for the nature of policy management institutions and processes. Historical influences are important considerations in Florida which has seen dramatic social and economic transformations.

Part I provides the analytical framework for the book. It also describes the broad architecture of the policy management system. In Chapter 1 Richard Chackerian sketches the historical development of governmental institutions in Florida since the Civil War and concludes that they have experienced significant reform under extraordinary social and economic pressures. The process of reform, however, is seen to be far from complete. "Local governments are at once deprived of central state leadership, while at the same time not given enough autonomy to solve problems on their own accord." On the other hand, he also concludes that "while Florida's institutional arrangements in fact badly lag the needs of the state, the environmental conditions which are so important for supporting and accepting change are largely in place." More

1

generally he concludes that "Florida . . . can be regarded as having some of the features of a developing state. It is a place where loyalties and commitments to state purposes are not strongly held and the public institutions not well shaped for public leadership. These conditions in turn are plausibly related to rapid cumulative changes, a rather weak tax base, and a tradition of failure to innovate."

Chapter 2, also by Richard Chackerian, describes current state government institutions responsible for making and implementing public policy. To make sense of these complex and highly disaggregated organizations, he finds it necessary to construct a functional typology. This conceptual experiment suggests that most of what state government does can be lumped into the following functional categories: (1) providing goods and services to citizens; (2) providing strategic direction; (3) providing technical support; and (4) providing administrative support. Examples of each type of organization are provided.

Part II focuses on the sources of external support and constraint on policy management. The external political environment as well as the legislature, governor, and cabinet are major forces providing strategic leadership and at the same time shape the policy management process and outcomes. Robert Crew, in Chapter 3, discusses the political environment. He traces the changes in the political environment, but concludes these have not had a dramatic impact on the conduct of political activities. "The dramatic social and demographic changes that have occurred in Florida in the twentieth century have had a modifying effect on selected elements of the Florida political environment. This upheaval has not created serious chasms in the basic contours of this environment." The only important change has been the proliferation of interest groups, a development which does not bode well for those in positions of strategic leadership who would like to integrate governmental institutions and policy. The disaggregation of the political environment is a natural complement of disaggregated government institutions.

Richard Scher focuses, in Chapter 4, on the governor and cabinet, the latter an institution unique in the 50 states. After reviewing the major types of influences on the governor's ability to act as a policy leader and manager and the varying ways Florida's governors have responded to these influences, Scher assesses the impact of the cabinet system. He comes to two somewhat surprising conclusions. The first is that the cabinet is not an important source of policy. The cabinet reacts to the initiatives of the governor and others; it doesn't have its own policy agenda. Second, the cabinet may actually help the governor's policy agenda rather than block his initiatives. "It is so fractured among its various roles that it can do little more than ratify decisions considered by the governor, legislature, bureaucracies, local government officials, and interest groups. It can also manage and oversee decisions made, if it chooses to invest the time and resources needed to do so. The problem is that it has not always shown a willingness to commit the necessary resources to carry out this purpose. . . ."

Augustus B. Turnbull III and John Phelps, in Chapter 5, discuss the role of the legislature in policy and administrative processes. In addition to documenting the very complicated structure of the legislature, they sketch the historical growth of its administrative apparatus and the impact this has had on administrative oversight. These general points are illustrated with two detailed cases covering the role of the legislature in higher education and human services.

Part III is a review of the most critical systems for implementing policy. The state bureaucracy, the people who run it, and the economic resources needed. Many of the themes introduced in prior sections are played out in greater detail. Common threads are changes in the social and economic environment, the essentially conservative posture toward institutional change and government, and the growing gap between institutional capacity and citizen needs.

Richard Chackerian, in Chapter 6, discusses the historical development of the state bureaucracy and attempts to reform it, paying particular attention to the reforms of 1968 and of 1990 to 1997. He concludes that "In some respects the [1968] reorganization of state government was a watershed in both the politics and administration of state government. The rapid growth and urbanization of the state was now reflected in the composition of the legislature. The reorganized state government, while certainly not the model of reformist ideology, was much closer to the ideal than before." Interestingly, however, these reforms strengthened the role of the legislature in policy implementation and thereby the intensity of the conflicts between the executive and legislative branches of government. After taking into account national patterns in intergovernmental authority and state fiscal resources, Chackerian speculates that organizational reforms will focus on rationalizing the state regulation of local activities rather than on a wholesale decentralization of state functions.

Frank P. Sherwood's and David Ferguson's discussion of the state personnel system, Chapter 7, is a detailed historical picture of its development. He does not come to very positive conclusions. It is an underfinanced, poorly organized system with little central leadership.

Chapter 8, "Planning and Budgeting," by William Earle Klay is a lukewarm endorsement of the existing arrangements: "Our budgeting process . . . does not prevent leaders from accomplishing change if the will exists to do so. Leadership in our state, however, is diffuse—

divided, scattered, and often transient." Critical to improving the situation, according to Klay, is to establish linkages between planning and budgeting. This is a formidable task under the fragmented institutional arrangements of Florida government, but certain matrix-like arrangements are suggested. The current "PB squared" efforts are noted.

Is the method of raising revenue to support state government fair? Is it adequate to meet legitimate public needs? These are the questions discussed by Gloria Grizzle in Chapter 9. Her answer to the adequacy question is that it was adequate until the early 1970s, but it has not been since then. She also presents evidence that the system is unfair because it tends to impose the heaviest burdens on those who can least afford it. This is consistent with Crew's general conclusion that the political environment is moderate to conservative and not highly participative.

Part IV deals with the relationships between governments in Florida and the important issues that face local governments. The state has always depended on local governments to deliver services and has in various proportions been willing to pay for them or to mandate their provision without state revenue. The level of fiscal support, the degree of discretion allowed local governments, the degree of service delivery competition, and the allocation of functions between governments are central issues discussed by Robert B. Bradley and Marcia Hosack in Chapter 10. These issues are very complicated and are not easily resolved by a uniform blueprint imposed by the state. They call for the use of incentives that recognize the diversity among local units of government and encourage them to come to grips with service demands.

Frank P. Sherwood's and Vivian Zaricki's "County Government in Florida," Chapter 11, discusses some of the same issues from the perspective of county government. De facto, county governments are increasingly expected to provide urban services, but they do not have the tax base to provide them. What are the options? The reforms affecting state government in the late 1960s also reached local governments and provided structural options to deal with some of these issues. Sherwood and Zaricki note some of the remaining problems in providing more local freedom to adopt structural and other changes, as well as the importance of improving the revenue base.

Jack M. Schluckebier, a city manager, looks at local government issues from a policy perspective in Chapter 12. "While some attention is given to structural issues, such as organization and finance, the majority [of the chapter] is focused on special issues of interest to municipal officials. These are annexation, special districts, growth management, and unfunded state mandates." The future of Florida's cities would be much brighter, according to Schluckebier, if unfunded mandates were reduced, annexation were less burdensome, and they were given more powers to manage growth.

Part V develops four policy management areas of particular importance to Florida: development management, tax policy, new forms of program delivery, and constitutional revision. Chapter 14, "Development Management: Balancing Growth Management and Economic Development," by Benjamin "Woody" Price and Richard C. Feiock, contrasts the pressures to stimulate and control economic growth. The seeming policy intractability stems in part from conflicting values and interests ranging from those supporting growth as a way to increase profits and tax base on the one hand and on the other to those which support a broader tax base and environmental protection.

Chapter 14, "Tax Policy: Factors Related to Success and Failure," by William Earle Klay, Joanne R. Snair, and Gloria Grizzle, traces the various attempts to reform the state tax structure and why they have either succeeded or failed. Where tax reform has succeeded, it has had strong gubernatorial leadership. "If tax reform is to occur, political common sense must be accompanied by both political courage and persistence. These have been the ingredients of successful reforms in the past and they will be needed in the future as well."

Chapter 15, by William Tankersley and Richard Chackerian, explores the wide variety of alternative forms of service delivery in addition to the usual use of governmental bureaucracy. The authors explain why there has been increasing attention to these alternatives and the circumstances under which one or the other of them might be useful. They conclude, ironically, that successful use of alternatives to government bureaucracy requires a highly competent government bureaucracy.

The final chapter in this part, by Lance deHaven-Smith, examines the constitutionally mandated constitutional review. He focuses on the nature of the process and the issues that are in the forefront.

The book's concluding chapter, by Richard Chackerian and William Earle Klay, lays out the vision that has guided the development of institutions and policy in Florida. Although there have been significant changes in the social and economic environment, the vision guiding the state, in their judgment, has not changed sufficiently. They suggest the necessity of a radical break from the old to a new vision if Florida is to have a brighter future.

INTRODUCTION

PART I

GROWTH, REFORM AND
THE PUBLIC POLICY MANAGEMENT SYSTEM

GROWTH AND REFORM IN FLORIDA
THE SETTING AND ANALYTICAL FRAMEWORK:
FLORIDA AS A DEVELOPING STATE

RICHARD CHACKERIAN

INTRODUCTION

Florida is an interesting case of governmental and administrative underdevelopment emerging from rapid change. As recently as the late 1950s Florida was a relatively poor, rural Southern state with a small population burdened with the cultural and legal aftermath of the Civil War. Today it is a mega-state in several senses. In just four decades it has become highly urbanized with a large population, the fourth largest in the nation. It has also developed a robust economy, significant wealth, and a degree of social and ethnic heterogeneity characteristic of Northeastern States. For those assessing conditions in the Sunshine State, it has been a habit of mind to compare it to other states in the Southeast: Alabama, Georgia, the Carolinas, Mississippi, etc. The new realities of Florida make such comparisons less appropriate. Florida's peer states are California, Illinois, Indiana, Massachusetts, Michigan, New York, Ohio, Pennsylvania, and Texas. These are the states with which comparisons must be made. We must recognize that Florida is now a large, urban, diverse, moderately wealthy state.

The thesis of this chapter is that Florida can be regarded as having some of the features of a developing state including underdeveloped governmental institutions. While it may seem farfetched to see this mega-state as in some ways analytically similar to a less developed country, the analogy can be helpful. Before exploring this perspective and its relationship to the development problems of Florida, it will be useful to explore, briefly, the history of Florida's development and its current condition.

Many of the governmental and administrative issues faced by the state are rooted in its history. This is a history that in some respects has burdened the state with institutions out of sync with the new realities. This can be seen when one compares Florida's social conditions to states of similar size. What is the state of the state? The answer is, in many important respects, "not good."

Florida is in the midst of significant social disorganization. Whatever indicator of social health one might use, the picture is not pretty. The property and violent crime rate in 1994 was nearly twice the national rate per 100,000 population and its total crime rate was one and a half times higher (*Florida Statistical Abstract* 1992, 591). (See Table 1-1.) Compared to other states it ranked as the most crime ridden (GAP 1996, 20). It also has one of the highest suicide rates: 15.1 per 100,000 population; and one of the highest abortion rates: 27.6 per 100 pregnancies (Department of Health and Rehabilitative Services 1996, 43 and 55). For a long time, Florida also had the highest rate of infant mortality. For example, in 1988, the rate was 11.3 per 1,000 live births compared to national average of 9.2 (Department of Health and Rehabilitative Services 1988, 10). By 1996, the rate had gone down substantially to 7.5 per 1,000 live births thanks to efforts by the Chiles administration to improve health services for children in the state. Other problems such as traffic congestion, school dropouts, environmental degradation, and water shortages are additional indicators of crisis. Why is this the case? How does one account for these grim conditions and what do they imply for those who are interested in governmental institutions and governmental reform?

Table 1-1

PROPERTY AND VIOLENT CRIME RATES IN FLORIDA AND THE UNITED STATES

1990 (per 100,000 population)

	All Crime	Property Crime	Violent Crime
Florida	8,811	7,567	1,244
United States	5,820	5,089	732

PROBLEMS OF DEVELOPMENT IN A RAPIDLY CHANGING ENVIRONMENT

These are not easy questions to answer, but at a general level governments in Florida, while undergoing very significant change, have not been able to catch up with the changes in society. If one were to ask an informed citizen why Florida is experiencing these problems, a likely answer would be "rapid population growth." This growth has expanded the scope and importance of public policy issues. It is hard to be unaware of the scale and immediate impact of population growth in Florida. In every decade since 1830 the population has increased by no less than 29% and in the decade from 1950 to 1960 it increased 80% (Florida Statistical Abstract 1995, 4). Migration is a big contributor to this growth. In 1994 there was a net population increase from migration of 718,518 accounting for 76.4% of total population increase in the same period (Florida Statistical Abstract 1995, 52). When one adds the nearly 40 million tourists and intrastate moves, the picture is of massive mobility. The growth has created huge demands for infrastructure and social programs, but it has also resulted in a citizenry too often uninformed and uncommitted to resolving public problems.

Associated with massive migration and a lack of popular commitment to resolving public problems is a lack of trust in government and a reluctance to support a tax base sufficient to provide for the needs of an expanding state population. Savings institution assets per capita in 1984 in Florida were 26% above the national average and Florida's rank among the 50 states in average personal income, in 1994, was 21st from the top. But, it ranked 37th in state taxes and 27th in local taxes (GAP 1996, 95). As implied above, because of the large number of in-migrants, a large proportion of Floridians were educated in and developed commitments to other states and even to other nations. In addition there is a disproportionately large number of older people who have retired to Florida. For example, 18.5 % of the state's population is above the age of 65 compared to a national average of 12.8% (*Florida Statistical Abstract* 1995, 25). It is often alleged that senior citizens vote against tax levies for schools and other public purposes because neither they nor their children have benefitted from them in the past. It is also important to recognize that there probably never has been a political culture in Florida which exhibited high levels of trust in government although the reasons for the reluctance have changed.

Daniel J. Elazar (1970) described Florida's political culture up to the early 1960's as "traditional." A traditional political culture reflects an older, pre-commercial attitude that accepts the ordered nature of things. It supports the idea that those at the top of the social structure should take a special and dominant role in government. It accepts government as an actor with a positive role in the community. It tries however, to limit that role to securing the continued maintenance of the existing social order. To do so, it functions to confine real political power to a relatively small and self-perpetuating group drawn from an established elite who often inherit their right to govern through family ties or social position. These conclusions are largely consistent with those of Claire Gilbert (1984, 149). Writing about the same time as Elazar, she concluded that in comparison to other regions of the country, governments in the South tend to be less pluralistic in power structure. They tend to be surrounded by fewer separate influence hierarchies in distinct issue areas and within each issue area leadership is less differentiated. The pattern of leadership associated with this political culture is essentially conservative.

Where the traditionalistic political culture is dominant in the United States today, political leaders play conservative and custodial rather than initiatory roles unless pressed strongly from the outside.

    . . . [T]raditional political cultures tend to be instinctively anti-bureaucratic because government bureaucracy by its very nature interferes with the fine web of informal interpersonal relationships that lie at the root of the political system and which have been developed following traditional patterns over the years (Elazar 1970).

Consensus on social values provides the integration which in other circumstances is provided by competitive political parties. Support of public purposes is assured by a general acceptance of social values. These values, in turn, are inculcated by primary socializing institutions such as religious organizations, schools, and work (Chackerian and Abcarian 1984). Traditional political culture and anti-governmental attitudes are important parts of Florida's political heritage.

    Conservative traditions which predate the Civil War, were reinforced by the experience with Reconstruction and its aftermath. This is illustrated by the constitution adopted in 1885 (Doyle, Laird, and Weiss 1954), important elements of which are embodied in the current constitution adopted in 1968. The constitution of 1885 was substantially a reaction to the Reconstruction constitution of 1868. The 1868 constitution was adopted by forty-six delegates chosen from nineteen electoral districts designated by the federal military governor. Conditions precedent to readmission to the Union after the Civil War included adoption of the Fourteenth Amendment to the Constitution of the United States and adoption of provisions prohibiting the limitation of the right of franchise because of race or color. The 1868 Reconstruction constitution provided a strong executive. The governor was authorized to appoint his cabinet subject to confirmation by the senate. The governor also was authorized to appoint local officers who had previously been elected. Later the governor was given the item veto and the power to appoint members of the supreme court.

    Two types of changes characterized the anti-Reconstruction constitution of 1885: (1) it restricted the right of Blacks to vote, and (2) it placed substantial restrictions on the powers of the governor. The governor was limited to two terms, but the now-elected cabinet would not be so restricted. The secretary of state, attorney general, comptroller, treasurer, superintendent of public instruction, and commissioner of agriculture were independently elected in statewide elections with no restriction on the number of terms. The governor also lost the power to make local appointments, although the constitution did not provide local home rule.

Governmental institutions have not remained as they were in the 1885 constitution, or even as they were after the 1969 reorganization. As noted, there have been significant changes in society and in institutional structure. There have been two waves of substantial institutional reform, the 1968 constitutional revision and state government organizational changes during the Chiles administration, 1991 to the present. These changes have significantly increased the power of the executive and somewhat increased the powers of local government. When Joseph A. Schlesinger ranked the strength of the governor's formal powers in 1971 (i.e., tenure potential, appointments, budget control and veto), he concluded that Florida ranked forty-seventh of the fifty states (Schlesinger 1971, 183). By 1983 the powers of the governor had expanded somewhat, the Florida governor being ranked moderately powerful according to the Schlesinger rating system (Beyle 1990). Given the changes during the Chiles administration, the relative power position of Florida's governor probably would be even higher on the Schlesinger index, although still not among states such as New York which give their governors extensive powers.

While the governor's powers have increased, the political culture of the state legislature was significantly transformed by the U.S. Supreme Court decision in *Baker v. Carr* (1961). The Baker decision required that legislative districts more accurately reflect the principle of "one man one vote." The Florida legislature was one of the most malapportioned legislatures in the country giving rural North Florida disproportionate legislative representation. The State Supreme Court, in *Swann v. Adams* (1966), following the U.S. Supreme Court precedent in *Baker v. Carr* (1961), declared the apportionment provisions of the Florida Constitution of 1885 null and void. The 1967 legislature was the first elected from reapportioned districts and provided more representation to urban constituencies and significantly less to rural districts that previously had dominated. Reapportionment was the beginning of the end of the traditional political culture in the legislature although not the end of political institutions associated with that culture.

In place of the traditional culture a new breed of politics has emerged with a more individualistic emphasis. This trend also characterizes many of the large, growing, urbanized states and the U.S. Congress. As Elazar has suggested, the individualistic political culture emphasizes the importance of private concerns and places strict limits on governmental intervention.

13

Government action is to be restricted to those areas, primarily in the economic realm, which encourage private initiative and widespread access to the marketplace (Elazar 1970, 172).

This is a conservative posture in that government officials are reluctant to make bold initiatives and exercise political leadership. Rather, they tend to be very sensitive to what the public wants (Elazar 1970, 173). The transition from traditionalism to individualism does change the pattern of political leadership, but not the appropriate role of government in society. Common to both traditionalism and individualism is an absence of moralism about the responsibilities of government. The government is not seen as a major influence on citizen virtue or community well being (Sandel 1996). Public interest and similar symbols of the general welfare are regarded with suspicion and in any case are products of private and non-profit institutions.

GOVERNMENTAL RESPONSES TO SOCIAL CHANGE: THE RECORD

Demographic changes, citizens who distrust their government and significant social disorganization have been responded to by governance changes. There have been major attempts to adapt government institutions to these new circumstances. The pattern of reform, however, can not be expected to be uniform given the complex unfolding of events associated with rapid social transformation. Some reform attempts have been successful, others not. Reapportionment of the legislature was probably the most important institutional change. Following from this were other changes and attempted changes that also must be recognized.

In 1972 significant legislation on intergovernmental coordination in planning, infrastructure finance, and developments of regional importance was adopted. There also was legislation requiring discussions of public policy issues be held in public (viz., the Sunshine Law). The staffing of the legislature was greatly strengthened and information systems for policy making greatly expanded. Important changes also were made in educational policy, with new minimum standards established for progression and matriculation.

Along with these successful attempts to bring institutional and policy change, were a large number of failed attempts. In 1974 the provision of human services was radically reorganized so that services previously delivered by many state agencies were consolidated into a single agency while deconcentrating the management of these services to local districts

(Martin, Chackerian et al. 1983). By 1997 the pendulum had swung back to a fragmented human services system. Florida, along with many other jurisdictions, attempted to establish a Planning Programming Budgeting System in the early 1970s, but the effort largely failed because of its complexity and cost. There have also been two major abortive attempts to reform the tax structure: the unitary tax was passed and quickly repealed during the Democratic Graham administration (1979–1986), and later the services tax was passed and repealed during the Republican Martinez administration (1987–1990). There also have been major failures in the area of human resources management. The Senior Management Service (SMS) was established to encourage the development of a highly professional set of career administrators in state government. By all accounts this has not been its effect. Rather than encouraging the development of a highly committed and professional senior civil service, the SMS has made senior managers more responsive to prevailing partisan interests (Auditor General 1984, 1987). The executive branch is highly divided although gubernatorial powers have been significantly increased. The strengthening of the governor has been paralleled by a strengthened legislature, leaving the state with highly divided leadership and an inability to integrate major political interests to deal with the social crises faced by the state. Local governments remain the stepchild of the state, but there has been some expansion of local home rule powers outside of fiscal matters. Overall, the failure to adapt sufficiently should not be taken as a failure of effort. There have been repeated attempts at institutional reform in the areas of finance and budgeting, and organization and human resources management. If the lag in institutional change cannot be accounted for by a lack of effort, what other explanations might be available?

GOVERNMENTAL RESPONSES TO SOCIAL CHANGE: AN ANALYTICAL INTERPRETATION

At a more abstract level, these observations about change in Florida are closely parallel to those made by experts on development in Third World nations (Heady 1979, 83–112). The idea of development has been used primarily to interpret the experiences of less-developed nations, but there is some precedent for its application to American states (Sharkansky 1982). The formulation which seems most useful for understanding the issues facing Florida is provided by Almond and Powell (1966). They suggest that all states face four general types of problems: (1) state building, (2) nation building, (3) participation, and

(4) distribution of welfare. State building is the process of building political institutions which are capable of integrating the political activities of all significant political elements in the society. Nation building emphasizes the cultural commitments of people in the society, particularly their loyalty and commitment to the system. Participation is indicated by the extent to which groups are allowed to be involved in the process of making policy decisions. Finally, distribution of welfare suggests the role of the state in using its coercive powers to redistribute resources to less advantaged elements of the population.

STATE-BUILDING

Florida has made significant progress toward state building since the 1969 reorganization by increasing the powers of the governor and creating other governmental processes such as work load and revenue estimating conferences in the legislature and agency strategic planning which brings together a variety of interested parties to develop consensus estimates and plans. Tentative steps have also been made in the direction of giving local communities a formal role in human services policy making and thereby providing an opportunity to integrate local interests.

The number of interest groups with registered legislative lobbyists has exploded since the early 1970's. This may indicate that there is a belief that access to policy makers is possible and fruitful. On the other hand there is the perception that interest group representatives do not include substantial influence for minorities and for the poor. Some have also suggested that the increased size and influence of legislative staff, since the 1969 reorganization, has further weakened the representative process by moving power and influence to staff and away from elected representatives. The passage of limits on the number of terms that may be served by elected officials is likely to further increase the influence of interest group representatives and legislative staff because elected representatives will be less experienced and therefore more reliant on the longer tenured professional staff and lobbyists.

NATION-BUILDING

Nation building emphasizes the cultural commitments of people in the society, particularly their loyalty and commitment to the system. We have already noted that Floridians have very marginal commitments to their governments. Population growth, migration, immigration and an individualist political culture have been major forces slowing the growth of a common identity and sense of commitment. This may be both a cause and consequence of relatively low levels of participation.

Voter registration in presidential election years has been among the lowest in the country. The state ranked 42nd to 47th in 1980 and 1994. (U.S. Statistical Abstract 1996, 290.) Florida has recently implemented the Federal "motor voter" registration procedures which reduce the burden of voter registration by allowing citizens to register to vote when they are registering their automobile. This will increase voter registration, but it remains to be seen to what extent newly registered voters will actually vote. A brighter spot is the representation of non-whites among elected state officials. In 1980 only 3% of elected officials were minority, but by 1995 the proportion reached 12%, five percent below the general population proportion of 17% (GAP 1996, 100). In the state civil service, progress has been achieved in the representation of women in the higher echelons, but there has been little change in the racial composition. The percentage of women in the state Senior Management Service (SMS) rose from 16% in 1986 to 24% in 1992. However, the racial balance worsened in the same period with a fall in the representation of blacks from 7% in 1986 to 5% in 1992. There was a similar trend in the Selected Exempt Service (SES) which mainly comprises professionals such as attorneys and physicians and assistant directors and bureau chiefs. Female representation rose from 19% to 33% between 1988 and 1992, but the proportion of blacks remained stagnant at 5% (OPPAGA 1995).

This chapter started with a brief discussion of the social disorganization endemic to Florida. High rates of crime, suicide, and abortion are indications that the state is not as effective as other states in dealing with important social problems. A fragmented state with a weak sense of citizen identity and which is still struggling to provide opportunities for political participation to the least advantaged, is not likely to be effective in dealing with its most important social problems. How do we account for the relatively poor performance? Again, the literature on developing nations (Almond and Powell 1966) is useful for understanding why some states may be more successful than others. The capacity to deal with problems of development depends on four major factors: (1) whether the problems come successively or cumulatively; (2) resources available to the system; (3) the orientation to accepting change; and (4) the creativity or stagnation of political leaders.

CONDITIONS SLOWING DEVELOPMENT

The rapidity of change in Florida has created an environment in which the problems faced have come cumulatively rather than successively. In a mere forty years Florida has moved from a largely rural Southern state to a highly urbanized state. The transformations in population size, nature of the economy, political culture, and representation have been dramatic. The resources available have been very limited if they are defined in terms of the tax revenue. Florida makes relatively little effort to tax its resources, which are in fact significant. The resource question is also important for the issue of innovation. Organizations that are most likely to innovate are those that have significant slack resources. Where resources are tight, as they always have been in Florida state government, it is very difficult to innovate. Experimentation is virtually impossible because resources are committed to essential services (Morgan 1986, 233–72). The 1994 state constitutional limitations (Article VII, Section I) on government revenues and the individualistic political culture tend to support the more general 1969 findings of Walker that Florida is not one of the innovating states, ranking 30th out of the 48 evaluated (Walker 1969). Since Walker's studies many reforms have been tried, but, an unfortunately large number of them failed (Chackerian, Berry and Wechsler 1996). The judgement that development and change have been limited in Florida should be put in perspective. Since the time of Walker's study, some conditions supporting development may be emerging.

CONDITIONS SUPPORTING DEVELOPMENT

Resources available to the system are critical, and it doesn't help that there is in place a constitutional amendment which limits tax revenue growth. However, the underlying economic reality is that Florida is becoming an increasingly wealthy state, now 21st among the states (GAP 1996, 67). The population will continue to grow, but at a decreasing rate. In the decade between 1980 and 1990 the population grew by approximately 13%, but by 1995 the rate was down to 9% (GAP 1996, 4). The slowing rate of population growth is likely to slow the rate at which problems pile on top of one another, thus allowing a more sequential resolution of policy problems. Reapportionment and urbanization as well as national trends in partisan alignments have created a competitive two party system. The era of the single party "court house gang" has come to an end, allowing greater access to the policy process. Competing policy positions will more often be debated and citizens will more often be given a role in their outcome.

THE DEVELOPING STATE AND THE POLICY MANAGER

This book is about how the policy management systems work and what changes might be made in them to improve performance. Much contemporary analysis is split between that which focuses on how administrative institutions and practices influence public policy and that which focuses on how administrative institutions maintain themselves. The intellectual roots for this distinction are deep and can be traced to the turn of the century.

PUBLIC POLICY AND INSTITUTIONAL MAINTENANCE

The public policy literature assumes that what needs explanation is policy: how it gets on the agenda of public discussion, how it is shaped, and what ultimately is implemented. There is a certain attractiveness to the policy focus, particularly if one is committed to serving human needs. On the other hand most policy analysis treats administrative institutions as a cause of policy and essentially ignores the internal environment of public organizations. The institutional maintenance literature focuses on how administrative systems respond to their internal and external environments to maintain support. Public policy is an environmental condition that has consequences for organizational survival. Policy must be shaped, adapted to, and even developed, but from the perspective of organizational survival rather than from the perspective of consequences for the public. The details of policy are ignored while the elements of intraorganizational behavior are given detailed attention.

PUBLIC BUREAUCRACY

An interesting marriage of these perspectives is based on the assumption that a public bureaucracy pursuing maintenance also is pursuing good public policy. The representational relations between public organizations and their clients, the public service orientation of bureaucrats, and the ambiguity of legislative mandates, combined with the drive for organizational survival and power, lead in this view to good policy (Long 1949).

It is not difficult to argue that public bureaucracy assumptions do not always correspond to the facts of organizational life. The automatic, equilibrium quality of the public bureaucracy argument seems to ignore subsets of power among external interests. Public organizations are responsive to external environments, but often this may be to narrowly defined interests, leaving non-elites without access. Public organizations pursuing their interests in institutional maintenance do not necessarily focus on a more general public interest. What is needed is a perspective which deals with organizational maintenance without ignoring general policy consequences.

POLICY MANAGEMENT IN A DEVELOPING STATE AND THE ORGANIZATION OF THIS BOOK

Policy management is a perspective that has been used to combine the analytical objectives of organizational maintenance and policy (Lynn 1987; 1996). This is not a fully developed set of ideas, but certain useful elements can be articulated. The first useful element is that both policy and maintenance are treated from the perspective of policy leaders, people who in formal and behavioral terms have responsibility for public policy and public management. The descriptive issues are how policy managers carry out their responsibilities in these domains.

The second useful element in the policy management perspective is that neither policy nor management is, strictly speaking, a matter of purely objective action. Policy is the retrospective interpretation of actions by those affected. The meaning of an action is constructed by a large number of actors who may attribute quite different meanings to it. Policy managers are also involved in the process of interpreting their own actions to themselves, to their organizations, and to the public. They play an important role in developing a culture which supports certain interpretations of public needs and actions. In addition, the process of translating popular perceptions into administrative expectations for performance involves the perceptions of a wide variety of actors including interest groups, professional associations, media, legislative and political elites, and administrative leaders.

Policy management should not be considered from the perspective of a single organization. Policy as perceived impact suggests that policy management must include consideration of inter-organizational networks and how they influence policy outcomes. Relations in networks are characterized in terms of power relations, communication patterns, status differences and policy outcomes (Benson 1975). The policy management perspective, then, is distinguished from the pure policy orientation because it takes a macro-organizational view, but also because it focuses on policy managers in the performance of their policy and management roles. Also, unlike the maintenance orientation, although the process for acquiring and deploying resources required for organizational survival are examined, it is not seen as unrelated to policy consequences.

Policy management can be linked to development by emphasizing the role of the policy management in shaping and being shaped by the problems faced by all developing states, namely (1) state building, (2) nation building, (3) participation, and (4) distribution of welfare (Almond and Powell 1966). The level of development in each of these areas influences how policy management takes place. An understanding of policy management in a developing state for the purposes of this book includes a description of the following:

1. the institutions, organizations, roles and processes that constitute the policy management system;
2. the conditions that provide the context for system operation; and
3. reforms that might increase the level of development and performance.

The remainder of Part I sketches the network of organizations and institutions that constitute the policy management system. Part II describes the environment of the policy management system, most notably the general political environment and elements of the institutional environment including the office of the governor and Cabinet and the Legislature. Part III describes internal organizational and institutional processes with special attention devoted to information, money, planning and staffing. Parts IV and V are devoted to the special role of local governments and their relations with the state and to special policy management issues including development management, tax policy, alternative service delivery and constitutional revision.

REFERENCES

Almond, Gabriel A. & G. Bingham Powell, Jr. (1966). *Comparative politics: A developmental approach.* Boston: Little, Brown & Co.

Auditor General (1984). *Performance audit of the senior management service system administered by the Department of Administration.* Tallahassee: State of Florida, Office of the Auditor General.

Auditor General (1987). *Performance audit of the senior management service system administered by the Department of Administration.* Tallahassee: State of Florida, Office of the Auditor General.

Baker v. Carr, 369 U.S. 186 (1961).

Benson, J. Kenneth (1975). The interlocking network as a political economy. *Administrative Science Quarterly, 20,* 229–49.

Beyle, Thad L (1990). Governors. In Virginia Gray, Herbert Jacob, and Robert B. Albritton (Eds.), *Politics in the American states: A comparative analysis* (5th ed.). Illinois: Scott Forseman/Little, Brown and Co.

Bureau of Economic and Business Research (1995). *Florida statistical abstract.* Gainesville, Fl, University Press of Florida.

Chackerian, Richard & Gilbert Abcarian (1984). *Bureaucratic power in society.* Chicago: Nelson-Hall.

CHAPTER 1

Chackerian, Richard, Fran Berry, Bart Wechsler (1995). *Comprehensive administrative reinvention: Resources, synergy and tradeoff.* Prepared for Presentation at the Eighth National Public Productivity Conference, November 9–10, 1995, Washington, D.C.

Cohen, Carol E. (1989). State fiscal capacity and effort: An update. *Intergovernmental Perspective,* 15, 17.

Department of Health and Rehabilitative Services (1988). *Patterns and trends of alcohol and drug abuse in Florida.* Tallahassee: The Department.

Department of Health and Rehabilitative Services (1996). *Florida vital statistics: 1995 annual report.* Tallahassee: The Department.

Doyle, Wilson K., Angus McKenzie Laird, and S. Sherman Weiss (1954). *The government and administration of Florida.* New York: Thomas Y. Crowell Co.

Elazar, Daniel J. (1970). Market place and commonwealth and the three political cultures. In Ira Sharkansky (Ed.), *Policy analysis in political science.* Chicago: Markham Publishing Company.

GAP (1996). *The Florida benchmarks report.* Tallahassee: Florida Executive Office of the Governor.

Lynn, Laurence E. (1987). *Managing public policy.* Boston: Little, Brown & Co.

Lynn, Laurence E. (1996). *Public management as art, science and profession.* Chatham, New Jersey: Chatham House Publishers.

Morgan, Gareth (1986). *Images of organization.* Newbury Park, CA.: Sage Publications.

Office of Program and Policy Analysis and Government Accountability (OPPAGA) (1995). *A longitudinal study of Florida's executive system.* Tallahassee: OPPAGA.

Pierce, A. C. (Ed). (1992) *Florida Statistical Abstract* (1996). Gainesville: University of Florida.

Sandel, M. J. (1996) *Democracy's discontent: America in search of a public philosophy.* Cambridge, Massachusetts: The Belknap Press of Harvard University Press.

Swann v. Adams, 87 SCT. 569 (1966).

U.S. Bureau of the Census (1995). *Statistical abstract of the United States* (115th ed.) Washington, D.C.: The Bureau.

Walker, Jack L. (1969). The diffusion of innovations among the American states. *American Political Science Review,* 63, 880–99.

CHAPTER 2

THE POLICY MANAGEMENT SYSTEM

RICHARD CHACKERIAN

The institutions and roles that constitute the policy management system are the structure in which the policy manager and the policy process operate. It is important to understand this structure because it both constrains and supports actions of political leaders and the desires of the public. We would all like to have strong and good leaders who would wave their wands of good policy to improve our condition. In truth however, the process of affecting the quality of life is highly constrained and complicated. Many of these constraints are associated with the structure of the policy management system. The meaning of these arrangements is somewhat obscure because Florida government is such a large, complex, and dynamic enterprise. The Florida Cabinet system is unique in the fifty states. It is a chameleon-like institution, transforming itself into the Administration Commission, the State Board of Education, the State Board for Vocational Education, or the Board of Trustees of the Internal Improvement Trust Fund depending on the decision requirement of the moment. In a more orderly world there would be more stable patterns of leadership and authority. The complexity which is so much a part of Florida's social and political history is reflected in its governing institutions. Some sense of the structure is given by the pattern of formal authority as indicated in Figure 2-1, but it falls far short of being a sufficient description.

The purpose of this chapter is to give a general sense of the structure and meaning of the policy management system. It focuses on the major institutions that constitute the system and the functions they perform. "Function" is used in various ways in the literature, but here we depend on the work of Henry Mintzberg (1979), which emphasizes the problems that must be addressed by the system, although modifications to his model have been made. Organizational functions can be divided into four groups. Generally speaking these functions are to provide: (1) strategic direction, (2) goods and services to citizens, (3) administrative

Figure 2-1
STRUCTURE OF THE EXECUTIVE BRANCH OF FLORIDA GOVERNMENT

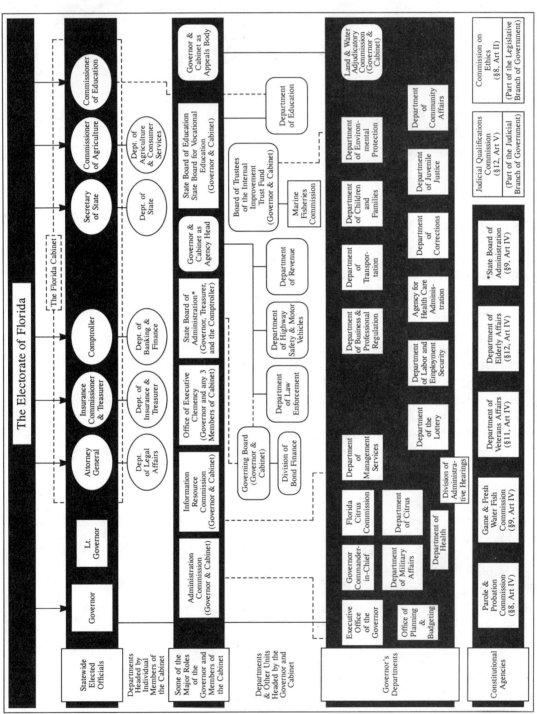

Adapted from an earlier draft developed by George H. Meier, November 1994.

support to those who provide strategic direction, and (4) technical support to those who provide strategic direction. These functions are at times performed by specialized organizational units, but in other instances a single organization may perform a set of functions. In Florida government there are also many instances in which many organizations perform the same function. These functions can be used to characterize the general mission of an entire agency or units within agencies. That is, each agency, whether its central mission is to provide direction, operations, or support, will have units which perform one of these functions for internal agency purposes rather than for another agency. Before describing the functional configuration of the policy management system, it is important to more fully define each functional type.

The function of *strategic direction* is performed by units at the "strategic apex." Normally the strategic apex is at the very top of the authority system, although it is sometimes scattered among a variety of government units. These units are heavily involved in the policy making process and to some degree involved in monitoring performance. The performance of these functions brings them into close contact with other policy-making units as well as external interests.

The function of *operations* is the production of goods and services. Normally these units are at the bottom of the governmental authority system, but increasingly they are entirely outside it. In some cases production is by other state government agencies, other levels of government (local or federal) or by for-profit and non-profit groups. In cases where the operating core is outside the state agency hierarchy, the relationship between the agency and the operating core is usually defined through formal contracts, franchise agreements, or regulations.[1]

Administrative support is budgetary, fiscal and personnel services to other units. These units are not normally in the chain of command between the strategic apex and the operating core, but play an advisory role to those in the strategic apex.

Technostructure units provide *technical support* and enforce operations performance standards. The position of these units is similar to administrative support units because they are not usually in the chain of command over operations. They do have, however, a significant advisory role in monitoring performance and making policy. In some cases government agencies will have very small technostructures of their own, instead depending on a central technostructure agency. Examples typical of state governments are the provision of legal, construction, and purchasing services by a central agency.

POLICY MANAGEMENT SYSTEM CONFIGURATION

Conventionally, discussions of the policy management system configuration are limited to agencies directly under the control of the governor and to other elected executives such as the comptroller and secretary of state. Here the discussion is broadened to include the management systems of the judicial and legislative branches because of their recently developed large scale and their roles in policy implementation as well as in policy development.

The legislative staff in Florida is one of the largest in the country with 1,354 positions in 1996. There are 337 positions in the Senate; 669 in the House of Representatives; and 348 in joint House/Senate committees. The judicial branch also has developed a formidable bureaucracy that accounts for about 2% of the nearly 147,000 employed by the state in 1996.

The largest proportion of positions, 66%, are allocated to the governor's 15 agencies. The other elected members of the Cabinet control about another 22% of the total positions, and agencies controlled jointly by the Cabinet account for another 8%. Commissions, boards, councils, and legislative and judicial staff round out the remaining 5% (see Table 2-1).

SOURCES OF STRATEGIC DIRECTION

Strategic direction is the responsibility of the Legislature and legislative staff, the governor and the Executive Office of the Governor, and the elected agency heads sitting as the Cabinet with the governor. These are the key institutions and positions because they decide the content of state policy and are the ultimate sources of responsibility for the effective performance of the public's business.

Since Reconstruction, Florida's governor has been relatively weak compared to other state governors. Although the reforms associated with the 1969 constitution broadened the scope of control over the bureaucracy and budget, the administrative capacity of the legislature also has been greatly expanded. In addition there is the continuing countervailing role of the Cabinet and cabinet agencies. As a consequence, sources of strategic direction are scattered throughout the government.

THE LEGISLATURE AND LEGISLATIVE STAFF

The structural arrangements important for the functioning of the Legislature will be discussed in greater detail in Chapter Five. Here it only is necessary to suggest that the constitutional reforms initiated in 1969 greatly increased the influence of the legislature in administrative

Table 2-1

POSITIONS BY BRANCH OF GOVERNMENT AND AGENCY

Governor	#	Cabinet	#	Legislative	#
Agency for Health		Agriculture	3,562	Senate	377
Care Admin.	1,904	Banking and		House	669
Business &		Finance	916	Joint Senate/	
Professional Reg.	1,749	Education	858	House	348
		Insurance	1,410	Auditor	
		Legal Affairs	901	General	616
		State Univer-			
Children & Family		sities	24,094		
Services*	29,098*				
Community Affairs	487				
Corrections	29,780				
Elder Affairs	316				
Environmental					
Protection	4,255				
Governor	294				
Health	2,536*				
Juvenile Justice	4,782				
Labor	7,614				
Lottery	738				
Management Services	1,770				
Military Affairs	247				
Transportation	10,588				
Total	**96,158** (65.5%)		**32,558** (22.2%)		**2,010** (1.4%)

Governor and Cabinet	#	Constitutional	#	Judicial	#
Law Enforcement	1,519	Veterans Affairs	268	Supreme	
Revenue	5,095	Citrus	160	Court	167
Highway Safety	4,974	Public Service		District Courts	
		Commission	380	of Appeals	403
		Game and Fish		Circuit	
		Commission	940	Courts	1,387
		Parole		County	
		Commission	164	Courts	520
Total	**11,588** (7.9%)		**1,912** (1.3%)		**2,477** (1.7%)

TOTAL ALL AGENCIES	146,703

Sources: Governor's Office of Planning and Budgeting, Budget Management Unit; Joint Legislative Management, Personnel Office; Auditor General, Personnel Office. Data reported as of June 30, 1996.

*Effective January 1, 1997, the Department of Health and Rehabilitative Services (HRS) was redesignated the Department of Children and Family Services and a new and separate Department of Health was created. These numbers are approximate.

matters by strengthening its staff and therefore its ability to oversee the actions of the executive branch. This role is captured in the title of the article, "Congress as Public Administrator," by James L. Sundquist (1987). His analysis focuses on the presidency and the Congress, but the main argument is equally applicable to the states.

Presidents may see themselves, as Franklin D. Roosevelt did, as general managers by constitutional intent. But the Congress sees them as agents of the Congress, very much as in a corporate board of directors-general manager relationship (Sundquist 1987, 262).

As a consequence, the Congress as well as the Florida Legislature have established a number of oversight committees. Some of these committees are in the House, others in the Senate, or joint between the House and Senate. Of particular importance are the following joint committees:

1. *The Administrative Procedures Committee* reviews statutory authority upon which administrative rules are based as well as agency actions under the Administrative Procedures Act. It can request agencies to repeal rules that are inconsistent with the constitution or statute.
2. *The Legislative Auditing Committee* appoints the Auditor General, who directs the operations of the Office of the Auditor General. With a staff of 616 and the power to require response to its audits of executive agency operations, it is a potent instrument of legislative oversight.

More specifically, the Auditor General is responsible for making annual financial audits of state agencies, district school boards, and the boards of trustees of community colleges. These audits are designed to assure that funds have been expended only for legally authorized purposes. In addition, the Office of the Auditor General is responsible for performance audits, which differ from financial audits in that they are designed to evaluate the efficiency and effectiveness of state and local government operations. Audits with agency responses are made available to the appropriate legislative committees for review and appropriate legislative action. These actions may include new substantive legislation on administrative practices or on budget allocations.

A relatively new, but important instrument for administrative oversight is the Office of Program Policy Analysis and Government Accountability (OPPAGA). Essentially, the portion of the Auditor General staff that was involved with evaluating the efficiency and effectiveness of government programs was split from the Auditor General and placed in a newly created OPPAGA. The main consideration in this shift was to facilitate the use of program evaluations for program monitoring and policy development by the legislative leadership. The 1997 session of the Legislature established a number of "super" committees in the House of Representatives which serve as gate keepers for the more specialized committees. It is to soon to judge whether or not these will become a permanent feature.

THE CABINET AND ASSOCIATED BOARDS AND COMMISSIONS

A second major source of strategic direction is the Cabinet, which as cabinets in many other states is composed of separately elected officials. The unique feature of Florida's Cabinet, however, is that it directly supervises the activities of three agencies. These departments are distinct from those supervised by the governor and from those directed by individual elected Cabinet members.

The Cabinet is a very complex institutionally because it plays several distinct roles. The positions that constitute the Cabinet are: the attorney general, insurance commissioner and treasurer, comptroller, secretary of state, commissioner of agriculture, commissioner of education, and governor. These elected officers provide executive direction to: (1) their own agencies, (2) Cabinet agencies, and (3) units within Cabinet agencies, as well as to (4) certain constitutional commissions.

The Cabinet agencies are: the Department of Law Enforcement, Department of Highway Safety and Motor Vehicles, and Department of Revenue. Each of these agencies is subject to the overall direction of the governor and Cabinet with day-to-day management by an executive director.

To carry out its functions, the Cabinet or portions thereof sit as several distinct commissions or boards. For bond finance, it sits as the Governing Board for the Division of Bond Finance; for executive clemency, the Office of Executive Clemency; for state lands, the Board of Trustees of the Internal Improvement Trust Fund; for fiscal and budgetary matters, the Administration Commission; for regional development and water issues, the Land and Water Adjudicatory Commission; for information resources management, the Information Resource Commission; and for education, the State Board of Education and the State Board for Vocational Education.

The administrative and technical support and operation for each of these roles is also very complex. In some cases each role is associated with its own administrative structure, but in other cases support is given by an executive agency. For example, bond finance functions are carried out by the Division of Bond Finance which receives administrative support from the State Board of Administration. Executive clemency is carried out by the Parole and Probation Commission. The Administration Commission is staffed by the governor's Office of Planning and Budgeting (OPB) and the director of OPB is secretary of the Commission. The Information Resource Commission has its own staff, but is housed in the Department of Management Services (DMS). This means that the IRC operates independently of strategic direction from the governor, but utilizes the services of DMS for budget processing, personnel and acquisitions matters.

THE GOVERNOR AND THE EXECUTIVE OFFICE

The governor now requires a relatively large administrative staff to perform the strategic duties of leadership, policy development, and executive oversight of the governor's agencies. The Executive Office of the Governor is critical to the effective performance of these roles. Since the 1969 reorganization, the governor has been responsible for submitting to the Legislature an executive budget covering all state programs. Because the governor is the most visible state political leader and is able to capture the attention of the mass media, the governor's policy preferences carry significant weight in the legislative process.

The position of the governor has been weakened by the growth of legislative staff and procedural changes which require all agencies to submit their budget requests simultaneously to the legislature and governor. It has already been noted that the governor exercises formal authority directly over only 66% of the state work force. The governor's weakness is not due simply to the limited number of agencies directly controlled. It also is affected by the types of agencies. In states with strong governors, the governor supervises virtually all agencies responsible for providing technical and administrative support to government operations. In Florida the governor must share these responsibilities with a wide variety of other elected officials including the Cabinet.

PROVIDING ADMINISTRATIVE AND TECHNICAL SUPPORT

THE CENTRAL CONTROL AGENCIES

Six units of government are primarily concerned with providing administrative and technical support to other units of state government these are: the Department of Legal Affairs, Department of Management Services, Department of Revenue, State Board of Administration, Administration Commission, and the Office of Planning and Budgeting in the Executive Office of the Governor.

The most important of the governor's administrative and technical support roles are played by the Office of Planning and Budgeting, but even here the planning and budgeting roles are affected by Cabinet influence. The Cabinet, sitting as the Administration Commission, exercises ultimate control over budgetary transactions dealing with the transfer of general revenue appropriations between funds, authorizing additional government positions, or authorizing budget cuts in cases of revenue shortfalls.

Revenue and investment management are in the hands of the Cabinet, which uses the Department of Revenue and the Administration Commission as its instruments. Control over state agency expenditure practices is exercised by the elected comptroller of the Department of Banking and Finance. Legal opinions and advice are in the hands of the elected attorney general.

THE OPERATING AGENCIES

Gubernatorial control over operations is also fragmented because each agency has its own technical and administrative control system which may not share the control orientation of the central control agencies. Examples are found in the usual claims of operating agency personnel and budgeting units for more positions and funds. These tendencies toward expansion are often balanced by the tendency of central agencies such as the Department of Management Services and the Office of Planning and Budgeting to be skeptical of such requests. The importance of support units within operating agencies is suggested by the fact that in 1978 and 1988 15% of state agency positions were in non-operating line units. There is great variation between agencies in these proportions. For example, in 1988, the range was from 2% for the Department of Corrections to 100% for the Department of Lottery. Much of this variation can be accounted for by the types of control problems faced by an agency given its size, function and service delivery system.

An agency can deliver a service directly using persons employed by the government. This is the most frequent method. Of the 25 agencies for which data is available, fifteen of them, in the main use direct delivery. This method and the associated organizational form is illustrated by the organization chart for the Department of Labor and Employment Security (see Figure 2-2). Direct delivery is to be distinguished from those methods which depend on non-government personnel to perform operating functions. These methods include delivering services by: (1) other governments, (2) non-profit agencies, and (3) for-profit agencies.

Some state government services are delivered entirely by the private sector. The best example of this is the Department of the Lottery (see Figure 2-3). Lottery tickets are sold and money collected entirely by private businesses for a fee. The role of the Department of Lottery is to regulate the conditions under which tickets are sold and money collected and to promote the sale of tickets by contracting with the private advertisers. The effect of this delivery system is to place all agency positions in the roles of strategic direction, administrative support or technical support. The entire operating line is in the private sector. A less extreme

31

Figure 2-2
DEPARTMENT OF LABOR AND EMPLOYMENT SECURITY

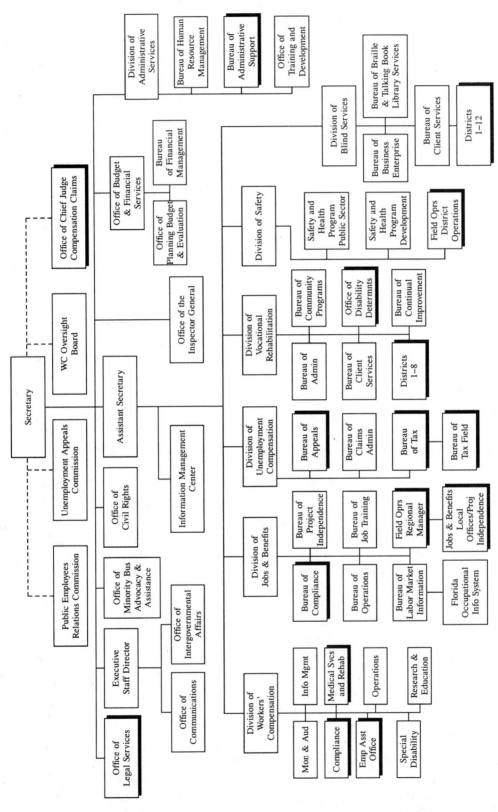

*Shadowed boxes indicate units also have field sites.

Source: Florida Department of Labor and Employment Security, October, 1996.

Figure 2-3

FLORIDA LOTTERY ORGANIZATION STRUCTURE

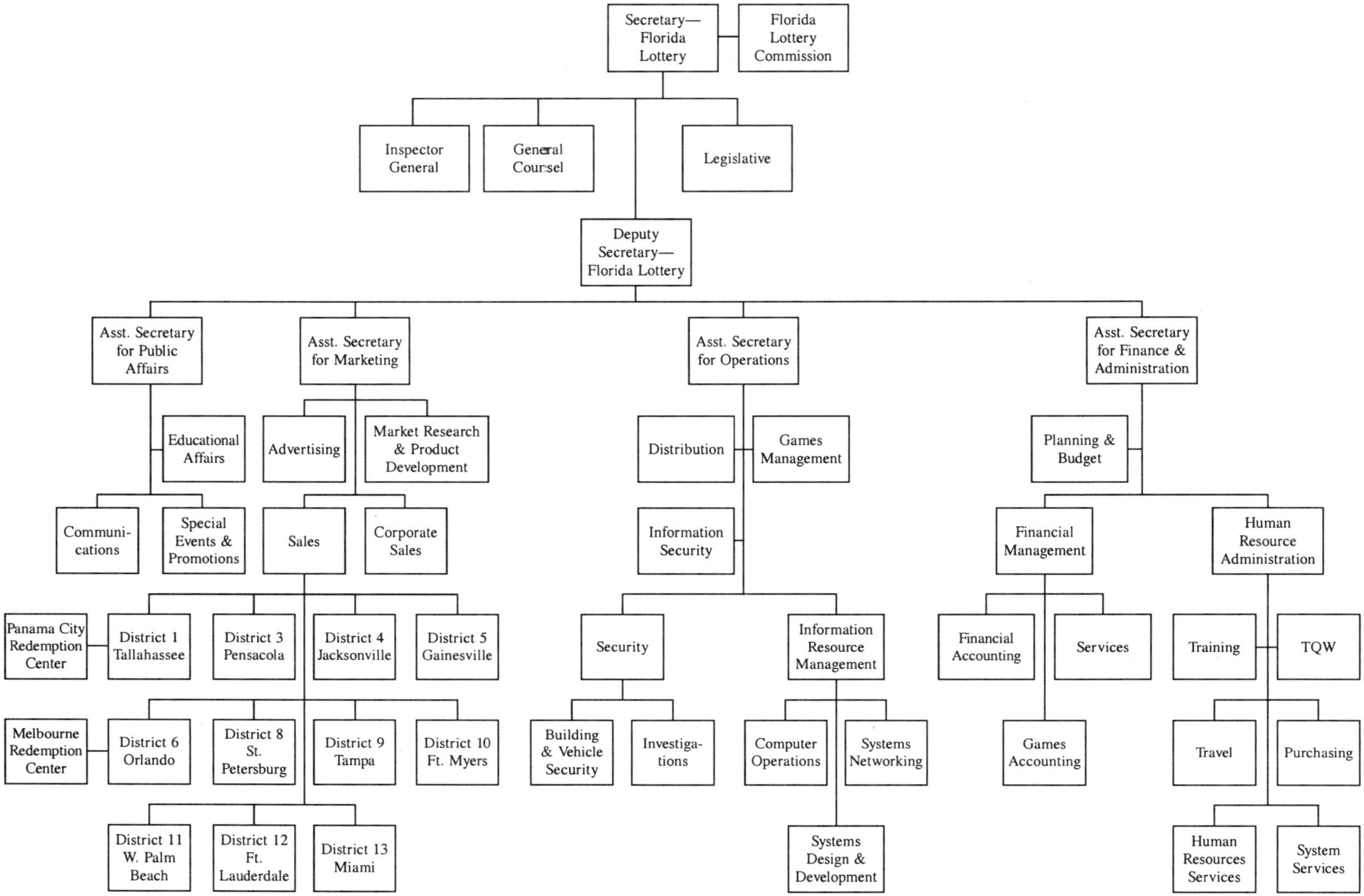

- Florida Lottery Commission
- Secretary—Florida Lottery
  - Inspector General
  - General Counsel
  - Legislative
- Deputy Secretary—Florida Lottery
  - Asst. Secretary for Public Affairs
    - Communications
    - Educational Affairs
    - Special Events & Promotions
    - Sales
      - District 1 Tallahassee
        - Panama City Redemption Center
      - District 3 Pensacola
      - District 4 Jacksonville
      - District 5 Gainesville
      - District 6 Orlando
        - Melbourne Redemption Center
      - District 8 St. Petersburg
      - District 9 Tampa
      - District 10 Ft. Myers
      - District 11 W. Palm Beach
      - District 12 Ft. Lauderdale
      - District 13 Miami
  - Asst. Secretary for Marketing
    - Advertising
    - Market Research & Product Development
    - Corporate Sales
  - Asst. Secretary for Operations
    - Distribution
    - Games Management
    - Information Security
    - Security
      - Building & Vehicle Security
      - Investigations
    - Information Resource Management
      - Computer Operations
      - Systems Networking
      - Systems Design & Development
  - Asst. Secretary for Finance & Administration
    - Planning & Budget
    - Financial Management
      - Financial Accounting
      - Services
      - Games Accounting
    - Human Resource Administration
      - Training
      - TQW
      - Travel
      - Purchasing
      - Human Resources Services
      - System Services

example was the Department of General Services (merged into the Department of Management Services), which had a little more than 20% of its staff in control positions. The major mission of General Services was building management, which is usually done by the for-profit sector through contracts with the state. Therefore a significant portion of its staff must be involved in control roles such as writing and monitoring contracts.

Another class of agencies with a large proportion of control roles is composed of those that depend on other governments to provide goods and services. The clearest case of this is the Department of Education (see Figure 2-4). The Department of Education does not directly provide educational services and has nearly 70% of its positions in technical, administrative and strategic direction roles.[2] Educational services are provided by local school districts controlled by locally elected school boards and school superintendents and in significant measure funded through local sources. The state Department of Education provides money, performance standards and technical assistance. To a lesser extent the Department of Community Affairs and the Department of Law Enforcement also depend on local governments to provide services, and as one might expect have a relatively large proportion of their positions in control roles, 30% and 53% respectively.

The Department of Community Affairs (see Figure 2-5) is an interesting case because, unlike the Department of Education, it probably achieves its greatest local impacts through its regulatory roles in land-use planning and growth management.[3] Like the Department of Education, Community Affairs is involved in providing money to local governments, but in this case for housing and energy saving programs.

The evidence suggests that agencies which depend on other governments or on non-profit and for-profit organizations to perform operating functions tend to have relatively large control structures. These structures are needed to keep the external service delivery organizations accountable. If the services were being delivered directly, other mechanisms of control would more likely be used. Two of the most common alternative control methods are rules and procedures and direct hierarchical supervision.

Interestingly there are cases where there is significant external dependence for service delivery, but the proportion of control positions is relatively small. The Department of Transportation (see Figure 2-6) is one of the state's largest agencies, with nearly 11,000 employees. The recently eliminated Department of Health and Rehabilitative Services was even larger, with over 43,000 positions. A feature these large agencies share is that they have very diverse service delivery systems. In both

Figure 2-4
DEPARTMENT OF EDUCATION

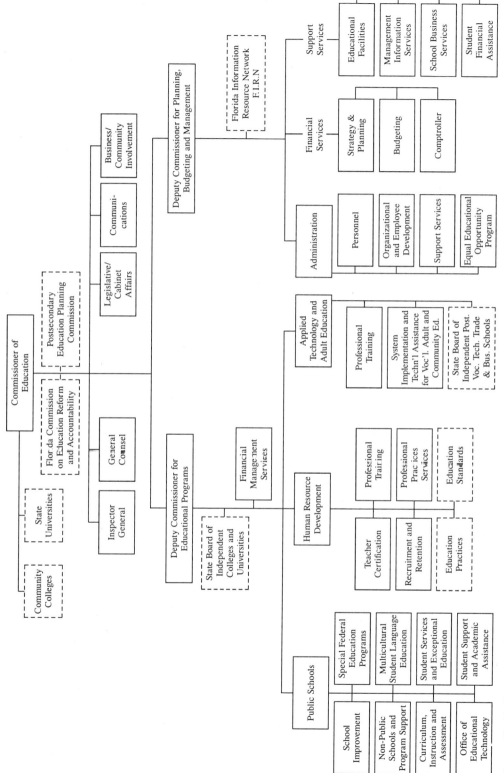

Source: Florida Department of Education, February, 1997.

Figure 2-5
DEPARTMENT OF COMMUNITY AFFAIRS

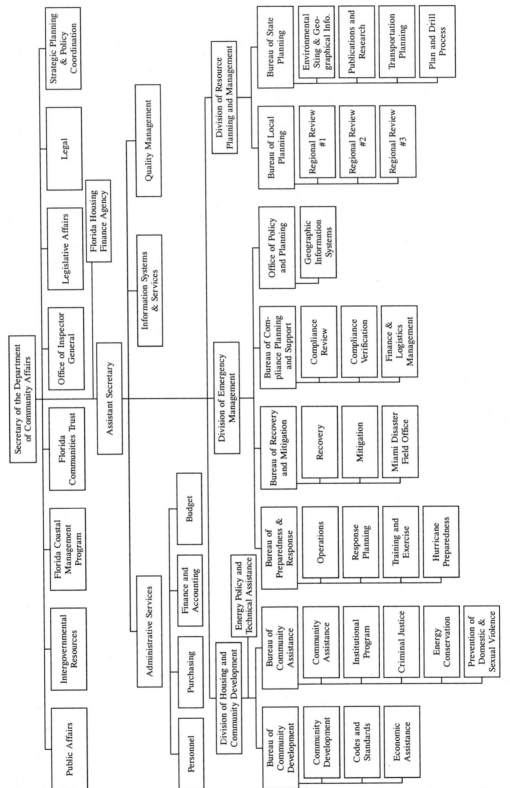

Source: Florida Department of Community Affairs, July, 1997.

Figure 2-6
DEPARTMENT OF TRANSPORTATION

Transportation Commission

Secretary

Office of Inspector General

Office of General Counsel

Quality Management Office

Office of Communications & Governmental Affairs

Asst. Secretary Finance & Administration
- Office of Comptroller
- Office of Administration
- Office of Operations
- Office of Information Systems
- Office of Management & Budget

Asst. Secretary District Operations
- District One Secretary Bartow
- District Five Secretary Deland
- District Two Secretary Lake City
- District Six Secretary Miami
- District Three Secretary Chipley
- District Seven Secretary Tampa
- District Four Secretary Ft. Lauderdale
- Turnpike District Secretary Tallahassee
- Motor Carrier Compliance Office
- Production Management Office

Asst. Secretary Transportation Policy

State Transportation Planner
- Office of Policy Planning
- Systems Planning Office
- Transportation Statistics Office

State Highway Engineer
- Office of Design
- Office of Right of Way
- Maintenance Office
- Office of Construction
- Engineering/CADD Systems Office
- Safety Office

Public Transportation Administrator
- High Speed Transportation Program
- Rail Office
- Transit Office
- Aviation Office

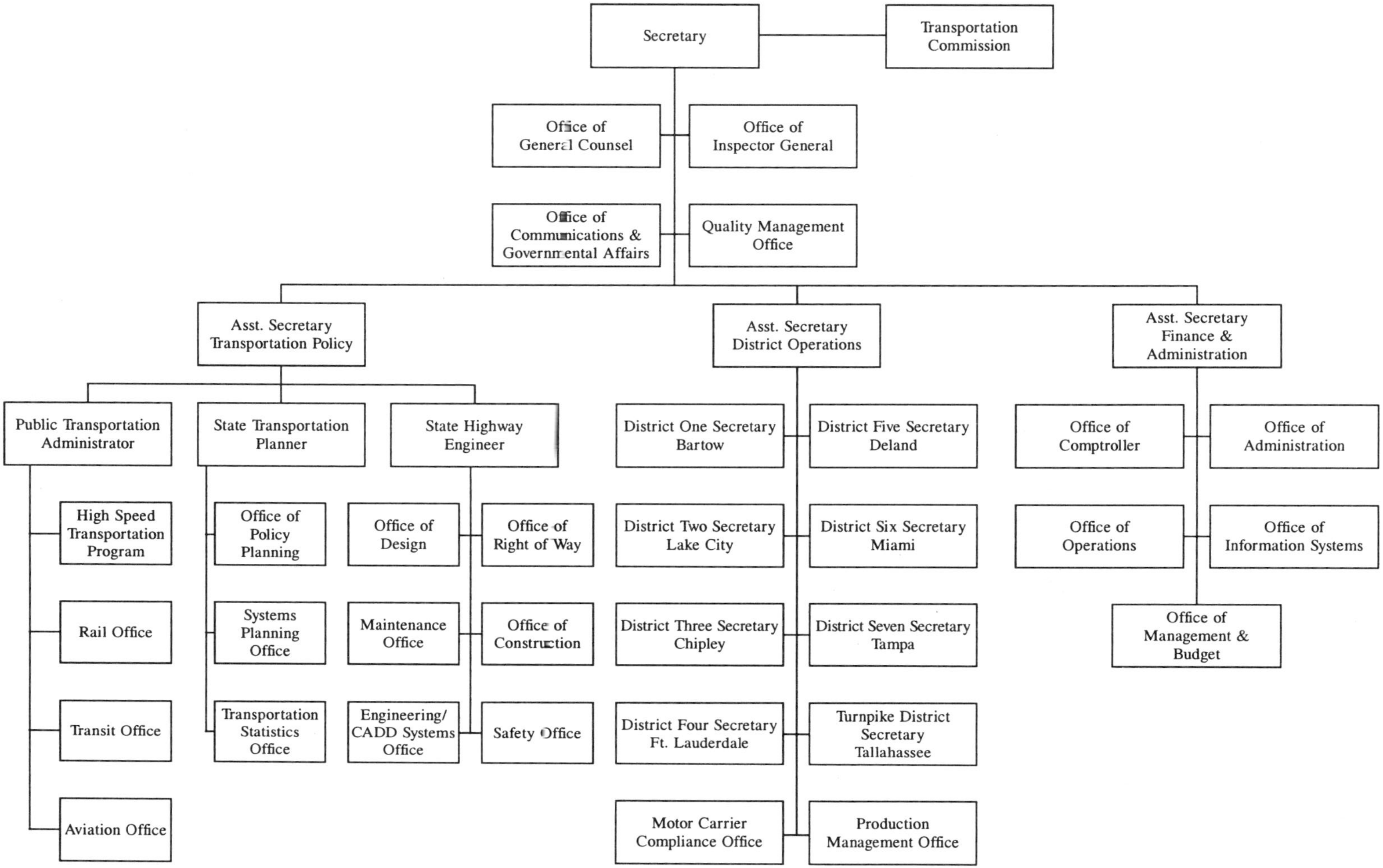

Source: Florida Department of Transportation, October, 1996.

cases services are delivered directly by the agency, but also there is extensive use of contracting. In the case of the Department of Transportation virtually all road construction is done by for-profit contractors. The primary direct operations functions of the Department are in road maintenance. Similarly, the Department of Children and Family Services (see Figure 2-7) delivers some services directly, but many others are provided through contract with non-profit and for-profit agencies and other governments.

One would expect under these circumstances that these agencies would have large control structures, but in fact they are relatively small; Transportation is at only 7%.[4] One explanation for this departure from expectations is that the operating core of both agencies has been decentralized to districts which together cover the entire state. This suggests a complicated control structure that is scattered throughout the state as well as in the central office.

The Department of Corrections (see Figure 2-8), which is responsible for the administration of the state prisons, has the lowest proportion of control positions, 2%. As with the Department of Transportation, there is a very large decentralized system (viz., over 29,780 positions).

Figure 2-7
DEPARTMENT OF CHILDREN & FAMILIES

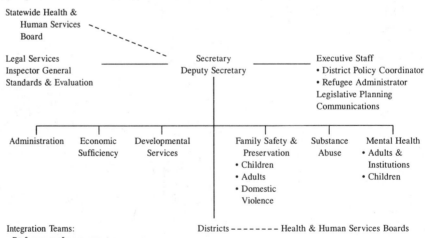

Source: Department of Children and Family Services, July, 1997.

Figure 2-8
DEPARTMENT OF CORRECTIONS

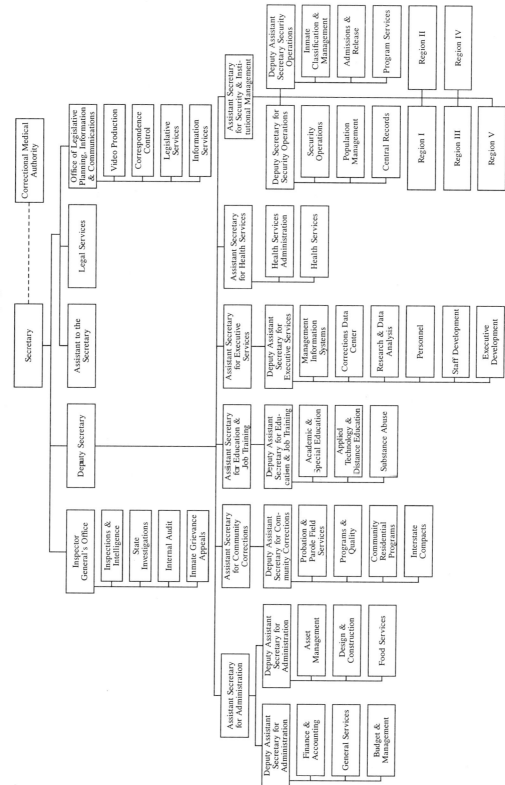

Source: Florida Department of Corrections, September, 1996.

CHAPTER

2

In this case, however, the decentralization is to local correctional institutions that are scattered throughout the state. Another significant difference is that these institutions are governed by strict operating rules and procedures covering virtually every aspect of institutional life (Goffman 1962). The elaboration of rules is possible because the mission of the Department of Corrections is relatively simple. It must keep criminals confined in facilities that meet the standards of custodial care mandated by public policy and the courts. This clarity is to be contrasted with the enormous complexity and ambiguity of human services welfare functions. Making citizens "self sufficient" often involves unclear technologies and conflicting operating standards. A very large array of groups and interests make claims on the limited resources available. The aged, children and families, developmentally disabled, and the poor receive separate organizational recognition.

The comparison of corrections and human services for welfare suggests that control functions are performed in different ways largely because of differences in the complexity and clarity of their respective missions. It has also been suggested that agency size and the decision to use other governments or non-government entities for operations can also have a significant effect on the configuration and control strategies.

CONCLUSION

The system of public institutions in Florida state government for providing policy guidance and implementation is large, complex and uncoordinated. There are multiple centers of policy impulse and control, but with only the most rudimentary methods of rationalizing the diversity. As we saw in Chapter One and as will be further developed in subsequent chapters, these institutional conditions are the product of cultural inheritance, rapid population growth, and national political trends. On the one hand our political leaders are constrained by these institutions, but the institutions themselves are subject to larger forces of stability and change.

In Chapter One it was suggested that the capacity to deal with problems of development depends on four major factors: (1) whether the problems come successively or cumulatively; (2) resources available to the system; (3) the orientation to accepting change; and (4) the creativity or stagnation of political leaders. Of these factors, in Florida the only one where there may be some reason for optimism is political leadership and here the record is mixed. As we shall see in Chapter Three, Florida has had some effective governors, but just as often its governors have not been progressive forces.

REFERENCES

Goffman, Erving (1962). *Asylums.* Chicago, Aldine Publishing Co.

Holden, Mathew, Jr. (1966). Imperialism in bureaucracy. *American Political Science Review,* 60 (December), 943-51.

Mintzberg, Henry (1979). *The structuring of organizations.* Englewood Cliffs: Prentice Hall.

Office of Planning and Budgeting (1990). *Florida's ten-year summary of appropriations data 1980–81—1989–90.* Tallahassee: State of Florida, Executive Office of the Governor.

Sundquist, James L. (1987). Congress as public administrator. In Ralf Chandler (Ed.), *A centennial history of the American administrative state.* New York: Free Press.

ENDNOTES

1. Chapter 16, "New Forms of Service Delivery" provides a more detailed discussion of alternative operation forms.

2. The discussion excludes the State University System which, while technically in the Department of Education, is controlled by the Board of Regents.

3. See Chapter 14 for further discussion of the Department of Community Affairs' role in land management and community development.

4. These proportions are based on 1988 data.

CHAPTER

2

PART II

SOURCES OF SUPPORT AND CONSTRAINT ON POLICY MANAGEMENT: THE EXTERNAL ENVIRONMENT

THE POLITICAL ENVIRONMENT
POLITICAL PARTIES, PUBLIC OPINION
AND INTEREST GROUPS

ROBERT E. CREW, JR.

Chapter 1 began, as do virtually all general accounts of Florida politics and government, with a description of the staggering demographic changes that have occurred in Florida since World War II. Observers of these remarkable changes have seen them as definitive for politics in the state. They have, implicitly at least, linked demographic upheavals to rather substantial changes in the state's political environment—in the nature of public opinion and political participation, in the behavior of political parties, and in the actions of interest groups. They contend that a "new" political environment arose from the demographic upheavals, one that created demands on governmental institutions different from those of the environment of the thirties and forties, and that set new constraints on policy management (Gannon 1993, 139–156; deHaven-Smith 1995). This hypothesis is examined in this chapter. The purpose is to describe the nature of the contemporary political environment in Florida, to examine the extent of the change in that environment which has occurred in the post-World War II period, to show the interaction between demographic change and political change, and to speculate about the impact of the political change on policy management.

PUBLIC OPINION AND IDEOLOGY

Public opinion, particularly the population's views on politics and governmental policy, is one of the basic ingredients in the complex recipe for successful policy management. People's basic values about the purposes of government and politics (their ideology), their attitudes about particular policies, leaders, and parties, their perceptions of political events, and their expectations about the future simultaneously create demands and provide constraints on the policy management system. Changes in public preferences about these issues bring about new policies in response (Page and Shapiro 1983). Thus knowledge of public opinion about government and governmental policy is essential to an understanding of the nature of government and public policy. What is the opinion of the Florida public on the important political and social issues? What is their political ideology? How has opinion and ideology changed over the period 1960 to the present? Are the changes that have occurred affecting policy direction and policy management? In what fashion? These questions guide this portion of the discussion.

POLITICAL IDEOLOGY

Political ideology is a set of beliefs about what government should do regarding public issues. In America ideological beliefs are usually labeled liberal, conservative, and moderate. Liberals tend to favor activist government and social-welfare policies that promote the well-being of specific segments of the population. They also show tolerance of social change and diversity. Conservatives typically prefer private rather than public initiatives, personal liberty, and weak rather than strong government. Moderates favor a mixture of the elements of these two ideologies.

The literature on government and politics in Florida during the early part of the twentieth century consistently described—generally without the benefit of opinion polls—the state's political ideology as conservative. Certainly most political candidates fostered this view by describing themselves in such terms.

Perhaps the state was conservative during this period, but as opinion polls came into widespread use, this characterization had to be refined. Not all Floridians, nor even a plurality of them, think that they are conservatives. Measures taken in 1968 (Gatlin 1973a), and 1976 (Wright, Erikson & McIver 1987) show self-identified liberals to be in a decided minority, but conservatives and moderates or middle-of-the-roaders to be almost equal in numbers. While the percentages in each category are somewhat different, the general distribution of liberals, conservatives, and middle-of-the-roaders in Florida is quite similar to that in the nation as a whole. This characterization has changed very little over subsequent decades and continues into the 1990s. (This supposition is confirmed by Florida's midpoint ranking among all the states on Wright, Erickson and McIver's (1987) index of ideological conservatism developed from data covering the period 1976–1982. On this index Florida ranked 19th among the 47 states for which data were reported.) Data on political ideology in Florida are presented in Table 3-1.

Since the ideological disposition of state electorates is strongly related to the content of state policies (Wright, Erickson & McIver

Table 3-1

IDEOLOGY AMONG FLORIDIANS

(In Percent)

	1968	1980	1981	1982	1983	1984	1985	1986	1987	1988	1989	1990	1991	1992	1993	1994	1995	1996	1997
Conservative	43	41	40	42	40	38	41	41	38	40	42	38	42	40	39	47	42	45	43
Middle of the Road	42	42	42	37	43	43	42	39	45	45	45	46	40	42	46	35	41	37	41
Liberal	16	17	18	22	17	19	17	20	21	16	13	16	16	18	16	18	15	20	17

Sources: Survey Research Laboratory, Florida State University 1980–97: Gatlin 1973a.

1987), we should not expect to find aggressive solutions to policy problems in Florida, a state where most people see themselves as moderates or conservatives. On the other hand, truly conservative proposals to "dismantle the state" will also be somewhat suspect. Thus a relatively limited set of policy options is, and always has been, available to policy managers in the state. The policy consequences are straightforward. Florida places in the middle to low levels among the states on a composite ranking of state government activism (Erickson, Wright & McIver 1989) and on specific measures of state "effort" to resolve the problems faced by its citizens. Thus the state can perhaps better be described as moderate, leaning toward conservative than as strictly conservative.

PUBLIC OPINION: VIEWS ON SPECIFIC ISSUES

While political ideology sets the general boundaries of public policy, elected officials are also influenced by the public's concerns about specific issues or problems. Because of their concern with re-election or their desire to represent public views, public officials actively address policies that are important to the interests of their constituents. Thus the issues that concern Floridians concern elected officials and public managers in the state.

Two issues form the bedrock of political conflict in the state and have focused political debate in Florida throughout the state's history. The first issue is race. The second is economic development and the use of the state's natural resources. The nature and impact of these issues on Florida government and politics is discussed in the following paragraphs.

THE POLITICS OF RACE

The issue that most dramatically has affected the political environment of contemporary Florida is that of race and civil rights. The point of contention has been the extent to which black and other minority Floridians are able to participate as full citizens in society. The bitter controversy over this issue split the Democratic party and laid the base for two-party competition in this state and in the remainder of the South.

The 1964 presidential election marked the decisive turning point on this issue. "With the nomination of Barry Goldwater the Republican Party—the party of Lincoln and emancipation—turned its back on one hundred years of racial progressivism and instead undertook a strategy designed to attract the support of racially disaffected Democrats" (Carmines & Stimson 1989, 47). Using a thinly disguised racist strategy, "go hunting where the ducks are," Goldwater won five southern states and 48.9% of the Florida vote and set the campaign tone for Republican candidates thereafter. The race issue has been used with more or less explicitness in all the Republican presidential campaigns since that time (Carmines & Stimson 1989; Black & Black 1987, 288–89) and has contributed substantially to the statewide victories that the Republicans have achieved in Florida in the past thirty years. The gubernatorial campaign of Claude Kirk in 1966 and his subsequent behavior as governor on the issue and the 1968 senatorial campaign of Edward Gurney appealed quite directly to the racist instincts of Floridians (Lamis 1988, 179; Colburn & Scher 1980, 83; Bass & DeVries 1976, ch. 6; Wagy 1985, ch. 14). Republican presidential politics from Nixon to Bush have reflected a continual commitment to the infamous "southern strategy" (Cosman 1966). Ronald Reagan especially became a "chief apostle of contemporary racial conservatism, breathing new life into the Republican's southern strategy," (Carmines & Stimson 1989, 54) and appeals to racial policy conservatism still forms the bedrock of Republican politics. (Van Wingen & Valentine 1988; Lamis 1988, 26; Strong 1971). It is the factor that led most directly to the restructuring of the political landscape in Florida. In the absence of this issue, the demographic upheaval in the state would have had far less profound effects on state politics. That is, in the absence of the "racist" or racially conservative Democrats who transferred their allegiance to the Republican party, not enough Republicans have moved into the state to make the Republicans into the majority party.

Ironically, Republican appeals to conservatism on race came at a moment when the Republican party was poised to reap the benefits of the enfranchisement of black voters. Eisenhower had carried black districts in Jacksonville in his 1956 campaign and in 1957 he sent federal troops to integrate the schools in Little Rock. Thus, given the opposition of Southern Democrats to black civil rights, Republicans had every right to expect to gain support in this community.

Barry Goldwater [and subsequent Republican presidential and gubernatorial candidates] destroyed this possibility . . . The national [political] surveys attest to the clarity of Goldwater's oratory: the percentage of Republican blacks dropped precipitously in 1964. When the

Voting Rights Act passed the next year and southern rural blacks, sometimes accompanied by federal marshals, began to register, they committed themselves to the national party that helped them. By 1968, over
ninety-seven percent considered themselves Democrats" (Van Wingen &
Valentine 1988, 137).

In Florida in 1992, 95% of the blacks registered to vote were registered as Democrats. To achieve electoral gains, then, the Republican
Party recast itself as a party in which white people who were either
opposed or indifferent to legitimate activities of black people would feel
comfortable. Adoption of this strategy accounts for a substantial portion
of the electoral success of the Republicans in Florida and in the South.

THE POLITICS OF ECONOMIC DEVELOPMENT

While perhaps less dramatic than race, the issue of economic
development and particularly the use and misuse of the state's natural
resources in such development has been, especially since the 1920's,
the focus of substantial political conflict. This dispute however, is not
between Democrats and Republicans. It goes beyond the usual party
labels and involves a one-sided battle between two factions of the
state's elite who disagree only on the speed of economic growth and a
small cadre of people who question the fundamental logic of continuing growth. The issue involved is how best to utilize the state's few
marketable resources, its climate and access to water, for economic
gain.[1]

The pro-growth proponents dominate this issue. The opposing side
has succeeded in stopping some, but by no means all, egregious projects
that would harm a major natural system like the Big Cypress Swamp.
They were also largely responsible for the adoption of the 1985 Growth
Management Act, which is among the most advanced pieces of land use
legislation in the nation. However, the logic that growth is the basis of
prosperity still drives political decision making in the state. Citing the
prospects of jobs and economic gain for their communities, local officials are reluctant to prepare land use plans, blame the Growth
Management Act for declines in housing starts and economic development, and, when they do require developers to meet the requirements of
the Act, pay close heed to the desires of builders. Even when county and
city commissioners bow to public pressure and impose the requirements
of the Act, they frequently amend them at a later date to accommodate
developers. Even destruction of wetlands is permitted, providing developers agree to set aside certain areas as undeveloped or to restore other
areas as "natural landscapes." This questionable practice has spawned a
whole industry devoted to ecological landscaping and has produced, at

best, piecemeal preservation of the natural environment, "pocket" wet-lands and habitats that often fail. The logic that growth equals prosperity has also resulted in shoddy construction of housing to meet the never-ending influx of population, unmet municipal infrastructure needs, and, particularly in central and south Florida, urban blight of the worst sort—gas stations and fast-food outlets at every corner, strip shopping centers, and climate-controlled malls lining the major thoroughfares.[2] To some, "South Florida has become a sort of American urban-frontier dream run wild" (Havard 1959). (For a fictionalized, but not inaccurate, descrip-tion of the growth phenomenon in Florida, see MacDonald 1977.) Thus:

> . . . during the past twenty years, while state politicians have enacted legislation they claimed would protect the environment and control growth, the state has experienced the most dramatic population increase in its history and acceleration of a precipitous decline in the quality of its water and the viability of its land (Derr 1989, 389).

The dominance of the pro-growth mentality has profound implica-tions for the nature of government and for policy management in Florida. Government in the state is seen both as an obstacle to the effi-cient operations of the free market and as a mechanism for promoting economic prosperity. Thus there is a strong anti-tax attitude and opposi-tion to governmental activism, except in support of economic develop-ment. To the extent that taxes are supported, they are those that will least affect the pocketbooks of individuals and organizations that can con-tribute maximally to economic development. Consequently, individual and corporate income taxes are opposed (individual income taxes are prohibited by the state constitution), and sales taxes and gasoline taxes, which shift the burden of government away from business and toward lower-income consumers and tourists, are supported. Substantial support can be provided to social programs only when they can be justified as providing a basis for improving the economy. Thus the state lags behind most states, and all large states, in its support for education, health care, assistance to children, and other programs that redistribute resources from better-off to less-well-off Floridians.

OTHER ISSUES

While the general outline of Florida politics has been structured by the issues of race and economic development (Key 1950, 5; Black & Black 1987; Carter 1974; Derr 1989), other problems have also con-cerned citizens of the state. Since 1979 the Survey Research Laboratory

Table 3-2

MOST IMPORTANT PROBLEM AREAS, 1995

at Florida State University has polled a cross-section of Floridians, asking the question, "What do you think are the most important problems facing the State of Florida?" Table 3-2 displays the 1995 response to this question and Table 3-3 the top three problem areas over the period 1979–1995.

Problem Area	Percent
Crime (crime, drugs, juvenile crime, other)	36%
Economic (unemployment, minimum wage, other)	9%
Social (immigration, health care, welfare fraud, other)	20%
Education (education, lack of funding, other)	11%
Government (taxes, other)	6%
Growth/Infrastructure (population growth, other)	5%
Environment	3%
Other Problems	4%
No Problems/Don't Know	6%

Source: Survey Research Laboratory 1996.2.

In 1993, for the only second time since 1983, the economy (unemployment, wages, other) ranked as the issue that concerned most Floridians. Problems related to crime came in second, and those related to education were third. Education emerged as an important issue in 1992 when it was perceived as the most important problem facing the state. This ranking constituted the first time since the survey began that education had been considered among the top three problems.

Many of the issues that appear over the course of the period—concern about the environment, issues of community development, and crime—are directly related to the growth that has come to Florida in the last half of the twentieth century. Community development problems have appeared as one of the top-three problems in all but one of the surveys conducted over the period, and the issue of crime has been a top three concern in every poll since 1982. Interestingly, the issue of taxes, which has been a focus of attention in the administrations of several governors, was not seen as a serious problem by the Floridians interviewed during this period.

Analysis of these data indicates that neither the Democrats nor the Republicans have benefitted disproportionately from these issues. Rather, they provide the grist for the policy mill of all elected officials and policy managers.

POLITICAL PARTICIPATION: TRANSLATING OPINION INTO ACTION

Democratic societies are distinguished by their emphasis on citizen participation. The concept of self-government rests on the proposition that ordinary people have a right, even an obligation, to involve themselves in the affairs of their governments. Further, a state that claims to operate in the interest of its citizens must provide meaningful opportunities to those citizens to participate in the decisions that affect them. To some extent, therefore, the extent of political participation—

Table 3-3
PUBLIC PERCEPTION OF TOP THREE POLICY PROBLEM AREAS
1979–1995

Year	Problem Area	Most Important	Second Most	Third Most
1995	Crime	36		
	Social Problems		20	
	Education			11
1994	Crime	45		
	Economic Problems		15	
	Social Problems			13
1993	Economic Problems	23		
	Crime		18	
	Education			16
1992	Education	26		
	Economic Problems		19	
	Government			15
1991	Economic Problems	32		
	Community Development		15	
	Government Management			10
1990	Economic Problems	27		
	Community Development		18	
	Energy			14
1989	Crime	27		
	Community Development		20	
	Environment			10
1988	Community Development	25		
	Crime		15	
	Economic Problems			14
1987	Community Development	23		
	Crime		21	
	Economic Problems			13
1986	Community Development	24		
	Crime		17	
	Social Problems			10
1985	Community Development	29		
	Crime		13	
	Social Problems			12
1984	Community Development	21		
	Economic Development		19	
	Crime			11
1983	Economic Problems	39		
	Crime		13	
	Community Development			12
1982	Crime	23		
	Social Problems		21	
	Economic Problems			16
1981	Economic Problems	25		
	Social Problems		17	
	Community Development			16
1980	Economic Problems	27		
	Community Development		18	
	Energy			14
1979	Economic Problems	32		
	Community Development		15	
	Government Management			10

Source: Survey Research Laboratory 1993; 1996.

that is, how much and by whom—is a measure of how fully democratic is a society (Verba and Nie 1972, 1).

Political participation is defined as "all behavior through which people express their political opinions" (Matthews and Prothro 1966, 3). These behaviors fall into two general categories: conventional activities that use the institutional channels of representative government, and extraordinary activities that challenge or defy government channels and thus are personally stressful to participants and their opponents (Janda et al. 1987). In this section we examine conventional political participation in Florida. We discuss the extent to which the state fosters such participation, describe the level of participation, and speculate about the policy management implications of the existing level of participation.

THE PARTICIPATORY ENVIRONMENT IN FLORIDA

A variety of factors affect the nature and level of political participation within a state. These include the socioeconomic characteristics of the residents, the nature of the political culture, and the laws that structure access to information and decision making and to the ballot. Actions of the state can have minimal effect on some of these factors—for example the socioeconomic characteristics of its population—but great effect on others—for example, ease of access to registration and voting.

The State of Florida has a mixed record with regard to fostering the participation of its citizens in public activities. It has made substantial efforts to ensure citizen access to public meetings and to provide for public access to legislative bill calendars, floor action agendas, and committee hearing schedules (Common Cause 1978). The Florida "sunshine laws," which govern the manner in which public officials conduct their business, are widely regarded as among the strongest in the nation. The state also has passed significant open records and freedom of information laws (Advisory Commission on Intergovernmental Relations 1979, 244–45) and has made relatively strong provisions for citizens to pursue their policy interests through initiative and referenda (Council of State Governments 1977, 176, 216–18). Thus, citizens interested in the affairs of the state have an excellent opportunity to inform themselves about issues confronting government, to witness and participate in the deliberations surrounding their resolution, and to initiate their own policy actions in the event that they disagree with the direction of policy as formulated by elected officials.

Florida has not, however, made access to the ballot as easy as it might be. The state's election laws contain some provisions that inhibit easy voter registration and voting, and thus deflate voter turnout. Current laws do not make it easy to register in the evening or on Saturday and require the closing of registration thirty days prior to the date of election. In states in which these (and other) impediments are lifted, voter registration is much higher (Wolfinger and Rosenstone 1980). Further, surveys conducted among Florida citizens suggest that

> . . . there might have been a small percentage point increase in voter turnout (in 1988) had the polls been open longer on election day, or election day were a holiday or, in general if access to the polling stations had been easier" (Gatlin 1989, 24).

This same research estimates that perhaps 500,000 more Floridians could be added to the registered voter rolls by improving the mechanics of voter registration (20). Newly passed federal legislation on this subject—the so-called "Motor Voter" law—has had an important impact on this problem. Nearly 1 million new voters were added to the rolls in the immediate aftermath of this law.

THE LEVEL OF POLITICAL PARTICIPATION IN FLORIDA

To this point, we have focused on things that affect the nature and extent of political participation in Florida. We turn now to an examination of actual participation levels. Three types of participation are examined: (1) voter registration, (2) voting, and (3) other forms of participation.

When possible, we compare the levels of participation in Florida to those in other states and in the nation.

VOTER REGISTRATION. In order to be eligible to vote, Floridians must register prior to election day. In the section above, we cited evidence that Florida's election laws may minimize voter turnout. These laws combine with other factors to produce much smaller percentages of registered voters in Florida than in other states. Although data are not available for every state in every year, there is no doubt that Florida fares poorly with regard to voter registration. Eligible voters in Florida register in smaller percentages than citizens in all but a handful of other states; only five states and the District of Columbia have lower average registration figures. Further, the demographic changes that have swept the state have had very little effect on registration figures, and the change that has occurred has been downward. A slightly smaller percentage of the voting-age population was registered in 1988 than was registered in 1960.

VOTER TURNOUT. Since one must be registered in order to vote and since relatively small percentages of Floridians are registered, it should come as no surprise to find that voter turnout in the state is low. In fact, turnout in Florida during the past thirty years has been, on average, 13.4% below the national average, and during the period 1960–1988 was the 10th lowest among the states and the District of Columbia. In the average year during this period, only 43.8% of Florida's voting age population actually cast ballots in the presidential elections. In 1988, just four states and the District of Columbia had a lower turnout rate than Florida (Council of State Governments 1991, 266).

In non-presidential years, the figures are even more depressed. The average turnout for gubernatorial or senatorial races during the years 1962–1988 was only 33.6%. A variety of factors—socioeconomic characteristics of the population, political culture, and party competition—affect voter turnout. Clearly many of these variables converge negatively in Florida, for Floridians do not take their responsibility to vote very seriously, especially when it comes to offices other than president. Once again, little change is observed over the nearly thirty years involved.

PARTICIPATION THROUGH INTEREST GROUPS. As an avenue of political participation, interest groups in Florida provide opportunities for persons who want more active involvement than is provided by the simple act of voting. Such groups provide interested citizens a mechanism for bringing their concerns directly to their elected representatives. While Floridians have been availing themselves of this opportunity more aggressively over recent years, the percentage of citizens involved is relatively low. Table 3-4 displays, for the period 1955–1988, data that touches on the topic. These data describe the numbers of people who register with the state legislature in order to lobby on behalf of a particular interest. Since the registration period changed over the years involved, the data are divided into three separate categories and are not strictly comparable. They do, however, provide a general picture of the level of involvement in lobbying. In the first year in which Florida law required persons who sought to influence state government to register their intent to do so (1955), 501 individuals were listed. By 1988 this number had risen to 5,833 individuals.

It is difficult to determine just how many individuals other than registered lobbyists are active in interest groups. However, in 1988–1990, 3,300 separate groups were registered with the state legislature. If we assume that each group has at least 100 members, then at least 330,000 people during the period 1988–1990 participated in Florida state government and politics in this fashion. Thus, a relatively large number of Floridians (but a small percentage of the total population) find this avenue of participation to be attractive. The major complaint about such participation is that it is skewed toward those whose resources permit either them or their representative to spend substantial amounts of time and money in efforts to influence public officials. These individuals and groups are thus able to exert influence on public policy that is out of proportion to their numbers within the state as a whole.

POLITICAL PARTICIPATION AND POLICY MANAGEMENT

Political participation is a technique used by citizens to influence the setting of goals, the choice of alternatives, and decisions about what resources to commit to goal attainment. Evidence suggests that public officials tend to be better informed about and more in agreement with the opinions of persons most active in politics than with the views of the rank and file of the citizenry (Verba & Nie 1972, 18). Those more active in politics are likely to be better represented through appointments to public positions; they are more apt to be involved in the implementation and evaluation of public programs; and they are likely to be better informed about and influential in the budget process. Thus, the relatively low levels of participation through voting in Florida skews public policy in the state. This problem of representativeness is compounded by the skewed distribution of participation through interest groups.

Low levels of voter turnout mean that elected officials in the State of Florida may exercise their power in different ways than elected officials

Table 3-4

LOBBYISTS REGISTERED IN FLORIDA

	Period	Number Registered
Biennial Period	1955	501
	1957	587
	1959	524
	1961	576
	1963	640
	1965	778
	1967	886
Yearly Period	1969	809
	1970	872
	1971	929
	1972	1,218
	1973	1,395
	1974	2,236
	1975	2,050
	1976	2,998
	1977	2,560
	1978	3,329
Biennial Session Only	1978	4,009
	1980	3,895
	1982	4,382
	1984	4,297
	1986	4,601
	1988	5,833

Source: Compiled by the Office of the Clerk 1990.

in high turnout states. It may not matter who exercises power if the political preferences of those who vote in Florida and those who do not are substantially the same, but limited evidence suggests that these preferences may not be the same. For example, registered voters trust government in both Washington and in Florida more than those who are not registered (Gatlin 1989, 13). Thus we do need to worry about the representativeness of our elected officials. It is also important to remember that "over the long pull, governments that must win the consent of the masses will differ from those that can hold on to power by the support of a small proportion of the people" (Key 1950, 489).

POLITICAL PARTIES

Political parties constitute an important element of the political environment of any democratic system. Parties tie the public to the government, loosely organize the government, set the agenda for debates on public policy, and provide a way to hold elected officials accountable for their actions.

Parties also transform conflict over society's goals into electoral competition in which the losers recognize the winner's right to take the lead in making policy decisions. While these roles are played imperfectly by the political parties of Florida, parties are a primary mechanism through which partisan preference is given some permanence and durability. When changes occur in that preference, the nature of the party system will also change.

This kind of change has been one of the most commonly cited characteristics of the Florida political environment. The massive population influx into Florida over the past fifty years has been accompanied by some important alterations in the nature of the state's party system. We turn now to an examination of that change and to a discussion of the relationship between the change in the nature of Florida's population and the change in the party system.

THE PARTY IN THE GOVERNMENT

There are at least two measures of the extent to which political parties command support within a political system: the number of party members who hold governmental office and the degree of psychological identification with the parties on the part of citizens. While the two are related, they measure separate dimensions of the party system and warrant separate analysis. This analysis begins with an examination of the extent to which the major political parties share public office in Florida. The focus is on federal and state offices.

The party system in Florida has undergone substantial recent change when judged on the party-in-government dimension. From a time in the 1950s when the system was controlled almost totally by Democrats, the late 1980s became a period when Republicans could point to substantial gains in public office. In 1993 Republicans had a five-seat majority in the U.S. House of Representatives. Over the past 40 years, they have also elected two governors, three U.S. senators, and two members of the cabinet, and have made significant gains in the State Senate and State House of Representatives. In 1992 voters elected equal numbers of Democrats and Republicans to the Senate and in an agreement between the parties, the Republicans were permitted to select the Majority Leader and the committee chairs to govern the first two years of the term, with the Democrats gaining control in the final two years.[3] While neither of the two governors and one of the two U.S. senators who have campaigned for re-election has been re-elected, this kind of electoral strength would have been unthinkable until the mid 1960s.

Table 3-5 provides a picture of the nature of the change in party fortunes that has occurred in Florida. It demonstrates that Republican gains have come largely in the Congress of the United States. Comparing party competition at the state level only, during the periods 1962–73 and 1974–80, Charles Barrilleaux (1986) found a decrease of 15%; that is, the Democrats were stronger in the second period than in the first. However, between the same two periods, competition for U.S. House seats increased by 7%; that is, Republicans became stronger over time. This pattern continued over the decade of the 1980s but has changed slightly in the early 1990s as Republicans have become more competitive at both the state and the federal levels.

THE PARTY IN THE ELECTORATE

A second way to determine the level of support for political parties within a nation or state is to ascertain the extent to which competing parties command the psychological loyalty of citizens. That is, regardless of how they vote, an issue is to what extent do people

Table 3-5

FLORIDA PARTISAN REPRESENTATION: STATE LEGISLATURE AND CONGRESS

| | FLORIDA LEGISLATURE | | | | U.S. CONGRESS | |
| | SENATE | | HOUSE | | | |
	REP	DEM	REP	DEM	REP	DEM
1962	1	37	7	88	1	7
1964	2	43	16	109	2	10
1966	19	29	39	80	1	11
1968	16	32	42	72	3	9
1970	15	33	38	81	3	9
1972	14	25	43	77	3	9
1974	12	27	34	86	4	11
1976	9	30	28	92	5	10
1978	11	29	31	89	5	10
1980	13	27	39	81	3	12
1982	8	32	36	84	4	11
1984	8	32	43	77	6	13
1986	15	25	44	76	7	12
1988	17	23	45	75	10	9
1990	17	23	46	74	10	9
1992	20	20	46	74	13	8
1994	20	20	46	74	12	11
1996	22	18	57	63	15	8

Sources: Compiled by the author from Morris, various years: and *The Clerk's Manual,* various years.

identify themselves as Democrats or Republicans. For nearly sixty years the concept of party identification has been used by political scientists as a measure of party support. Data on this phenomenon in Florida, gathered in polls taken over a long period of time, are utilized to place the changes in party strength described above into perspective. Have the gains made in the government by Florida Republicans during the past fifty years been reflected in gains in psychological attachment to the party? Do more people in Florida now think of themselves as Republicans than in previous years?

The answer is yes. The data in Table 3-6 show that in 1964, 70% of Floridians thought of themselves as Democrats, 19% as Republicans, and nine percent as independents. In 1996 the figures were 32% Democrat, 33% Republican, and 35% independent. These data indicate substantial changes in support for the Democrats and Republicans, and very strong growth in the number of independents. In 1964 the Democrats were the majority party; that is, more than 50% of Floridians identified themselves psychologically with the Democratic party. In 1996 the Republicans and the Democrats were virtually tied as the favored party in the state. While Republicanism has not yet risen to the ranks of majority status (indeed in the past four years the Republicans have lost nine percentage points support within the electorate), the change in Democrat-Republican fortunes is quite dramatic. Equally dramatic is the change in numbers of independent voters. Beginning in 1991, independents became the largest "party"; that is, the numbers of persons who see themselves as independent of either party now outnumber those who view themselves as either Democrats or Republicans. Thus in 1993 the Democratic Party, the party of Thomas Jefferson, Andrew Jackson, Franklin Delano Roosevelt, John F. Kennedy, Harry Truman, Lyndon B. Johnson, and Jimmy Carter, and of LeRoy Collins, Reubin Askew, Bob Graham, Lawton Chiles, and Claude Pepper—the longest-lived political party in world history—had lost command of the hearts and minds of most Floridians.

Table 3-6

PARTY IDENTIFICATION IN FLORIDA: 1964–1995

	DEMOCRAT	INDEPENDENT	REPUBLICAN
1964	70	9	19
1968	49	29	22
1970	64	10	23
1972	43	30	22
1980	44	35	21
1981	40	31	30
1982	40	27	33
1983	41	30	30
1984	40	30	30
1985	36	29	35
1986	32	30	39
1987	33	30	37
1988	35	30	35
1989	33	24	42
1990	31	28	40
1991	32	37	32
1992	28	36	36
1993	32	35	33
1994	32	34	33
1995	27	34	38

Sources: Louis Harris Poll 1964, 1972; Gatlin 1973b; Hamilton and staff 1976; Survey Research Laboratory 1980–95.

EXPLAINING THE CHANGES IN THE PARTY SYSTEM

The data described above show a change in the nature of the political party system in Florida over the past fifty years. The Republicans clearly have made inroads into both the government and the electorate. The changes have been so remarkable that one observer described them as "the first stage of a critical realignment in Florida. Barring a complete reversal in the climate of the times, there is good reason to believe a major and lasting transformation of Florida politics has taken place" (Beck 1982, 435–36). A combination of factors explains these changes.

The Republican gains outlined above coincided with the substantial immigration to the state described in Chapter 1 of this book, and it is often assumed that the former is caused by the latter. Thus, a common explanation for the rise of Republicanism in the state is that most of the people who moved to Florida during the decades of the fifties through the eighties were Republican retirees from the northern, more heavily Republican states. There is truth to this characterization, and the core support of the Republican party as it emerged in the 1960s did derive from migrants. However, not all of these migrants came from the North, nor were they all Republicans (Gatlin 1973a). Thus other factors have also contributed to the change in the party's fortunes.

A second explanation for the increase in Republican office holders has been the activism and success of the party organization. Following a model conceived by Republican national chairman Ray Bliss, Florida Republicans have adapted modern technology to political purposes and have greatly improved their ability to assist their candidates in political campaigns and to enroll their partisans in challenges to the Democrats. The party has been especially successful in registering its voters.

Between the years 1960 and 1995, Republican registration increased from 338,340 to 3,077,416. During the same time, Democratic registration increased at a much slower rate. Therefore, at the end of the period Democrats outnumbered Republicans by "only" 1.5 million registered voters. Thus the Republicans have achieved a substantial gain in supporters at least in part because of the organizational efforts of the party.

While the voter registration effort has been a source of pride for the Republicans, current voter registration figures indicate a potential future problem for the party in an increasingly heterogeneous state. Not surprisingly given the party's stance on race and civil rights, the Republican increases have come almost entirely within the white population, leaving the party woefully weak in the remainder of the population. In 1992, the Republican Party was 96.9% white. Only 3.1% of registered Republicans were from races other than white and only 2.2% of registered Republicans were black.

CHAPTER

3

To further limit their appeal in a rapidly changing state like Florida, the Republicans are also ideologically homogeneous. Almost all Republican party officials rate themselves as either moderate, somewhat conservative or conservative. Fewer than 3% see themselves as liberal or somewhat liberal (Kelly 1993).

The Democratic party, meanwhile, has sustained its historic support among African-American and "other" races. In 1992 registered voters from these races constituted 12.8% of the Democratic total. And 86.8% of all non-white voters in the state are registered as Democrats (Department of State 1960, 1992). Further, Democrats are quite dispersed along the ideological (liberal to conservative) dimension. While most Democratic party officials see themselves as somewhat liberal or liberal, many also view themselves as conservative or somewhat conservative (Kelly 1993).

Several other hypotheses have been posited to explain the change in the party system of Florida. The first is that the state is becoming more conservative and therefore more likely to be amenable to the blandishments of the Republican party. A second, and related, explanation is that Floridians are moving closer to the issue positions of the Republicans. Finally, structural changes in the electoral system have been credited with improving Republican representation in the legislature.

We have dealt with the first of these issues in an earlier section of this chapter. Floridians are not markedly more conservative now than they have been in the past and, therefore, increasing conservatism cannot account for growing Republicanism in the state. Further, Floridians are not following the Republican lead on any policy issues except those related to race. Of course, positions on this issue are definitive and explain most of the rise of Republican party strength in the state.

The Republican Party has argued for years that the nature of the electoral system in Florida discriminates against their candidates and that structural changes in that system, through reapportionment and a change from multi-member to single member legislative districts would improve their fortunes. While legislative reapportionment has produced more Republican districts (as one might expect given the increase in Republican registrants in the state), the change in 1982 to single-member districts did not positively affect their electoral fortunes. More accurately, the gains state candidates made appear to be attributable to their riding on the coattails of Republican candidates for national office, particularly Ronald Reagan.

Other scholars have also suggested the popularity of President Reagan as an explanation for the shift in party fortunes in Florida and in the South generally. They have argued that "Reagan's performance in office revised the feelings of millions of southern whites about the Republican and Democratic parties" (Black & Black 1987, 240). Suzanne Parker (1988) found this phenomenon in Florida. She demonstrates that the popularity of the former president was the impetus for shifts in party fortunes in the 1980s. Reagan's popularity in Florida increased during his term of office; people identified with him and through him with the Republican party. This identification helps explain the recent growth in Republicanism in the state.

PARTY CHANGE AND POLICY MANAGEMENT IMPLICATIONS

The changes in the party system of Florida described above will have substantial implications for policy management in the state. First, and most obviously, the rise of the Republican party should interject new or modified issues into the political debate that structures public management. A major function of a political party is to aggregate the demands of its supporters and try to convert them into public policy. As Republicans continue to challenge for supremacy within Florida, their articulated views of what is best for the citizens of the state continue to be different from those of Democrats. Since political parties have at least some range of choice in the specific content of policies they adopt, they can shift policy grounds to adapt to the "attack" of competitors. Policy managers will inevitably be caught up in this debate and affected by its outcome.

We should not expect, however, fundamental shifts in the nature of public policy in Florida to emerge from the increase in party competition in the state. The rise of Republicanism does not mean that a group that had been heretofore under-represented in Florida politics is now better represented. Increases in the number of Republicans simply gives the dominant interests a more conservative vehicle through which to pursue their goals, and it is only these interests which are adequately represented in the existing party system. In the absence of the kind of economic development that produces interests whose goals are more progressive than are the goals of those represented in the existing party system and who can organize themselves effectively, policy outcomes in Florida are likely to remain relatively stable.

While political parties are concerned about the issue positions of the electorate, party competition is more than a policy game, with each party articulating competing views of the good life. Strategies to defeat the opposition party may take precedence over strategies to enact a consistent policy program. Such actions can have substantial effect on policy management.

We are likely to see such behavior in emerging two-party systems such as that in Florida (Gatlin 1973b). We can anticipate actions of parties designed to place their opponents in an embarrassing light or to force them into defense of a position that they would prefer to avoid. They may adopt strategies "to divide the opposition party if possible, to place it in an untenable parliamentary position, and to force it into actions and pronouncements likely to be unpopular in the eyes of the electorate" (Gatlin 1973b, 41).

The absorption of public officials in such actions will detract from their attention to substantive policy issues (Dye 1984; Crew 1969). Public managers will be drawn into these debates, and citizens will criticize both these public managers and elected officials for being more concerned with defeating the opposition party than with solving the problems faced by the state.

INTEREST GROUPS

"Interest groups are any association of individuals, whether formally organized or not, which attempts to influence public policy" (Hrebenar and Thomas 1990, 1). Group interests are the animating forces in the political process and an understanding of politics in any state requires a knowledge of the chief interests in the state and their positions on public issues.

Interest groups, along with political parties, are the major mechanisms linking citizens with the government. Groups aggregate and articulate the needs and policy preferences of their members to government. They provide information to policy makers, an essential role in the policymaking process, and they participate in the electoral process in at least three ways: by recruiting candidates, providing campaign support in the form of workers and other services, and raising and contributing money to the parties and to individual candidates. Thus interest groups are a critical element of the political environment of any political system.

The activities of interest groups overlap those of political parties. Both aggregate and articulate the views of interests within a state or society; both participate in the electoral process; and both seek to secure political benefits for their members. This overlap produces competition between the two, and some scholars compare the states in terms of this interrelationship, arguing that the stronger the parties the less freedom interest groups will have; and the weaker the parties the greater the impact of groups (Zeller 1954, 190–91; Fenton 1966; Morehouse 1981; Hrebner and Thomas 1990). Using this framework, states can be characterized as strong party states or strong interest group states. Florida is ordinarily grouped into the strong interest group category. Nevertheless, to make government effective and responsive, both groups and parties are necessary. In some aspects parties and groups complement each other, while in other ways they are in competition.

THE INTEREST GROUP STRUCTURE IN FLORIDA

The variety or range of interest groups working to affect public policy in a particular state tells much about the nature of politics within the state. An examination of the groups active within a state and of the interests from which they arise throws light on the demands that public officials must manage and on the problems with which they must cope. Thus a first task in any effort to understand the impact of interest groups on the management of public policy in Florida is to come to an understanding of the number and nature of interests that are represented in Florida state government.

Table 3-7 provides some very basic longitudinal information on the interest group system in Florida: the number of groups registered to lobby the state legislature, the number of individuals who represent these groups, and the amount of money reportedly spent in efforts to promote their interests. This table indicates that the late 1970s was a high point in group activity in Florida, with 3,488 groups registered in 1976 and $213,000 spent on their behalf in 1977. Group activity surpassed the 1977 number only in 1990. The number of lobbyists peaked in 1988–1990, but both the number of groups and the number of lobbyists began to decline after that date as laws enacted in 1991 required lobbyists and groups to pay a fee to register took effect.

Table 3-7
INTEREST GROUPS IN FLORIDA

	Period	Number of Groups	Number of Lobbyists	Dollars Spent by Registrants
Biennial Period	1955	NA	501	NA
	1957	NA	587	NA
	1959	NA	524	NA
	1961	NA	576	NA
	1963	NA	640	NA
	1965	NA	778	NA
	1967	NA	886	NA
Yearly Period	1969	NA	809	$ 57,833
	1970	1,069	872	76,152
	1971	1,127	929	82,511
	1972	1,484	1,218	76,868
	1973	1,622	1,395	129,688
	1974	2,622	2,236	169,112
	1975	2,274	2,050	167,227
	1976	3,488	2,998	195,268
	1977	2,852	2,560	213,679
	1978	1,249	3,329	206,800
Biennial Session Only	1978–1980	1,815	4,009	$ 709,009
	1980–1982	1,618	3,895	852,853
	1982–1984	1,891	4,382	1,507,220
	1984–1986	2,278	4,297	1,618,444
	1986–1988	2,599	4,601	1,919,961
	1988–1990	3,300	5,833	2,283,432

NA = not available

Source: Florida House of Representatives.

A second way of illuminating the nature of the Florida interest group system is to categorize the active groups according to the number that represent broad elements of the society. Such a description provides insight into the numerical weight of each of these elements in the society. The public officials of a state in which manufacturing groups are predominant may behave in quite different ways from those in a state in which social groups predominate. Table 3-8 provides a picture of the Florida interest group system, categorized by elements of the group system, at two periods: November 1978–December 1979, and October 1988–June 1990. The table also provides comparable 1980 data for 44 of the 50 states.

Table 3-8 shows the Florida interest group system, at least in 1978–79, to be quite different from the average state group system of that time. Social and trade groups make up at least 10% more of the system in Florida than they do in other states. And finance/insurance, and mining make up at least 5% less of the Florida system than comparable groups in other states. Table 3-8 also shows some change within the Florida system in the past ten years. Trade groups have increased by 12% and services have declined by nearly 13% between 1979 and 1990.

Table 3-8

INTEREST GROUP STRUCTURES: FLORIDA AND UNITED STATES

Sector	Florida 1979	US 1980	Florida 1989
Social	26.4%	17.2%	28.6%
Government/Politics	14.7	14.4	16.5
Manufacture	2.4	7.4	0.9
Trade	18.1	7.1	30.1
Finance/Insurance	8.1	13.3	7.4
Agriculture	2.2	3.0	1.8
Services	20.1	15.3	7.7
Construction	2.5	5.8	2.4
Transport/Utilities	5.0	10.6	4.3
Mining	.01	6.2	.3

Sources: Joint Legislative Office on Lobby Registration;
Lowery & Gray 1990.

The descriptions provided above offer a starting point for understanding the Florida system of interest groups. However, they leave unanswered the question of the relative influence of the groups. Which group (or groups) are most influential and how can the general pattern of relationships among the groups be characterized? We address the latter question first.

The research of Harmon Ziegler and Hendrick van Dalen (1976) provides a framework for examining the power relationship within the Florida state interest group system as a whole. They identified four ways in which influence relationships among interest groups in a state can be described.

First is dominance by a single interest. In this pattern, one group, because of its importance to the state's economy, dwarfs all other groups in political importance. A second pattern is the alliance of dominant interests. In this pattern, a few groups have relatively equal power and these three or four interests dominate all others. A third pattern is conflict between two dominant groups. This pattern exists in an economy dominated by a single industry—such as automobile manufacturing—that is divided into two groups competing for power—such as labor and management. The final pattern is the triumph of many interests. This pattern is likely to occur in a state with a diverse economy that stimulates multiple groups with relatively equal influence.

While the relationships among interest groups within a state may fit into more than one of these patterns over the course of time, for the past ten years Florida has fallen into the fourth category. The most recent research on interest groups in the state suggests that at least twelve groups were "consistently influential (in the politics of Florida) over the latter half of the 1980s" (Hrebner & Thomas 1990). And Sarah McCally Morehouse (1981) found nine groups to be "significant" in 1980. Such numbers qualify the state for listing in the category of triumph of many interests.

We come now to the second question about interest group influence in Florida. Which groups are most powerful or influential? The research of three scholars, using somewhat different methods, helps provide the answer. These people, working at two different periods, attempted to specify the most "significant" groups in the Florida system. The results of their assessment are shown in Figure 3-1. In 1980 five specific groups and eight types of interests were deemed influential. In 1990 eleven specific groups and eight other types of interests were in the influential category.

Figure 3-1

SIGNIFICANT INTEREST GROUPS IN FLORIDA

1980	1990
• Associated Industries	• Florida Association of Realtors
• Utilities— Florida Power Corporation Florida Power and Light	• Associated Industries
	• Trial Lawyers
• Farm Bureau	• Florida Association of Insurance
• Bankers	• Governor's Office
• Liquor interests	• School teachers— FTP/NEA Florida Education Association
• Chain stores	
• Race tracks	• Homebuilders and Contractors Association
• Phosphate Council	• Health groups— Florida Medical Association Florida Dental Association Florida Hospital League

(Left axis label: Interest Groups)

Sources: The 1980 data are from Morehouse 1981, and the 1990 data from Hrebner & Thomas 1990.

CHANGE IN THE INTEREST GROUP SYSTEM

The growth in population and economic activity that has occurred in Florida in the past fifty years clearly has had an impact on the nature of the interest group system in the state. First, as indicated in Table 3-7, the number of groups involved in activities designed to influence state government has grown dramatically over the years. The numbers have nearly doubled just since 1978, from 1,815 to 3,300.

Second, the groups defined as influential have changed. Only one group—Associated Industries—was influential in both 1980 and 1990.

Thus, while the interest group system remains unchanged—it was and is in the category of triumph of many interests—the influence of groups within the system has changed.

Further, the interest group system in the Sunshine State is becoming more dense or cluttered; that is, relative to the size of the state's economy, there are more interest groups than one would expect. The interest group system in Florida, along with those in Minnesota and Pennsylvania, is "far more dense than expected" (Lowery and Gray 1990, 17). In most states, as size increases, interest group density declines because many older interest groups, such as the Chamber of Commerce, need not be replicated as the economy grows. Any growth in the number of interest groups, therefore, must come in the form of new interests or in the specificity of representation of old interests (3). For some reason the economic change that has occurred in Florida over the past ten years has had the opposite effect on the state's interest group system. As the size of the state's economy has increased, the number of interest groups has also increased, and at a faster rate than the economy. Thus the changing economy and the interest group system are clearly interrelated, but in an unexpected way.

Despite these changes, the general characterization of the system has not been altered. The system has been and continues to be characterized as a "triumph of many interests." No single interest can expect to command exclusive attention from policy makers in Florida. Conversely, policy makers must be prepared to balance the competing demands of a range of groups.

REGULATING GROUP ACTIVITY

That interest groups play an important role in Florida state politics makes them widely viewed with some skepticism. A major fear is that the economic resources that they control will permit them to bring unwarranted influence on the government. Combined with evidence of illegal and questionable ethical behavior on the part of some representatives of these groups, this fear has led to several attempts to regulate group activities. These attempts include: the passage of legislation requiring lobbyists to register as agents of specific interests; limiting the amounts of campaign funds groups can provide to individual candidates; requiring the disclosure both of campaign contributions made to public officials and of money spent in attempts to influence the behavior of public officials (meals, gifts, etc.); and prohibiting certain kinds of activities. Spurred by the gubernatorial campaign of Lawton Chiles and the investigations of State Attorney Willie Meggs, the Florida State

Legislature in 1991 amended previous legislation on the topic. Effective in May 1991, interest groups and their representatives in Florida are constrained in their efforts to influence public policy in the following ways: (1) they must register their intent to seek political influence with both the House of Representatives and the Senate; (2) they are prohibited from providing gifts valued in excess of $100 to public officials; (3) they must file semiannual reports identifying gifts that were valued between $25 and $100 to public officials; and (4) they are prohibited from making contributions in excess of $500 to the electoral campaigns of any candidate for public office and they must file semiannual reports of these contributions.

CONCLUSION

The political environment in which public officials operate molds their behavior. The extent to which citizens participate in politics, the nature of citizen views about public officials and political issues, the level of partisan competition in existence at a given point in time, and the strength of specific mechanisms designed to structure citizen interaction with public officials profoundly influences both the policy positions taken and the strategies and tactics adopted by those officials.

Political environments—like those of nature—evolve and change. Also like the changes in the natural environment, the changes that occur in the political environment do so slowly. While the political environment in Florida today differs from that at the turn of the century, the evidence provided in this chapter supports the view that continuities in the environment are at least as prevalent as changes. Following are several generalizations about the current political environment that illustrate the continuities.

Florida's political ideology is moderately conservative.

Participation is low in important political activities in Florida.

Interest groups are more effective than political parties at influencing public policy and public management.

The interest group system in the state can be characterized as one in which several interests have relatively equal influence.

These generalizations indicate the extent to which the broad currents of politics in Florida have been sustained despite the tremendous social and demographic changes that have occurred over the past fifty years. Indeed, the continuities identified above dictate a modification of the oft-repeated phrase that the "nature and breadth of these changes have profoundly affected the state's politics in the twentieth century"

(Colburn & Scher 1980, 11). The modification is reflected in the following generalization:

The dramatic social and demographic changes that have occurred in Florida in the twentieth century have had a modifying effect on selected elements of the Florida political environment. This upheaval has not seriously altered the basic contours of this environment.

The political effects of social and demographic change can be seen most directly in two areas: (1) attitudes toward and competition between the political parties, and (2) the nature of the interest group system. The changes are reflected in these generalizations about the existing political environment:

Political competition between Democrats and Republicans is substantial. The Republican party is a viable entity in Florida.

Three factors, listed in order of importance, have contributed most to the new alignment in partisan identification: the positions of the two parties on the issue of race, the personal appeal of former President Ronald Reagan, and the demographic changes that have taken place in the state.

The number of interest groups has increased faster than has the size of the state's economy, and there are now more interest groups in the state than one would expect, given the size of the economy.

The political environment in Florida remains moderately conservative. The only issue that divides substantial numbers of citizens is that of race. Political competition exists, but takes place within a relatively small segment of interested citizens. These people channel their views through groups who represent their special interests. A government founded on democratic principles becomes some other sort of regime when circumstances such as these exist.

REFERENCES

Advisory Commission on Intergovernmental Relations (1979). *Citizen participation in the American federal system.* Washington, D.C.: U.S. Government Printing Office.

Bass, Jack & Walter DeVries (1976). *The transformation of southern politics.* New York: Basic Books.

Barrilleaux, Charles. (1986). A dynamic model of partisan competition in the American states. *American Journal of Political Science, 30.*

Beck, Paul (1982). Realignment begins? The Republican surge in Florida. *American Politics Quarterly, 10.*

Black, Earl & Merle Black (1987). *Politics and society in the South.* Cambridge: Harvard University Press.

Carmines, Edward & James Stimson (1989). *Issue evolution: Race and the transformation of American politics.* Princeton, NJ: Princeton University Press.

Carter, Luther J. (1974). *The Florida experience.* Baltimore: Johns Hopkins University Press.

Colburn, David & Richard Scher (1980). *Florida's gubernatorial politics in the twentieth century.* Tallahassee, FL: University Presses of Florida.

Committee for the Study of the American Electorate. (1962–1988). *Non-voter study.* Washington, D.C.: the Committee.

Common Cause (1978). *State open meeting laws.* Washington, D.C.

Cosman, Bernard (1966). *Five states for Goldwater.* University, AL: University of Alabama Press.

Council of State Governments (1977). *Book of the states 1976–77.* Lexington, KY: the Council.

Council of State Governments (1990). *Book of the states 1989–1990.* Lexington, KY: the Council.

Council of State Governments (1991). *Book of the states 1990–1991.* Lexington, KY: the Council.

Council of State Governments (1992). *Book of the states 1991–1992.* Lexington, KY: the Council.

Crew, Robert. (1969). *State Politics: Readings on Political Behavior.* Belmont, CA: Wadsworth Publishing Co.

deHaven-Smith, Lance (1995). *The Florida Voter.* Tallahassee: The Florida Institute of Government.

Department of State, Elections Division, State of Florida, (1960, 1990, 1992). *Registered Voters in Florida.* Tallahassee, FL: the Division

Derr, Mark (1989). *Some kind of paradise.* New York: William Morrow.

Dye, Thomas. (1985). *Politics in States and Communities 5th ed.* Englewood Cliffs, NJ: Prentice Hall.

Douglas, Marjory S. (1978). *The Everglades: River of grass.* New York: Rinehart and Co.

Erikson, Robert, Gerald Wright, & John McIver (1989). Political parties, public opinion, and state policy in the United States. *American Political Science Review,* 83, 3.

Fenton, John (1966). *Midwest politics.* New York: Holt, Rhinehart and Winston.

Florida Department of State, Elections Division. (1960, 1990).

Gannon, Michael (1993). *Florida: A Short History.* Gainesville: University Presses of Florida.

Gatlin, Douglas (1973a). Florida. In David Kovenock, James W. Prothro and Associates (Eds.), *Explaining the vote.* Chapel Hill, NC: Institute for Research in Social Sciences.

Gatlin, Douglas (1973b). The development of a responsible party system in the Florida legislature. In Robinson, James (Ed.), *State Legislative Innovation*. New York: Praeger.

Gatlin, Douglas (1989). *Voter Participation in Florida,* STAR Project No. 88-006. Tallahassee: Florida Institute of Government.

Hamilton & Staff (1976). Washington, D.C.: the Staff.

Harvard, William C. (1959). Notes on a theory of constitutional change: The Florida experience, *Journal of Politics,* 21.

Hrebner, R. J. & C. S. Thomas (1990). Interest groups in the states. In V. Gray, H. Jacob, and R. Albritton (Eds.), *Politics in the American States* (5th ed.). Glenview, Illinois: Scott, Foresman.

Janda, Kenneth, Jeffery Berry & Jerry Goldman (1987). *The challenge of democracy.* Boston, Massachusetts: Houghton, Mifflin.

Kelley, Anne E. (1993). Party images in Florida: A comparative analysis of three organizational levels. *Governing Florida,* 3.

Key, V. O. (1950). *Southern politics.* New York: Alfred Knopf.

Lamis, Alexander (1988). *The two party South.* New York: Oxford University Press.

Louis Harris Poll (1964, 1972). Chapel Hill, NC: University of North Carolina.

Lowery, David & Virginia Gray (1990). *The deep structure of state interest group systems.* A paper presented at the Annual Meeting of the American Political Science Association, San Francisco.

MacDonald, John D. (1977). *Condominium.* New York: Fawcett Crest.

Matthews, Donald & James W. Prothro (1966). *Negroes and the new southern politics.* New York: Harcourt, Brace and World.

Morehouse, Sara (1981). *State Politics, Parties and Policy.* New York: Holt, Rinehart and Winston.

Morris, Allen (1993). *The Florida Handbook.* Tallahassee, FL: Peninsular Publishing Co.

Office of the Clerk, House of Representatives, State of Florida (1993). *The Clerk's Manual.* Tallahassee, FL: Florida House of Representatives.

Page, Benjamin & Robert Shapiro (1983). The Effects of Public Opinion on Policy. *American Political Science Review,* 77.

Parker, Suzanne L. (1988). Shifting Party Tides in Florida: Where Have all the Democrats Gone? In Robert Swansbrough and David Brodsky (Eds.), *The South's New Politics.* South Carolina: University of South Carolina Press.

Strong, Donald (1971). Further Reflections on Southern Politics. *Journal of Politics,* 33.

Survey Research Laboratory, Florida State University (1980–1991, 1993). *Florida*

Annual Policy Survey. Tallahassee, FL: the Laboratory.

Survey Research Laboratory, Florida State University. (1993). *Florida Annual Policy Survey: 1993.* Tallahassee: the Laboratory.

Van Wingen, John & David Valentine (1988). Partisan politics: One-and-a-half, no-party system. In James F. Lea (Ed.), *Contemporary Southern Politics.* Baton Rouge, LA: Louisiana State University Press.

Verba, Sidney & Norman Nie (1972). *Participation in America.* New York: Harper and Row.

Wagy, Tom (1985). *Governor LeRoy Collins of Florida.* University, AL: University of Alabama Press.

Wolfinger, Raymond & Steven Rosenstone (1980). *Who votes?* New Haven: Yale University Press.

Wright, Gerald, Robert Erikson & John McIver (1985). Measuring state partisanship and ideology with survey data. *Journal of Politics,* 47.

Wright, Gerald, Robert Erikson, & John McIver (1987). Public opinion and policy liberalism in the American States. *American Journal of Political Science,* 31.

Zeller, Belle (Ed.) (1954). *American state legislatures.* New York: Crowell.

Ziegler, Harmon & Hendrick van Dalen (1976). Interest Groups in State Politics. In Herbert Jacobs and Kenneth Vines (Eds.). *Politics in the American states* (3rd ed.). Boston, MA: Little, Brown & Company.

ENDNOTES

1. See Douglas (1978) and Carter (1974) for a discussion of the nature and origins of the efforts to exploit the state's resources.

2. See chapter 7 in Lance deHaven-Smith, *The Florida Voter,* for a discussion of growth management issues in Florida.

3. The tie in the state Senate does not have dramatic policy implications since for nearly 20 years a coalition of conservative Democrats and Republicans has controlled that body.

CHAPTER

3

THE GOVERNOR AND THE CABINET:
EXECUTIVE POLICY-MAKING AND POLICY-MANAGEMENT

CHAPTER 4

RICHARD SCHER

"The judgment evidenced by the [governor's] opportunities will determine whether the state will enjoy four years of politics or four years of capable government."
—*Governor Millard Caldwell, 1947*

While conceptions of policy-making and policy-management vary considerably, students of state politics are in general agreement that governors, and other state political executives, are critical actors in these processes. Their exact roles, of course, differ from state to state. They may also change over time and, for that matter, across different subject areas. Yet the centrality of the governor, and executive branch, for policy initiation, design, agenda setting, implementation, and management can scarcely be overstated. Indeed, while there are many factors which influence the popular prestige and reputation of a given gubernatorial administration, there seems little doubt that how it conceives and articulates state "policy" are key determinants of what journalists, pundits, other state officials, legislators, subsequent governors, and scholars say about it.

Florida has often been said to be "the different state," (Key 1949, ch. 5; Dauer 1972, ch. 3; Dauer 1984) and perhaps in no other area is this more obvious than in its politics of the executive branch and their impact on policy-making and policy-management. Unlike any other state, Florida has a "two-headed" executive branch, consisting of the Governor and the Cabinet, each of which has major influences over policy development and implementation. The Governor, of course, is the popularly elected "chief executive" of Florida. But the Cabinet is a constitutionally-defined group of six state political executives, all separately elected, who serve as a collective decision- and rule-making body for the State. True, the Governor sits and votes with the Cabinet. And it is also true that the Governor has influence and authority over public policy independently of his role as a Cabinet member.

CHAPTER

4

But Florida's system in which there are two separate executive political institutions which have major policy roles is without parallel elsewhere in the other forty-nine states. Indeed, it is an oversimplification to say that Florida has a "two-headed" executive branch. This is true only in structural terms. For the purposes of policy development, implementation, and management, Florida has had a truly decentralized, even fragmented, executive branch, which only in recent years has seen significant change. This structural and political idiosyncracy still has enormous consequences for the role of the executive branch in public policy development and management in this state.

In this chapter we shall examine the nature of the Florida executive, focusing on the Governor and Cabinet, and discuss its unique role in policy-making and management. We shall begin by looking at the politics of the Governor's office, from both historical and contemporary perspectives. Our purpose will be to explore how the Governor influences policy in this state. We shall then move to a consideration of the Cabinet system, and indicate its policy role. We shall conclude with an assessment of the system, as well as with suggestions for its possible streamlining and modernization.

"Policy," "policy-making," and "policy-management" are terms commonly used in political science and public administration, often without precise meaning. Yet this is not as troublesome a problem as might be expected, because intuitively, as well as in everyday life, their meanings are often quite clear. "Policy" refers to overall goals and directions which government (or parts of government) pursue. "Policy-making" involves political and administrative efforts to establish those goals and directions. "Policy-management" is the process of renewing, reviewing, implementing, and evaluating the goals and directions originally sought.

From the standpoint of the politics of the executive branch in Florida, these terms overlap. The Governor and the Cabinet worry about "policy," "policy-making," and "policy-management." But they do not make sharp distinctions among them. In this chapter we shall seek to keep the terms separate for analytical purposes, but the reader should remember that when the Governor and/or Cabinet act, they may be "doing" a great deal that concerns "policy" in a variety of ways, all at once.[1]

THE FLORIDA GOVERNORSHIP IN HISTORICAL PERSPECTIVE

Writing in the late 1960s, Joseph Schlesinger examined the relative strength of the American governorships in the 50 states. He created a scale based on formal gubernatorial powers through which he was able to assess the capabilities of the office, and rank the states based on total values assigned to each power. The powers he chose were: tenure potential; appointment powers; budget powers; veto powers; and cumulative totals (Schlesinger 1971, 220–234).

Based on this study, the Florida governorship ranked 47th among the 50 states in terms of its relative strengths and capabilities. The office was seen to be average in tenure potential (3 of 5 possible points); weak in appointments (receiving only 2 of 5 points); very weak in budget authority (1 point); and average in veto power (3 points). Its cumulative total was 9 points, compared to 20 for the governorship in New York, Illinois and Hawaii, and 19 in California, Michigan, Minnesota, New Jersey, Pennsylvania, and Maryland.

Schlesinger's study took place at a time when the Florida Constitution was being re-written. The new Constitution, adopted in 1968, strengthened the Office of Governor in Florida, as we shall see. Thus, Schlesinger's study is of historical interest only. But in fact for much of this century the Governorship in the Sunshine State was structurally very weak. Its formal powers were among the puniest in the nation. Combined with the Cabinet system, which deliberately sought to diffuse gubernatorial powers and authority, the Office of Governor has generally been a major handicap to those few governors interested in policy initiation and development. It also served as a shield and protection to the majority of Florida governors in this century, whose views of and ambitions for the Office were more modest.

Why the Office of Governor in Florida was deliberately made weak rests on historical circumstances and the political culture of the State. During Reconstruction, Florida had a powerful governor's office. But when the post-Reconstruction Constitution of 1885 was written, its authors sought ways to ensure that a strong, centralized governorship was avoided. A weak office, and the Cabinet system, were designed in order to limit gubernatorial authority over politics and policy in the State. The decentralized executive branch prompted the ascendency of the Legislature, and the emergence of a potent constellation of interest groups, as major actors in state affairs. Indeed, throughout the twentieth century it has been a fact of political life in Florida that the Legislature and interest groups have often successfully competed with the Governor as major political decision-makers in Tallahassee (Morris 1995, 100–103).

Additionally, the political culture and traditions of the state contributed to the relative weakness of the Governor's Office. At the beginning of this century, Florida was the least populous southern state.

75

Geographically large and demographically relatively urban and diverse compared to other southern states, Floridians have been uncertain about looking to the Governor as the major focus of problem-solving and policy initiation. Instead, the Legislature and Cabinet have been viewed as virtually co-equal with him in importance to the policy process, the latter in fact even sharing, by Constitutional mandate, authority with the Governor.

Even local, especially county, government in Florida also developed a tradition of impacting the policy process, including at the state level. This sometimes created a tension between state and local authorities in terms of setting priorities and addressing public needs. On the other hand, the decentralized policy structure at the state level permitted additional access points for local government officials, members of interest groups, and influential private citizens, to have a significant impact on policy initiation, development, and management in Tallahassee.

The effect of this was to create a decentralized, generally uncoordinated system of policy development and management. Given the rough-and-tumble, frontier quality of the state that existed prior to World War II, it was difficult for Governors to assert their powers or assume the mantle of policy leadership. Combined with conservative, southern Democratic rule, the fragmented, even isolated, nature of state politics fostered an ideology of low taxes and services that few governors were willing to buck.[2]

The political culture and leadership tradition of Florida strongly influenced the type of Governor who was elected, and how he would behave once in office (Colburn and Scher 1980, ch. 2; Scher and Colburn 1984, 105–107). In fact, most Florida governors had a very limited view of the office. In the process of gubernatorial "recruitment," most had been well socialized into the prevailing political norms of the State, and its "acceptable" views of what the Florida governor was supposed to do. The vast majority of Florida's chief executives in this century were "Chamber of Commerce" governors,[3] who were in office to protect entrenched economic and political interests, and/or to act as cheerleaders for the business community.

Few even tried to rock the boat or use the Office for policy development. One study suggested that only 5 of the 23[4] governors in this century—William Sherman Jennings (1901–1905), Napoleon Bonaparte Broward (1905–1909), Millard Fillmore Caldwell (1945–1949), LeRoy Collins (1955–1961[5]), and Reubin Askew (1971–1979)—saw that the Office contained possibilities and potentialities which could be used to advance public policy in the State.[6] Most, instead, either could not or would not see beyond the liabilities and weaknesses of the Office, or used structural limitations as an excuse to do little or nothing.

THE MODERN FLORIDA GOVERNORSHIP

In 1968, Floridians adopted a new Constitution which changed the nature of state politics, and strengthened the Office of Governor. A recent up-dating of the original Schlesinger study by Thad Beyle shows that the Florida Governor now ranks in the "moderate" category, in terms of formal gubernatorial powers, on a par with such states as Arizona and Kentucky, and just behind California, Colorado, Georgia, Mississippi, Washington, and Wisconsin (Beyle 1990, 228; Beyle 1996, 221–238).

Major changes were made in each of the categories originally outlined by Schlesinger. In terms of tenure potential, the Governor, who for most of this century could not serve consecutive four-year terms, was permitted to do so.[7] Thus the possibility increased of his having a substantial impact on politics and policy in the state, if only because the Governor was "around" longer. This had special relevance to his relations with the Cabinet, as well as the Legislature, which also began to meet annually instead of biennially.

The new Constitution also strengthened the Governor's appointment role. Prior to 1969, the Florida Executive branch consisted, at its most fragmented stage, of some 150 administrative agencies. Not all of them were under the aegis of the Governor—some were independent, while others were controlled by the Cabinet. But the Governor was responsible for several thousand appointments to state agencies. The most important of these were called the "Little Cabinet," so named because it was conceived to be solely within the purview of the Governor, as distinct from the full Cabinet, which is not. The Little Cabinet consisted of some 23 boards and agencies (Colburn and Scher 1980, 120).[8]

Appointments to these numerous and disparate boards and agencies gave Florida Governors plenty of patronage opportunities. The problem was that there were so many of them—and the Little Cabinet was just a fraction of the whole—that the Governor had difficulty controlling or administering his own executive branch. The concept of policy management, then, was virtually unthinkable under this system, as the governor usually had trouble grasping all of the agencies with which he had to deal, much less was able to create a sense of administrative order, control and priorities.

After 1968, however, the executive branch of state government was reorganized. The Governor directly controlled major administrators of 12 "super agencies." Some subsequent restructuring took place so that by 1990, the Governor's departments included the Department of

Administration, Department of Professional Regulation, Department of Citrus, Department of Labor and Employment Security, Department of Environmental Regulation, Department of Corrections, Department of Transportation, Department of Health and Rehabilitative Services, Department of Community Affairs, Department of the Lottery (Morris 1989, 1). In 1993 a significant reorganization occurred, in which the Departments of Business Regulation and Professional Regulation were merged into a new Department of Business and Professional Regulations under the Governor. The Departments of General Services and Administration were merged into the Department of Management Services. Also, the Department of Environmental Regulation was combined with the Department of Natural Resources into a new agency, the Department of Environmental Protection.

In 1994, the legislature created a new Department of Juvenile Justice under the Governor. In 1996, the Department of Health and Rehabilitative Services (HRS), once the nation's largest social services agency with some 38,000 employees and a budget of $4.4 billion, was split into two smaller ones: a Department of Health and a Department of Children and Family Services. In addition, in 1996 the Department of Commerce was abolished with the support of the Governor and Secretary, its major functions (recruiting tourists, outside investment capital, and new business and industry for the state) handed over to Enterprise Florida, a public-private organization based in Orlando which can operate free of the red tape that hindered many Commerce activities.

Five state agencies continue to operate independently of the Governor, or answer to him and the Cabinet jointly, since they have constitutional status: the Parole and Probation Commission; Game and Fresh Water Fish Commission; Department of Veterans Affairs; Department of Elder Affairs; and the State Board of Administration. The Governor must share with the Cabinet oversight of the Departments of Law Enforcement, Highway Safety and Motor Vehicles, Veterans Affairs, and Revenue Information Resources Commission (Morris 1995, 7–13; Citizens Commission on Cabinet Reform 1995).

The number of disparate appointments to major state agencies which the Florida Governor must now make has been reduced as a result of Constitutional and legislative changes. Yet this has strengthened his hand, for he has more direct control over the administrative branch. Appointments are more visible, sensitive, and accountable than they were formerly. Good ones can improve the Governor's ability to dominate the executive branch, and strengthen both his policy-making and policy-management tasks. True, the continued existence of the Cabinet remains a major administrative weakness of the Governor from the standpoint of appointments and control. But there is no question that administrative reorganization has improved the Governor's overall appointment power, and his ability to direct the executive branch of state government.

Perhaps nowhere did Constitutional change improve the Governor's powers more than in budgeting. Prior to 1968, Florida did not have an executive budget. Rather, the budget was designed by the entire Cabinet, sitting in one of its many roles, that of State Budget Commission (Colburn and Scher 1980, 121, 149–152; Scher and Colburn 1984, 116–120).

Under this system, the Governor could not dominate the budget process. Nor did it necessarily reflect his priorities, but included those of his colleagues on the Cabinet. Moreover, given the close ties between members of the Cabinet, the Legislature, and interest groups, it was difficult for the Governor to have a major impact on the budget.

Thus, the concept of the budget as an instrument of administrative control or policy management was unheard of in Florida prior to 1968. After Constitutional reform, however, both became possible. The Florida Governor now has the responsibility for designing and submitting the budget to the Legislature. This does not mean the Governor necessarily or always dominates the budget process. State agencies, for example, must submit their budget requests via computer to the Legislature even as they negotiate with the Governor. The Legislature continues to play a powerful—some might even say determinative—role in creating the budget. The Cabinet, while not involved formally, can act as a major lobbying instrument during budget decisions, and also plays a role during emergency budget proceedings (for example, if a budget cut-back is required prior to passage of a new budget). Interest groups, officials of local government, and non-Cabinet agencies also lobby hard during budget negotiations.

Yet it is also true that the Governor in Florida is now at the center of the budget process. He sets its priorities and overall parameters. His office is fully staffed (the Office of Planning and Budgeting is part of the Executive Office of the Governor) with professionals to examine, analyze, systematize, and redirect budget requests. Other participants in the budget process look to the Governor to initiate budget discussions, and it is generally his document and his Office, which constitute the focus of negotiations.

Constitutional reform in 1968 did not weaken the Governor's veto powers. Unusual majorities are still required for the Legislature to override a gubernatorial veto. And the Governor retains the "item veto," by which he is able to "knock out" individual line item appropriations in the budget with which he does not agree, without having to veto the entire bill. These are not absolute powers, of course: vetoes, and especially item vetoes, can have costly political consequences for the Governor. Yet, both the veto and the threat of a veto can improve both the legislative and administrative powers of the Governor.[9]

The Legislature, ever jealous of the Governor's budget and fiscal powers, in recent years has sought to oversee and review his use of the item veto. However, the State Supreme Court has consistently upheld the right of the Governor to exercise control over the budget and other expenditures, including use of the line item veto. Thus, it is fair to conclude, the veto power has become another mechanism whereby the Florida Governor can exercise some policy management capabilities. He retains the option of vetoing whole bills he does not like, while the probability of their being overridden is remote (Wiggins 1980).[10] And the item veto allows him some capacity to tailor the state budget to suit the policy and management priorities of his administration, not necessarily those of other actors in the policy-management processes.

THE FLORIDA GOVERNOR IN POLICY-MAKING AND POLICY MANAGEMENT

To this point we have focused our attention on those aspects of the Florida Governor's office which have influenced its potential strength to direct policy initiation, creation, and management at the state level. We must now take a broader view, and examine the Governor's role in the processes of policy-making and policy-management in Florida.

A brief explanation of a fundamental assumption is in order. It is that government generally, and Governors and the executive branch in particular, now exist primarily to address public problems. Thus, by its very nature, the modern Governorship is not only a problem-solving institution, but the Governor has become both an architect and manager of public policy. It is, after all, through public policy, programs to implement policy, and the effective management of policy, that the state can make serious efforts to resolve public problems and questions.

Following this line of reasoning leads to a conception of effective gubernatorial leadership that can be used in our discussion: what political forces are at play which influence the Florida Governor as policy-maker and policy manager? What comprises the behaviors and activity that go into these endeavors? How can we assess the job which the Florida Governor does, and make intelligent, defensible judgments about the quality of his policy leadership?[11]

In this chapter we shall not be concerned with this latter question. But we do need to understand what is involved in the policy roles of the Florida governor. The following schema will help the reader grasp what these are, and help show the major influences which shape the way in which the governor carries them out.

The political environment serves an envelope within which the Florida Governor acts as policy-maker and manager. Some of the political environment is abstract: it consists, in part, of the set of political traditions and public expectations in Florida about the way in which the Governor is to carry out his job. Other aspects of the environment are more concrete and immediate: for example, possible "mandates" from, the Governor's election as well as economic conditions strongly influence what is likely to be done.

Specific instances abound to illustrate the importance of the political environment as both facilitator and brake on policy initiation and development. As noted earlier, most Florida Governors accepted the traditional view that the Office was not to be used vigorously for policy-making. Bob Martinez, for instance, entered office in 1987 after specifically campaigning on the premise that he would be primarily a manager, and largely ran his administration on that basis. Reubin Askew, whose first administration was marked by energetic policy movement in race relations, education, and environmental protection, was faced in his second term with a severe state-wide recession which significantly hindered additional policy initiatives.

The second major force shaping gubernatorial problem-solving and policy-making in Florida is the nature of the Governor's Office itself. We have already discussed the manner and extent to which it has been modernized and strengthened through Constitutional reform in the late 1960s.

A third set of influences on gubernatorial policy-making and management in Florida results from individual characteristics of the Governor. Personal qualities make a difference in what Governors do and how they do it; the problem is identifying those characteristics which seem truly significant, and are analytically useful, in helping us understand gubernatorial behavior. While the list is potentially long, several stand out as crucial: the incumbent's view of the office; the ability to adapt to changing circumstances; personal interests, preferences, and ideology; and style.

The Governor's own view of the Office is perhaps most important. What is it for? Does the Governor conceive of it in active ways, in which it is to be used for energetic policy leadership? Does the Governor have a managerial view, in which the chief executive referees a variety of

81

struggles going on around the executive office? Or does the Governor see the Office in fairly passive terms, dealing only with issues and problems when they cannot be avoided? (Barber 1985; George 1974, 234–282). Clearly, the way in which the Governor conceives of an appropriate role within the Office significantly influences expectations for the administration as well as what is ultimately done. The Governor's conception of the chief executive's role thus determines what are the policy-making and management responsibilities of the Office.

Most Florida Governors in this century have tended toward the "passive" end of this continuum. The traditions of the Office, public expectations concerning the Governor, and their own political socialization and recruitment, shaped their policy-making behaviors in this way. Governors such as Cary Hardee, John Martin, and Fred Cone were barely noticeable in office, as they had remarkably passive views of what they wished to do.

Others were more managerially oriented, such as Dan McCarty and Bob Martinez. Yet a few Governors, such as LeRoy Collins, Reubin Askew, and Bob Graham, actively looked for issues to confront and problems to solve. Their policy agendas were extensive, and while their reach sometimes exceeded their grasp, these Florida Governors were notable for the vigorous, energetic ways in which they conceived of, utilized, and stretched the powers of the Office they occupied.

Personal conceptions of the Office could be modified by a variety of factors. Some Governors, such as Fuller Warren and Claude Kirk, had vigorous views of the Office, but lacked the political skills and temperament needed to effectuate their initial agendas. Frequently too, changing circumstances and times influence what a Governor can do, especially in policy development. All Governors have to cope with problems and crises of greater or lesser proportions; the question is, were they paralyzed into inaction, or galvanized, by unforeseen circumstances? Were they mastered by events, or did they become their master?

Here, too, the variation among Florida Governors is considerable. John Martin seemed completely befuddled by the collapse of the Florida land boom and severe hurricanes of the late 1920s; his administration foundered as a result. On the other hand, Bob Graham, confronted by a host of severe crises in his first term, especially the Mariel boatlift of thousands of Cuban refugees, found ever-greater measures of self-confidence as he successfully coped with the problems landing on his doorstep, problems which no-one had anticipated and which were not an original part of his policy agenda. Yet the confidence which he and his administration gained from mastering these crises enabled him, late in his first administration and throughout his second term, to push policy development in the State ever further, especially in public education and growth management.

The Governor's own personal interests and ideology also help determine his policy role. Millard Caldwell, with whose quotation we began this chapter, was passionately interested in upgrading the quality of Florida government, and repeatedly sought ways to improve administrative performance. LeRoy Collins and Reubin Askew were deeply concerned about the lack of opportunity and racial discrimination affecting Florida's black citizens, and each had notable records in civil rights policies. Bob Graham achieved a reputation as Florida's "education governor," because of his personal convictions concerning the importance of public education to the quality of life in the State. And Bob Martinez, whose administration ultimately lost the confidence of the citizens of Florida, nonetheless was nationally recognized for his policy leadership on environmental issues and drug interdiction, in both of which he repeatedly expressed considerable personal interest.

Finally, a Governor's style affects his policy roles. Space prevents a detailed discussion of this important personal quality, but a few comments are essential. Gubernatorial style is an expression of the incumbent's political identity, his *persona*. Thus, the Governor's style influences the perception which other actors in the political system have of him and affect how they relate to him. How the Governor comes across to others, how they feel about the incumbent, how each reacts to the other, can significantly affect the Governor's policy roles.

For example, Claude Kirk had a very vigorous view of the Governorship, and was personally very interested in Constitutional reform and environmental protection. Yet his style was so flamboyant, erratic, and abrasive, that other state policy-makers found working with him difficult. As a result, his relations with both the Legislature and the Cabinet ranged from poor to disastrous, and his policy agenda suffered accordingly.[12]

Other Governors used a different operating style. Askew was low-key, serious, and cooperative; while other state officials found him somewhat formal and distant, they had little trouble working with him. Bob Graham, whose style was initially perceived as rather rigid, later became warmer, more relaxed, and more effective. Bob Martinez, who was viewed as friendly and pleasant, nonetheless was also seen as indecisive and uncertain; as a result, legislators and members of the Cabinet did not always grasp what his priorities were, and his policy role, as well as his public reputation, suffered. Lawton Chiles' long service in the U.S. Senate evidently taught him a good deal about coalition building, enabling him to create and use a political style which many public officials, and indeed most Floridians, found palatable, even ingratiating. Indeed, the comment was sometimes heard that Chiles' style was sometimes too laid-back, conveying the erroneous impression that the Governor was not fully involved in the affairs of his own administration.

The last part of our schema which shows the influences on the Florida Governor's policy-making and management roles concerns the ways in which he carries out the most important tasks of the Office. For the purposes of this chapter, three such tasks are most important: the Governor's symbolic roles, legislative tasks, and administrative duties.

Given the traditional weakness of the Florida Governorship, it is not surprising that the Governor's symbolic roles have actually been among his most important. Indeed, for a significant number of Governors, including the most active and policy-oriented, their accomplishments in this area have been at least as noteworthy as their more "substantive" ones.

Symbolic roles consist of a range of activities (Rossiter 1963, ch. 11) but the most critical for our purposes are those of shaping public opinion and moral leadership. We say these are "symbolic" in nature because they do not always lead to specific policy results. Yet they both can serve as major forces for shaping the policy agenda in the State, often for years following the expiration of the Governor's administration.

As the Florida Governor acts as molder or shaper of public opinion, he directs the attention of the public, as well as that of other actors in the policy process, toward specific problems, policies, and solutions. In this capacity the Governor conveys his sense or vision of the future, how the State should use its resources, and what the priorities of State action should be. He says, in effect, "Let us commit ourselves to this purpose, and work towards these goals in these ways, for the benefit of the State and its citizens."

This is not a trivial task, for shaping public opinion can force the State to consider the kind of future it wants, and how it should work to achieve it. Millard Caldwell was the first modern Florida Governor to recognize that rapid population and economic growth after World War II meant opportunities as well as obligations, and the State needed to prepare for both. LeRoy Collins, who was largely unsuccessful in his efforts at Constitutional reform and legislative reapportionment during his term, nonetheless succeeded in establishing these as major priorities for the State long after he left office. Askew and Martinez forced Floridians to confront the necessity for environmental protection and preservation, expensive though it is, while Bob Graham did the same for K–12 and public higher education.

Moral leadership is of a similar importance. The Florida Governor is in a unique position to define what is right and wrong, acceptable and unacceptable, at least in terms of the standards of the State. This, too, has important policy consequences. Thus, when both Collins and Askew publicly announced that continuing segregation violated the moral principles of the State, they were able to pursue vigorously (although not fully successfully, especially in Collins' case) policies aimed at removing racially discriminatory practices from the public life of the state. Likewise, Graham invoked the moral tradition of the State and Nation while opening the doors of Florida to the Cuban Marielites, in spite of the obvious expense, inconvenience, and public resentment it created.

Molding public opinion and establishing high moral standards may not always have direct programmatic consequences. Yet policy leadership, including both policy-making and policy-management, includes more than what occurs in the immediate short term. It can also be long-term, and refer to the legacy of a gubernatorial administration. Certainly this is true in the case of both Caldwell and Collins, whose symbolic roles left unfinished policy agendas which influenced subsequent administrations, and the entire state, for twenty years and more, after they were gone. The same is likely to be true of Askew and Graham, and even Martinez, especially in drug enforcement, crime prevention, and environmental protection.

Increasing the Governor's tenure potential, and improving his budget capabilities, have greatly aided him in carrying out his symbolic roles. They have been at least as important in enabling the Florida Governor to strengthen his hand in dealing with the Legislature.

The Governor's legislative record is an important indicator of his policy leadership, but by no means the only one. Indeed, the whole nature of the legislative "scorecard" is suspect, since it does not indicate anything of the substance of the Governor's legislative agenda, or how he seeks to ensure its passage. Florida Governors such as Haydon Burns have been known to "inflate" their "scorecard" by proposing relatively non-controversial legislation. Others, such as Collins, had relatively low "batting averages," but it was because the nature of the proposals he put forward on race relations, reapportionment, and Constitutional reform were so complex, far-reaching, and controversial that they went beyond the limits of political feasibility, at least when they were initially put forward.[13] But even though Governors such as Burns had a higher legislative "batting average" than Collins, it would be difficult to sustain the position that therefore he was a less effective or important policy leader than they were.

CHAPTER
4

Nonetheless, there is no question that the policy leadership of the Governor depends heavily on his relations with the Legislature. "Policy" is much more than the bills passed by the Legislature and signed by the Governor, or allowed to become law without his signature. Yet these same bills, and the programs and budgets they contain, are integral elements of state policy.

Another chapter in this book details the impact of the Legislature on state policy-making and management. Yet a few characteristics of legislative organization and politics need to be mentioned here, for they bear on the Governor's own policy roles.

Traditionally, the Florida Legislature has been a jealous body, one defensive of its own role in state politics and not opposed to taking an adversarial position to the Governor, even one seen as relatively cooperative. Legislative leadership has often been strong—the Speaker of the House of Representatives and President of the Senate are considered among the most powerful members of State government, and not infrequently these officials have subsequently become candidates for Governor, U.S. Senator, or U.S. House of Representatives. Yet the Legislature itself has often been fragmented, dominated by powerful individual members, especially in the Senate, who parlayed longevity and/or important committee chairmanships into positions of great leverage virtually independent of the leadership.

Too, the Legislature has been the locus of important sectional cleavages in Florida. The most important of these have been North-South, and urban-rural, splits. The so-called Pork Chop Gang, infamous in the Florida Senate from the late 1940s until reapportionment in the late 1960s, was the embodiment of these cleavages. Interest groups, also, have had special access to the Florida Legislature, particularly those associated with dominant economic interests such as land development, banking and insurance, the tourist industry, the business sector, and agri-business.

All of this has made policy life difficult for the Florida Governor. He has had relatively few resources with which to deal with the Legislature. Partisanship and party organization, available to Governors in states with relatively strong parties, have been of only limited help to the Florida Governor in the past decade. Legislative leaders may choose to compete with, or oppose, the Governor instead of cooperating, which hinders his ability to push his own policy agenda. Powerful interest groups, independent legislative "barons," and sectional/economic cleavages can also disrupt the Governor's policy and programmatic purposes, well conceived and planned though they may be.

The Florida Governor has some "weapons" with which to confront these problems. His speeches, especially the "State of the State" speech opening the Legislature, are crucial in establishing the legislative agenda. He can supplement them with other forms of publicity aimed at marshaling public opinion behind him, such as press conferences, alliances with other state leaders and officials of local government, personal visits and media events, etc. He can try to identify individual legislators (whether in leadership positions or not) willing to act as his emissaries, as well as his eyes and ears, in the Legislature.

The reorganization of the executive branch, and centralization of some of the Governor's appointment powers, also has had a positive effect on his legislative roles. The reason is that under the old administrative structure of Florida state government, with its jumble of departments, agencies, and bureaus, the Legislature could use a "divide and conquer" strategy in dealing with the executive branch. Since the Governor was scarcely in charge of anything outside of his immediate Office, legislators could build tight alliances with administrative agencies, and largely ignore him as they dealt directly with agency personnel. Coupled with their ties to interest groups, "iron triangles" were common, and were very difficult for even the strongest Governor to confront successfully.

But with reorganization, and an increased professional staff in his own Office, the modern Florida Governor finds that the old "divide and conquer" strategy of the Legislature is less commonly used. The Legislature knows that it must attend to the Governor even as it negotiates with agencies, and the Cabinet. This has somewhat strengthened the Governor's administrative control, and also given him a bit more leverage with the Legislature.

But ultimately the Governor has to negotiate with members of the Legislature, whether individually or in small groups. Indeed, this is the heart of the problem for the Governor as policy leader. It takes tremendous time and energy for him to secure the continuing support of a majority of legislators so that his agenda is accepted in an identifiable form. Moreover, the process of legislative negotiations inherently is a disjointed, fragmented, often ad-hoc one, ultimately acting as a centripetal force on the Governor's policy agenda. The result of this activity can significantly diffuse and dilute what may have been originally a cohesive, coherent set of policy proposals.

Some Florida Governors have proven adept at dealing with the Legislature, for example through sophisticated, on-going systems of negotiations and bargaining (such as those employed by Askew and Graham). Others have used different techniques, such as cajoling or scolding the Legislature, sometimes with indifferent success. Caldwell

was not opposed to strong-armed techniques; he once held the Legislature in special session for 50 days during the brutal heat and humidity of a Tallahassee summer (this was before the Capitol was air-conditioned) until it agreed to a modest reapportionment bill.

Most Governors, though, sensing the difficulty of dealing with the Legislature, submitted only modest agendas. This of course paralleled their limited view of the Office. Some, such as Dave Sholtz, Fred Cone, Farris Bryant, and Haydon Burns, despaired of the legislative process, and declined to submit any but the most modest legislative proposals, or those they felt certain would pass.

Part of the problem which Florida Governors prior to the mid-1960's had in dealing with the Legislature was a simple matter of timing. By Constitutional language, the Legislature is only in session for sixty days. Moreover, before the mid-1960s, it met only every other (odd-numbered) year.

As a result, there was only a limited "window of opportunity" for the Governor to get much from the Legislature. But there was an additional political problem, inherent in the political culture of the State, which adversely affected his policy roles. It was essential that the Governor prompt the Legislature to follow his policy and programmatic leadership in his first year in office (always an odd-numbered year) if he were serious about his proposals. By the second legislative session the Governor was already a lame duck. Floridians began to forget the incumbent Governor, and take an interest in the beginning contest for the new administration, even during the last two years of a sitting Governor. And of course there were likely to be at least several potential candidates for the Governorship in the Legislature, so media and public attention was directed at them, and away from the occupant of the Office, during the final twenty-four months.

There is one more aspect of the Florida Governor's tasks influencing his policy-making and management roles worth our attention: administrative duties. Throughout this century, Florida Governors have recognized the importance of being the state's "chief executive." It has been very common during gubernatorial campaigns, or in an inaugural or some similarly important address, for the Governor to compare himself to the CEO of a private corporation, or to refer to the "business" of state government (Colburn and Scher 1980, ch. 3, 5; Scher and Colburn 1984, 108–112).

The problem for the Florida Governor, although it is not unique to him, is that from a structural standpoint it was virtually impossible for him to act as a "chief executive officer." The reason is that the executive branch, as we saw earlier, is fractured and disjointed. The major weapon with which Governors sought administrative control was through appointments and other forms of patronage. Appointments were supposed to allow the Governor to have "his" people in key slots; it will be recalled that even with the existence of the Cabinet, the Governor still had his "Little Cabinet," and a host of other agencies, to which he could make appointments. And patronage was a mechanism whereby the Governor could secure cooperation by providing inducements to agency heads, as well as to legislators and lobbyists for key interest groups.

Florida Governors used different approaches to matters of appointments and patronage. Indeed, they could be placed on a continuum whose ends are defined as "merit system" on the one hand, and "spoils system" on the other. Those favoring the former, such as Millard Caldwell, Reubin Askew, and Bob Graham, sought to fill state offices, and use state patronage, to provide "good" government. Those favoring a "spoils system" approach to appointments and patronage, such as Sidney J. Catts, Fuller Warren, Charley Johns, Haydon Burns and Claude Kirk, regarded administration as a playground for rewarding friends and punishing enemies. They were less concerned with the quality of government than with making sure that their allies and supporters benefitted from their tenure in office. Other Governors fell in between these extremes (Colburn and Scher 1980, 128–147; Scher and Colburn 1984, 112–116).

Was one of these approaches "better"? The "merit system" Governors did much to improve the professionalism of state government. And some of the excesses of the spoils system Governors, especially Catts and Johns, diminished the stature and prestige of the Florida Governorship. But the evidence that one "style" was "better" than another, in terms of increasing the Governor's administrative control, is inconclusive. As many governors remarked, and as the evidence substantiates, both appointments and patronage, however approached, were problematic. Once the governor made a decision, and placed the appointment or ordered the contract let, many different things could happen, most of them not good for the governor. The appointee could be inept, disloyal, or worse; the contractee could be dishonest or perform shoddy work. Moreover, bad appointments could not easily be remedied; the Florida Governor can suspend, but not remove, appointees.[14] And lurking in the background were the Legislature, the Cabinet, and the media, all waiting for the Governor to slip, make a mistake, or show a weakness which they could exploit.

Policy-making and management, from an administrative standpoint, were thus very uncertain under this system. The Governor was forced to spend a great deal of time negotiating with members of his own executive branch, rather than planning, designing, executing, managing, and overseeing policy development. Indeed, for much of this century, the Florida Governor, when acting in a purely administrative capacity, seldom had the luxury of dealing with "the big picture." He was so concerned with operating on a case-by-case, individual agency basis, in attempting to secure their cooperation, that he scarcely had time for anything else.

Reorganization of the executive branch, increased tenure potential, and a substantially increased budget authority, have aided the Governor's administrative control. The modern Florida Governor has also generally utilized the "chief of staff" structure within his own Office, which has provided him with a trusted deputy possessing substantial administrative authority. This, in turn, has permitted the Governor to spend less time on day-to-day administrative considerations, allowed him more opportunity to design and plan new policy initiatives, and manage policy decisions already made and in place.

It is of interest that one modern Florida Governor—Bob Graham—began his first term as an administrative interventionist. He initially spent a great deal of time with the daily affairs of departments and agencies under his control. Later on, he backed away from this activity, after realizing that his intense regular scrutiny did not ensure agency cooperation, and that it took irreplaceable amounts of his time and energy. The consensus of observers of state politics was that Graham actually became a better administrator, and more adept policy planner and manager, when he allowed his deputies and appointed agency heads to do their jobs, and report to him, rather than when he himself became personally involved in agency activity (Scher 1986, 97–98). Governor Chiles also took a considerable interest in administrative reform. While he seldom was directly involved himself—he preferred to establish gubernatorial commissions, or utilize members of his administrative branch such as the Lieutenant Governor—to effect reform. It is entirely likely that one of the positive legacies of the Chiles administration will be its commitment to revisiting both the administrative structure of state government and the rules and regulations under which it operated.

THE FLORIDA CABINET

In theory, the Cabinet is but one part of the executive branch of Florida state government. But in fact, it exists as such a powerful force in Florida government and politics that it virtually serves as a fourth branch. While the Governor is part of the Cabinet system, he seldom dominates it, at least for any extended period or across any significant range of issues. Long the bane of Governors, almost all of whom have publicly complained about it, the Cabinet has successfully resisted all efforts to abolish it. Like death and taxes, it is likely to remain a part of the Florida political scene for the foreseeable future.[15] On the other hand, recent changes in the Cabinet—especially the requirement of term limitations—might alter some of the traditional power relationships between Governor and Cabinet members.

For the reader unfamiliar with the Florida Cabinet, the name might prove misleading. It should not be assumed that it bears any relationship to the British or Canadian cabinets, or to the U.S. President's Cabinet. The latter, for example, is an extra-Constitutional body that exists by custom, and essentially is the creation of the President, to be used however he wishes. The Florida Cabinet is a product of Constitutional language, and has very specific duties and responsibilities which derive from its Constitutional status.

The Florida Cabinet is a mechanism exquisitely designed to prevent consolidation of political power in the hands of the Governor, and to weaken his capacity as policy leader and manager. It is also unique in the United States. No other state has any Constitutionally-sanctioned body analogous to the Cabinet that exists to share broad executive powers with the Governor.[16] It was first established in the Florida Constitution of 1885, a time when other Southern states were seeking ways to curb the power of Reconstruction Governors; no other state arrived at quite such a baroque design to achieve this purpose. The Cabinet was preserved under the Constitution of 1968 as well.

The Cabinet consists of six separately elected state executives: Attorney General; Secretary of State; Treasurer (also serving as Insurance Commissioner); Comptroller (also the Banking Commissioner); Commissioner of Agriculture; and Commissioner of Education (formerly called the Superintendent of Public Instruction). The Governor sits with the Cabinet, and votes with it, but is not officially a Cabinet "member;" it is correct, however, to refer to the "Cabinet system" which includes the Governor. Cabinet members serve four year terms, with one re-election permitted. The limitation on terms served by Cabinet members was not adopted in Florida until 1992.

Each of the Cabinet members heads a major Department of state government: Legal Affairs (Attorney General); Department of State (Secretary of State); Banking and Finance (Comptroller/Banking Commissioner); Insurance (Treasurer/Insurance Commissioner); Agriculture and Consumer Services (Agriculture Commissioner); and Education (Education Commissioner). It is important to emphasize that each of these departments is solely under the direction of the Cabinet member who heads them. They are not responsible to the Governor (except for the purposes of the executive budget) nor to other members of the Cabinet, except to the extent that the individual member may wish to apprise his colleagues of affairs in his department.

In itself, this creates significant problems of policy-making and policy-management for the Governor. To the extent that he wishes to propose new policy directions, or consolidate existing functions, in any area under the purview of these other elected executives, he must negotiate and bargain with them in order to secure their cooperation. They may or may not wish to comply, as they all have their own independent constituencies and power bases, and have a good deal of latitude in terms of how they wish to deal with the Governor.

Moreover, time spent negotiating and bargaining with his fellow state executives is time that he cannot use for something else, such as dealing with the Legislature, members of his own administrative agencies, local government officials, the media, lobbyists, visitors ranging from dignitaries to troops of Boy Scouts, or any of the other individuals, groups, and institutions that want the Governor's attention. Clearly, then, this fragmented executive makes the Florida Governor's administrative tasks, and policy roles, more difficult.

On the other hand, none of what has been discussed so far is especially unique to Florida. In virtually every other state, North and South, Governors are confronted by other state executives, some of whom are elected separately from him, and who may choose to compete, instead of cooperate, with him. Indeed, the Council of State Governments has identified eighteen state executive offices which often exist independently of the Governor.[17] Sometimes mitigating circumstances might exist which create alliances between the Governor and other elected executives. For example, partisanship might tie them together. Or several might join with the Governor to form a "ticket" for the purposes of election, and if successful they become mutually interdependent once in office.

No such circumstances exist in Florida. Cabinet members do not join with the Governor during electoral campaigns. The political culture, which stresses individual action and frowns on collective electoral activity or "dynasties," ensures that each candidate for a Cabinet position, whether an incumbent or not, runs and pays for his own campaign entirely separately from the Governor's race. Nor is partisanship an effective linkage, since until 1986 all members of the Cabinet system except Sidney Catts and Claude Kirk were Democrats; Republicans Bob Martinez and Jim Smith (Secretary of State, a Cabinet member) joined the Cabinet system in 1987.[18] Weak party organization and ongoing party factionalism within the state, moreover, militate against party as a unifying force on the Cabinet even today.

Thus, on the face of it, the Cabinet is a major decentralizing force within the Florida executive branch. But matters extend much further. What is unique about the Cabinet, and what has frequently been so maddening to Governors, is that the six members plus the Governor serve, by Constitutional mandate, as a collective policy-making, policy-management, and decision-making body that deals with a broad range of state issues.

Originally, the Cabinet served as twenty-two separate boards and commissions. By the 1940s, the number had grown to thirty.[19] During Cabinet meetings, which generally occur weekly, members would "switch hats" to re-constitute themselves as one or more of these boards in order to transact state business. To complicate things further, not every Cabinet member (including the Governor!) sat on each board. In the 1940s, the Governor sat on nineteen of the thirty boards and commissions; Secretary of State, ten; Comptroller, thirteen; Treasurer, seventeen; Superintendent of Public Instruction, seven; Commissioner of Agriculture, ten; and Attorney General, seventeen. A sort of "program" or "scorecard" was needed to ensure that the "right" members were present, and voting, so that the business of the various boards and commissions could be transacted!

In 1968, the Cabinet system was reorganized by the new Constitution, which reduced the number of boards and commissions. Currently there are 16 of them.[20] In addition, there are several quasi-independent Cabinet boards, such as the Office of Executive Clemency and the Elections Canvassing Commission. As before, not every member of the Cabinet sits on each of these individual boards and commissions.

Whether under the "old" system or the "new" one, the Florida Governor finds that his administrative authority over Cabinet agencies is fragmented and limited. Earlier we noted that he could not intervene directly into major departments headed by Cabinet members. But he also is not able to have a direct impact on those other executive boards and commissions of which he is not a member! True, he is "first among equals," and traditionally has been regarded as such. Nonetheless, on matters of broad policy, he has had to "clear" them with other members of the Cabinet. These individuals have had important allies in the Legislature, and among powerful interest groups, who could sabotage the Governor's agenda if they were not appropriately consulted. Sometimes they would merely disapprove of Gubernatorial initiatives, either directly at Cabinet meetings, or indirectly in the Legislature. The result, in either case, was potentially disastrous for the Governor's proposals.

In truth, the record shows that the Cabinet did not and does not always oppose the Governor. On matters of little concern, indifference, or where there was little controversy, other members will not block him. Cabinet members have also recognized that while the Governor is but one of them, the public expects him to attend to a broad range of issues and concerns. Thus, he has been given latitude to speak out or to make proposals, especially if their general feeling about the Governor is that he is willing to cooperate with them.

This latter point is important. Some Cabinet members have proven difficult colleagues. Tom Watson, the Attorney General during the 1940's, was an especially irascible official who repeatedly argued with Governors Spessard Holland and Millard Caldwell; he and Holland almost came to blows on at least one occasion. Fred Cone refused to cooperate with his Pardon Board, publicly stating that since he didn't make the Board's rules he saw no reason to follow them. The worst Governor-Cabinet relations probably came during the Kirk administration. Kirk was openly hostile to his colleagues, at one point referring to them as "the six dwarves." He later refused to sign expense vouchers for them and 15 Cabinet aides, and had individual members followed and spied on by the private police force he employed (Colburn and Scher 1980, 124–127).

How the Governor treated his Cabinet colleagues appears to be a key determinant of his success with them. If he has been willing to recognize their role in administration and policy-making, and invest the necessary time and energy in negotiating and consulting with them, he enhances the likelihood of achieving his policy and administrative goals, or at least in moving significantly towards them. On the other hand, if he has a negative view of the Cabinet, and shows that attitude towards them, they have been likely to resist, even overtly oppose, him.

Lengthy terms of service by Cabinet members have also created difficulties for Governors. Unlike the Governor, other Cabinet members could succeed themselves indefinitely. Between 1900 and 1970, members served an average of 12 years, some much longer. R.H. Gray was Secretary of State for 30 years; Nathan Mayo, Commissioner of Agriculture for 37; and Doyle Conner in that same office, 24.

Because of this longevity, Cabinet members developed close working relationships and mutual sets of understanding with one another. They created similar relationships with members of the Legislature, their own Departments, interest and clientele groups, and local officials. They were used to seeing Governors come and go; to some, in fact, the Governor's seat in the Cabinet Room was just a game of musical chairs. The "mobilization of bias" which this arrangement created was very hard for Governors to dislodge. The Cabinet developed "its" way of doing things, including methods of "non-deciding" or resisting through passive, or aggressive, means policies and proposals from the Governor which members saw as unacceptable (Bachrach and Baratz 1970a, 1970b; Schattschneider 1975).

This historical pattern no longer holds. Governors are now potentially in office for eight years; they can no longer simply be ignored by other Cabinet members. He forwards the executive budget to the Legislature, and while they maintain close ties to that body, the Governor does have the item veto which potentially can adversely affect their Departments. Moreover, Cabinet members wish to maintain positive relations with the Governor so that during the process of creating the budget he will include their full request; or, during leaner years, needed cuts will not come heavily at their expense.

Even more importantly, Cabinet members are now subject to eight year term limits, just like the Governor. They no longer have the luxury of "waiting out" the Governor until he becomes a lame duck or his term expires. Cabinet members wishing to make a significant mark on state policy are thus on the same timetable as the Governor, and it therefore is in their interest to find a *modus operandi* with the chief executive, as well as their Cabinet colleagues, in order to advance their policy agendas. If one or more Cabinet members have further political ambitions—and as of late 1996 at least three sitting Cabinet members have their eyes on the Governor's office—it is additionally important that they reach working alliances with the Governor and Cabinet to establish a statewide record on which to launch their further ambitions.

Thus, the modern Florida Governor enjoys some additional influence in the Cabinet that his earlier colleagues did not. Moreover, the Cabinet has sometimes proven to be a major asset to the Governor. On those occasions when the Governor needs political allies, the Cabinet can be most helpful to him if he is able to secure its support. For example, in the late 1950s, during a period of great racial tension in Florida, a jury convicted Walter Lee Ervin of raping a white woman, and he was sentenced to death. Governor Collins and his Cabinet colleagues on the Pardon Board were not convinced that the sentence was justified on the basis of the evidence presented in trial. They commuted Ervin's death sentence, and immediately were the target of substantial public criticism. Involvement of the Cabinet diffused some of the anger away from Collins (Colburn and Scher 1980, 123).

During Bob Graham's administration upgrading the public schools received a very high priority. Graham's ideas, however, were both controversial and potentially expensive. In order to secure public support, Graham first enlisted the Cabinet as major allies, along with the business community. As a result, his proposals were ultimately passed into law (Craddock 1983, 44–48; Craddock 1985, 92–94; Koenig 1986, 47–50). Thus, the Cabinet is not always an "albatross" for the Governor. When approached appropriately, his colleagues on the Cabinet can actually help him secure his political and policy objectives.

The Cabinet System: Executive Policy-Making and Management in Florida

From the standpoint of the executive branch, then, how does the Cabinet system influence policy-making and policy-management in Florida? The answer is that the Cabinet system does not initiate policy. In Florida, policy initiation tends to come from other governmental arenas (including the Governor, Legislature, individual members of the Cabinet, departments and agencies, local governments, and interest groups). It is somewhat more useful in policy-management, for it can review and monitor policy decisions already made.

The most important policy role for the Cabinet is unquestionably that of legitimization. Seldom does an idea get to the full Cabinet for action unless it has been aired elsewhere in state government and in the media. Seldom will the Cabinet discuss or vote on a policy item unless it has been fully "cleared" with all members, and with other actors in the policy/political process as well. Thus, by the time the Cabinet acts, a consensus within, and often outside, that body will have developed. The Cabinet ratifies the decision that has already been made, if only informally, in other political arenas.

It is not difficult to understand why the Cabinet functions in this way. It is a highly fragmented body whose members act first to protect themselves and their territories. Their loyalties come first to their respective offices and departments, and secondarily to the Cabinet.

The range of tasks which the Cabinet performs also militates against policy initiation. The situation is better now than formerly, when the Cabinet acted as thirty different boards and commissions. But sixteen is still a significant number. Cabinet meetings remain disjointed as members rush to get through agenda items for all the different boards they comprise. Often any given matter receives but a few moments of consideration. The press of business and the great diversity of issues requiring attention act to prevent any real ability of the Cabinet to plan and design policy in any broad sense, and seriously limit its capacity to manage it. Policy legitimization is perhaps its inevitable role. The vast number of appeals on a range of very diverse subjects which the Cabinet hears further emphasizes a legitimizing role for decisions largely worked out elsewhere.

No one dominates the Cabinet. The Governor is the most prestigious and influential part of the Cabinet system, if only because he is the most visible, and has greater budget authority than any other member. Also, through his legislative roles, and the variety of bills he can submit, he can push the Cabinet's attention in directions he wants.

Governors also have wide latitude to determine what their Cabinet role will be, and how they play it. Individual personalities, interests, and commitment, as well as their own conception of how they should play their role, seem most important in making this determination. Bob Graham was an activist, continually prodding his colleagues and directing Cabinet meetings to suit his purposes. But Bob Martinez was much less assertive or direct, often giving few cues as to where his preferences lay. Yet both enjoyed good relations with their colleagues, and generally were regarded as effective with their Cabinets. Without permanent, firm leadership, it is difficult to see how the Cabinet can act as a policy initiator or manager, or indeed do much more than legitimize. But there is at least one more factor which emphasizes this role: the Cabinet staff.

Each Cabinet member has at least one staff member assigned primarily to Cabinet duties (Morris 1995, 18). These are highly trusted aides who are crucial for conducting Cabinet business. The reason is that the aides communicate members' preferences with one another, engage in negotiating and bargaining, inform one another of agenda items and priorities, and so forth. Thus, when the Cabinet is ready to decide, aides have almost always already arranged the decision. It is then simply ratified by the formal body.

There are exceptions. Sometimes a Cabinet member will push an item directly. Or occasionally negotiations among aides fails. Sometimes a "confrontation" between Cabinet members occurs, often because of political pressures, or the need for media attention. All of this is rare. Most "votes" on the Cabinet are unanimous, because they have been arranged in advance by staff, and/or are reflections of a consensus reached in other parts of state government. Again, this simply re-emphasizes the legitimization role which the Cabinet plays.

A final factor which promotes policy legitimizing activity on the Cabinet is the strong norm of deference to which members strictly adhere. Significant respect is paid to subject specialization, as it is to "territoriality." This is even true on highly controversial matters. It is not the case that Cabinet members never oppose one another. Rather, it is that, other things being equal, they will defer to the priorities and expertise each brings to the table, and they will only oppose when there is

97

significant reason to do so. Of course, members then expect that when it is their turn to bring a major issue forward, colleagues will show them the same deference!

In sum, then, the major policy role of the Cabinet is indirect, rather than direct. It is so fractured among its various roles that it can do little more than ratify decisions considered by the Governor, Legislature, bureaucracies, local government officials, and interest groups. It can also manage and oversee decisions made, if it chooses to invest the time and resources needed to do so. The problem is that it has not always shown a willingness to commit the necessary resources to carry out this purpose; rather, it tends to move on hurriedly to the next item.

It has sometimes been alleged that because of the role which the Cabinet system plays in policy development in Florida, it is a body which is fundamentally negative in character. That is, it tends to act as a "veto-ing" agency, disallowing policy initiatives that it finds unacceptable, rather than serving in a more positive, creative way. Is this view justifiable?[21] Honest disagreement is possible over answers to this question. We have noted in several places that the Florida Governor sometimes feels frustrated over the Cabinet system because he must share much of his policy role with it. Additionally, the Cabinet does balkanize policy development within the State to such an extent that the public interest is often difficult to define or pursue. As a result, special, localized, and parochial interests acquire additional entry points into the policy process, and exert sometimes undue influence in decision-making. On the other hand, one of the original, and most important, purposes of the Cabinet, besides preventing a concentration of power in the hands of the Governor, was to provide a collective executive voice in state decision-making. In this sense, the Cabinet has been successful.

Following this line of reasoning leads to a major conclusion about the Cabinet's policy role in the State: while it may at times act as a "veto-ing" agency, more commonly it defines the limits of political acceptability, from an executive standpoint, for policy questions in Florida. It sets parameters as to what is desirable, and possible, in terms of addressing issues at the state level. The Cabinet will deal with, and accept, ideas and proposals which have reached a consensus within those parameters; it will not for those outside of them.

Whether or not this is a "positive" or "negative" contribution to the politics of Florida depends heavily on one's viewpoint, what one expects the Governor to do, and how coordinated and coherent one wants policy development to be. Yet if one is to understand how policy is made, and managed, in Florida from an executive standpoint, this critical role of the Cabinet must be understood, and appreciated.

Conclusion: Is There a Better Way?

Earlier we noted that there have been repeated efforts to modify, even abolish, the Cabinet system. None has been successful. Moreover, it seems unlikely that future efforts to rid Florida of its Cabinet will prove fruitful. Floridians are used to it. The Legislature, interest and clientele groups, local governments, and the bureaucracies like it. The six Cabinet members themselves like it, because it gives them a constitutionally-based role in state affairs. Private citizens who like multiple access points to state government favor it. Only the Governor, joined perhaps by students of public administration and others interested in a more "streamlined" governmental structure, do not.

Yet some possible modifications can be made which might serve to increase the policy-making and management roles of the Cabinet. For example, the Cabinet might elect, or appoint, one of its members (preferably the Governor) as its true head. This individual would have much more control over the Cabinet agenda, and enable it to focus more of its attention on crucial matters, instead of giving them short shrift, which so often they receive now.

Another possible change is to restructure meetings so that fewer agenda items are included. As noted, the Cabinet now must work its way through 16 different boards and commissions each time it meets. A way to divide these could be found, so that at any given meeting the Cabinet could attend to a narrower range of matters, and concentrate its collective attention more sharply.

Perhaps most importantly, the Cabinet needs a professional staff, with an executive director. We noted that individual members have Cabinet aides. And while there is a Cabinet staff (composed of a few lawyers and other generalists), it is woefully small, and it cannot compete in importance or professional sophistication with individual members' cabinet aides, or the professionals within the Departments themselves. An executive director and professional staff would improve the self-identity of the Cabinet, and assist the members in gathering and understanding needed materials to cope with the press of business. At a minimum, a professional staff would organize and expedite the work of the full Cabinet.

Some of these proposed changes are quite controversial. Governors, in particular, are likely to oppose plans which seem to give the Cabinet additional policy authority. The concept of a professional staff for the Cabinet, for example, is not one which many Governors might like; it would rival their own professional staff in the Executive Office of the Governor.

CHAPTER

4

On the other hand, at least some Florida Governors might appreciate a more professional Cabinet, one whose level of consistency and predictability would increase. Governors whose views and style of policy development tend more towards regularity and procedural neatness might actually prefer a system in which staff can build a better foundation and framework for executive decision-making than currently exists.

In 1995 the Cabinet appointed a blue-ribbon committee to examine the Cabinet system and suggest possible reforms. Called The Citizens Commission on Cabinet Reform, it was headed by two former Governors (Askew and Martinez), and included as members a number of state luminaries.

Perhaps to the surprise of many, the Commission did not recommend abolition of the Cabinet. In its December, 1995, Report[22] it offered some 46 recommendations, most of which were narrow and technical in nature. However, its most controversial structural recommendations included moving the Departments of Revenue, Law Enforcement, and Veterans Affairs directly under the Governor, and abolishing the Department of Highway Safety and Motor Vehicles by breaking it into a separate Department for the Highway Patrol and transferring the Division of Motor Vehicles and the Division of Driver Licenses into the Department of State. It also recommended abolishing the Information Resource Commission, transferring its functions to the Department of Management Services. The Commission further recommended significant changes in the way the Cabinet handles growth management and environmental issues.

The following section from the letter of transmission written by the Commission Chair, Reubin Askew, is worth quoting, as it suggests the rationale for the significant changes proposed by the Commission (Commission 1995, 2–3):

- The Governor and Cabinet have a number of collegial responsibilities which they should continue to perform, but the Governor and Cabinet should stop functioning collegially as the head of various agencies. All departments currently, by statute, reporting to the Governor and Cabinet should be assigned to report to the Governor or one of the Cabinet Officers.
- Relieve the Governor and Cabinet of as many narrowly administrative decisions as possible. The Commission identified over 200 statutes where responsibilities currently assigned to the Governor and Cabinet could either be shifted to a lower level of decision-making or be eliminated altogether.
- Refrain from adding new responsibilities to the State Board of Administration. This Board should remain focused on financial matters and should not have its role blurred.

- Because of significant citizen interest in acquisition and management of public lands, the duties of the Board of Trustees of the Internal Improvement Trust Fund should remain largely unchanged.
- The collegial responsibilities of the Governor and Cabinet in growth management should be reduced. Because of the technical nature of policies in this area, the Commission recommends an in-depth study to frame detailed reforms.

In his letter Askew went on to note that the suggestions, ". . . if implemented, would reduce costs and increase accountability. The collegial workload of the Governor and Cabinet would be cut by one-fourth to one-half. This would allow the remaining collegial responsibilities, some of which are constitutional in nature and therefore beyond the purview of this Commission, to be discharged more effectively" (Commission 1995, 3).

The Commission's far reaching report received only modest press coverage. If adopted, it would assuredly streamline Florida's executive branch. It would increase the Governor's role in executive policy making and policy management, and would probably serve to make the Cabinet system much more workable by assigning primarily administrative tasks to lower level officials, permitting the Cabinet to focus on broad issues of policy. While the recommendations would not eliminate all of the difficulties inherent in the Cabinet system—as Askew noted, some are constitutionally based and difficult to change—the proposal offered by the Commission would serve to modernize and streamline Florida's creaky executive branch.

While the Commission's report was not immediately acted upon, it did play a role in Florida's constitutional revision in 1997. In the past, many proposals concerning the Cabinet were either so marginal as to make little difference, or too drastic for Floridians to accept (such as abolishing the whole apparatus). The Commission's report, however, as well as other suggestions currently aired (such as the ones mentioned above in this chapter) gave members of the Constitutional Revision Commission reasonable alternatives to consider as they go about making suggestions for changing the state executive branch. Of course, whether or not the voters accept the proposals remains to be seen.

The Cabinet is unlikely to go away. But it may not have to. Some changes are possible which can increase its role in policy-making and policy-management, and help it reach its original promise of providing a variety of executive voices in policy development in the State. In addition, the impact of term limits may force the Cabinet to become more focused and coherent in its approach to policy-making and administration. Although the Cabinet has been present in Florida politics for over 100 years, in some respects it has never really discovered a role which allows it to be seen and understood as a creative, positive force for policy-making and management in the state. But it is still not too late to turn the "idea" of the Cabinet, or "Cabinet-ness," into a reality which is truly beneficial to all of Florida's citizens. This could well be a valid, and valuable, use of Floridians' time, energy, and resources, in the years ahead.

REFERENCES

Bachrach, Peter and Morton Baratz (1962). Two faces of power. *American Political Science Review,* 56, 947–952.

Bachrach, Peter and Morton Baratz (1963). Decisions and non-decisions. *American Political Science Review,* 57, 632–642.

Barber, David (1985). *The presidential character* (3d ed.). Englewood Cliffs, NJ: Prentice Hall.

Bass, Jack and Walter DeVries (1976). *The transformation of southern politics.* New York: Basic Books.

Beyle, Thad (1968). The governor's formal powers. *Public Administration Review,* 28, 540–45.

Beyle, Thad (1990). Governors. In Virginia Gray, Herbert Jacob, and Robert B. Albritton (Eds.), *Politics in the American states* (5th ed.). Glenview, Illinois: Scott Foresman/Little, Brown.

Beyle, Thad (1996). Governors. In Virginia Gray and Herbert Jacob (Eds.), *Politics in the American States* (6th ed.). Washington, D.C.: CQ Press.

Beyle, Thad (1996). Being governor. In Carl E. Van Horn (Ed.), *The state of the states* (3rd ed.). Washington, D.C.: CQ Press.

Black, Earl (1975). *Southern governors and civil rights.* Cambridge: Harvard University Press.

Burns, James McGregor (1979). *Leadership.* New York: Harper and Row.

Citizens Commission on Cabinet Reform (1995). *Tallahassee.*

Colburn, David R. and Richard K. Scher (1980). *Florida's gubernatorial politics in the twentieth century.* Tallahassee: University Presses of Florida.

Colburn, David R. and Richard K. Scher (1984). Florida politics in the twentieth century. In Manning J. Dauer (Ed.), *Florida's Politics and Government* (2d ed.). Gainesville: University Presses of Florida, 35–56.

Collins, LeRoy (1971). *Forerunners courageous.* Tallahassee: Colcade Publishers.

Council of State Governments (1988). *Book of the states, 1988–1989.* Lexington, KY: the Council.

Craddock, John (1983, August). The bid for better schools gets a rude reception. *Florida Trend,* 44–48.

Craddock, John (1985, May). Education needs reform, but whose plan should we use? *Florida Trend,* 28, 92–94.

Dauer, Manning J. (1972). Florida: The different state. In William C. Havard (Ed.), *The Changing Politics of the South.* Baton Rouge: Louisiana State University Press.

Dauer, Manning J. (1984). *Florida's politics and government,* (2d ed.). Gainesville: University Presses of Florida.

Dror, Yehezkel (1983). *Public policymaking reexamined.* New Brunswick, NJ: Transaction Books.

Dye, Thomas (1988). *Politics in states and communities* (6th ed.). Englewood Cliffs, NJ: Prentice Hall.

Elazar, Daniel J. (1994). *The American mosaic.* Boulder: Westview.

Ellis, Richard J. (1993). *American political cultures.* New York: Oxford.

George, Alexander (1980). Assessing presidential character. *World Politics,* 234–82.

Goggin, Malcolm et al. (1990). *Implementation theory and practice.* Glenview, IL: ScottForesman/Little, Brown.

Havard, William C. and Loren Beth (1962). *The politics of mis-representation.* Baton Rouge: Louisiana State University Press.

Havard, William C. and Loren Beth (1972). *The changing politics of the south.* Baton Rouge: Louisiana State University Press.

Huitt, Ralph K. (1968). Political feasibility. In Austin Ranney (Ed.), *Political Science and Public Policy.* Chicago: Markham.

Kallenbach, Joseph E (1966). *The American chief executive.* New York: Harper and Row.

Key, V. O. (1949). *Southern politics.* New York: Vintage.

Koenig, John (1986, June). Round three in the debate over education reform. *Florida Trend,* 47–50.

Lindblom, Charles E. (1968). *The policymaking process.* Englewood Cliffs, NJ: Prentice Hall, Inc.

Lipson, Leslie (1939). *The American governor.* Chicago: University of Chicago Press.

Lynn, Laurence E., Jr. (1987). *Managing public policy.* Boston: Little, Brown.

Morris, Allen (1989). *The Florida handbook, 1989–1990* (22d biennial ed.). Tallahassee: Peninsular Publishing Co.

Morris, Allen (1995). *The Florida handbook 1995–1996* (25th biennial ed.). Tallahassee: Peninsular Publishing Company.

Peirce, Neal R. (1972). *The megastates of America.* New York: Norton.

Peirce, Neal R. (1974). *The deep south states of America*. New York: Norton.

Prescott, Frank (1950). The executive veto in the American states. *Western Political Quarterly,* 3, 98–112.

Ransone, Coleman (1951). *The office of governor in the south*. University, AL: University of Alabama Press.

Ransone, Coleman (1956). *The office of governor in the United States*. University, AL: University of Alabama Press.

Ransone, Coleman (1982). *The American governorship*. Westport, CT: Greenwood Press.

Rossiter, Clinton (1987). *The American presidency* (2d ed.). New York: Time Inc.

Sabato, Larry (1983). *Goodbye to goodtime Charley* (2d ed.). Washington, D.C.: CQ Press.

Saffell, David (1987). *State and local government* (3d ed.). New York: Random House.

Schattschneider, E. E. (1975). *The Semisovereign people*. Hinsdale, IL: Dryden Press.

Scher, Richard and David Colburn (1984). The governor and his office. In Manning J. Dauer (Ed.) *Florida's politics and government.* Gainesville: University Presses of Florida.

Scher, Richard (1986). The incumbent wins: The politics of gubernatorial reelection in Florida. In Thad Beyle (Ed.), *Reelecting the governor: The 1982 elections.* Lanham, MD: University Presses of America.

Scher, Richard (1992). *Towards the new south*. New York: Paragon House (2d ed. forthcoming, Armonk: M.E. Sharpe).

Schlesinger, Joseph (1971). The politics of the executive. In Herbert Jacob and Kenneth N. Vines (Eds.), *Politics in the American States* (2d ed.). Boston: Little, Brown.

Wagy, Tom (1985). *Governor LeRoy Collins of Florida*. University, AL: University of Alabama Press.

Wiggins, Charles (1980). Executive vetoes and legislative overrides in the United States. *Journal of Politics,* 42, 1110–17.

ENDNOTES

1. For some useful literature, both classic and modern, see Lindblom (1968); Dror (1983); Lynn (1987); and Goggin, et al. (1990); Ellis (1993); and Elazar (1994).

2. On the political and policy consequences of traditional southern political culture, and its relevance to Florida, see Key (1949); Havard and Beth (1962); Havard (1972); Black (1975); Colburn and Scher (1980), ch. 1; Colburn and Scher (1984), 35–56; Scher and Colburn (1984), 105–123; and Scher (1992), chps. 2, 3, 9 and 10.

3. The term is from Havard and Beth 1962, 28; see also Colburn and Scher (1980), ch. 11; Scher and Colburn (1984), 105; and Scher (1992), ch. 10.

4. Not included is Wayne Mixon, who served for a few days in 1987 upon the early resignation of Bob Graham, who entered the U.S. Senate that year.

5. Collins was chosen in a special election in 1954 to fill the unexpired term of Dan McCarty, who died in office. He was then elected to a full four-year term in 1956.

6. Colburn and Scher (1980, ch. 11). Another study adds Graham to this list; see Scher (1986), ch. 6.

7. Interestingly, in other southern states the Governor, beginning in the late 1960s or early 1970s, also became eligible for a second four-year term Texas and Arkansas even moved away from the two-year term to a four-year one, with one consecutive re-election permitted. Currently only Virginia, among the southern states, continues to hold onto a single four-year term. See, for example, Lipson (1939); Ransone (1951); Ransone (1956); Kallenbach (1966); Ransone (1982); Sabato (1983); Scher (1992), ch. 9.

8. Offices which comprised the Little Cabinet consisted of the State Road Department, State Racing Commission, State Board of Health, Game and Fresh Water Fish Commission, Milk Commission, Beverage Commission, State Board of Control, State Auditor, Improvements Commission, Industrial Commission, Citrus Commission, State Chemist, Livestock Sanitary Board, Board of Forestry and Parks, State Marketing Bureau, Hotel Commission, Tuberculosis Board, Advertising Commission, Crippled Children's Commission, Council for the Blind, State Library Board, Budget Director, and Adjutant General.

9. See, for example Prescott (1950), 98–112; Beyle (1968), 540–545; Schlesinger (1971); and Wiggins (1980), 1110–1117. See also Dye (1988), 197–199; Saffell (1987), 139–140; Beyle (1990), 224–226; and Scher (1992), ch. 9.

10. During the 1996 legislative session, a substantial effort was made by tobacco and other business interests to have the legislature overturn a gubernatorial veto of a bill which would have eliminated the ability of the State to sue tobacco companies to recover the state's health-care costs of tobacco-related illnesses. Governor Chiles made sustaining the veto a centerpiece of his legislative agenda, and designed and carried out an elaborate lobbying plan of his own to counteract the powerful one on the other side. In the end, the Governor was victorious, and his veto was sustained. This example indicates how vetoes and the politics of vetoes can substantially influence the policy-making process.

11. There are many conceptions of the nature of leadership which have important consequences for gubernatorial politics For example, see Burns (1979) and Barber (1985). For a discussion of this point with relevance to the Florida governorship, see Colburn and Scher (1980), chps. 1 and 11. See also Scher (1992), ch. 10.

12. It should be noted, however, that without Kirk's unswerving support, constitutional reform in Florida would not have taken place in 1968. Likewise, he paved the way for major environmental legislation ultimately passed in the Askew administration. See Colburn and Scher (1980), 111, 216–218.

13. See Huitt (1968), ch 11. See also LeRoy Collins' own book (1971); and Wagy (1985).

14. The Senate has the power of removal.

15. There are many discussions of the Cabinet See, for example, Key (1949), ch. 5; Havard and Beth (1962); Dauer (1972); Peirce (1974), 435–494; Peirce (1974), 435–494; Bass and DeVries (1976), ch. 6; Colburn and Scher (1980), chps. 5, 6, and 11; Scher and Colburn (1984), 108–112; and Scher (1992), ch. 9. Helpful interviews on the Cabinet were also held with knowledgeable state officials, including Theodore Mannelli, Howard E. "Gene" Adams, Martin Young, and Dr. Bob Bradley (all Tallahassee, November 19, 1990); the author expresses his sincere thanks to these individuals for sharing ideas and information, but emphasizes that he alone, not they, is responsible for the views expressed in this chapter.

16. Other states do have various boards and agencies which share powers with the Governor, especially on budget matters. None, however, has the range of authority which the Florida Cabinet does.

17. Council (1988), 53–54. Not including the governor and lieutenant governor, the other potentially independent state executives are secretary of state; attorney general; treasurer; adjutant general; head of administration; commissioners of agriculture, banking, budget, civil rights, commerce, community affairs, computer services, consumer affairs, corrections, economic development, and education; comptroller; and elections supervisor. Not all of these offices are found in each state, of course.

18. Following the election of 1994, Republicans constituted half of the Cabinet: Secretary of State Sandra Mortham; Comptroller and Banking Commissioner Robert Milligan; and Commissioner of Education Frank Brogan.

19. The major ones were: Budget Commission; Board of Commissioners of State Institutions; State Board of Education; Trustees of the Internal Improvement Fund; Board of Administration; Pardon Board; Board of Pensions; State Board of Conservation; Board of Drainage Commissions; Labor Business Agents Licensing Board; and Agricultural Marketing Board (Colburn and Scher (1980), 121).

20. State Board of Administration; Veterans Affairs; Information Resource Commission; Highway Safety and Motor Vehicles; Law Enforcement; Revenue; General Services; State Board of Education; State Board of Vocational Education; Administration Commission; Land and Water Adjudicatory Commission; Environmental Regulation; Marine Fisheries Commission; Canal Authority; and Trustees of the Internal Improvement Fund.

21. I am indebted to Mr. Richard R. Alexander, former Graduate Student in the Department of History, University of Florida, for raising this crucial issue.

22. The Citizens Commission on Cabinet Reform, Final Report. December, 1995. Tallahassee.

THE LEGISLATURE AS POLICY MANAGER

CHAPTER 5

AUGUSTUS B. TURNBULL, III AND JOHN B. PHELPS[1]

O
ther chapters in this book describe policy management issues in Florida, the systems by which policy implementation takes place, and the other governments affected. This chapter describes the Florida Legislature itself as a principal participant in Florida policy management.

The perspective of Florida as a developing state affected by specific "nation-building" events as presented in Chapter 1 can also be useful in describing the Florida Legislature. Its balance of strength in relation to the Executive Branch has remained fundamentally unchanged since the 1885 Constitution, but discontinuous events of the last 35 years have altered its capabilities and responsibilities as a policy leader and arguably its ability to integrate the activities of significant components in the state's political and social systems.

DISCONTINUITY AND LEADERSHIP

IMPACT OF REAPPORTIONMENT AND THE 1968 CONSTITUTION

From its entry into the Union in 1845 until the State Supreme Court's 1967 decision in *Swann v. Adams,* apportionment of the Florida Legislature reflected struggles over the representation of geographic areas versus population. It also had specific impact on the political forces that held power according to 29 members of the State House of Representatives in the 1950s:

> . . . we have been forced to the firm conclusion that the underlying reasons for defeat of reapportionment are the refusal of some members of the Senate to give up their personal political control over state, city and county government, and their personal political

control over laws affecting large segments of the business interests of the State (Havard and Beth 1962, 56).

Reapportionment led to a substantial decline in the political power held by the representatives from rural Florida.[2] Prior to reapportionment less than 13 percent of the population elected a majority of the legislators (Dauer 1980, 141). Reapportionment brought about a sweeping change in the membership of the legislature with both the House and Senate receiving a substantial number of new members.[3]

Another development impacting the power position of the legislature vis-à-vis the Executive Branch was the election in 1966 of Republican Governor Claude Kirk, which heralded the return of two-party politics to Florida for the first time since Reconstruction. Former state legislator, U.S. Congressman, and present Lieutenant Governor Buddy MacKay gives Governor Kirk credit for motivating the legislature to take charge of policy development:

> . . . [B]asically what he did was he scared the hell out of the Democrats who had had it up there for over a hundred years. . . . he was the catalyst who pushed us over the top (Rosenthal 1990, 48).

The rise in influence of urban representatives was dramatized by the election in 1970 of Richard A. Pettigrew of Miami as the Speaker of the House. During this period of sweeping change, the Executive Branch was "modernized" by the Constitution of 1968 which limited the number of state departments to 25 and for the first time charged the governor with responsibility for budget development. Between 1968 and the mid-1970s, the Florida Legislature raised the salaries of its members (resulting in a major battle with Governor Kirk), established a modern professional staff reporting only to legislators, introduced computers into bill drafting and budget analysis, and established a year-round pattern of operations while shifting from biennial to annual sixty-calendar-day regular sessions. These changes, however, left undisturbed a pattern of leadership in which both chambers of the legislature vested enormous, though time-limited, power in their presiding officers.

TWO-YEAR "SUPREME COMMANDERS"

The prevailing pattern, albeit with minor variations between chambers, has been for the House and Senate to select a speaker and president for one two-year term and to confer upon them vast authority over the legislative process and thus over the outcome of legislation. The presiding officer's powers include: appointment of committee members and chairs and vice chairs, approval of the budgets and expenditures of the chambers including members' travel, employment of all staff, control of office space allocations and parking, interpretation of all rules, reference of bills to committees, and procedural control of the daily legislative sessions. Through their appointive and budgetary authority, the presiding officers are able to promote program goals and objectives and establish the direction of interim activity by the standing committees.[4] Through their bill referral authority, influence over the Rules & Calendar Committees,[5] and authority to preside over daily sessions, the presiding officers have control over the flow of legislative business during a session to the degree they choose to exercise it. So complete is the speaker's control that the available recorded history of the House in this century cites no instance of a speaker's ruling being reversed by appeal to the House.[6]

LEADERSHIP IN THE HOUSE OF REPRESENTATIVES

Following reapportionment, as power shifted from rural to urban members, leadership elections followed suit. Since the election in 1969 of Speaker Frederick H. Schultz of Jacksonville, only three of the eleven people chosen as speakers (Tucker, Thompson, and Johnson) have been from smaller North Florida districts.

From 1978 to 1986 the speakership was in the hands of a coalition of progressive leaders first assembled by Representatives J. Hyatt Brown and Samuel P. Bell III. These two Daytona Beach-area, urban legislators resisted the plan of two-term Speaker Donald L. Tucker of Tallahassee to pass the speakership on to a rural Florida Panhandle colleague, Representative Edmond M. "Ed" Fortune of Pace. With the clear threat of the Fortune candidacy before them, Representatives Brown and Bell organized an effort which quickly gained signed pledges of support for Representative Brown's speakership from a majority of the Democratic representatives. With the majority in hand, Representative Brown requested and was granted by Speaker Tucker a meeting of the Democratic caucus, which changed its rules and proceeded to designate Representative Brown as its nominee for the 1978–1980 term as speaker.

The practice of would-be speakers and presidents soliciting advance pledges for support, often years in advance, has been a subject of concern

Table 5-1

SPEAKERS OF THE HOUSE
1968–1998

Frederick H. Schultz	1968–70
Richard A. Pettigrew	1970–72
T. Terrell Sessums	1972–74
Donald L. Tucker	1974–76
Donald L. Tucker	1976–78
J. Hyatt Brown	1978–80
Ralph H. Haben, Jr.	1980–82
H. Lee Moffitt	1982–84
James Harold Thompson	1984–86
Jon L. Mills	1986–88
Tom Gustafson	1988–90
T. K. Wetherell	1990–92
Bolley L. "Bo" Johnson	1992–94
Peter R. Wallace	1994–96
Daniel Webster	1996–98

and occasional ridicule. Members have not always been pleased to be asked to take sides in a leadership race several years in advance, particularly when its conclusion is subject to disruption by intervening elections. A notable example occurred when Representative Bell, Democratic speaker-designate for 1990–1992, unexpectedly lost his bid for reelection in 1988, thus leaving vacant "his" speakership. The coalition rallied and quickly named Representative T. K. Wetherell, also of Daytona Beach, as speaker for that term (Representative Wetherell had taken retiring Representative Brown's legislative seat.).

The Brown coalition lost control of the speakership when Representative Steve Pajcic of Jacksonville was defeated by Representative Jon L. Mills of Gainesville in a contest for the 1986–1988 term. Representative Mills was personally more liberal than the group which supported him and later became part of his leadership team, but his team still largely represented urban rather than rural interests.

LEADERSHIP "PROGRAMS" IN THE HOUSE OF REPRESENTATIVES

Each speaker leads according to his own view of the office. Some have used its considerable powers to promote a substantive program. Other speakers have dispersed among the members most programmatic control over legislative outcomes, being content to let the chairs of standing committees compete for leadership in their functional areas. Recent Speakers Ralph H. Haben, Jr., of Palmetto and James Harold Thompson of Quincy fit the latter mold; Speakers Richard Pettigrew, J. Hyatt Brown, and Jon Mills fit the former.

The continuation of leadership control by the same team of House members into a second decade has in some degree overcome the discontinuity one would expect from a tradition of one-term speakers. New members of the House have been oriented to leadership patterns and practices and have been coached and evaluated for future leadership positions by senior members of the coalition. The new members have then assumed leadership positions and helped select newer members for such roles.

The tradition of selecting leaders far in advance is likely to cease now that term limitations are imposed by a constitutional amendment adopted in November 1992.[7] House members and senators are now prohibited from serving in their chamber more than eight consecutive years.[8] This new condition of service is likely to cause members to push for leadership roles much earlier than before. With only four consecutive terms available to House members and two available to senators, there is much less time to await one's turn for a leadership role. Another possible outcome of term limitation might be a move to constrain the powers of leadership over the legislative process and thereby allow new members to be more influential earlier in their legislative careers.

Since the demise of the progressive Brown/Bell dynasty, the most historic change in the House has been a decided shift away from new and expanding government programs and toward scaled back, limited government. The shift in Florida has reflected the national pattern and has been led by the strong electoral performance of the Republican Party. In just six elections, from 1984 to 1996, the Republican Party has gained enough seats to be a numerical majority in the House and Senate (23/17 in the Senate and 61/59 in the House).

PROFESSIONAL STAFF OF THE HOUSE OF REPRESENTATIVES

A force for continuity in the legislature has been its stable professional staff. Other than the speaker and the speaker pro tempore, the members of the House elect only one other officer, the Clerk of the House. Allen Morris served in that role from 1966 to 1986 and continued as clerk emeritus/historian until his retirement in 1996. He was succeeded as clerk in 1986 by John B. Phelps who has held the office for five terms.

The clerk, a constitutional officer, has a number of formal duties focused on creating an accurate record of the actions of the House and on advising the leadership on parliamentary procedure. The clerk also retains a key informal role as archivist of its traditions and history.

All leadership offices (speaker, speaker pro tempore, majority leader, and minority leader) and the standing committees maintain a professional support staff. While some adjustment occurs every two years as speakers and committee chairs change, there has nonetheless been a substantial holdover of staff. Many serve the same committee year after year, thus acquiring institutional memory and enabling them to provide legislators the information necessary to make policy judgments without having to rely exclusively on advice from the Executive Branch.

LEADERSHIP IN THE SENATE

The Senate has had a more fluid leadership history, marked simultaneously by the long-term influence of Senator Dempsey J. Barron of Panama City and the three-way or four-way

Table 5-2
PRESIDENTS OF THE SENATE
1970–1998

Jerry Thomas	1970–72
Mallory E. Horne	1972–74
Dempsey J. Barron	1974–76
Lew Brantley	1976–78
Philip D. "Phil" Lewis	1978–80
Wyon D. "W. D." Childers	1980–82
N. Curtis Peterson	1982–84
Harry A. Johnston II	1984–86
John W. Vogt	1986–88
Robert B. "Bob" Crawford	1988–90
Gwen Margolis	1990–92
Ander Crenshaw	1992–93
Pat Thomas[9]	1993–94
James A. Scott	1994–96
Toni Jennings	1996–98

struggle for influence of Republicans, conservative and liberal Democrats, and Hispanics.

Before, during, and after his term as president, Senator Barron was widely regarded as the principal "power broker" in the Senate. Paradoxically, a major source of his strength was that he rarely, if ever, sought anything for himself, but was always in a position (e.g., president, rules chair) to help a fellow senator. Some long-term observers believe he preferred the role of a behind-the-scenes power as rules chair over the more visible one as president.

Senator Barron's visible influence has diminished since he left office in 1988. Filling this leadership vacuum has been a team of young, mostly urban Republican senators, who have succeeded in pushing conservative programs. The Republican Party gained control of the Senate by a two-seat majority in 1994.

SENATE STAFF ROLES

In the Senate too, the staff has provided continuity in the midst of change of presidents and committee chairs. The Secretary of the Senate, Joe Brown, has served in that role since 1974 and has provided the Senate the same support services that the clerk has provided the House. Authority over the Senate staff has traditionally been more centralized than in the House. Howard Walton, executive director of the Senate from 1974 to 1991, was the *de facto* chief of staff under Senate presidents of varied political persuasions. In dealing with both strong and weak standing committee chairs, Walton successfully maintained a consistent style of staff operations and a very stable committee staff structure. In part because only half of the Senate is elected at each general election (Senators have four-year terms.), Senate standing committee staffs and staff directors have usually remained even if chairs changed. This continuity of personnel has provided considerable continuity of policy and relationships with the executive agencies.

POLICY MANAGEMENT DYNAMICS

As noted in Chapter 1, the policy management perspective includes the analytical objectives of organizational maintenance and policy. It is concerned with the actions of policy leaders who are linked in an interorganizational network that produces decisions characterized as "policies" by the retrospective interpretation of those involved. In the "strong-legislature" State of Florida, any analysis of policy management must include the actions of the Florida Legislature, its officers, its committees, its staff, and its members. In this section, the procedures by which the Florida Legislature develops policy will be described.

POLICY INITIATION

Where does Florida public policy originate? Individuals in both the private and public sector can and do originate ideas that become public policy when passed into law. A common path is for these ideas to be conceived, and then, if deemed appropriate, advanced for legislative consideration by private sector lobbying organizations or by public agencies, including local and regional governing bodies and associations.

THE ROLE OF LOBBYISTS

Lobbyists in Florida have been defined as "all persons (except legislators and authorized staff) who seek directly and indirectly, to encourage the passage, defeat or modification of any legislation" (Morris 1977, 47).[10] They form an integral and an increasingly regulated element of the legislative process. They are a basic mechanism through which the representative character of the American political process is affected.

One can, and statutes do, quibble over definitions and classifications of lobbying. But the lobbying function in practice differs very little in fundamentals—whether the lobbyist is a highly paid representative of a major industry, or organization of industries, or a volunteer citizen representing a category of clients served by the state's human services program.

FOURTEEN GUIDELINES FOR EFFECTIVE LEGISLATIVE LOBBYING

The character of lobbying as a profession gives insight into how policy is made in the legislature. Done well, it provides a critical source of information for legislators. These tried and true lobbying guidelines have been suggested by Representative Marjorie Turnbull of Tallahassee,[11] who formerly served as a legislative analyst, committee staff director, and executive assistant to the Speaker of the Florida House of Representatives.

- Know the legislative process. Know how a bill progresses through the system. Valuable time can be lost in following a bill if you do not understand the committee system, the appropriations process, the manner in which the calendar is set, and the differences between the various calendars.
- Learn who the key legislators are on an issue. You do not have to convince all 120 members of the House and all 40 senators that the bill is a good one, if you can convince the members whom their colleagues regard as the experts in a particular area. The chair of the substantive committee(s) through which the bill passes is always a key member.

- Pinpoint your opposition early. Be aware of the issues that will create conflict and the groups that will oppose your legislation. If possible, try to resolve the differences before a bill is introduced. If this is not possible, then be prepared to build coalitions in order to overcome opposition. Anticipate arguments against your bill and be prepared with information in response.

- Develop coalitions in support of your legislation. Look for a balance among your supporters (i.e., consumer and advocacy groups and providers).

- In developing a broad base of support, have local people contact their local legislative delegation before the legislative session. Legislators tend to be more responsive to local constituencies.

- Learn to work with staff. Staff has the advantage of a close working relationship with members. It has the trust of the members. If a trusting relationship with staff is built, then that will be translated to members. Building a trusting relationship is simple: Be honest, give good, solid factual information, and provide it in a timely manner. Leave a brief written list of your most important points for future reference.

- Know the filing dates for legislation and be alert to both the formal and informal legislative calendars. Be aware of and meet legislative time lines for reports and information. Remember, legislators and staff operate within very short deadlines.

- Be brief. Brevity is important whether in written information or in the time you spend with staff or a member. Remember you may have only one minute of time to explain your entire program. Learn to make your arguments in that period of time.

- Never play one house against another. Always make certain that you state the same position in both houses. If you find that, in fact, you have lost one house and intend to try to recoup your losses in the other, make it clear that this is your intent. Do not appear satisfied with the outcome in one house and then go to the other and work for change.

- Do not make distinctions among "powerful" legislators. Remember that each legislator is equally important in his or her district. Power in the legislature shifts from session to session and issue to issue.

- Develop a reputation for trust. Let people know they can tell you something in confidence and that you will maintain that confidence. There is a terrible urge when you have inside information to share it with someone else. Assume that anything you tell someone will be passed on.

- Be appreciative. Legislators and staff work very hard. Sometimes members take personal political risk to support your legislation. When it is over, even if you are not pleased about the outcome, let members know you appreciate their efforts.
- Do not take issues personally. During the session tempers are hot, and sometimes things are said that should not be said. Never try to get even. When the session is over, forget all the negatives and only remember the positives. If you win, enjoy your victory with humility. If you lose, figure out why and restructure your approach for next year.

THE ROLE OF LEGISLATORS AND STANDING COMMITTEES

A second source for the initiation of policy is legislators themselves and legislative standing committees. Despite its sixty-calendar-day limitation on regular sessions, the legislature operates in fact on a year-round basis. Except for holiday periods and during election years, both chambers routinely schedule committee meetings on a monthly basis. The interim between regular sessions is a time for committee staff to conduct interim studies, which include traditional academic research,[12] oversight visits to executive agencies, statewide public hearings designed to gather public input on a topic of interest to the legislature. The ideas for such interim projects can originate from staff, from committee members or chairs, or from the leadership of the chamber. A well-designed interim study often results in legislation. At one time, such legislation usually took the form of a regular bill offered by a member of the committee or the chair. In recent years, it has become more common for committee staff to develop a "committee bill" which incorporates through the committee process the collective ideas of the members assisted by the staff.

POLICY CONSTRUCTION

A complete understanding of the legislative policymaking process requires a detailed review of how a bill becomes a law or, more inclusively, how an idea becomes public policy. Legislative ideas or proposed policies first take form when ideas are converted into bills for formal consideration by the legislature.[13]

THE ROLE OF LEGISLATIVE COMMITTEES

Committees are the hub of most of the day-to-day activities of the legislature. By rule, all bills are referred to at least one standing committee for review and, as noted above, committees may take the initiative of creating bills. There are several categories of committees, which are created by rule or authorization of the presiding officer. Standing or substantive committees deal with topical areas of continuing interest to the legislature. Fiscal committees deal with revenues and the expenditure of funds. The Committee on Rules & Calendar sets the agenda of the chamber and resolves disputes over procedure.[14] During the last two decades, the number of standing committees has ranged from 18 to 30 in the House and has remained in the 16 to 17 range in the Senate.[15]

The 120 members of the House and the 40 members of the Senate are assigned to an average of four committees.16 (See Table 5-3) Committees in the House average 17 to 21 members, while the smaller Senate averages 9 or 10. The key Appropriations Committee is typically larger. In 1994–1996 there were 38 House Appropriations Committee members and 35 Senate Appropriations Committee members.

Committees are governed by the rules of the House and Senate, respectively. They can have both formal and informal (workshop)[17] meetings. To avoid scheduling conflicts for members, an established calendar controls the timing and length of meetings during the regular and special sessions of the legislature. Interim meetings are more flexible, although normally scheduled during a time set by the leadership for committee meetings each month.

Each committee has nonpartisan professional staff—typically a staff director, one or more legislative analysts, and clerical support staff. Committees will occasionally employ outside consultants, though for most bills the permanent staffs are considered experts in key policy areas.

After filing with the House clerk or Senate secretary, bills are referred by the presiding officer to at least one standing committee. The subject matter of the bill normally determines the committee of reference, though presiding officers may do otherwise as the circumstance dictates.[18] However, the rules require bills affecting appropriations to have a reference to the Appropriations Committee and those with an impact on revenue to the Committee on Finance and Taxation. The chair of the Appropriations Committee, by raising a "point of order" on the floor of the chamber, can pull a bill into committee if it might affect state appropriations.

Scheduling bills for consideration is the prerogative of the committee chair. For other strategic purposes, a chair may resist placing a bill on the committee agenda or may hold it for a meeting late in the session. This makes it more difficult for the bill to move through the remaining stages of the process. Bills must be acted upon favorably by each committee of reference before being forwarded to the full house.[19] Committees are required by rule to give public notice[20] before bills may be voted upon.

Table 5-3
COMMITTEES OF THE HOUSE OF REPRESENTATIVES AND SENATE
1997

Standing House Committees

Group I—Governmental Services Council
- Health Care Standards & Regulatory Reform
- Health Care Services
- Children & Family Empowerment
- Long Term Care

Group II—Academic Excellence Council
- Education Innovation
- Education/K–12
- Community Colleges & Career Prep
- Colleges & Universities

Group III—Economic Impact Council
- Business Development & International Trade
- Transportation
- Financial Services
- Regulated Services
- Tourism
- Business Regulation & Consumer Affairs
- Utilities & Communications

Group IV—Justice Council
- Corrections
- Crime & Punishment
- Law Enforcement & Public Safety
- Juvenile Justice
- Civil Justice & Claims
- Real Property & Probate
- Family Law & Children

Group V—Governmental Responsibility Council
- Governmental Operations
- Governmental Rules & Regulations
- Environmental Protection
- Water & Resource Management
- Community Affairs
- Agriculture
- Election Reform

Group VI—Fiscal Responsibility Council
- Education
- General Government
- Criminal Justice
- Health & Human Services
- Transportation & Economic Development
- Finance & Taxation

Group VII—Procedural Council
- Joint Committee on Intergovernmental Relations
- Joint Administrative Procedures
- Joint Legislative Auditing
- Joint Legislative Information Technology Relations
- Reapportionment
- Rules, Resolutions & Ethics
- Joint Everglades Oversight

Select Committees
- Select Committee on Educational Facilities
- Select Committee on State Employee Health

Standing Senate Committees

- Agriculture
- Banking and Insurance
- Children, Families and Seniors
- Commerce and Economic Opportunities
- Community Affairs
- Criminal Justice
- Education
- Executive Business, Ethics and Elections
- Governmental Reform and Oversight
- Health Care
- Judiciary
- Natural Resources
- Regulated Industries
- Rules and Calendar
- Transportation
- Ways and Means

Joint Committees

- Administrative Procedures
- Everglades Oversight
- Florida Legislative Committee on Intergovernmental Relations
- Legislative Information Technology Resource
- Legislative Auditing
- Legislative Management

Votes by a committee must occur in an open meeting with the decision of each member recorded by name.[21] Bills are reported in one of several prescribed formats: favorably, favorably with committee amendment, favorably with committee substitute,[22] or unfavorably (House Rule 6.34). To further complicate the process, many House committees and some Senate committees use a subcommittee system. The procedure for bills in full committee is identical for bills referred to subcommittee.

Often referral of a bill to the Appropriations Committee becomes a major procedural problem since that committee often decides not to consider substantive legislation until work has been completed on the general appropriations bill (usually week four or five of the regular session).[23] This process allows an argument to be made against scheduling a bill because no funding has been provided for it in the appropriations bill and all available funds have been earmarked. This "Catch 22" has doomed many bills.

THE RULES COMMITTEE AND SPECIAL ORDERS

Once a bill has been reported favorably by all committees of reference, a report is filed with the House clerk or Senate secretary and the bill is available for consideration by the full House or Senate. Since the late 1940s, it is almost unheard of for a chamber to take up bills in the order in which they were reported to the clerical officer.[24] Instead, the daily schedule of bill consideration on the floor is determined by the Special Order Calendar, which is established for each daily session by the Rules & Calendar Committee. This committee may schedule a series of bills on similar subjects but the order of consideration is more often based on the unstated priorities of the majority or minority leadership.

Sponsors and supporters may petition the Rules & Calendar Committee for a slot on the Special Order Calendar while opponents may quietly urge that the bill not be scheduled. If the speaker or president intervenes, a bill can be advanced or retained. Although a Special Order Calendar is technically a recommendation of the whole committee, it is in reality the work product of the chair of the Rules & Calendar Committee and staff and the minority leader and staff. In the House, the bills on the Special Order Calendar not reached during a daily session are carried over to the next daily session, unless a new Special Order Calendar is received.

Although technical and traditional differences between House and Senate practice in managing the special order calendars exist, the principles are fundamentally the same. Likewise, the politics of getting a bill on the Special Order Calendar are more alike than different.

The critical power over the daily schedule of the House or Senate makes the position of Chair of the Rules & Calendar Committee one of the most powerful positions in the legislature. It is usually ranked just below the speaker or president (although some Rules chairs have come close to eclipsing their presiding officer). One indication of the importance of the position is that since 1980, House Speakers-designate Ralph H. Haben, Jr., James Harold Thompson, Bolley L. "Bo" Johnson of Gulf Breeze, and Peter R. Wallace of St. Petersburg have served as Rules & Calendar chairs just prior to their scheduled term as speaker. In the Senate, Dempsey J. Barron's long-term effective power as Rules chair differed little from that he held as president.

It is also acknowledged that the year before one becomes the presiding officer is often one's most influential year. The membership will follow a designated officer's lead because they are anxious to have preferred committee assignments and to be in the good graces of the speaker-apparent or president-apparent in the following two years. Once a presiding officer has named the committees and their chairs, the members' attention slowly begins to drift in the direction of the "next leader."[25]

FLOOR CONSIDERATION

The Florida Constitution requires that bills be "read" three times on three separate days.[26] "First reading" usually occurs at the time of the bill's introduction when its title is printed in the *Journal of the House of Representatives* or in the *Journal of the Senate.* When the bill comes up for consideration on the Special Order Calendar for a daily session of the House or Senate, it is read a second time by title[27] and is subject to the amendatory process. If committees have recommended amendments, these are taken up first. Member amendments are then considered after being filed with the clerk or secretary in accordance with deadlines established by rule.

The debate on second reading is the most crucial step in the passage of a bill. It is the point at which a bill is subject to the most critical scrutiny, and the policy consensus of the full house membership is determined by votes on amendments and motions. If a bill is controversial, its sponsor needs to have a command of legislative procedure and detailed knowledge of a bill's substance.

A firm grasp of political strategy and tactics as well as knowledge of the psychology of the legislative process are also of great importance at this stage. Members tend to specialize in certain policy areas and to develop well-known philosophical leanings on specific legislative topics. Other members come to rely upon the experience of these specialists and often vote in tandem with the expert having political views similar to their own. Thus, for example, on a complex tax bill, conservative members may follow the lead of a conservative expert and liberal members *vice-versa*.[28] Since most voting is electronic and visible on an electronic tote board, it is relatively easy for members to "follow the buttons" of others.

There are procedural limitations on amendments. Each must be in writing, germane to the subject embraced by the bill before the chamber, and technically accurate as to form and content. Once the amendatory stage of consideration is completed, the bill is rewritten by the chief clerical officer to reflect amendments adopted by the respective house. This "engrossed" bill is read a third time.[29] The chamber then votes on the bill as amended. If passed, it is formally transmitted by the clerk or secretary to the other house as a "Message."

CONSIDERATION BY THE "OTHER" HOUSE

To become an act, the same bill must be passed in identical form by both the House and the Senate.[30] This requirement governs many strategic and tactical considerations for a bill's sponsors and opponents. Because a regular session is limited to 60 calendar days, it is important that supporters secure the introduction of identical bills in each of the two houses and then push for parallel action on both bills by each chamber. If, for example, the House has passed a bill, and its companion bill (a bill with identical intent and virtually the same wording) is taken up in the Senate, the Senate sponsor may move to substitute the House bill for the Senate bill and have the Senate move to immediate floor consideration of the House bill. Lacking such parallel progress, the normal course of action would be to receive the House bill in the Senate and refer it to a Senate committee for review. Unless passed by at least one chamber by the sixth week of the nine-week session, it is unlikely that a routine bill, without a companion in the other house, will have the time to complete the remaining hurdles and become law.

As the session draws to a close, much legislative action on the floor begins with a motion "that the rules be waived" for a bill to be taken up "instanter" (i.e., immediately) without reference to a committee and without adherence to normal notice requirements. This is most common when a companion bill from one house has passed and has been transmitted to the other house where procedures are waived so the companion bill can be taken up. Sometimes, the progress of a bill is slowed by the leadership, until its language is acceptably revised. Another practice, used to gain leverage in negotiations between houses, is the "holding hostage" in one chamber of key legislation wanted by the leadership of the other chamber.

While sponsors seek passage in identical form by both houses, bills are sometimes passed between the houses several times, with one chamber or the other adding amendments and disagreeing with amendments adopted by the other chamber. If the two houses disagree on a complex bill of major importance, it may be assigned to a conference committee[31] composed of both senators and representatives. The report of a conference committee cannot be amended—only voted up or down as an entirety in each of the two chambers.

In the hectic final days of a regular session, especially the final 24 hours, the technical skills of members and lobbyists become critical. Passage of many major bills, usually including the general appropriations bill,[32] occurs in the last week. Multiple bills may be held hostage to bring pressure to bear for passage of other bills. Bills that have failed to move may suddenly appear as amendments to another bill. A bill may become a "train" (i.e., used as a vehicle to pass a number of bills as amendments). A constitutional provision requires that an amendment be on the same subject as the bill,[33] but this limitation is sometimes given only fleeting consideration.

Caught up in this intense-end-of-session political struggle between the House and Senate[34] are dozens of routine bills that have reached the final stages of passage, but need skilled attention to overcome the final political or procedural hurdles. For several days, they may languish on the special order calendar, never having been placed high enough to be reached in that day's session.

Many bills may "die in messages" (i.e., in transit between the chambers) because of the press of higher priorities. Securing timely passage may be as simple as knowing to request "immediate certification" (i.e., transmittal) to the other chamber, or knowing whom to ask to expedite the physical conveyance of the bill[35] to the other chamber. It may involve having the clout and knowledge of when it is permissible within the traditions of the chamber to have a bill removed from committee and placed on the calendar by the required two-thirds vote of the membership. In sum, it is often critical to have skilled teamwork and support in both chambers in order to secure the advancement of a bill.

ACTION BY THE GOVERNOR

After passage by both chambers, a bill is enrolled, signed by the constitutional officers[36] of the legislature, and presented to the governor for his or her assent. Skilled supporters of a bill do not take this step for granted. In some cases, they will have secured the governor's tacit, or perhaps open, support much earlier in the process. But if a bill has not yet come to the attention of the governor and his or her staff, it is important to show it

121

as reasonable and consistent with the governor's views in order to avoid a veto. This is especially important if the bill has fiscal consequences and was not part of the governor's budget recommendations.

VOLUME OF LEGISLATION

Given this intense process, in which the intended effect of the rules and procedures is to prevent most bills from becoming law, what is the actual volume of legislation and what percentage of bills filed actually become law? Table 5-4 shows that the number of bills and joint resolutions introduced in the House has varied over a narrow range for a 50-year period.

Legislative leaders have made efforts to restrict the number of bills a member may file and to adopt rules governing deadlines after which bills may not be filed.

Table 5-5 indicates that less than 16 percent of the bills filed during the 1989 and 1990 sessions of the legislature actually became law. This percentage has drifted within this approximate range over the past 20 years, but is deceptive because it counts as dead, bills that may actually have passed in the form of an amendment or whose companions may have become law.

POLICY AND THE BUDGET: EXECUTIVE LEGISLATIVE TENSIONS

The most consistent and reliable instruments of policy formulation are the annual Legislative Budget Request [LBR] developed by the agencies and recommended to the legislature by the governor and the annual general appropriations bill, which gives effect to the annual agency operating budgets.[37] The governor's LBR gives him particular influence over executive agencies that do not report to him,[38] and in broad outline the legislature often accepts the governor's recommendations. On the other hand, in the fine tuning of a governor's recommendations, and in implementing its own policy initiatives, Florida's strong legislature puts its own stamp on the appropriations bill. Each chamber of the legislature maintains strict independence and control over the computer system that produces its appropriations bill and subsidiary "legislative work papers."[39]

The detail work of the appropriations committees is usually handled by subcommittees in each chamber with approximately parallel jurisdiction: education, human and social services, transportation and general government, and criminal justice and corrections.[40] (Because of their influence over detailed budget questions, appropriations

Table 5-4

HOUSE BILLS AND JOINT RESOLUTIONS INTRODUCED

1943–1993

Year	Number of House bills and resolutions introduced
1943	708
1953	1618
1963	1274
1973	1847
1983	1090
1993	1039

subcommittee chairs are usually viewed as having higher status than many standing committee chairs.) The chair of the full Appropriations Committee assigns an expenditure allocation to each subcommittee. Because the Constitution requires the state budget to balance, the subcommittees and full Appropriations Committee must match

Table 5-5

GENERAL AND LOCAL BILLS INTRODUCED IN THE HOUSE AND SENATE, PASSED AND BECOMING LAW, 1989–1990

Calendar Years	1989	1990
General and Local Bills Introduced	3158	3215
Passed......................................	559	519
Vetoed	21	18
Becoming Law	538	501

estimated revenues with expenditures in the general appropriations bill.[41] At the committee stage and in full floor sessions, budgetary balance is ensured by a rule requiring that amendments adding dollars to a line item must also include a line item from which those dollars will be subtracted (House Rule 11.13).

In the closing days of a session, the speaker and president, along with appropriations leadership and possibly the finance and tax leadership, meet with the governor and his or her representatives to seek a compromise on the overall level of revenues and expenditures together with a resolution of major specific disagreements on proposed expenditures. In much of the 1970s and 1980s it was common for several (even tens or hundreds of) millions of dollars to "appear" in a revised revenue estimate or adjusted estimate of agency spending. These dollars would be just enough to break the log jam and allow the legislature and governor to reach a compromise. In recent years, however, the likelihood of extra dollars appearing has greatly diminished as the revenue estimating process has become more participatory, open, and exact.

In the appropriations process, the Florida Legislature's policy-making independence has often been at odds with the governor's assertion of authority as chief executive. Legislative tactics, in the form of appropriation line items,[42] provisos[43] in appropriations bills, details in the letter-of-intent,[44] legislative work papers, and a relatively new device, the appropriations implementation bill,[45] have been met by gubernatorial objections and even vetoes on the grounds that they exceed the legislature's authority to appropriate funds. The argument reached the Florida Supreme Court, which ruled in support of both the governor's formal authority and the legislature's *de facto* power over what course of action executive agencies will ultimately follow. From the agencies' perspective, concern over what the legislature will do to them "next year" tends to overcome the governor's arguments on matters of principle.

POLICY OVERSIGHT

It has long been clear that the simple civics textbook dichotomy of the legislature establishing policy and the executive carrying it out is so distant from reality that it confuses rather than contributes to understanding. In truth, in Florida as elsewhere, the political struggle over policymaking supremacy has blurred lines presumed to separate the executive and legislative branches. A recent national review of governors' and legislators' respective influence over administration concludes that in many states executive agencies are more responsive to legislatures than to the governors (Rosenthal 1990, 167–69). There is only one governor per state, but there are dozens, even hundreds of legislators, organized into a committee structure that typically reflects the agency structure of the state. The result is that a governor, even aided by a competent staff, can pay only occasional and passing attention to a single agency while most legislatures and their committees have continuing and focused interest on their activities.

The Florida Legislature's capacity to oversee the administrative performance of agencies has been greatly enhanced by its professional staff. Governor Reubin Askew (whose term of service coincided with the advent of the Florida Legislature's professional staff system) notes:

> You wind up staffing the legislative branch in order to give it some independence. Then the staff has to have something to do. So they end up really usurping the authority of the executive branch under the guise of oversight (Rosenthal 1990, 186).

There are many mechanisms of legislative oversight. These include a single member's "casework" on behalf of a constituent, hearings and program reviews conducted by committees and their staffs, formal fiscal audits conducted by the Auditor General, and program audits conducted by the recently created Office of Program Policy Analysis and Government Accountability.[46] The Administrative Procedures Act imposes a structured public rulemaking process upon all agencies and gives the legislature a role in evaluating the detailed rules that implement general statutory law.[47]

OVERSIGHT OF EDUCATIONAL POLICY AND ADMINISTRATION

The arena of education offers an illustration of the extent to which Florida's legislative oversight process can influence executive policy decisions. Governmental reorganization in the late 1960s created a comprehensive Department of Education headed by the State Board of Education.[48] Florida Constitution Art. IX, s. 2 authorizes the legislature to delegate policymaking powers to the Board and to the Commissioner of Education.

Within the Department of Education are the Division of Public Schools,[49] the Division of Community Colleges,[50] the Division of Applied Technology and Adult Education, the Division of Human Resource Development, the Division of Administration, and the Division of Universities. The State University System consists of the eleven state universities and the Board of Regents.[51] Regents primarily establish policy and provide oversight for the universities.

Like most states, education is the most far-reaching and costly enterprise of Florida government. The original 1991–1992 education appropriation was $8 billion for operating costs plus $1.2 billion for capital outlay. The specific appropriation that funds the major part of the public school budget, the $4 billion Florida Education Finance Program, is the largest single item in the state budget. One can understand why this scale of appropriation attracts considerable legislative interest.

For at least 30 years, the Florida legislature has taken an activist posture toward educational policy. In the mid-1970s, Senator Robert D. Graham of Miami Lakes (who later became governor and then U.S. Senator) chaired the Senate Education Committee, and Dr. Richard S. Hodes of Tampa chaired the House Education Committee. Their committees produced the Public Education Act of 1975 and the Educational Accountability Act of 1976, the first of many statutes and procedures originated within the legislature to better integrate and make more accountable the public educational activities of the state. In 1990 a new generation of legislative leaders, assisted by some of the same staff present in the early 1970s, were in conflict with Governor Lawton Chiles and Commissioner of Education Betty Castor over a new and presumably improved version of "accountability."

Computer technology now affords the legislature and its staff access to detailed data about the operations of schools and colleges. Because these systems are structured primarily to conform to legislative interests, much information about school-level activities is organized and formatted to meet legislative needs rather than provide information useful to educational administrators. As a consequence, the State University System data files are organized by program categories that do not conform to the managerial structures of the universities. For example, the program "Social Sciences" does not include the same set of disciplines/ departments that comprise the College of Social Sciences at Florida State University (or others). The College of Social Sciences departments are actually spread across at least three different state/federal program categories.

To get data useful at the dean's level, the legislatively mandated state reports must be adjusted to obtain the relevant disciplines while dropping the irrelevant ones. Yet in the real world, these adjusted management reports are often not available because the first priority is placed upon legislative requirements. Even if the adjusted managerial data are available, confusion can result because administrators and legislative policy makers, while using the same terminology, may be talking about different numbers, events, or programs.

Another difficulty is that legislators or other policy makers, such as the Board of Regents, may attempt to direct policy outcomes by adjusting resource inputs by program categories without realizing that the necessary budget linkages simply do not exist to effect the desired changes. For example, the legislature for several years provided special funding for "enhancement of undergraduate education" in the university system. Along with money for new faculty positions came explicit mandates on maximum class sizes in certain disciplines and levels of instruction (e.g., freshman mathematics and sophomore English) together with mandated reports and legislative hearings to see whether the universities had "closed the loop."[52]

Several practical problems ensued. First is a fundamental difference in perspective. A new faculty "hire," even using newly appropriated undergraduate enhancement funds, over many years will inevitably result in a mixed program result. Universities hire permanent faculty with the expectation that over a career these individuals will provide a variety of services—instruction, research, advisement, administration, etc., in a distribution of effort among tasks that will vary from term to term. An expectation that success in meeting legislative intent on faculty effort can be measured with a semester-by-semester reporting system, balanced against a once every 25-year or 30-year hiring decision, does not mesh well with reality.

Also clouding the accountability picture is the relative size of the specific appropriation to the task at hand. By one calculation, the total "undergraduate enhancement" funds over five years constituted less than a 10-percent increase in the State University System budget for providing instruction and research and was accompanied by a simultaneous increase of 18 percent in number of full-time equivalent students enrolled.

Viewing policymaking efforts over a number of years, a cyclical pattern emerges. The philosophy behind the early 1970s legislation was to provide public access to information about public school performance coupled with school-building-based management. This was grounded in the theory that a better informed public would demand improved performance from school managers who had the decentralized authority to affect performance by their students.

What actually happened was that better information about failures to perform led to the invention, often by the legislature, of new programs and new funding to "cure" the particular problem so identified. After 15 years of loading such "corrective" programs on top of each other, the thrust in the 1990s has been to simplify mandates, consolidate funding, require school-level accountability based on outcome measures, and even contract for public education from nonpublic sources (e.g., charter schools). Despite widespread agreement on the goals, however, there is considerable difference of opinion on how to achieve them. It is clear that the legislature will insist on being an active participant in the process and will continue its oversight activities.

OVERSIGHT OF HUMAN SERVICES PROGRAMS

Also in the mid-1970s, the legislature took a close look at Florida's second most expensive area of programs, human services, and passed the nation's most comprehensive human services programs reorganization act. This 1975 legislation reorganized the Department of Health and Rehabilitative Services (HRS) described as follows 10 years later (National Academy 1986, 1):

> . . . [HRS] is characterized by consolidation of programs under common management in Tallahassee and service delivery through eleven districts with the aim of integrating a range of programs at both state and local levels.
>
> The statutory reorganization . . . marked a radical break with the 1969 organization of the department which was designed to consolidate state social service agencies into a single administrative entity. The 1975 reorganization established a structural framework within which health and human services could be decentralized, client-oriented and coordinated.
>
> * * *
>
> . . . changes in policies and practices toward the support of the concept of services integration, philosophies and responses of management, use of contractors, relations with the advocacy groups and composition of staff have continued to occur during the last ten years. . . . [D]imensions of the Department . . . give rise to a unique organization which is increasingly under fire for being too large, too unresponsive, too ineffective, and too bureaucratic.

It is significant that in the more than 25 years (and five governors) since the creation of the department, there has been continuous and intense legislative interest in the department. In 1996, the legislature, after years of frustration over perceived inefficiencies, finally created a separate Department of Health.[53] Again the legislature, not the executive, originated the idea.

These examples of ongoing oversight in the education and human services arenas demonstrate the legislature's long-term institutional commitment to policy management in the two most expensive areas of state programming. This commitment has continued through the administration of successive governors, House speakers, and Senate presidents. There is every indication that this practice of detailed and continuous legislative participation in managing Florida public policy will continue.

REFERENCES

Burns, John (1971). *The sometime governments.* New York: Bantam Books.

Colburn, David R. and Richard K. Scher (1980). *Florida's gubernatorial politics in the twentieth century.* Tallahassee: University Presses of Florida.

Doherty, P. C. (1991). *Development and impact of legislative involvement on selected aspects of state university system operations 1954–1990.* Unpublished doctoral dissertation. Tallahassee: Florida State University.

Dauer, Manning J. (1980). Florida's Legislature. In Manning J. Dauer, (Ed.), *Florida's Politics and Government.* Gainesville: University Presses of Florida.

Havard, William C. and Loren P. Beth (1962). *The politics of mis-representation: Rural-urban conflict in the Florida legislature.* Baton Rouge: Louisiana State University Press.

Morris, Allen (1977). *The language of lawmaking in Florida.* (3rd ed.). Tallahassee: Office of the Clerk of the House of Representatives.

National Academy of Public Administration (1986). *After a decade: A progress report on the organization and management of the Florida department of health and rehabilitative services.* Washington, D.C.: The Academy.

Rosenthal, Alan (1990). *Governors and legislatures: Contending powers.* Washington, D.C.: CQ Press.

ENDNOTES

1. The original of this paper was prepared by Augustus B. Turnbull. Following his death in November 1991, the paper was edited for publication by John B. Phelps, Clerk of the House. Dr. Turnbull had worked closely with Mr. Phelps throughout the drafting of the original paper. Mr. Phelps also completed revisions for the second edition.

2. These rural legislators were first called the "Pork Chop Gang" in a *Tampa Tribune* editorial in 1955 according to Allen Morris (1977, 63).

3. David R. Colburn and Richard K. Scher note that in the April 1967 session one-third of the Senate and over half of the House were freshmen (1980, 111).

4. Interim activities often result in major legislative policy initiatives during the next regular session. In this way, the legislature is able to conceive its own approach to policy making independent of the executive.

5. As discussed below, these committees determine the daily agenda of the House and Senate.

6. This is perhaps the best point to begin to interject the role of the Clerk of the House and Secretary of the Senate as the "institutional memories" of the chambers, among many other vital duties. Current Clerk John B. Phelps is my source for the above information. He has also been kind enough to review the entire manuscript to help me avoid misstatements of procedural fact. Any opinions or value judgments remain entirely mine and must not be ascribed to him, for he is far too wise to be led into such non-clerkly comments. Senate Secretary Joe Brown, in addition to holding a certificate in public administration from a major Florida university, was also wise enough to be out of town when most of this writing was done, so no blame can be ascribed to him!

7. *Florida Constitution* Art. VI, sec. 4.

8. Senators and House members elected in 1992 and serving consecutive terms will be unable to run for reelection in the year 2000. (Fla. Const. Art. VI, sec. 4)

9. The Senate was equally divided (20-20) after the 1992 election, which led to an agreement to divide the presidency over a two-year period with Republican Ander Crenshaw of Jacksonville presiding over the first year and Democrat Pat Thomas of Quincy over the second.

10. The legal definition of "lobbying" and associated reporting requirements were adopted by joint action of both houses in 1991 and have been subsequently amended.

11. Representative Turnbull was elected to the House in 1994 to serve a part of Leon County. She served as a Leon County Commissioner from 1988 to 1994.

12. These projects are often carried out by the professionally trained staff members of the substantive, or less-frequently by the appropriations, committees. On occasion, university faculty or other experts are employed for particular research projects. (See the further discussion of legislative oversight in the following section.)

13. Much of the formality of legislative procedure revolves around the subject of bills. While they can be proposed and drafted by any individual or organization, only members of the legislature or legislative committees may sponsor (introduce) bills. Keeping track of bills requires familiarity with a very specialized terminology. The Clerk has determined there are currently in use for bills six formal prefixes, eleven functional classes, and thirteen descriptive names. Several of these will be introduced in the section that follows.

14. There are also committees on administration of the chambers, and select, ad hoc, and joint committees, which are established from time to time.

15. Statistical and quantitative data on the legislature in this chapter, unless otherwise referenced, are taken from unpublished tables maintained by the Clerk of the House of Representatives.

16. House speakers and Senate presidents and their "shadow" equivalents in the minority party will sometimes be relieved of committee service to concentrate on their leadership duties.

17. Both types of meetings usually provide public notice.

18. Such so-called "negative references" have not been used in recent years but remain as a potential power of the presiding officer. Upon appeal to the chamber, a reference may be changed.

19. By a two-thirds vote of the House, a bill can be removed from committee. Although rarely used, this is a power available to overcome a resistant committee chair.

20. In the House, for example, two days notice is required during the first 45 days of the session, and two hours notice thereafter. Permission to waive the rule can be granted by the House upon request of the committee chair.

21. Earlier legislatures allowed votes to be taken by polling members on the floor or by proxy. This practice was seen as a violation of the "open meetings" principle and has since been prohibited by rule.

22. A Committee Substitute (CS) is a new bill offered in the name of the committee itself. Usually, a bill substantially amended by action of a committee will be offered as a committee substitute.

23. The often-expressed reason is that until the committee knows how much money is available for overall state priorities, individual special appropriations should not be considered.

24. It is so rare for this to happen that on one occasion when it did, the normally well-prepared Clerk's staff had to scramble to determine which bill was next on the regular order and to get it into the appropriate posture for consideration. In recent times, the House has simply adjourned upon completion of the Special Order Calendar.

25. Although on rare occasions, members who found themselves in major conflict with the presiding officer have had their assignments changed during the session.

26. *Florida Constitution* Art. III, s. 7.

27. Usually this and all readings by title include a statement of the prime sponsor's name, the bill's number, and its relating clause (which summarizes the bill's subject).

28. This is called "following a member's button."

29. Engrossing is the process of incorporating amendments adopted by the chamber into the body of the bill. Engrossing is handled by the Clerk for House bills and by the Secretary for Senate bills even when dealing with amendments adopted by the opposite body. Bills may be engrossed more than once if further amendments are approved after the first engrossment. A bill is "enrolled" after it is passed by both houses, thus becoming an act. Once signed by the constitutional officers of the House and Senate, it is sent to the governor.

30. It is not sufficient, therefore, for the House and the Senate to each pass identical but separate bills. At some point in the process, both chambers must affirmatively act on the same bill.

31. Conference committees are rare in the Florida Legislature. Usually, not more than four or five will be appointed during a regular session.

32. A constitutional amendment adopted in November 1992 requires that an appropriations bill be placed before a house for 72 hours prior to a vote on final passage.

33. *Florida Constitution* Art. III, s. 6 requires that each bill may have but one subject.

34. Or between key leaders within either the House or Senate!

35. We note again for emphasis that a bill is an actual physical document that must be present whenever action is being taken on it. It has been alleged that years ago some bills simply disappeared into a chair's pocket at critical moments in the proceedings or were physically assembled after passage and adjournment of the legislature.

36. Speaker and clerk in the House and president and secretary in the Senate.

37. See Chapters Eight and Nine, which provide a much more detailed perspective on the financial procedures of the State of Florida.

38. For example, Department of Education, Department of Agriculture and Consumer Services, Department of State, etc.

39. These are computer printouts produced by the legislature to provide details on objects of expenditure and program categories, which add up to the summary numbers contained in the actual appropriations bills. These details are closely guarded by appropriations staffs during the deliberative process and may not become available for agency guidance until days or weeks after the legislature has adjourned a session.

40. The actual number of subcommittees and their agency jurisdictions has changed slightly from year to year in one chamber or another, but this appears to be the "normal" center of gravity.

41. *Florida Constitution* Art. IV, s. 13, Art. VII, S. 1(d), and Art. III, s. 19(h).

42. The governor has authority to veto legislative line items.

43. These are narrative comments in the appropriations bill dictating how certain sums (or portions of large sums) are to be spent or otherwise directing action by executive agencies, e.g., "From the funds in item 456 the department shall conduct a study of xyz."

44. This is a document issued by the two appropriations chairs several weeks after the close of the legislative session to "clarify" and "correct" the appropriations bill itself. It does not have the force of law, but agencies are well advised to heed its directions since they must return for support in subsequent sessions.

45. This is a bill which makes statutory changes that are necessary in order to effect provisions of the appropriations bill. It is viewed as a technical document produced by staff in the closing hours of the session, and has been known to contain some surprises.

46. For example, increasingly, the Postsecondary Education Planning Commission [PEPC] has been assigned interim research projects on higher education issues through provisos in the annual appropriations bill.

47. Sections 11.60 and 120.545, Florida Statutes, as amended by chapter 96-159, Laws of Florida. The Administrative Procedures Committee is a joint standing committee of the legislature.

48. The State Board of Education is composed of the Governor and Cabinet, which includes the Secretary of State, Attorney General, Comptroller, Treasurer, Commissioner of Education, and Commissioner of Agriculture.

49. Actual school administration in Florida is in the hands of 67 countywide, elected school boards.

50. The Division of Community Colleges oversees 28 community colleges that are operated by multicounty boards appointed by the governor and confirmed by the Senate.

51. Regents are appointed by the governor, approved by three cabinet members, and confirmed by the Senate.

52. This is a term of art favored by some key legislative staff and feared by many university officials. In its most extensive conception, it assumes that the programmatic results of all dollars appropriated for specific functions in the university can be measured and linked back to the original legislative intent. For example, faculty effort devoted to instruction or research or academic advising would match resources provided through the funding formula for those activities.

53. The department name was changed to Children and Family Services after a number of its functions were removed and a new Department of Health created.

PART III

SYSTEMS OF IMPLEMENTATION

THE BUREAUCRACY: HISTORICAL DEVELOPMENT AND REFORM

RICHARD CHACKERIAN

The role of government in society, particularly its power is one of the major preoccupations of citizens and scholars alike. The functional scope, effectiveness and control of government bureaucracy are particularly important aspects of this larger issue. Government bureaucracies, perhaps more than private sector organizations, are faced with profound tensions in the values they are expected to serve. Governments often are attacked as being a fundamental threat to individual freedom and as being inherently ineffective. It is argued that they tend to be ineffective because they normally provide services without market competition. The threat they present to civil liberties is said to be grounded in the fact that they are the only institutions in society which can legitimately use force.

The constitutional separation of powers between the legislative, executive and judicial branches of government and between federal, state and local governments is part of the formula for reducing the threat of improper use of government power. A basic assumption of our constitutional system is that by dividing government power the threat to individual liberties is reduced. As we shall see the governmental and bureaucratic arrangements in Florida reflect a strong commitment to this assumption.

The assertion that government organizations are not efficient is usually based on the argument that governments do not face market competition. As a consequence they have little incentive to work hard, be innovative and to improve the effectiveness of operations. As with private organizations individuals seek to maximize economic reward, but in a governmental setting that is said to be accomplished by increasing the number of employees and the size of the bureau's budget. This view of government ineffectiveness lead critics to focus on keeping taxes low. If governments and their bureaucracies are inherently ineffective, the waste is minimized by reducing the tax burden. Again, Florida is an example of a state that has worked hard and successfully at keeping taxes low.

A competing view of the relationship between government and individual freedom is that government action can provide certain conditions for the expansion of human freedom and development. Education, law enforcement, transportation, and justice are services all would agree are essential to civil society. Those supporting an active role for government argue further, however, that these services cannot be provided effectively by the private sector. There are a variety of reasons given for this, including the inability to put a monetary value on certain goods such as air, and the inability of certain groups to compete in the marketplace for essential goods such as food, shelter, and health care because they are poor.

In recent years a middle-ground developed on these issues which depends on the distinction between the provision and production of public services. The argument is that the government must be responsible for the provision of certain services but not necessarily their production. A private or non-profit agency may, under contract with the government, actually deliver the service or good, but the government is responsible for defining the nature of the goods to be delivered and to be sure that the non-government provider does a good job. A related strategy is public regulation of private activity to assure that in private provision public concerns are taken into account. Examples include fines for pollution and required contributions by health providers for indigent health care. When we examine the delivery systems and structures used by Florida's bureaucracies, it will become clear that they are heavily invested in the strategy of public provision and private production.

Even if one concedes government bureaus are less effective than for-profit organizations, government bureaucracies play a critical public policy role which private organizations are not expected play. Public administrators manage programs and policies in addition to managing people. They implement the will of citizens as it is expressed by elected officials. This role involves public administrators in the resolution of conflicting social values. It is not unusual for there to be a variety of views on what ought to be done to deal with a given problem in society. Government bureaus are heavily involved in making suggestions to resolve these conflicts. The involvement may take the form of proposed legislation, administrative rules and procedures, or informal agreements with interested parties. This process involves attempts at reconciliation of interests before, during and after the adoption of legislation.

The results of the public manager's policy role may include (1) making public managers cautious in the decision-making style; (2) absorbing valuable resources; and (3) leaving the organization with imperfectly reconciled interests and conflicting goals. Obviously this is not an environment which encourages technical efficiency but it is inevitable for public bureaucracies in a democracy. Bureaucratic power is mitigated through constitutional division of government roles, but also through informal representational roles of government bureaucracies. Responding to external demands and interests may reduce the technical efficiency of government bureaus, but it is part of the process of minimizing the danger inherent in government power.

The implication of this debate over government bureaucracies is not whether we should have them, but their appropriate scope and control systems. Public policy issues tend to focus on the form and characteristics of public bureaucracies and their relationship to bureaucratic accountability and effectiveness. Much of the effort to reform government bureaucracies attempts to reconcile these values.

THE THEORY AND PRACTICE OF BUREAUCRATIC REFORM MOVEMENTS IN FLORIDA

The theory of bureaucratic hierarchy as a method of efficiently and effectively coordinating administrative activities was well developed in the United States by the 1920's. One of its most articulate spokesmen in state governments was A.F. Buck (1938). Buck usually is considered to be the originator of the traditional theory as it specifically relates to state executive branch reorganization. In his, *The Reorganization of State Governments in the United States* (1938, 14–15), he provides a succinct statement of the general theory:

Through administrative reorganization it is possible to simplify the machinery of complicated and poorly organized state governments and thereby bring about better and more economical management. Such reorganization usually involves the consolidation of various offices, boards, commissions, and agencies which administer the state's affairs into a few orderly departments, set up along general functional lines. This process of reconstruction has developed . . . certain standards with respect to the organization and integration of state administration. These standards are no longer theoretical, but are based upon experience and supported in whole or in part by actual practice in a number of states. They may be enumerated as follows: (1) concentration of authority and responsibility; (2) departmentalization, or functional integration; (3) undesirability of boards for purely administrative work; (4) coordination of the staff services of administration; (5) provision of an independent audit; (6) recognition of a governor's cabinet.

The approach taken by Buck and other early classical reformers prescribes that there should be a clear, unbroken line of formal control from a single chief executive to the lowest level of the organization. These were called *monocratic* hierarchies. The logic is rather simple. If the chief executive is given control over the operations of a bureau, s/he can be held responsible for its operations. In-so-far as control and authority are diffused by boards, commissions, and other forms of multiple direction, administrative accountability is made difficult. Since no single individual is in charge, it is difficult to place responsibility when things don't go well.

An additional advantage of monocratic hierarchies for control, it was argued, is they are more efficient than hierarchies which allow multiple lines of control and supervision. Every subordinate, having one supervisor, would receive clear and unambiguously defined responsibilities. The unbroken chain of command from the top to the bottom of the organization also would simplify communications within the organization.

An underlying premise of the monocratic hierarchical approach is that there is one best way to implement a program or policy. That is, under all circumstances monocratic hierarchies are the best way to organize. Further, there is the premise that knowledge is held at the top of the organization and that duties necessary to achieve organizational objectives should be delegated from the top to subordinate positions. There is little consideration given to the possibility that knowledge may be scattered throughout the organization, including the lowest levels.

The ideal classical model of organization for a very short period of time reflected the reality of government organization in Florida and in academic circles has long been discarded as the only way to organize. Significantly however it is an ideal that even its critics cannot completely disregard. In the world of practicing administration, departures from the classical model are attributed to "politics" and other parochial interests. The realities of course are much more complicated and this is amply illustrated in the case of Florida.

Florida operated under the anti-Reconstruction constitution of 1885 until 1968 and in some measure is still influenced by the ideas that were important for that document. The reorganization movements before

1968 were not implemented but they provide a sense of the logic and culture of change in Florida. The post-Reconstruction reform efforts were based on the premise that strong executive leadership represented a danger and that means must be found to minimize the burden of taxes. It wasn't until the reforms of 1968 that the long standing interest in minimizing taxing and spending was linked to structural consolidation and the desirability of monocratic hierarchies.

In 1930 Governor Carlton appointed a Finance and Taxation committee to find ways of making the state tax structure more fair. The Commission was heavily influenced by the Great Depression, which began in 1929, and the inability of many home owners to pay their property taxes.

> By 1932 Florida was deeply mired in the national depression. The hurricanes of 1926 and 1928, the failure of the land boom, and the fruit fly pestilence had devastate the state's economy well before the onset of the depression. The financial collapse of the nation merely added the final coup de grace to Florida's economic trials (Colburn and Scher 1980, 70).

Under these circumstances it is not surprising that the Commission's administrative recommendations were an attempt to implement a local tax system based on the ability to pay, but its recommendations that a state Tax Commission be established for these purposes was defeated in the Legislature.

In 1934 the Special Committee on Taxation and Public Debt was established by Governor Sholtz. It criticized the state's revenue system and its administration as "haphazard and without regard to sound principles of finance. . . ." (Doyle et al. 1954, 103). These recommendations, although clearly aimed at economy issues, had a distinct administrative cast. For example the Committee recommended (Doyle et al. 1954, 103).

1. All state appropriations should be under a single budgetary authority and earmarked funds abolished.
2. All state tax administration should be consolidated under a proposed state fiscal authority.
3. The state fiscal authority would be able to impose a uniform accounting system on local authorities, equalize local tax assessments and supervise all local property tax administration.
4. A constitutional amendment was proposed that would permit the state to levy a personal income tax and to adopt a business privilege tax based on net income.

These recommendations are extraordinary in the extent to which they embrace the ability to pay principle, but more importantly for our purposes, the extent to which they support the centralization and consolidation of fiscal functions at the state level. The Tax Inquiry Council (1940–41) and a study by the Florida State Planning Board (1942–43) made recommendations which were similar to the earlier reports. They placed primary focus on revenue and on the most appropriate implementing administrative arrangements. In each instance the administrative recommendations were to consolidate and unify administrative direction.

The emphasis shifted in 1943 when the Legislature created the Special Joint Economy and Efficiency Committee which worked through 1945. The significance of this study is that it was the first time the Legislature showed an interest in administrative questions. Previously, the governor took the initiative in these matters, and understandably, because the governor was the most likely beneficiary of greater administrative consolidation. The committee proposed (Doyle et al. 1954, 104–105).

1. Creation of an executive department consisting of the governor and the following administrative heads appointed by the governor: budget director, personnel director, director of revenue, director of public safety, director of planning and a director of purchases. Although it recommended that more power be given to the budget director, it left the final major budgeting decisions with the Budget Commission.
2. Creation of a state-wide merit system under the supervision of the personnel director.
3. Consolidation of tax administration under the supervision of the director of revenue.
4. Abolition of a large number of boards, commissions, and other agencies and consolidation of their functions under departments that would be under the supervision of the governor, including a department of conservation, a department of business regulation, and a department of professional licensing and examining.
5. Creation of a legislative post audit, with the state auditor appointed by and accountable to the legislature.
6. Limitation of the comptroller to accounting and fiscal control functions, the state treasurer to the custody and payment of state funds and the custody of securities, the commissioner of agriculture to purely agricultural functions, and the transfer of certain functions from the secretary of state. The committee made no recommendations that would change the constitutional standing of the members of the state cabinet.

While these recommendations also were not adopted, they were consistent with many of the main recommendations that were adopted a quarter of a century later. The themes and recommendations of the earlier commissions and councils were largely repeated in the recommendations of subsequent post war advisory groups. The Citizen's Tax Committee (1945–47), the Joint House-Senate Tax Survey Committee (1947–1949), the Legislative Council (1949–1951) and the Legislative Council (1951–1952) were governed by the premise that there ought to be consolidation of departments, particularly in the fiscal area to increase efficiency and fairness.

In 1954 the governor of Florida was weak in comparison to the powers held by other governors. State budgeting was still highly decentralized and directed by the Cabinet sitting as the Budget Commission. A budget director was appointed by the governor, but the Budget Commission held final authority. Accounting and control of expenditures was split between the controller and state treasurer with post-auditing in the hands of the state auditor appointed by the governor. In addition there was no central personnel system (Doyle et al. 1954, 108).

> A central personnel program exits only for the employees of the departments and agencies that receive Federal aid, namely, the Industrial Commission, the State Department of Health, the state Department of Public Welfare, the Crippled Children's Commission and the Hospital Division of the Florida State Improvement Commission; administrative supervision of the program rests with a council appointed by the agencies concerned.

Tax functions were assigned to forty-seven different agencies with four collecting about 90 percent of the total. The administrative structure of Florida was an object lesson in poor organization from the perspective of organizational reformers. To say that it was decentralized doesn't adequately describe the arrangements because it was never centralized but rather grew in response to highly particularized pressures for governmental action.

THE POLITICAL AND CULTURAL CONTEXT OF REFORM

V.O. Key Jr., writing about the same time as Doyle and his colleagues argued that politics in Florida was different from other states (Key 1949, 82).

> Florida ranks high in political atomization. In its politics it is almost
> literally every candidate for himself. Ordinarily each candidate for
> county office runs without collaboration with other local candi-
> dates. He hesitates to become publicly committed in counties for
> state office lest he fall heir to all the local enemies of the state-wide
> candidate.

Key further observed that Florida politics is not only unbossed, but
also unlead with the consequence that anything can happen. The underlying reasons offered for the lack of political coherence are geography
and social structure. The large physical size of the state and the disbur-
sal of political centers made it difficult to centralize leadership. This was
added to the fact that Florida had an unusually large proportion of non-
natives with few attachments to the state, its political leadership and
institutions.

Key's analysis must be seen in the context of southern politics
which has been traditional and conservative. As was suggested in Chapter
One, Florida's political culture in this period was *"traditionalistic."*
Thus while there may not have been a great deal of political organization,
there was also the widely shared political premise that the role of government in society ought to be severely limited. When this premise is widely
shared, strong leadership is seen as unnecessary. The history of reform
effort failures suggests that the fragmentation of the governmental structures was not seen as a problem demanding action. The central concern
was essentially economy, not disaggregated governmental arrangements.
Ultimately however factors beyond economy were needed to make significant changes in governmental and administrative arrangements.

The successful effort for constitutional and administrative reform
began in 1965 when the legislature established a Constitutional Revision
Commission. The report of the Commission was submitted to the legislature in 1967 but was not acted upon because in January 1967, the
United States Supreme Court declared in *Swam v. Adams* that the legislature was illegally apportioned. The court ordered that new elections be
held based on the principle of "one man one vote" (Colburn and Scher
1980, 111).

The 1967 elections greatly increased the number of representatives
from Florida's metropolitan areas. They had been kept out of influential
positions of influence in the past, but were now empowered and ready
for change. It was also important that the first Republican governor since
Reconstruction, Claude Kirk, understood that his Republican party
would benefit from constitutional change. The Cabinet had been over-
whelmingly Democratic. Any constitutional revisions which might

increase the power of the Republican governor was an obvious advantage for the Republican party. Kirk called three special sessions of the legislature and on July 3rd it adopted a document which was submitted to the electorate for approval. The new constitution went into effect in January, 1969.

Many of the early reform efforts focused on saving money and adopted the language of reform that had dominated these movements since the 1920's. The fragmentation of authority and organization lessened both the efficiency and economy of governmental operations and also made the government less accountable to the public. It is apparent however that there were other considerations which were critical in Florida.

In Chapter One it was argued that Florida is in some respects a developing state whose administrative arrangements lag significantly behind its needs. Mosher suggests that (1967, 494)

> Many organization structures, or parts thereof, originally set up in eminently rational and efficient forms in response to the needs of their times, become gradually less efficient and less in tune with the needs as the years go by. Ultimately, major modifications are necessary.

Mosher's observations are highly relevant to Florida. In addition to the pressures of population growth, the role of state government was also undergoing significant change. The 1960's was a period of significant expansion of Federal outlays and dependence on state governments to implement Federal policy. James Reichley was not atypical in his concern over the capability of states like Florida to respond to these new responsibilities (Reichley 1964, 198).

> Another handicap to effective state government, at least as serious as legislative malapportionment, is posed by the often paralyzing division of administrative powers within the governmental structures of many states.

The impact of reformist thinking and movements also can be seen in the remarks of Professor Parker to the Joint Committee on State Government Reorganization on December 7, 1968. This committee took a lead role in reorganizing state government in conformance to the then recently enacted mandate to reduce the number of departments to not more than twenty five (Dennis 1974, 243).

Ten years after Florida's admission into the union the legislature designated the governor and the officers of "the several departments" (a secretary of state, attorney general, treasurer, controller, and registrar of public lands, all elected by the legislature) as the Board of Trustees of the Internal Improvement Fund.

The constitution of 1868 created three ex officio cabinet boards: the Board of Commissioners of State Institutions, the Board of Education (the Superintendent of Public Instruction, the Secretary of State, and the Attorney General), and a Pardon Board made up of the Governor, Attorney General, and the justices of the Supreme Court. The Constitutional Convention writing the 1885 charter provided for the same three boards. . . .

Today there are at least 35 ex officio boards in almost every phase of administration, most of the boards existing by statutory authority.

Habit, chance, lack of understanding and lack of time for understanding, lethargy, and vested interests have provided a combination of circumstances that have made it easy for legislators to create another ex officio board to take care of another administrative need.

It is clear from this description of the state's organizational arrangements that the number and consequent lack of coordination between agencies was a source of great concern. It is not difficult to read into Parker's remarks the organizational principles developed by A. E. Buck (1938): (1) concentration of authority and responsibility; (2) departmentalization, or functional integration; (3) undesirability of boards for purely administrative work; (4) coordination of the staff services of administration; (5) provision of an independent audit; (6) recognition of a governor's cabinet.

The importance of efficiency and effectiveness is reflected in the connections made between the needs of society and the development of government bureaus (Dennis 1974, 243).

Florida's vast sprawling disintegrated host of executive agencies of all types, structures, sizes and nomenclature has had its main growth since 1900. Until the 1890's the constitutional executives were almost personally adequate to take care of the regular administrative activities. A separate board of medical examiners was set up in the sixties, and the ex officio Board of Trustees for the Internal Improvement Fund had been created in the fifties [1850's].

After 1885 there appeared the Railroad Commission (at first appointed, but elected after 1897), the Reform School Board, the Commission on Uniformity of Legislation, the State Board of Health, the State Board of Pharmacy.

The minutes of the Board of Commissioners of State Institutions reveal the relatively simple nature of state administration before 1900. In the seventies and eighties meetings of the Board were generally few and far between, with months often elapsing between recorded meetings. After 1900, the state faced new problems connected with technical advancement, urbanization, industrialization and increased population; agencies were set up to meet the problems and provide the required state services, no task being considered too menial or too tremendous for an executive agency.

Between 1965 and 1975 twenty two states, including Florida, significantly revised their constitutions and consolidated agencies. They also eliminated large numbers of boards and commissions consolidating them under functional entities such as human services, transportation, administration, public safety, etc. There was also a tendency to consolidate staff services under the governor. This was particularly pronounced in the case of budgeting, planning, personnel, and procurement (ACIR 1985, 143–150).

FLORIDA'S 1969 REORGANIZATION

The reorganization effort in Florida was *"significant"* but not extreme in its adoption of the reformist ideas. The number of agencies was drastically reduced from over 150 to 23, a number quite comparable to other states undergoing reorganization in this period. It also increased significantly the powers of the governor by placing responsibility for budget preparation, personnel and planning directly under the governor and purchasing (General Services) under the governor and cabinet. Previously these management functions had been scattered throughout the government.

The executive however remained plural. The Cabinet retained elective status for Agriculture, Education, Legal Affairs, Banking and Finance, State, and Insurance/Treasurer. Other agencies were put under the joint direction of the Governor and Cabinet. General Services, Highway Safety and Motor Vehicles, Criminal Law Enforcement, Natural Resources and Revenue were cabinet agencies. The governor was given direct responsibility for his Executive Office and Administration, Business Regulation, Commerce, Community Affairs, Health and Rehabilitative Services, Military Affairs, Transportation and Professional and Occupational Regulation.

The type of reorganization model followed in Florida has been described as *"traditional"* or *"standard"* (Garnett 1980, 179). This type is contrasted to *"cabinet"* and *"secretary-coordinator."* In traditional reorganizations the number of agencies after reorganization is relatively large, more than seventeen, and less than fifty percent of existing units are consolidated into single function agencies (Garnett 1980, 179). It is also characteristic of traditional reorganizations that less than fifty percent of the post-reorganization department heads are appointed by the governor.

Florida departed from the traditional model and more approximated the secretary-coordinator model in the low proportion of post reorganization agencies with plural executives (e.g., boards and commissions). In 1950 Florida had 26 ex officio boards and 21 examining boards. The 1969 reorganization eliminated nearly all of them (ACIR 1985, 148).

In some respects the 1969 reorganization of state government was a watershed in both the politics and administration of state government. The rapid growth and urbanization of the state was now reflected in the composition of the legislature. The reorganized state government, while certainly not the model of reformist ideals was certainly much closer to it than before.

The 1968 constitution provided for a Constitutional Revision Commission in ten years and every twenty years thereafter. The Commission that prepared the 1978 proposed constitution did not return it to the legislature for approval but placed it directly before the voters. All eight propositions were defeated including the one which would have eliminated the six elected cabinet members and provided for their appointment by the governor.

The defeat of the 1977 reorganization proposals had little to do with the proposals themselves but with procedure. By referring the recommendations directly to the voters, the Commission failed to get legislators committed to the proposals. As a consequence the proposals lacked political support and leadership which made passage of the 1968 revisions possible (Dauer 1980, 95–96). In 1997 the constitution revision process began again and reorganization of the Cabinet is on the agenda.[1] Indeed, the Askew Commission has recommended significant reductions in the scope the Cabinet's responsibilities.

FLORIDA'S REFORMS IN NATIONAL CONTEXT

In some respects the 1968 Florida revisions reflected needs and trends that had already reversed themselves at the national level. The 1978 defeat may not only have been a consequence of procedure, but also of national trends which increasingly focused on keeping government bureaucracies accountable. Herbert Kaufman recently suggested that the doctrines of reform embrace, over time, the goals of neutral competence and executive leadership. These values are linked respectively to extension of merit personnel systems on the one hand and more centralized powers for executives on the other (Kaufman 1990, 484).

Kaufman raises an important question: "Is it really feasible to enlarge the chief executive's authority over the administrative apparatus of government and still insulate that apparatus from political influence [through the extension of merit personnel systems]?" The answer is "it all depends." At the national level there had been no substantial conflict between these principles of administration from the New Deal until the Eisenhower administration because the federal bureaucracy was controlled by administrators with essentially Democratic party sympathies. The prospect of extending merit protection to them did not create conflicts between the need for accountability to the president and the need for neutral competence.

President Eisenhower, in 1956, took office after 20 years of Democratic presidents, and was confronted with a bureaucracy largely Democratic in its sympathies. His response was to increase the number of positions not subject to civil service protection. Controlling the administrative apparatus became an important part of executive leadership and some have suggested that under these circumstances neutral competence was sure to suffer. Interestingly the struggle to establish executive leadership continued through subsequent Democratic and Republican administrations, each reducing the tenure protection of government employees in the name of making the bureaucracy responsive and accountable.

Ironically, the attempt of presidents beginning in 1956, to exert leadership was occurring at the same time as federal functions were being decentralized to state governments. Given the logic noted above, it is not surprising that it was president Nixon who pushed the expansion of sharing federal revenue with state governments. The reasons for this move are complex, but the effects were ironic. Revenue sharing raised the question of state government capability. Could the states with highly disaggregated governing and administrative structures efficiently and effectively spend federal money? Many felt that they were by and large,

147

not capable because they failed to measure up to the reformist ideal of administrative organization which emphasizes executive leadership and neutral competence. In a larger sense then the reform movement which swept through the states beginning in the late 1950's reflected the federal inability to reconcile conflicts between neutral competence and executive leadership inherent the reformist model.

THE ROLE OF THE LEGISLATURE IN ADMINISTRATIVE CONTROL

The tendency to focus on executive leadership in the states was not unambiguous with respect to patterns of organization. Executive leadership really meant gubernatorial control. In Florida however the Legislature was also interested in a greater role in controlling administrative activity. When the 1968 constitutional reform package was adopted Florida had its first Republican governor since Reconstruction but the legislature was solidly Democratic and committed to making changes in how the government was run. It is not surprising then that the legislature would be effective in asserting its interest in administrative control.

In the late 1960s the Florida legislature transferred the state auditor from the executive branch to the legislative branch. The new Office of the Auditor General was charged with making sure that agencies spent their funds in accord with legislative intent and that the funds were spent efficiently. Agency heads were required to respond to audit criticisms to the appropriate legislative committee and to the Legislative Auditing Committee. Performance audits, audits concerned with efficiency and effectiveness, in the traditional reform model were the responsibility of the chief executive. In Florida this role was transferred to the legislatively controlled auditor general and to the legislative staff.

The legislative staff also expanded. In the early 1970's the Florida legislature was rated by the Eagleton Institute as one of the best organized and staffed in the country (Smith 1970, v.)

> Compared to most state legislatures that we have studied closely or observed from a distance, Florida's is in splendid shape. In fact, Eagleton's consultant . . . was so impressed by legislative modernization in Florida that he posed the obvious question. "Why did the legislature ask Eagleton to made a study of its organization. . . ?

By 1989 the Florida legislature had 1,013 professional legislative staff, only surpassed by New York (2,140) and California (1,773)

(Rosenthal 1990, 46). The significance of this expansion was that in the pre-1968 period the bureaucracy was relatively free of legislative intervention while the legislature was not in session. The growth of a full time, highly professional staff changed that. One of the major responsibilities of legislative staff is administrative oversight. Interim staff studies and inquires are highly important for agency interests and are taken very seriously. All of this of course dilutes the ability of the governor to control his own agencies.

The legislature further restricted the powers of the governor to control the bureaucracy by reducing gubernatorial authority to transfer funds between programs and agencies. In Florida a transfer has to be authorized by the Cabinet sitting as the Administration Commission (Rosenthal 1990, 178–179).

> If an agency requests a transfer, a consultative process takes place, during which the legislature can object in writing. If it does so, two-thirds of the administration . . . [commission] is required to override the objection. But the governor generally will respect legislative wishes, because he cannot be sure of getting the votes of enough of his colleagues for an override.

Additionally, the Administrative Procedures Act was passed in 1974. It was another important element in the broader strategy of legislative administrative control. The act provides for a joint legislative committee which has the power to review administrative rules. Rules which are found to be inconsistent with legislative authority can be reversed by the Committee.

The 1968 reorganization of state government and the events associated with it focused the attention of the governor and legislature on administrative accountability. Both increased their control at the expense of the bureaucracy. Certainly the governor's control was enhanced by the consolidation of structural and procedural elements. On the other hand the revised staffing and control procedures also expanded control by the legislature, greatly reducing the autonomy of the bureaucracy and increasing the scope of interests to which it must be responsive. But where is Florida now? What are the current patterns of organization and control?

CURRENT PATTERNS OF ORGANIZATION AND CONTROL

Reorganization activity after 1969 was very limited until Lawton Chiles took office in 1990. The Department of Corrections was split

Figure 6-1
RESTRUCTURING SINCE 1969:
SPLITS, CREATIONS AND CONSOLIDATIONS

Current Agency		Change Year	Source Agency	
Agency Name	Accountability		Agency Name	Accountability
SPLITS				
Corrections	Governor	1975	Health and Rehabilitative Services	Governor
Labor and Employment Security	Governor	1978	Commerce	Governor
Veterans Affairs	Commission/ Constitutional	1990	Governor	Governor
Elder Affairs	Governor/ Constitutional	1990	Health and Rehabilitative Services	Governor
Health Care Administration	Governor	1992	Health and Rehabilitative Services	Governor
Juvenile Justice	Governor	1994	Health and Rehabilitative Services	Governor
Children and Family	Governor	1997	Health and Rehabilitative Services	Governor
Health	Governor	1997	Health and Rehabilitative Services	Governor
CREATIONS				
Environmental Regulation	Governor	1975		new*
Lottery	Governor	1987		new
CONSOLIDATIONS				
Business and Prof. Regulation	Governor	1993	Business Reg. Prof. Reg.	Governor / Governor
Environmental Protection	Governor	1993	Environmental Reg. Natural Resources	Governor / Cabinet
Management Services	Governor	1992	General Services Administration	Cabinet / Governor
DELETIONS				
Commerce	Governor	1996		
Health and Rehabilitative Services	Governor	1997		

Merged in 1993 with Natural Resources to form Environmental Protection.

from the Department of Health and Rehabilitative Services (DHRS)in 1975 and the Department of Labor and Employment Security (DLES) was split from the Department of Commerce in 1978. Two new agencies were created one in 1975 and another in 1987, Environmental Regulation and the Lottery respectively. Each of the agencies involved were subject to gubernatorial control. The reorganizations did not involve the Cabinet agencies or the principle of divided executive control (see Figure 6-1). It also is apparent in retrospect that the thinking rationalizing these changes were different than those driving the 1969 reorganization.

The creation of Lottery was a response to the decline in state revenues and citizen opposition to increased taxes. The lottery was seen as a way to stem the tide of red ink while avoiding higher taxes.

In each of these cases consolidation, a central aspect of the 1969 reform and of the classical Progressive reform movement, was not central. It probably reflected a belief that the consolidated agencies were not particularly efficient or responsive to the public because consolidation is associated with large size, complexity and problems of communication and control.

The decline in the emphasis on consolidation continued with the Chiles reorganization proposals but with important exceptions.

The importance of constituency driven reorganizations continued into the 1990's. Two constituency organizations were created by constitutional amendment in 1990, Veterans Affairs and Elder Affairs. Veterans were unhappy with the arms length treatment veterans affairs were receiving when this function was in the Office of the Governor. A petition put the issue on the ballot which provided a Department of Veterans Affairs joining only four other operating administrative units with constitutional status. The logic for the creation of Elder Affairs was similar to that of Veterans Affairs. During the 1990 gubernatorial campaign, Chiles committed himself to implementation of the idea. The creation of the Department of Health in 1997 is a special case of a constituency driven reorganization in that the constituency in this case is a professional group, namely physicians, who were never very accepting of the merger of Health with social services in the Department of Health and Rehabilitative Services.

The creation of Health Care Administration in 1992 is classified here as a split from the Department of Health and Rehabilitative Services, but it could as easily be seen as a new agency. It was a way to give emphasis to a policy area particularly important to the governor. Health, a division in the huge Department of Health and Rehabilitative Services was not thought flexible enough or committed enough to health care reform to drive policy changes through the legislature and to implementation.

In 1992 the Department of Management Services (DMS) was created. Creation of this agency, as well as the creation of the Department of Business and Professional Regulation (DBPR) and of the Department of Environmental Protection (DEP) was distinctive. Unlike the other post-1969 reorganizations, these were not splits from existing agencies but resulted from combining existing departments. In addition, they were unique in that they involved Cabinet as well as gubernatorial agencies. Management Services combined the Cabinet agency Department of General Services and the gubernatorial agency Department of Administration under the control of the Governor. The new Environmental Protection, established in 1993, combined the functions of the Governor's Department of Environmental Regulation with the Cabinet Department of Natural Resources. Finally, in 1993 the Department of Business and Professional Regulation combined the functions of the Department of Business Regulation and Professional Regulation.

These agencies are essentially regulatory. In the case of DBPR and DEP the focus of regulation is on activities external to the government. In the case of DMS it is on government management activities. Over-regulation and irrational regulation are sentiments that have grown steadily since the early days of the Reagan administration.

These mergers, the Governor suggested, would allow the reduction of regulations and allow more focus on making regulations consistent. It is also significant that in the Department of Management Services the regulatory functions of the Department of Administration were reduced. In this agency at least, the merger supported the position taken by the Chiles administration that the regulation of state personnel should be decentralized to the operating agencies. What better way to expedite this process than to weaken the organizational position of the central regulatory agency? The merger of the governor's regulatory agencies for business, professions and environment was heavily influenced by the political logic of reducing the burden of regulation.

WAYS OF LOOKING AT THE REASONS FOR REORGANIZATION

At the outset it should be said that giving the reasons for reorganization is not as simple as it might first seem. At the most obvious level the reasons for reorganization are to be found in the statements of those who seek the change. Typically this will involve claims that the changes will increase economy, efficiency, responsiveness or some other public virtue. In fact, of course, the public rhetoric and political motives may not overlap a great deal.

To this point I have emphasized political interests, such business, some of which reflect interest group pressures from labor, veterans, medical professionals, and the elderly. In other instances the political forces reflect a general policy shift, as in the separation of Corrections from HRS or the creation and later merger of the environmental agencies. The consolidation of agencies which are responsible for administrative functions within the government, such as General Services and Administration into Management Services, also can be seen as a political interest of the governor in getting control over the state bureaucracy.

From the political interest perspective, it is hard to predict an overall logic for reorganizations. (Lipson 1939; Garnett 1980, 161). Garnett concluded his 1980 study of state government reorganizations by suggesting that

> State executive branch reorganizations occur as a result of a variety of forces acting at different times under different conditions. Even based on this preliminary and incomplete research, it appears

clear that no single, dominant perspective is the best predictor of Adoption Decision. . . .

The reason for reorganizations at this level of explanation is they are the product of idiosyncratic political influences. A more complete understanding however also must consider the institutional environment and long waves of social and economic change.

LONG WAVES OF SOCIAL AND ECONOMIC CHANGE

The Civil War and Reconstruction had a profound effect on the governmental arrangements of Florida. A weak executive and a relatively strong legislature were the products of these experiences. This is well known and well documented in Florida and other Southern states. The persistence of these structures in the face of the enormous social and economic changes is extraordinary.

Florida has always been a high population growth state, but it was not until the end of World War II that population growth, economic growth, and urbanization reached record breaking levels. In addition, the 25 to 35 year long waves of economic growth and decline also have had a measurable effect on the initiation of government reorganizations. Chackerian's research on state government reorganizations between 1900 and 1985 indicates that during long waves of economic decline, the rate of reorganization increases and declines as the long economic wave turns to growth. The reasons for the correlation are not clear but it probably is influenced by the need to respond to the need for greater efficiency in periods of declining government revenue (Chackerian 1996).

Until 1969 Florida did not have a single major reorganization, thus defying the national pattern of reorganizations in response to economic conditions. After World War II several legislative committees and governors made reform proposals which went down to defeat in spite of the fact that there was no central control over revenue raising and spending. Why was it that the national pattern did not begin to show itself in Florida until 1969? The best answer is that general social and economic trends will not have their effect unless institutional conditions are in place. It wasn't until 1963 that these social and economic trends started to be linked to the governmental reform. The linkage was made possible by an important change in the institutional environment.

CHANGES IN THE INSTITUTIONAL ENVIRONMENT

A variety of institutional factors have been shown to facilitate or block the political agenda of leaders and interest groups. These include institutional age, party competition and legislative/gubernatorial alignment.

On average, state governments have undergone major changes in structural arrangements approximately once every 25 years between 1900 and 1985 (Chackerian 1996). Interestingly, the survival rates of the state governments are strikingly similar to private organizations (Starbuck and Nystrom 1981, xv). The shape of the curve describing this form of "organizational death" is also similar. In the initial years after the creation of an institutional arrangement, there is relative stability, followed by a relatively rapid mortality rate, and finally for those that get beyond the middle years, the prospect of a rather prolonged existence.

The theory behind these trends is not well developed, but the general argument is that new organizations are subject to considerable risk. They must establish political support and technical competence. The early years after a reorganization are often exciting but trying times. At the other end of the continuum, the older organization has its own set of problems. The risks of old age are rigidity and low energy levels. In both of these situations the inability to perform makes the organization vulnerable to political agendas aimed at changing the organization.

By 1969 Florida had one of the longest periods of institutional stability of any state government, not having reorganized in any significant way since the Anti-Reconstruction constitution of 1885. In statistical terms, Florida was long overdue for a reorganization in 1969. The long survival of the governmental arrangements suggested the extent to which they were imbedded in the state's political institutions.

As noted above, a key aspect of the institutional structure is the extent of party competition and legislative/gubernatorial party alignment. Reorganization proposals, and policy innovations generally, are more likely to emerge where there is strong party competition. Florida, of course, had been a one-party, Democratic, state since Reconstruction. The Democratic party was highly fractionalized and not a vehicle for clearly articulated policy initiatives.

Legislative reapportionment and the election of the first Republican governor since Reconstruction signaled a shift in political institutions that allowed reform to find its way to the governmental policy agenda. Representatives from the newly enfranchised urban areas, influenced by reformist ideals, led the transformation of governmental arrangements. It was also important that Republican Governor Claude Kirk, the first Republican governor since Reconstruction, saw reorganization as an opportunity to strengthen his role. The fact that he faced a legislature now dominated by urban Democrats who wanted government reorganization was also important for getting the government reorganized.

The next major wave of reorganization in Florida began 23 years after the first, almost exactly at the average of reorganizations for all states from 1900 to 1985. Why did the second wave occur "on time" while the first wave was 59 years over due? My hypothesis is that governmental institutions prevented change in the earlier period, but it was not an impediment in the more recent period because of the constitutional changes that were implemented in 1968. Perhaps it was predictable that, as parties become more competitive and more dynamic, interests would gain access to the policy process, and reorganization processes would follow a "normal schedule."

Florida state government, even after the 1969 reorganization, was classified as a "traditional" organization by Garnett (1980). The dimensions of this classification system are outlined in Figure 6-2. Traditional forms have more organizational units, are more likely to be headed by a plural executive; are less functionally consolidated; and are less likely to have an agency head appointed by the governor. Of the three types, the traditional is the least likely to approximate the ideals of Progressive reform. The secretary-coordinator form most closely approximates the Progressive reform model with the cabinet form falling mid-way between the two extremes.

The changes that have occurred since 1969 have not substantially changed the classification of Florida. There have been five agency splits and two new agencies, which have increased functional specialization, but there have been only six mergers. The governor's appointment

Figure 6-2

GARNETT TYPOLOGY OF STATE GOVERNMENT ORGANIZATION

ORGANIZATION TYPE/ DIMENSIONS	TRADITIONAL	CABINET	SEC./COORD.
number of agencies	high >17 FLORIDA	moderate 9–16	low 1–8
functional consolidation	low <50% FLORIDA	moderate >50% in single function	high >50% in broadly defined functions
gubernatorial appointment of head	low <50% FLORIDA	moderate 50%–65%	high >66%
plural executives	high >24% FLORIDA	moderate >9–24%	low >0–9%
retained authority by transplanted agency*	high >50% keeping	low >50% losing	moderately high >50% keeping some but losing other authority

Data on this dimension is not available for Florida.

Source: Garnett (1980).

power has been somewhat increased because Natural Resources is now combined with Environmental Regulation, in Environmental Protection, a gubernatorial appointment. Also, the new agencies have been put under the governor, with the exception of Veterans Affairs.

Since the turn of the century, most major reorganizations have been within organizational types rather than among them. Between 1900 and 1975, with nearly 120 major state reorganizations, the traditional type has lost 5 cases, one going to the cabinet form, and 4 to the secretary-coordinator type. While many would like to believe that reform moves in the direction of the secretary coordinator form, the evidence does not support this trend and Florida is a case in point.

What Have Been the Consequences of Reform?

There is little evidence available on the consequences of the recent reorganization efforts or, for that matter, of the 1969 reorganization. Systematic studies have not been done in Florida, and this is typical in the overwhelming majority of reorganization cases. (Meier 1980; Thomas 1993). To the extent that general evidence exists, the main effects of agency consolidations are to increase the ability of the chief executive to achieve accountability and control. Claims for economy, efficiency, effectiveness, reliability, equity or public trust are either discredited or unknown.(Thomas 1993, 484) The general evidence concerning splits is equally inconclusive. There is some indication that they may increase public participation and involvement, but whether this in turn increases economy, efficiency, or public trust is unknown.

Certainly in Florida there is little evidence to suggest that the reorganization efforts have had beneficial effects. In fairness it must be emphasized that there simply hasn't been enough time to evaluate the results from the most recent changes. The unwillingness of the public to assume higher taxes and the governor's marginal popularity suggest that recent reorganizations have had little impact on public trust.

Conclusions

There are constant political pressures to restructure government because it suits the needs of political interests to gain access to agency resources and programs. Whether these changes are actually made, however, depends on there being appropriate institutional conditions, particularly the state of partisan political competition and the age of the organizations in question. If conditions combine older institutions with a relatively high level of political competition and economic decline, one can expect a major reorganization about every 25 years, on average, in the United States.

The importance of these reorganizations is that they institutionalize new patterns of influence over policy making and implementation, including the degree of control exercised by the governor over operating departments. Institutions set very general parameters within which the game of government and policy is played. They make a difference in specifying who has access to decision opportunities and the types of solutions that are seen as legitimate. They are also important for establishing premises that influence the implementation of policy. The connection of these broad institutional changes to higher levels of economy, efficiency, effectiveness, or responsiveness is problematic although it is often claimed as justification for reorganizations. Florida's political leaders, in this respect, tend to follow the national pattern.

REFERENCES

Advisory Commission on Intergovernmental Relations (1985). *The question of state government capability.* Washington, DC: ACIR.

Buck, A. E. (1938). *The reorganization of state governments in the United States.* New York: Columbia University Press.

Chackerian, Richard (1996). "State Government reorganization: 1900–1985." *Journal of Public Administration Research and Theory,* vol. 6, 25–47.

Colburn, David R. and Richard K. Scher (1980) *Florida's gubernatorial politics in the twentieth century.* Tallahassee: University Presses of Florida, a Florida State University Book.

Dauer, Manning (1980). Florida's Constitution. In *Florida's Politics and Government,* edited by Manning Dauer. Gainesville: University Presses of Florida.

Dennis, James Milton (1974). *State executive branch reorganization: The case of Florida.* Ph.D. dissertation, University of Florida.

Doyle, Wilson K., Angus McKenzie Laird, and S. Serman Weiss (1954). *The government and administration of Florida.* New York: Thomas Y. Crowell Company.

Osborne, David E. and Ted Gaebler (1992). *Reinventing government: How the entrepreneurial spirit is transforming the public sector.* Reading, MA: Addison Wesley Press.

Garnett, James L (1980). *Reorganizing state government: The executive branch.* Boulder: Westview Press.

Kaufman, Herbert (1990). The end of an alliance: Public administration in the eighties, in *Public Administration: The State of the Discipline,* edited by Naomi B. Lynn and Aaron Wildavsky. Chatham, NJ: Chatham House Publishers.

Key, V. O., Jr. (1949). *Southern politics*. New York: Vintage Books, A Division of Random House.

Lipson, Leslie (1939). *The American governor: From figurehead to leader.* Chicago: Greenwood Press.

Meier, J. Kenneth (1980). Executive reorganization of government: Impact on employment and expenditures. *American Journal of Political Science,* 24 (August): 396–411.

Mosher, Frederick C., editor (1967). *Governmental reorganization: Cases and commentary.* Indianapolis: Bobbs-Merrill.

Nystrom, Paul C. and William H. Starbuck (1981). Designing and understanding organizations, in *Handbook of Organizational Design,* edited by P.C. Nystrom and W.H. Starbuck. Oxford, England: Oxford University Press.

Reichley, James (1964). *States in crises.* Chapel Hill: University of North Carolina Press.

Rosenthal, Alan (1990). *Governors and legislatures: Contending powers.* Washington, D.C.: CQ Press.

Tolbert, Pamela S. and Lynne G. Zucker (1983). Institutional sources of change in formal structure of organizations: The diffusion of civil service reform, 1880–1935. *Administrative Science Quarterly,* 28 (March): 22–39.

Smith, C. Lynwood (1970). *Strengthening the Florida legislature.* New Brunswick, NJ: Rutgers University Press.

ENDNOTE

1. See Chapter 16 for a full discussion of constitution revision.

STAFFING STATE GOVERNMENT: A PUBLIC POLICY ISSUE

FRANK P. SHERWOOD AND DAVID S. FERGUSON*

STAFFING AS A POLICY ISSUE

The government of the state of Florida touches the lives of its citizens in multitudinous ways. But it is not a case of a behemoth hovering over a tiny atom. Rather, there are many relationships that are much more individualized and one-on-one. Nearly 150,000 employees of the state government have contact with one or more of 12 million citizens.

It is within this context that the competence, motivation and values of those in the service of the state of Florida assume significant dimension. These are not just hired hands, in the normal sense of doling out hamburgers at McDonald's. While they are paid from the public treasury, their salary costs are only a small part of the equation. It is their capacity to influence and even direct the quality of life of all the state's citizens that makes them pivotal. In a very real sense state employees are hired to perform regulative and supportive tasks, which can be obtained from no alternative sources. We are stuck with the people we hire.

Because it has long been understood that the public servant lives in a world with vastly different tasks and responsibilities than does the employee of General Motors; there has been a notably political dimension to the conduct of public employment affairs. There is recognition that the occupation of positions in a government provides a sure and clear path to power. Further, as governments have become more complex, the realization has grown that there are many elements of power in the system. Large numbers of positions must be occupied to secure influence. Such dominance may be utilized to secure personal, self-interested goals or broader, public-interested ones. One continuing question, then,

---

*David S. Ferguson added new material to this chapter to provide a more current picture of human resources management in state government.

is how the state bureaucracy, which is where the very great bulk of state public servants work, should be constituted to make it reflective of the diverse, sometimes conflicting, interests of the society.

While the composition of the public service in Florida is a basic public policy issue, there are other issues that make the seemingly routine business of hiring and firing people far more complex in the governmental setting. One involves the way in which most people feel about public employment, namely that it is essentially a right of citizenship to have equal access and opportunity to government jobs. In some degree everyone pays for, and is affected by, public employees; in consequence, everyone ought to have an equal prospect of becoming one of its employees. The pursuit of such equality, even though seldom achieved, has undoubtedly hobbled personnel agencies with arcane procedures and bountiful red tape. It is not, for instance, a matter of hiring a qualified person; it is the problem of making sure that every interested, qualified person has an equal crack at the job. Getting out the message that a position is available becomes a major task. Control mechanisms must be established to be sure that all opportunities are shared.

In an earlier, simpler day, there were no such problems. In the first years of the Republic, however, the emphasis on human resources was substantial. The nation was a fledgling and needed its best talent. Political parties had not yet been institutionalized. As parties began to assume greater significance in the mobilization of interests at the end of the first quarter of the nineteenth century, the issue of rewards for participation arose. At that time the government had less involvement with its people, who were primarily farmers. There were not the contracts, the regulatory favors, and the outright gifts that have made control of governments attractive today. In effect, the big reward was a government job with some cash income. Thus, it was inevitable that Andrew Jackson, or someone like him, would carry the process to its logical extreme; namely that the real purpose of public employment is to provide rewards to the party faithful, rather than to perform valued services.

The idea of spoils thus emerged and has been a highly important part of the political firmament for more than 150 years. In the last century, however, the increasing complexity of the society, with its urban transformation, has markedly changed the role and scope of governments. An alternative view of public employment has consequently emerged that recognizes the need for a continuing, permanent group of employees with sufficient skills to handle the complex business of government. Political neutrality, professionalism, and merit are important elements of such an orientation.

THE ATTRIBUTES OF A MODERN CIVIL SERVICE

Today a national consensus has been forged that specifies the attributes of a modern civil service. The Federal Government's 1978 Civil Service Reform Act codified the principles that govern such a system. So seriously are they honored that a Merit Systems Protection Board has been established to insure their observance.

The civil services principles, as stated in the 1978 act, are found in virtually every textbook on public personnel.[1] Ingraham and Rosenbloom have commented that these principles can be summarized as: fair and open competition for jobs, admission to the competitive service only on the basis of neutral examination, and protection of those in the service from political influence and coercion (Ingraham and Rosenbloom 1990, 1). The principles should be regarded as a reference point. The continuing query is the degree to which they have been recognized and honored in the personnel system of the state of Florida.

The health and integrity of the civil service depends in considerable degree on institutional arrangements. Experience throughout the nation indicates that governors generally do not see themselves as general managers of a large, purposive enterprise; they are not prepared or oriented toward these responsibilities, and tend to ignore them. Unlike the situation in the large private companies, government chief executives do not see the people in the organization as constituting the real key to success.

Inevitably, the burden of managing human resources is lodged in the bureaucracy and fails to secure public attention. Yet the management of human resources in the public sector is particularly complex. The administrative implications of a system that values equal opportunity and eschews arbitrariness are substantial. Uniform standards must be set; controls must be established; and enforcement pursued.

Issues of centralization and decentralization, which appear frequently across the landscape of state government, are particularly evident. The requirements of the civil service necessitate a central control agency; and its mission often collides with the more unique, decentralized imperatives of the operating agencies. Thus there is a particular burden placed on the personnel agency to perform particularly well. Its effectiveness is needed to reduce the costs of the control burdens imposed on the operating agencies.

Ineffectiveness on the part of the central personnel agency inexorably ratchets the demands of the operating units for freedom from onerous controls. The greater freedoms provided, the less comprehensive the civil service. There comes a time when there are so many leaks and fissures that the integrity of the civil service system has been destroyed. It is in terms of this kind of scenario that the experience with civil service in Florida must be examined.

A Pervasive Spoils System in Florida

To gain some appreciation of the tensions between the spoils of Florida's past and the relatively recent efforts to institute a civil service consistent with the national consensus, it is necessary to examine the conditions of public employment that existed only a few decades ago. Much of this history can be best understood through the behavior of governors in the last half century. This is true despite the fact that Florida governors have generally been regarded as "weak," or at best "moderate" in the sense that their capacities to control events within the executive branch have been relatively limited. St. Angelo and Gibson have pointed out that this was particularly true from 1885 to 1968, at which time a new constitution was promulgated. They observed that the organic laws in the earlier period ". . . mandated and encouraged a highly decentralized administration" (St. Angelo and Gibson 1980, 124).

The 1968 constitution retained a cabinet form of government, with six elected department heads, and thus restrained the formal powers of the governor. Symbolically, however, the governor has always been a powerful figure and the 1968 constitution did endow the chief executive with much greater formal capacity to function as the general manager of the system.

Patronage Appointments: Key to Gubernatorial Power

Despite the dispersion of power within the state government, Colburn and Scher have commented on the ". . . vast amount of patronage controlled by the Florida governor" in the pre-1968 days through the state commissions and boards appointed by him. They continue:

> Appointments are perhaps the most significant source of patronage because there are numerous positions to fill and numerous pressures exerted . . . This potentially affords the governor a tremendous opportunity to staff his administration with loyal supporters, or at least with individuals willing to follow his system of priorities (Colburn and Scher 1980, 127).

It was estimated that there were 4–5,000 appointments by the governor to such varied entities as the Road Board, Beverage Commission,

Racing Commission, Hotel Commission, Citrus Commission, and Game and Fresh Water Fish Commission. Just the recital of this list suggests the rural orientations of the state at the time. Of these entities, the most significant from the patronage perspective were the Road Board and the Beverage Commission. There was an uninhibited freedom to hire and fire; and not only did this provide many opportunities to reward the party workers but numerous contracts and other governmental favors were involved. Clearly, these two agencies alone did much to drive the political system.

MERIT-PATRONAGE CONTINUUM: GUBERNATORIAL ATTITUDES AND BEHAVIOR

Colburn and Scher analyzed the attitudes of several governors toward public employment on the basis of a civil service-patronage/spoils model. They noted, "The impact of patronage on a governor's administration is largely a function of the style that can be found on a continuum ranging from 'merit system' on one end to 'spoils system' on the other" (Colburn and Scher 1980, 128).

They declared that Spessard Holland (1941–45), Millard Caldwell (1945–49), Dan McCarty (1953), and LeRoy Collins (1955–61) tended to be at the civil service end of the continuum, emphasizing a "professional approach" and establishing qualifications for appointments. At the extreme patronage point were Fuller Warren (1949–53) and Charley Johns (1953–55), who rewarded friends and punished enemies, ". . . largely irrespective of costs and qualifications. Professionalism is downplayed and partisanship becomes a primary consideration" (Colburn and Scher 1980, 128).

Fuller Warren was elected because of the deep pockets of three supporters. Each contributed more than $100,000 to his campaign and insisted on a major role in staffing his administration. There were numerous reports on the situation. It was suggested that the most serious problem of the administration was the lack of "Warren men." Others declared there was no Warren administration but one subdivided into three spheres of influence established by his trio of supporters. As a result there were few individuals on whom the governor could rely. Colburn and Scher summarize, ". . . the conclusion is inescapable that some of the problems he [Warren] incurred from weak appointments were the results of poor judgement or accepting the advice of his political cronies" (Colburn and Scher 1980, 140).

State Senate President Charley Johns succeeded to the governorship in 1953 as a result of the untimely death of Dan McCarty. He is described as a ". . . prominent member of what later came to be known as the Pork Chop Gang" (Colburn and Scher 1980, 140).

163

Because Johns had not been elected, it was assumed that he would go slow in replacing McCarty appointees. But he did not. He called for resignations of key people and suspended those who did not comply. Dismissals were not restricted to the top people. Forty-six employees of the Tag department were personally fired by Johns, who ignored the department head in announcing the ousters. According to Colburn and Scher,

> . . . [P]ublic opinion generally had mobilized against Johns. There was tremendous hostility to what he was doing. McCarty had been seen as a highly competent and well intentioned governor following the inept Warren, and after his death this public impression remained strong . . . Morale among public employees sank incredibly low; as one analyst pointed out, the cloud of tension and fear among state employees caused by the prospect of instant dismissal prevented virtually all of them from working at anything even close to peak efficiency (Colburn and Scher 1980, 140–1).

The governors on the merit side of the ledger present a sharp contrast. There were few horror stories; instead, the record is one of attempts at reform, but within a political context. As Colburn and Scher observe, these men ". . . were every bit as 'political' in their use of appointments . . ." (1980, 143). The difference was that they were also struggling to make the state government an effective management institution. Perhaps Caldwell was the earliest governor to articulate the extent of these management-politics tensions. While he was concerned about upgrading the quality of state personnel, he also understood that the appointment power was an important source of gubernatorial influence. Given the weakness of his position, he had to be careful to husband his limited influence resources. Colburn and Scher comment that, ". . . other things being equal, he would regard the loyal supporter as a more desirable appointee than one who was not" (1980, 135).

One is reminded of a similar type of statement by a political leader: "I am not against civil service people. I just want my own." Thus, it is not surprising that Caldwell appeared to engage in contradictory behaviors. On the one hand, he sponsored the extension of the merit system, involving a consequent reduction in the amount of patronage available to him. On the other hand, he opposed the institution of a statewide merit system because the extreme limitation on his appointments would reduce his executive control over the system. The conflict Caldwell experienced, and with which he sought to deal, was a familiar one for succeeding governors. It is a recurring issue, not only in Florida, but in jurisdictions throughout the nation.

Dan McCarty was elected in substantial degree because of the dissatisfaction with staffing in the Warren administration. In his campaign he promised to "clean up the mess" and particularly to reform the civil service. Colburn and Scher write:

> In his attitudes toward patronage he went even beyond the criteria espoused by Millard Caldwell: While the faithful had to be rewarded, it had to be done in a businesslike, professional way, and certainly the spoils system could not he tolerated. In his inaugural address he said he would clean out the state government, and added, "I am determined that ours will not be an administration of 'sounding brass and tinkling cymbal'; nor one tainted with any kind of dishonesty.' By the next day he had eliminated 400 jobs from the Road Department and halted $6 millions in road projects (1980, 139).

It was a tragedy for Florida that one of its youngest governors died of a massive heart attack and was succeeded by Johns, who shared so little of McCarty's public agenda. The popular dissatisfaction with Johns did, however, lead to a gubernatorial campaign in which patronage and its place became a major issue. It was within this circumstance that Collins, a close McCarty ally and also a strong believer in professionalism as a way of achieving honest, effective government, was elected to office.

The cases of Warren and Johns made it quite apparent that there were limits to a governor's use of patronage. While it had always been a part of the Florida system and was still acceptable to a degree, times were changing. State government was now beginning to affect the lives of its citizens directly. Blatant disregard for competence, ethical standards, and effective performance were not acceptable to increasing numbers of voters. Those governors at the spoils system end of the continuum found that their behavior was politically costly.

Further, the concern for a quality public service redounded to the benefit of Holland, Caldwell, McCarty, Collins, Reubin Askew (1971–79), and Robert Graham (1979–87). Except for McCarty, who died, the others maintained solid political support. Holland and Graham, of course, went on to become U. S. Senators. The public has not been as supportive of Ferris Bryant (1961–65), Hayden Burns (1965–67), Warren, Johns, and Claude Kirk (1967–71), all of whom took major advantage of the spoils culture. Colburn and Scher conclude:

> It is not easy to determine whether governors who use the spoils system experienced administrative difficulties and a loss of public support for that reason alone, or whether they would have had

problems running the executive branch even if they had tried to be more "professional" in their appointments.

. . . It should be noted that the limits of public acceptability of different styles of patronage shifted after a period of excess. McCarty and Collins were regarded as much more professional in their patronage styles than either Warren or Johns . . . Askew was also perceived as upgrading appointments in the years following Bryant, Burns, and Kirk. Thus a sort of "ebb and flow" pattern marks the governors' use of appointments . . . (1980, 144).

The detailing of gubernatorial experience in the last half-century underscores the policy significance of public employment. It is not at all an issue of mechanics. As Mosher has pointed out with particular clarity, the way in which a state chooses to construct its public service has a great deal to do with the quality of its democracy (Mosher 1982, XVI, 251).

The people working in the system are the critical component and resource; their capacity and motivation to perform is a key consideration in the development of a management policy for the state government. The amount of attention directed toward these management policy issues are important predictors of the commitment of a governor to function as a general manager; and, as experience has shown, such management concern is likely to have significant political consequences.

THE EVOLUTION OF A CAREER SERVICE IN FLORIDA: 1936–67

An understanding of the way public employment has evolved to its present status requires an appreciation not only of the state's spoils roots but also of its civil service history. The chronology of events that led to a fairly comprehensive formal system of civil service coverage in 1967 and the issues that emerged in the management of that system suggest that the tensions between civil service and patronage have been persistent. From the beginning of the career service system in 1936, it took three decades to arrive at a point of fairly comprehensive coverage. The problems of the last quarter-century have been less formal and structural and more managerial. The governor, constitutional officers, and other top officials still struggle, either consciously or unconsciously, with managing a work force consonant with democratic expectations and imperatives for high quality performance.

Federal Grants-in-Aid Stipulations Bring First Civil Service Program in 1936

Given the general characterization of the federal government as an inept big brother, it is interesting that the first civil service system in Florida state government was the result of a direct Washington intervention. Early in the New Deal, a decision was made to utilize state and local governments to administer programs for which the national government had assumed responsibility, notably in health and welfare. Large amounts of federal tax dollars were to flow to a congeries of units in 48 states, some of them quality operations and others no more than courthouse gangs. Were the Roosevelt administration to tolerate extreme variations in administrative performance, with attendant problems of ethics and corruption, the survival of important social programs could have been put in jeopardy. It was within the terms of this realization that federal grants-in-aid grew strings. In effect, the only way the states and their localities were able to tap into such funds was to play by a specific set of civil service rules. These prescriptions were carefully specified and rather rigidly enforced by a small federal bureaucracy. Grant programs, with their strings, really launched career service systems in many states, of which Florida was one.

The first movement toward a civil service system in Florida occurred on June 29, 1936, and involved employees of the State Board of Welfare. At the time there was much anger with such federal infringement; but there was no alternative. If the Board wanted the money, it had to put its personnel on a civil service basis. The Florida Industrial Commission, established in 1937, also relied heavily on federal money and therefore had to place its people in a civil service program. Finally, the 1939 amendments to the nation's Social Security Act covered certain health programs, notably in maternal and child health, placing them in civil service.

For about 10 years, these civil service systems resided in pieces of organizations. It was Governor Millard Caldwell who sought to give some organizational integrity to the situation in 1946. Despite his misgivings about a statewide system, Caldwell did believe in the need for merit in specified agencies; he felt that an organizational integration was desirable; and argued that uniform standards of professionalism could be applied.

Establishment of the Florida Merit System

Caldwell's success came with the agreement of the Board of Health, the State Welfare Board, and the Florida Industrial Commission to consolidate their civil service programs and to establish the Florida Merit System. Included were activities primarily in public health, social welfare, and employment security.

The program established at that time embraced a structure and procedures that were gaining wide acceptance and adoption across the United States. From the organizational perspective, the key ingredient was an independent board which had essentially complete control over personnel matters. Its independence was to be achieved through the appointment of its five members for overlapping terms of four years. Its commitment to civil service was to be secured by a criterion that would restrict appointment only to those with a "known sympathy for merit."

The procedures adopted were traditional even at that time. Examinations had to be open and competitive with everyone to have an equal opportunity, at least insofar as the racial taboos of the time would permit. The openness and availability of opportunity were apparently taken seriously. Doyle, Laird and Weiss wrote a few years later, "For a number of years performance tests for typists and stenographers have been administered once or twice weekly in local employment service offices in 26 different centers in the state" (Doyle et al. 1954, 145).

On the basis of the examinations, registers of eligible candidates were developed and maintained. When a vacancy occurred, names on the register were certified to the agencies for possible appointment. The rule of three prevailed, which meant that one of the three at the top of the list had to be appointed. Once on board, employees enjoyed permanent tenure. Appeal procedures were established, both for those seeking entrance and also for those in the system experiencing problems of ratings, demotions, or dismissals. All in all, the Florida Merit System embraced the features that have continued to characterize civil service systems for the past 45 years. The structure of a more professional system was in place.

SLOW BUT STEADY EXPANSION OF CIVIL SERVICE PRINCIPLES

Candidates for governor in both 1948 and 1952 advocated a comprehensive, state-wide system. Bills were regularly introduced in the legislature and as regularly ignored. Finally, in 1953, Governor McCarty did get the legislature to provide funds and authorization for a two-year study of state employment. The purposes of the study reflect the list of concerns of a governor dedicated to the management of a large enterprise: attract persons of high character and qualifications; give reasonable security to employees; establish uniform practices of employment, discharge, compensation and leave; and consolidate retirement programs when practicable. Such concerns did not secure universal approbation from legislators. Doyle and his colleagues report, "During consideration of the measure there were statements by legislators that we do not want 'civil service' . . ." (1954, 154).

It should be noted that the state did not at the time have a general retirement system. There was a series of separate but unrelated plans.

Governor Collins' assumption of gubernatorial responsibilities signaled a new, invigorated drive toward merit system expansion. In his inaugural address he declared that the establishment of a statewide, professional personnel system was a major objective of his administration.

With his prodding, the 1955 legislature passed "An Act to Create a Merit System of Personnel Administration." The high-sounding label did not involve a significantly new departure. Yet it did represent movement in two directions. The first was to legitimate the existing Merit System Council in statute, whereas before its only status derived from a mutual agreement among the state departments participating in grants-in-aid. The second was to provide the possibility for an expansion of the system by permitting the governor to include such other agencies as he "may direct." It was estimated that about one-third of the state's employees (15,000) were covered by the new legislation (Morris and Waldron 1965, 29).

Although the essence of the system was little changed, and could not be because of the dominant presence of the federal government, a more elaborate structure was initiated. A State Personnel Board was created and essentially comprised another set of institutional hats to be worn by the governor as chair and the constitutional officers (viz., Secretary of State, Comptroller, Commissioner of Agriculture, Attorney General, Superintendent of Public Instruction, and Treasurer) as board members. The basic function of this board was to appoint the Merit System Council, which was to be constituted and function very much as it had in the past. In respect to criteria of appointment to the Council, there was the further proviso that members could not be active in partisan politics (CSG 1957, 171–2).

The Board also was conceived as having some role in extending the merit system. Theoretically, an agency on its own initiative could come to the Personnel Board and ask to be brought under the jurisdiction of the Merit System Council. Available data do not reveal whether the expanded commitment to professionalism produced any agency initiatives.

MAJOR REORGANIZATION OF FLORIDA STATE GOVERNMENT: A CENTRALIZATION THEME

The adoption of a new Florida constitution in November, 1969, brought major change to all three branches of the state government. Significant societal transformations in Florida were having their effects on the governance structure. The *Baker vs. Carr* decision that every citizen's vote should carry equal weight resulted in a major shift of power to the southern, more highly urbanized parts of the state. A system had to be developed that came closer to representing and reflecting the broad, diversified interests of the polity. The balkanized, decentralized form of traditional government that diffused responsibility among many individualized elements was seriously modified in the new constitution, instead placing more power and responsibility in the governor as chief executive and thus legitimating his role as general manager of the state bureaucracy. The Florida constitution followed a pattern that had been emerging in state governments across the nation in the previous 40 years.

THE STATE PERSONNEL SYSTEM WITHIN A POWERFUL DEPARTMENT OF ADMINISTRATION: 1969–79

The Executive Reorganization Act did, of course, bring a heightened presence to personnel as a central management function. While the coverage of the career service was greatly expanded by 1967 legislation,[2] the administrative structure remained roughly the same as before. The role of the State Personnel Board, composed of the governor and other cabinet members, was expanded to provide for more direct involvement in personnel policy, but the approach tended to be traditional. Further, the Career Service Council, whose name had been changed from Merit System Council in 1967, functioned isolated from top state management. It was a situation in which it would have been difficult for a governor, concerned to be a general manager, to gain any real control over the human resources of the state. The 1969 law brought the human resources system directly under the governor by abolishing the State Personnel Board and making the Career Service Commission, formerly Council, which had previously advised the Personnel Board on personnel policy and supervised the staff. The *Book of the States* issued by the Council of State Governments, took note of these changes and reported that the new arrangement covered "almost all state employees" (CSG 1970, 178).

From a widely dispersed system with many hiring arrangements, Florida had moved in two years to a situation of high integration and uniformity.

STRUCTURE OF THE DEPARTMENT OF ADMINISTRATION: EMPHASIS ON THE BUDGET

The Reorganization Act provided for the creation of a Bureau of Planning and one of Budgeting within Department of Administration's (DOA) Division of Planning and Budgeting. No bureaus were authorized in the legislation for the Division of Personnel and Retirement. Over time, a number of other functions were assigned to DOA, notably in the areas of criminal justice and of environmental planning. People who were staff members in the Department of Administration reported that the dominant concern was with the budget, stimulated by the governor's own sense of its importance to his chief executive responsibilities. Less urgent, long term issues in personnel and in productivity improvement simply did not receive the same attention. Thus the Department of Administration became primarily a budget office that also operated the state's personnel system.

CHANGES IN THE 1970s

In 1970 a number of changes occurred in the approach to retirement of state employees, leading to a single statewide, comprehensive system, which is now compulsory for employees of state agencies, counties, school boards, community colleges and state universities, and optional for cities and special districts. This expansion of function led to organizational change in 1972, when legislation was passed that created a separate division of retirement within the Department of Administration. A State Retirement Commission was also established within the Department of Administration in 1975.

The growing costs and significance of health benefits were recognized in 1972 when a statewide program was begun and lodged in the Department of Administration.

Finally, the role of employee unionism was confronted in 1974 with the creation of an office of labor relations in the Department of Administration, charged with representing the governor as the public employer in collective bargaining negotiations with state career service employees.

CRITIQUE OF HUMAN RESOURCES MANAGEMENT
IN THE ASKEW ADMINISTRATION

While the personnel responsibilities of the Department of Administration were expanding during the seventies, there was also criticism. The conclusion of Reubin Askew's eight years as chief executive meant there would be a transition in 1979. It seemed an appropriate time to re-examine the situation and to make suggestions for improvement. Certain faculty members of the Department of Public Administration at Florida State University undertook this task, and the Institute of Science and Public Affairs published their recommendations in November, 1979. The paper was entitled, *Improving Florida Personnel Practice: An Agenda for Action* (DPA 1979).

Noting that the problems of civil service in Florida were no longer "protectionist" and that corruption, patronage, and arbitrary treatment were under control, the call was for an "aggressively positive" approach. Sought was a changed image and increased prestige for the career system through better recruitment, improved and better rationalized pay systems, and greatly expanded training.

Recruitment and appointment processes came under particularly heavy attack. People seeking to identify employment opportunities faced a "complex maze." The report continued, "Even though the advertising of vacancies is more centralized for state than local positions, many candidates are uncertain as to how to determine whether it is a vacancy for someone with their skills and, if so, where it is located" (DPA 1979, 7).

It was commented that the system of listing job openings had "not been successful" and that the DOA needed to find a way to secure an up-to-date list of job openings. But the problem did not end there. Once a candidate discovered a job opening, there were great difficulties in securing the necessary qualifications certification from the Department of Administration so as to be available for appointment. "Some reasonable balance must be made," it was observed, "between a system of decentralized anarchy in which candidates have no idea where to seek information about openings and a centralized selection process that ignores the realities of agency needs. *Some observers suggest that Florida has the worst elements of both extremes* [italics added]" (DPA 1979, 15).

There were other major criticisms. On the one hand the Department was chastised for lack of effectiveness in position classification, a central function. There was a perpetual backlog of reclassification requests; action came slowly; and much of the processing was seen as arbitrary. On the other hand, the department was charged with failing to support the agencies in more decentralized functions. Training and development was particularly condemned. Here was a case where control was not an issue. The basic responsibility was with the agencies. Yet DOA was doing so little to be helpful that nothing could be criticized. There was simply no record of performance.

Although there were many specific suggestions in the report, its great significance likely lies in its appraisal of about a decade of experience with a much more centralized system of personnel management than had existed in Florida previously. Where St. Angelo and Gibson assumed that the formal structure had brought automatic centralization, the public administration professors characterized the system differently. They called it "mixed" and noted that the basic centralization-decentralization dilemma had not been resolved. DOA was decentralized to the point of

anarchy in recruiting and centralized to the point of stultification in classification and selection processes. While this latter analysis was likely the
more realistic, it is probable that St. Angelo and Gibson reflected the predominant feelings in the bureaucracy. The excesses of centralization are
more apt to be remarked than the inadequacies of decentralization. In any
case, it appeared that an organizational strategy for effectively managing
the state's human resources had not yet emerged.

GOING IT ALONE: PRESSURES ON DOA IN THE EIGHTIES

Surprising as it may seem, the report of the public administration
professors may have come at the high water mark in the effort to create
an integrated, managerially-oriented human resources program in
Florida. The personnel function at the time was in a department that had
the confidence and attention of the governor; further, it was a highly professionalized organization that symbolized the aspirations of a merit system. Finally, the clout of the budget undoubtedly strengthened efforts to
maintain an integrated, comprehensive process.

GRAHAM MOVES BUDGET AND PLANNING FROM DOA

Things changed, however, when Robert Graham became governor.
While the new chief executive had a deep respect and appreciation for
the career service, he perceived his more immediate need as one of
gaining control of, and full staff support for, his efforts to improve planning and budgeting in the state. He concluded that his imperatives could
best be realized by placing the budgeting and planning functions directly
under his wing. Legislation passed in 1979 therefore left the Department
of Administration as little more than a personnel agency.

Not only did budgeting and planning go to the new executive office
but also did certain management responsibilities, notably organization
planning which involved control of the structure at the bureau level and
below. Other major parts of the Department of Administration were
transferred to the Department of Community Affairs. A few small units
were directed to the restructured DOA.

In itself the change might have appeared to benefit human resources
management, which now had a departmental secretary to represent its
interests. The problem is that status alone does not always bestow influence. If a governor does not think of himself as a general manager of a
large, operating organization, calling the head of the personnel unit a secretary will not command much attention. The function of the department

has to be perceived as important and therefore requiring time and energy, just as do health, welfare, transportation, and corrections. Unfortunately, there was neither history nor tradition to suggest to Governor Graham and his successor that human resources matters should command substantial personal consideration.

The problem also involved the nature of the leadership of the Department of Administration. In the first decade the secretaries had primarily been people who had the confidence of the governor; indeed, for two years a lieutenant governor served as head of DOA. Also, a top career professional in budgeting had a stint as secretary. Throughout the decade the Division of Personnel was headed by a careerist with long experience in personnel. With the elevation of the personnel leadership role to the secretarial level, the division head was moved to a position within the department. A management consultant became secretary, brought in as a political appointment. Governor Graham's second DOA secretary was a career professional, Gilda Lambert, with rich personnel experience both in Florida and in the federal government. She was not reappointed by Governor Robert Martinez, however; and her successor, Adis Vila, was a lawyer with experience neither in personnel nor in Florida state government. Clearly, political considerations dominated. Suffice it to say, the elevation of the personnel function to departmental status had made the job of state personnel officer a political plum. Instead of having a leader who would serve as a model of merit and career professionalism, there was at least an equal chance that the secretary was a person who would have been comfortable back in the spoils days of the state government.

SENIOR MANAGEMENT SERVICE INCREASES EXEMPTIONS FROM CIVIL SERVICE

In 1980 it appeared that a major advance was to be made in the management of human resources in the state. The occasion was the establishment of the Senior Management Service (SMS), whose ostensible purpose was to provide an orderly mechanism by which the scarce top management resources in the state government could be identified, developed, and utilized effectively. The idea for such a service was clearly stimulated by the 1978 creation of the Senior Executive Service in the U.S. Civil Service Reform Act. As would be expected, the responsibility for managing this important new undertaking fell to the Department of Administration.

But the image of the Senior Management Service (SMS) was not quite its reality. To understand the forces that prompted the creation of the SMS, it is necessary to return to the outlook of Governor Millard

Caldwell. While he wanted a professionalized public service, Caldwell was also concerned that the presence of such people not diminish his power. Even in the best of circumstances, patronage clashes with the career service because of the power factor. There is a longstanding belief in the culture that the only way to secure responsiveness from an individual, and therefore to get one's way as boss, is to have the capacity to drop the guillotine. Also, it is generally more advantageous to hire a friend. Thus it was inevitable that the existence of a comprehensive civil service in Florida would arouse a counter movement to shrink the system through exempting positions from coverage. Those who valued traditional patronage, who believed executive influence that executive influence was basically exercised through the process of hire and fire, and who thought the red tape and delay in civil service processing was excessive coalesced to push for more positions open to political appointment. While the history of politics and fragmentation in government may have strengthened such tendencies in Florida, the trend toward exempt positions was nationwide. Even states with strong civil service traditions felt the need to open up their systems and to make them more politically responsible (Roberts 1988).

After the career service reforms of 1967 and 1969, bills were more often introduced into the Florida legislature to exempt so-called policy making positions from coverage. Finally in 1979 the legislature did substantially increase the number of exempt positions. It also created a Senior Management Advisory Committee to "conduct a study to examine the feasibility of an alternative system of personnel administration for the senior managers and exccutives of the state, to be known as the Senior Management Service."

A report from this group, in which the Department of Administration was a collaborator, was published in April 1980. Shortly thereafter, the legislature established the Senior Management Service. In effect, this was an elegant name for an exempt system. Criteria for entry into Senior Management were very general. Membership came from holding a job that was designated SMS. It was that simple. How were such positions identified? Essentially two ways were stipulated: (a) the functional nature of the job or (b) managerial judgement. In the former case, the legislature followed rather common approaches by specifying that positions should be "primarily and essentially policy making or managerial in nature" (Sherwood and Rainey 1983, 39).

A position, carrying no responsibility for the work of others but assisting a policy maker in some way, could qualify for entrance under these criteria. The second means of inclusion was even simpler. Each agency head was free to hire up to 10 people in positions that he or she could simply designate senior manager. "Thus a secretary or an administrative assistant (and probably even a janitor) could join the presumably exalted ranks of the Senior Management Service. Virtually anyone had the possibility of access to the service" (Sherwood 1988, 7).

A study of one department in 1988 showed 33 SMS members, 22 of whom held high level managerial jobs and 11 of whom were in exempt positions so classified by the director of the department.

While it was true that all the managerial positions at levels of bureau head and above were brought into the SMS, the roster was also a catch-all for a wide range of positions and responsibilities. By early 1985 there were about 1500 people in the Senior Management Service, with salaries ranging from $15,000 to $74,000 (Sherwood 1988, 8).

Not only was there substantial discretion in selecting the positions included in the system but also wide latitude in appointment. The boss was free to hire and fire as he or she pleased. There was no statement of qualifications developed by the Department of Administration for entrance into SMS; and DOA performed no review of appointments. It was a totally decentralized system completely free from any ties to the career service. In their study, Odell Waldby and Annie Mary Hartsfield concluded that there was no intent to create a centralized senior service system (Hartsfield and Waldby 1982, 2).

Membership in the SMS did carry some benefits in exchange for a more precarious tenure. The amount of time required to vest in retirement was cut in half; health insurance premiums were entirely financed by the state; annual leave arrangements were more generous and less bound in red tape; and there was the psychic satisfaction and resume benefit in calling one's self a senior manager. As it turned out, the benefits became a stumbling block to subsequent reform efforts. No one wanted to give up these advantages.

The Department of Administration, the titular manager of the SMS, did not have a significant influence on its affairs. Meetings of an advisory committee were sporadically convened, but the nature of the Senior Management Service was shaped in each individual agency. An important change in the state employment system had, therefore, occurred in 1980. The roughly 500 jobs at the top of the state bureaucracy were removed from the career service and any guarantees of job security; and about 1000 other jobs were made available to the political leadership on a patronage basis. The civil service had been substantially diminished in importance. Further, the opening of such a significant part of the bureaucracy to political influence really meant that employment security was threatened throughout the system and opportunities for career advancement within the civil service greatly limited.

CHANGES IN 1986 CREATE MORE EXEMPT POSITIONS

The formal configuration of the Senior Management Service was sufficiently unwieldy that a major structural change occurred in 1986. Digging below the formal trappings of the reform, however, reveals an even more elaborate patronage system operated on the same, decentralized basis. Legislation in 1986 split the old SMS into two parts: (a) a greatly reduced SMS that included only the top managerial jobs in the state government, numbering no more than 500, generally including division directors and above; and (b) a Selected Exempt Service (SES), which not only took in the remaining members of the old SMS but also a large number of professionals, including lawyers and physicians. Fringe benefits, which were a sticking point in the effort at reform, were generously handled. Those in the Selected Exempt Service got treated as SMS members had in the past. Those in the new Senior Management Service got even more benefits. The expansion in the number of employees in the two groups meant that the scale of political appointments had grown further, as the incumbents in both systems were appointed and served at the pleasure of the agency leadership.

With the SMS reforms, the Department of Administration had responsibility for three employment systems: the formal career service, with about 90,000 people; the Selected Exempt Service, with about 2500; and the Senior Management Service with about 400. It was hard to discover any significant way, however, in which the Department of Administration had substantial influence on the latter two systems. If civil service/merit values were to be found, it was strictly at the discretion of the agency heads. The fourth performance audit of the systems by the Auditor General in 1992 reported that statutory requirements for monitoring personnel practices in such SMS and SES areas as recruitment, selection, training and staff development ". . . have not been met" (Auditor General 1993, iv).

COLLAPSE OF COMPREHENSIVE CIVIL SERVICE IN 1988: DOA LOSES FORMAL CONTROL OVER HIRING

Perhaps the single, most significant setback to the comprehensive civil service in Florida occurred in 1988. At that time the formal authority of DOA over the state's hiring processes was withdrawn by the legislature. The result was that the 26 major agencies of state government set their own rules and carried them out as they saw fit.

DOA's inadequacies as the control point for state recruiting, examining, and certifying candidates were, of course, well known. A report by the State Auditor General in November, 1987, undoubtedly had a

great effect on attitudes in both the legislative and executive branches (Auditor General 1987).

First observing that the recruiting, examining, certifying and appointing processes were originally conceived as parts of a uniform and comprehensive system, the report went on to pronounce the system in serious disarray. It observed that DOA had not met ". . . its statutory responsibility to establish uniform Career Service selection policies and procedures, nor has it monitored the selection activities of the state agencies" (Auditor General 1987, ix).

The Auditor General therefore made it quite clear that a comprehensive hiring process, which is critical to the idea of the civil service, no longer existed in Florida. This state of affairs did not, of course, disturb the operating agencies. They had long struggled with DOA's ponderous, time-consuming, and often unavailing procedures for bringing in new employees. Now they enjoyed the delicious freedom of a decentralized system. Unfortunately, it could no longer be considered a comprehensive civil service.

There were also political fireworks that further jeopardized the possibility of solutions that would retain a comprehensive civil service. They focused on Adis Vila, the DOA secretary, and her relations with the legislators. Her truculence particularly offended the President of the Senate, John Vogt, who proposed legislation to abolish the Department of Administration. A political compromise permitted the continuation of DOA but so weakened its position as to erase even DOA's formal role of protector of the civil service.

Just what the failures of DOA over the years have meant to the civil service principle of equal employment opportunity can be seen in the way an individual must conduct a search for a state job. In the first place, there is no single place from which full information on job availabilities can be obtained. Second, there is no way to ascertain a person's qualifications for a group of jobs. The search for openings must go on at many sites and locales, principally in Tallahassee. Applications and the presentation of credentials must be made at the appropriate agency offices, and one then waits for a judgement. Feedback is given, however, only to the successful applicant in many agencies. There is no uniform practice of providing information on the fate of an application and reasons for non-appointment. Applicants cannot be sure they will get any information on how their qualifications are evaluated.

It is possible that a person could apply for jobs of a similar nature at four different agencies and be rejected at three and approved at one. Or exactly the opposite may occur, three approvals and one rejection. There is even difference in where these qualifications judgements are made in the agencies. In a considerable number of agencies the responsibility rests solely with the supervisor; in others there is review and final judgement by the personnel office (Burgess 1990).

In terms of traditional standards of civil service, there were three basic problems with these arrangements: (a) there could be no equal opportunity for employment because the availability of information varies significantly from situation to situation; (b) there could be little assurance that fairness and equity are honored uniformly; and (c) there could be small promise of appointing the most qualified person because employment pools are localized and qualifications decisions decentralized. Thus practices existing in Florida in 1990 gave no guarantee that the most deeply held values of the civil service idea in a democratic society will be observed.

The withdrawal from the concept of system comprehensiveness, which inevitably involves a certain degree of centralization, lies at the heart of these problems. The hiring process was now handled in many different ways, leaving individual applicants subject to a variety of different rules. Fewer people were covered by civil service. In 1990 there were approximately 2500 office holders in managerial and professional positions that were not hired in accord with civil service standards and enjoyed no job security. In 1990 it was revealed that the number of temporary employees had risen nearly 40% (from 26,000 to 36,000) during the administration of Governor Bob Martinez. Temporary, non-career service employees thus constituted about one-quarter of the total work force of nearly 150,000 (Cotterell 1990).

It has often been argued that temporary appointments, necessary as they are in certain circumstances, function for patronage purposes and against civil service principles.

THE CAIN CASE: A THREAT TO JOB SECURITY IN THE CAREER SERVICE

While the changes in civil service comprehensiveness and the move away from a uniform and equitable hiring process have been the major threats, there was an event in 1989 that was both worrisome and also reassuring in regard to the job security of those in the state career service. It involved a lower level manager in the Department of Administration, Carolyn Cain, and the DOA secretary, Adis Vila. Specifically, Vila fired Cain, disregarding her career service protections. Vila's action suggested a disregard in the Martinez administration for an essential principle of the career service.

The official reason given for the dismissal was inadequate job performance, as stated in her two most recent performance ratings. But the press reported a somewhat different story. Cain had been on the board of the National Association of Suggestion Systems, which involved her area of expertise, and requested travel authorization for a 1988 meeting at which she was to speak. Vila said she would replace Cain and make the speech. The Association demurred, suggesting both come but that Cain make the speech. Vila's decision was that no one would go.

From that point on, Cain's problems progressed. She had begun her state career 24 years earlier in a clerical position and had been in the Department of Administration for more than 10 years. Her position was hierarchically at the top of the career service; and her immediate supervisor was a member of the Selected Exempt Service with no tenure. In less than a year she had two supervisors, both appointed by Vila; and her performance evaluations suffered markedly. Up to that point she had never received an unsatisfactory rating. A number had been at the "exceeds performance standards" level; and a 1987 rating included the comment, "There are few who hold a candle to her in terms of dedication, mission orientation, participative leadership style and openness" (Cotterell 1989, May 16).

Further Cain's role put her in touch with many people throughout the government. Virtually without exception she was regarded as a competent, effective public servant.

One evaluation late in 1988 graded her work unsatisfactory and provided the following specifics: did not communicate well with her staff; failed to develop criteria for hiring people in her own four person office; was late with monthly reports; and slow in responding to suggestions for improved operations. Another evaluation in April, 1989, also rated her work unsatisfactory, and she was dismissed on April 25. Vila cited the poor evaluations as the basis for the firing; but the coincidence of the conflict in June and the beginning of the poor ratings could not be overlooked. Cain's evaluations had not suffered in the first year of the Vila administration; and, further, she had received a "team merit" award in June, 1988.

There seemed little doubt that Cain had aroused the ire of the Secretary, and she would have to pay a price. Her husband's exempt position as DOA budget officer, with his continued service totally dependent on Vila, appeared to weaken Cain's hand. She was sufficiently angered, however, to accept the risk that both would be fired. [He lost his job later.] She hired a lawyer and appealed the case to the state's Public Employees Relations Commission. Cain was also deprived of sick leave and annual leave accumulations, which gave the case additional importance.

The ouster was not immediately covered in the press. A major story appeared on May 16, however, and it then became apparent that the case constituted a threat to what little integrity was left in the career service system (Cotterell 1989, May 16).

Four days later it was reported that the governor's office had asked for the Cain file and was conducting a review. On June 7, 1989, the Governor intervened and ordered Cain rehired. The issue was described as a "personality clash," and the rationale for the intervention was to avoid a long and costly legal fight. It was, reported, however, that "some personnel officers and local Republicans had quietly advised Martinez the state would lose" (Cotterell 1989, June 8).

Cain was first assigned to a different job; then, when Vila resigned and moved to Washington, she returned to her old position.

There are both discomfiting and reassuring aspects to the Cain case. On the positive side, it is clear that the existence of the Public Employees Relations Commission does make a difference. It does provide an opportunity for a hearing. The press also played a major part in the case. Its substantial coverage made it difficult for the Governor to ignore the actions of his secretary.

On the other hand, there were concerns. Most worrisome was the fact that the chief personnel officer of the state would feel free to engage in exactly the kind of behavior civil service rules are designed to prevent. A second preoccupation was with the way in which the middle managers' lack of job security may have promoted arbitrary and inequitable treatment of a subordinate. Vila had full freedom to fire her bureau heads; and there certainly must be the suspicion that the sharp change in Cain's performance appraisals correlated with the secretary's attitude toward her. The assumption, too, that Cain would do nothing because of her husband's vulnerability suggests how important tenure is to the maintenance of a fair and open human resources system. Finally, it did take considerable courage for Cain to buck the system. Ideally, a subordinate should be able to appeal a management action without the risk of high costs.

THE CHILES PERIOD

In 1989 a gubernatorial election occurred in which the predominant issue was change in the role and performance of the state government. Lawton Chiles, a much respected former U.S. senator, overwhelmed the incumbent, Bob Martinez, on a platform that promised greater integrity and more effectiveness in state government. Elected as lieutenant governor was Buddy MacKay, a former congressman also regarded as a reformer.

Before the new team took office, several transition studies were commissioned. One dealt specifically with overhead functions, like human resources, and others with the more direct tasks of the state government. A common theme in these reports was criticism of the personnel system. Some of the views were extreme, in that they would ignore the national consensus and eliminate even the notion of a statewide system based on civil service principles. Others argued for even greater decentralization as part of a larger restructuring effort.

A former journalist, David Osborne, also had significant influence on the new administration. He was in the process of completing a new book on "reinventing government," and many of his ideas had already come to the attention of the Chiles-MacKay team. Some time later, MacKay was quoted, "While lots of folks have talked about David's theories, Lawton and I have been doing it." Officially, Osborne was enlisted as a consultant to the Government by the People Commission, appointed by Chiles to advise him on reform.

In his book, co-authored with Ted Gaebler and published in 1992, Osborne revealed much of the thinking that lay behind the actions of the new administration (Osborne and Gaebler 1992). The assumption was that civil service ideas had not changed over the many years since 1873 and the passage of the first Federal law, whose basic purpose was to control a politically corrupt system rather than to bring about better management. These controls had become nooses for public managers and had made it impossible for them to operate. The basic answer was to eliminate the controls and give managers wide freedom. There was no recognition that a national consensus on civil service policy had been forged over the many years since 1873.

Within this general orientation, Chiles-MacKay moved quickly. A first, ingenious step was to secure legislation "sunsetting" all personnel statutes, as of July 1, 1992. That created great pressure for reform by raising the threat of totally abandoning the personnel system, such as it was, roughly one year hence. Another major move, made easier by a rapidly deteriorating budget situation, was the "down-sizing" (later restated as "right-sizing") of state agency staffs. Particular emphasis was placed on reducing the size of the managerial cadres, thus using layoffs to reduce the layering in state organizations. Finally a Civil Service Reform Commission of nine members was created, three appointed each by the Governor, Senate President, and Speaker of the House of Representatives. It was to articulate the blueprint for the new civil service.

Refashioning the system proved a far more difficult task than implied by Osborne. The Civil Service Reform Commission, launched with great fanfare, emerged with proposals which were far from earthshaking. As Wechsler has written, ". . . the process was inherently more political than technical" (Wechsler 1993).

Much of the debate was around decentralization of the system, with little apparent recognition that it was already highly decentralized. Ultimately, the Commission issued a brief report in which it endorsed proposals of the Department of Administration for only modest statutory changes.

The legislation that ensued in 1992 did little to change the system in any fundamental way. It did, however, further downgrade the career service by adding another 300 exempt positions to the roughly 2500 which already existed at the top levels of government. It picked up on the very fashionable total quality management, a set of managerial ideas that advocates claimed would fix much of what was wrong with governmental management. The rhetoric in the preamble to the law was characteristically exuberant: ". . . the implementation of total quality management will provide the framework for agencies to develop their human resources through empowerment, training, and reward for productivity enhancement, to continuously improve the quality of services, and to satisfy the expectations of the public."

The legislation also possessed a strangely contradictory quality, on the one hand charging the Department of Administration to set broad policies and expectations for the state and on the other insisting that the management of the system fall to the individual agencies. Much was again rhetoric, as evidenced by the following statement: [The central agency] "maintains a central classification system for use by all agencies while continuing agency authority for classification and reclassification" (DMS 1992, 1).

The overall the effect of the legislation was to decentralize the human resources system further, particularly in the areas of classification and pay. Goals were set to reduce the number of job classifications from 1700 to 700, thus to provide greater discretion in hiring, in assignments, and in compensation. Further, it was reaffirmed the classification authority would rest with the individual agencies. In the same mode of decentralization, agencies were granted considerably greater freedom in setting salaries, both to become more competitive in the job market and also to reward individual performers.

At the same 1992 legislative session in which personnel reforms were passed, a major organizational change was also effected. The inept Department of Administration was merged with the better regarded Department of General Services into a new unit, the Department of Management Services, under the direct control of the governor. Although the reorganization considerably enhanced the power of the governor by removing the supervision of general services from the cabinet, the change was approved with little fanfare. The mandate that the new department would effect a 10% savings in personnel costs within a year seemed a sufficient argument. System-wide human resources management responsibilities were lodged in a new Division of Personnel Management Services.

Although there were few real changes effected in the system, civil service reform attracted considerable attention throughout the nation. At a meeting of the Democratic Leadership Council in May 1992, Osborne labeled the Chiles-MacKay reforms ". . . the most ambitious effort to reorganization state government I have ever seen" (Crawford 1992, May 2).

At the same meeting MacKay "delighted the crowd" with "examples of state reform, such as giving cash incentives to bureaucrats." It was also reported that MacKay ". . . argued that civil service rules must be set aside throughout state government before widespread reform is possible" (Crawford 1992, May 2).

Within the bureaucracy the picture appeared quite different in 1993, at least in part a consequence of the very tight budgets within which the Chiles-MacKay group had to contend. Data published in 1992 showed that 12.3% of the workforce earned less than the Federally established poverty level of a family of four of $14,672 (Cotterell 1992, May 4, 1A).

There was no question that pay was a big problem, with most employees going without even cost of living increases for three years. In 1992 salary increases were authorized by the legislature and then rescinded, as the state's financial situation worsened. In March 1993 the state court declared the employees' contract was violated but concluded that the increase was owed only for the six months remaining in the fiscal year. It ordered that lump sum payments be paid by July 1, 1993. However, it was reported that, as of July 12, 1993, a third of the employees had not received the back pay (Cotterell 1992, July 12, 3C).

In May, 1992, on the occasion of the state's Employee Recognition Week, the *Tallahassee Democrat* reported, ". . . more than most years, this Employee Recognition Week finds many workers tired, frustrated, and apprehensive about their future" (Cotterell 1992, May 4).

CONCLUSION

Government serves its citizens in many different ways. Yet there is often a failure to recognize that each of those services is performed by another human being. The people who make up the bureaucracy are typically regarded as cogs in a gigantic machine, unfortunately so perceived even by many in political leadership roles. In fact, public servants have the same aspirations as others in the society. They want to work in situations where they are valued, provided adequate rewards, and where there are opportunities for challenge and personal growth. They do not appreciate unfair treatment any more than anyone else.

The quality of the Florida public service has impacts well beyond any immediate services rendered. Its performance will, in substantial degree, dictate the attitude of citizens toward their government and affect their own sense of responsibility as citizens. A bureaucracy that is aloof and closed will not generate the trust and support that is desirable. Favoritism, even if not consciously practiced, in appointing people to state government will have its effect on trust levels. Any process that deprives the state of the very best people available will work against the capacity to perform services effectively and responsively.

It is within this context that a national consensus on civil service emerged over the last century. The principles evolved because governments do need qualified people who see their government service as a career and believe that they will be fairly and honestly treated.

After approximately 30 years of rather slow change, the basic principles of civil were adopted in Florida in 1969. Nearly all employees were covered in the system; and the governor had responsibility for its effective operation. The move in 1969 was a centralizing one by placing the governor in control. But uniform policies and procedures can become massive red tape; they can inhibit the effective operation of the many state agencies, with their unique needs and priorities. There was, as a result, the imperative that the management of human resources be given priority attention. What was needed was an operation so effective that it could provide the gains of civil service uniformity without the attendant losses of a centralized system.

In more than two decades the Department of Administration failed to achieve that important goal. At the end of its first decade it had maintained a comprehensive system and had protected against the flagrant violation of civil service norms. But it had failed to perform as a positive force and had become a drag on the operating agencies.

In the succeeding period, from 1979 to 1993, there has been a pronounced retreat from civil service concepts. Most importantly, the state abandoned uniform hiring policies and practices. Twenty-six different agencies began setting their own rules and practices. Not only were issues of equal employment opportunity raised but there was the corollary question whether the best available talent was being brought into the system.

The system also became far less comprehensive. An increased number of people came to employment outside career service procedures; and they generally enjoyed no job tenure. A large number of people, 2800, were members of the Senior Management Service and Selected Exempt Service, for which there were no recruiting procedures nor any job rights. As shown in the Cain case, the proliferation of such exempt positions can have substantial effect on those still in the career service. There is also the question whether the top 2800 people in the state government should not be recruited, utilized, developed, and dismissed in a more systematic manner. If regularized, orderly procedures are desirable for other public servants, are they not also for those at the top? The appearance of an increasing number of temporary appointments, nearly 25% of the workforce in 1990, also raises questions.

An attempt has been made in this chapter to provide both a perspective and historical insight on the development of the state's public service over the last half century. The system in 1993 was clearly unlike that contemplated in legislation in 1969. In considering changes that may be in order, the "central message" of the Volcker Commission report in 1989, *Leadership for America: Rebuilding the Public Service*, may be an appropriate departure point:

> In essence we call for a renewed sense of commitment by all Americans to the highest traditions of the public service—to a public service responsive to the political will of the people and also protective of our constitutional values; to a public service able to cope with complexity and conflict and also able to maintain the highest ethical standards; to a public service attractive to the young and talented from all parts of our society and also capable of earning the respect of all our citizens (VC 1989, 1).

In its first report, the National Commission on the State and Local Public Service, of which former Florida Governor Reubin Askew was a member, included approvingly the words of the Lieutenant Governor of New York, Stan Lundine:

> I do think government needs more flexible personnel systems. I strongly believe in collective bargaining. I strongly believe that public employees' rights have to be protected. But I think we could come up with a more rational structure and a better structure for public employees to work in; I envision an era of higher quality public service, better skilled and motivated workers, and as a result of that, more satisfied taxpayers (NCSLPS 1993, 25).

REFERENCES

Auditor General (1993). *Performance audit of the senior management service and selected exempt service systems.* Tallahassee: State of Florida, the Auditor.

Auditor General (1987). *Performance audit of the career service employee selection program administered by the Department of Administration.* Tallahassee: State of Florida, the Auditor.

Burgess, Susan B. (1990). *Eligibility determinations within Florida's career service: A demerit to the merit system?* Tallahassee: An Action Report Submitted to the Department of Public Administration.

Colburn, David R. and Richard K. Scher (1980). *Florida's gubernatorial politics in the twentieth century.* Tallahassee: University Presses of Florida, A Florida State University Book.

Cotterell, Bill (1992, July 12). At HRS, many still are waiting for their checks. *Tallahassee Democrat.*

Cotterell, Bill (1992, May 4). Why bother working for the state anyway? *Tallahassee Democrat.*

Cotterell, Bill (1990, August 26). State workers not a priority. *Tallahassee Democrat.*

Cotterell, Bill (1989, June 8). DOA Administrator fired by Vila is rehired. *Tallahassee Democrat.*

Cotterell, Bill (1989, May 16). I'm not going to crumble. *Tallahassee Democrat.*

Council of State Governments (CSG) (1970). *The book of the states 1970–71.* Lexington, Kentucky: the Council.

Council of State Governments (CSG) (1957). *The book of the states 1956–57.* Chicago: the Council.

Craword, J. Craig (1992, May 2). Florida reforms earn kudos. *Orlando Sentinel.*

Department of Management Services (DMS) (1992). *Career service rule changes.* Tallahassee: State of Florida, the Department.

Department of Public Administration (DPA) (1979). *Improving Florida personnel practice: An agenda for action.* Tallahassee: Florida State University, Institute of Science and Public Affairs, Florida State University.

Doyle, Wilson K., Angus M.Laird, and S. Sherman Weiss (1954). *The government and administration of Florida.* New York: Thomas Y. Crowell Co.

Hartsfield, Annie Mary and H. Odell Waldby (1982). *Effectiveness and efficiency of state recruitment services.* Tallahassee: Florida State University, Department of Public Administration.

Ingraham, Patricia W. and David H. Rosenbloom (1990, June). *The state of merit in the federal government.* Occasional Paper prepared for the National Commission on the Public Service.

Morris, Allen and Waldron (1965). *Your Florida government: 500 questions and answers.* Gainesville: University of Florida Press.

CHAPTER

7

Mosher, Frederick C. (1982). *Democracy and the public service* (2nd ed.). New York and Oxford, England: Oxford University Press.

National Commission on State and Local Public Service (NCSLPS) (1993). *Hard truths/tough choices: An agenda for state and local reform.* Albany, NY: Nelson A. Rockefeller Institute of Government.

Osborne, David and Ted Gaebler (1992). *Reinventing government.* Reading, MA: Addison Wesley Press.

Roberts, Deborah D. (1988). A new breed of public executive: Top level exempt managers in state government. *Review of Public Personnel Administration, 8* (Spring).

Sherwood, Frank P. (1988). Two state executive personnel systems: A comparative perspective. *State and Local Government Review, 20* (Winter).

Sherwood, Frank P., and Hal G. Rainey (1983). *Management policy in the state government of Florida: Managers' views, training policy, and the senior management service.* Tallahassee: Florida State University, Institute of Science and Public Affairs.

St. Angelo, Douglas with Bill O. Gibson (1980). Administrative and functional agencies. In Manning J. Dauer (2nd ed.). *Florida's Politics and Government.* Gainesville: University Presses of Florida.

Volcker Commission (VC) (1989). *Leadership for America: Rebuilding the public service.* Lexington, MA: Lexington Books.

Wechsler, Barton (1993). Florida's civil service reform. *Spectrum: The Journal of State Government, 66* (Winter).

ENDNOTES

1. One such book is Donald E. Klingner and John Nalbandian (1985). *Public personnel management: Contexts and strategies.* Englewood Cliffs, NJ: Prentice-Hall.

2. Most of the reorganization provisions are contained in Chapter 110, FS., 1967.

CHAPTER 8

PLANNING AND BUDGETING

WILLIAM EARLE KLAY

W hen a government is confronted by rapid growth and change, the practices of an earlier, simpler era no longer suffice. Florida has undergone rapid growth and change for most of this century. It is not surprising that the state has made numerous efforts to improve its planning and budgeting processes and to forge links between them.

As we enter the 21st century, it is imperative that we do a better job of thinking ahead in order to spend our limited resources wisely. What is emerging is a turbocharged economy, one that is driven by rapid change in advanced technologies in a context of global competition. The implications of the new era are best seen from the standpoint of Florida's largest industry, tourism. It is possible that advancements in virtual reality technology could render the technologies of places like Disney World and Universal Studios obsolete. Environmental degradation in the form of ozone depletion could cause tourists to fear exposure to the sun with devastating impacts on our sun based tourism. On the other hand, wise investments in technology and environmental protection could make Florida an attractive destination throughout the coming century. Making such a vision become real, however, will require foresight and wise investment of resources. Our ability to plan, and to link plans to reality through the budget, will greatly determine our success or failure in the new economy.

Planning is the process of government through which vision is formed. If it is lacking, threats become greater and opportunities are likely to be ignored. When vision is absent, it is likely that the public's money will be spent less wisely, upon lesser priorities. Budgeting, on the other hand, is the process of government where political power is most obviously manifest. Budgeting addresses the ancient question, "Who gets what?" Budgeting, a complex process that houses the maneuvers of powerful officials in their quest to affect resource allocations, has resisted the influence of planning.

Chapter

8

In spite of the inherent difficulties, Florida has a long history of trying to bridge the gaps between planning and budgeting. In some ways, Florida's experiences have been similar to those of other governments. The ways in which planning and budgeting innovations arise and are implemented in Florida, however, have often reflected our own unique peculiarities. Notable successes have occurred, but other efforts have either failed or lead to outcomes that were different than originally intended. For the most part, planning and budgeting in Florida remain separate processes. Their continuing separation imperils our ability to fashion opportunities in the new global, knowledge driven, economy.

Fragmentation of authority is a hallmark, a defining characteristic, of Florida's state government. An understanding of this fragmentation is essential to understanding why some innovations failed while others succeeded. What follows is a look at several innovations that have sought to link planning and budgeting. As will be seen, fragmentation manifests itself in numerous ways in Florida. There are also various ways to overcome fragmentation. For the most part, when fragmentation has been overcome, innovations have taken root. When it has not, innovations have waned.

THE EXECUTIVE BUDGET MOVEMENT COMES TO FLORIDA

In the late 19th and early 20th centuries, civic minded citizens became concerned that governments in the United States were being operated inefficiently and sometimes corruptly. The "good government" movement they formed sought to overcome these "evils" by introducing practices that would be conducive to sound management. One such practice was the selection of employees according to merit rather than political affiliation. Another practice that reformers espoused was the "executive budget."

Proponents of the executive budget believed that accountability is essential. They looked approvingly upon parliamentary systems where the prime minister proposed a budget, oversaw its implementation, and stood accountable for its results before a questioning parliament. The separation of powers contained in the American constitution and mirrored in the constitutions of the states, however, divided authority and, in so doing, diluted accountability. To lessen this effect, reformers proposed that the chief executive be given the authority to frame a proposed budget for an entire government and to oversee the execution of the budget following legislative appropriations.

Enhanced accountability was not the only rationale for the executive budget. Emphasis was given to the fact that the chief executive, whether the president or a governor, was the only official elected by all citizens. Efficiency would be enhanced by reviewing all competing claims from the standpoint of the jurisdiction as a whole, rather from that of narrower legislative districts. Being elected by all of the people, chief executives were also expected to exhibit more statesmanlike qualities than insular legislators. This is where planning entered the picture. Statesmanlike chief executives, concerned with their place in history and accountable to all the people, would propose budgets that could best guide the state or nation into the future.

The executive budget concept was adopted by the federal government in the Budget and Accounting Act of 1921. The president was given the authority to propose a comprehensive budget to the Congress. He was also given a staff to prepare and execute the budget. First located in the Treasury Department, the budget staff was subsequently moved to the Executive Office of the President where it resides today in the Office of Management and Budget. In the same year, 1921, Florida also adopted its version of the executive budget but it was a version that differed markedly from the model proposed by the reformers and adopted intact by the federal government.

In Florida's budget act (Chap. 8426, Laws of Florida, 1921) budget authority was vested in a body known as the Budget Commission. Comprised initially of the governor, comptroller, and treasurer, the Budget Commission was to receive budget requests from all state agencies and submit a comprehensive proposed budget to the legislature. The governor was designated as "the chief budget officer of the state," and was given authority to employ "competent budget assistants," but it was the commission, not the governor alone, who decided what to include in the proposed budget. In 1925, the composition of the Budget Commission was changed to include all members of the Cabinet (governor, secretary of state, comptroller, treasurer, attorney general, commissioner of agriculture, and state superintendent of public instruction).

Why did Florida decide that executive budget authority should be shared (or fragmented depending on one's point of view) when the primary purpose of the executive budget reform concept was to centralize accountability? The answer lies in the events that followed the Civil War, events that still affect the structure and processes of government in Florida. The constitution imposed by the Union, the reconstruction constitution of 1868, gave the governor extensive powers, especially to appoint state and county level administrative officials. Thus, gubernatorial authority became associated with memories of Reconstruction,

CHAPTER

8

Republican dominance, and black enfranchisement. The 1885 constitution was written to counter the effects of Reconstruction and included several features to limit the authority of the governor. Executive authority was divided among seven cabinet members, each of whom could be reelected indefinitely while the governor was limited to a single term in office. The weakening of gubernatorial authority also opened the door for the emergence of an independently minded legislature, a factor that has greatly influenced reforms in recent decades.

Even though Florida's version of an executive budget perpetuated the diffuseness of executive authority, the 1921 act did overcome some of the fragmentation. The appropriations committees of the House and Senate were required to sit jointly in open session to consider the budget. In addition, the staff of the Budget Commission also served as staff to the legislature when it was in session. Indications are that the staff was impartial and professional, thereby having credibility among both legislators and members of the Commission.

Section 8 of the 1921 budget act also specified a format for the Commission's proposed budget: "Opposite each item of the proposed expenditures the budget shall show in separate parallel columns the amount appropriated for the last preceding appropriation year, for the current appropriation year, and the increase or decrease." Modern observers of the legislative appropriations process will find a very similar format in use today. Requests are now arrayed by line-item category and parallel columns are used to compare increases and decreases between past appropriations and the proposals of the governor, House, and Senate. The durability of this format underscores the staying power of the established budgetary processes of the state.

The commission form of executive budget remained in place for nearly a half century, but did not go uncriticized. In 1945, a special Joint Committee on Economy and Efficiency recommended that gubernatorial authority over the budget be strengthened (Dennis 1974). Most of the committee's recommendations languished with one notable exception. The legislature amended Chapter 216, Florida Statutes, the chapter that specifies budgetary procedures, to authorize the governor to appoint a budget director and reaffirmed his authority to hire budget staff assistants (Chap. 22857, Laws of Florida 1945). Even though the governor alone could appoint the director and staff, they continued to work for the Budget Commission.

In addition, the 1945 act specified that the services of the budget director would be available to the legislature during the legislative sessions. Authority to propose and execute a budget remained divided in the executive branch. The legislature retained its independence, but coordination continued to be achieved through the use of a single budget staff. It is also notable that in the 1940's, most state appropriations were in the form of continuing appropriations that did not require reappropriation in each legislative session. In recent times, however, the legislature has sought to extend its control and oversight of executive activities through detailed annual reviews of agency budget requests.

In 1949, a study by the Public Administration Clearing Service of the University of Florida recommended that Florida fully institute an executive budget by giving full budgetary authority to the governor (Waterman 1949). They also suggested that the Budget Commission should be limited to an advisory role. The governor did not receive such authority for two more decades. The absence of exclusive budget authority, however, did not keep governors from having a substantial influence. Budget Commission members were reluctant to propose expenditures that would require new revenues without the support of the governor. If the governor opposed a revenue increase, other cabinet members were unlikely to support one. Moreover, in the days of biennial legislative sessions, the role of the Budget Commission in executing budgets was quite important and much of the attention of the public and press focused upon the governor.

THE GOVERNOR BECOMES THE SOLE BUDGET (AND PLANNING OFFICER)

Remembered more for his high jinks than his executive talents, Governor Claude Kirk was instrumental in establishing the governor as the state's chief budget and planning officer. It was he, for example, who pressed successfully to get the state's teacher retirement system funded on an actuarial basis. In the midst of his term, the legislature created an office of state planning and programming as a separate division under the renamed "State Planning and Budget Commission" (Chap. 67-157, Laws of Florida 1967). The governor was designated the "chief planning officer of the State," and was given the authority to appoint a director for state planning and programming.

The late 1960's were years of fundamental change in Florida's government. The legislature was reapportioned under federal court order, thereby opening the door to many more elected officials from urban areas. Some of these arrived in Tallahassee with ideas about government reform that were strongly influenced by the "good government" movement of an earlier era. The new constitution approved by the electorate in 1968, for example, called for the reduction of more than 175 boards, commissions, and similar bodies to not more than 25 state executive departments. The main supporters of this limitation were Chesterfield Smith and Richard Pettigrew, respectively the chairmen of the Constitutional Revision Commission and the reorganization committee of the House of Representatives. They believed that executive accountability should be clear and centralized (Dennis 1974).

In the struggles that ensued over reorganization, the "good government" view was espoused mainly in the House. The opposing group, located primarily in the Senate and Cabinet, favored retention of the cabinet system. State senator Lawton Chiles took the middle ground in this matter. He sponsored a bill to give budget recommendation authority to the governor. Chiles' bill was incorporated into the compromise that gave the governor primary authority for planning, budgeting, and personnel administration while allowing the cabinet to retain authority in many other areas.

The "Governmental Reorganization Act of 1969" (Chap 69-106, Laws of Florida 1969) was the vehicle that finally gave the governor sole authority to propose a budget. The act again designated the governor as chief budget officer, but required agencies to submit their "legislative budget" requests to the governor. The Department of Administration (DOA) was created that included a Division of Planning and Budgeting. The governor appointed the department secretary and the budget and planning staffs of the now defunct commission were transferred as career status employees into the newly created division. Later, during the Askew administration, the division was separated into a Division of Budget and a Division of State Planning. This separation was indicative of the divergent paths being taken by the planning and budgeting staffs.

In a period of about five years during the late 1960's and early 1970's, Florida's malapportioned and largely unstaffed legislature became one of the most reformed and well staffed in the nation. In 1967, the state auditor was moved from the executive branch to the legislative branch, thus increasing the legislature's oversight capacity. The 1969 reorganization act required the DOA to submit copies of the agencies' legislative budget requests, as well as the governor's proposed budget, to the House and Senate appropriations committees who no longer sat in joint sessions as they were required to do in 1921.

At the same time the legislature gave greater budget authority to the governor; it was taking steps to reduce its dependency upon the executive branch. The staff of the old Budget Commission had served as staff to the legislative committees. By 1975, however, the House Appropriations Committee was staffed by 9 professional and 2 clerical personnel (Kyle 1975). Other budget related committees were comparably staffed. Legislative staff were assigned to analyze agency requests, review the governor's recommendations, develop independent revenue estimates, prepare fiscal notes (forecasts of the financial impacts of proposed legislation), and develop independent budget recommendations for legislative consideration. Never again would the legislature be as dependent upon recommendations and staff from the executive branch.

PROGRAM BUDGETING AND COMPREHENSIVE PLANNING: SOME SUCCESS, MOSTLY FAILURE

The legislature was the primary proponent of Florida's experiment with the form of program budgeting known as PPBS (planning-programming-budgeting-systems). In the 1967 act that designated the governor as chief planning officer, the legislature mandated a state plan and annual development programs, including recommended financial schedules for each of the major programmatic areas of the plan. Specifically, section 2. (d) of Chapter 67-157 required the identification of "Alternate methods of accomplishing long and short range development plans including recommended financial schedules for each alternative method."

Program budgeting seeks to group together related activities, irrespective of the organizational structures through which the activities are carried out. Budgeters direct their attention to a "public safety" program, for example, rather than upon the separate budgets of a police and fire department. It is not surprising that Florida experimented with program budgeting in the late 1960's and early 1970's. PPBS, the most ambitious form of program budgeting, was developed in the Department of Defense earlier in the decade and it was the dominant governmental reform of that era. PPBS combined aspects of economics, systems analysis and computer technology. Its staunchest supporters sought nothing less than the rationalization of all budget decisions.

A report on governmental reorganization prepared for the House by the consulting firm of Booz, Allen, and Hamilton (1969) endorsed PPBS as an appropriate approach to executive budgeting. What is unique about Florida's effort is that the desire to do program budgeting came mostly from the legislature. In most governments, the initiative for program budgeting has come from the executive branch.

Program budgeting in Florida faced insurmountable obstacles and it was a failure. It failed for many of the same reasons it failed in other governments. It was overly ambitious and oversold, placing demands of calculation upon the planning and budgeting staffs that could not be met. Research elsewhere showed that program budgeting failed quickest where it lacked the active support of top executives (e.g., Doh 1971; Harper, et al. 1969). In Florida, neither the governor nor agency heads became active proponents and supporters (Tin 1971). Furthermore, even though the legislature called for program budgeting, it did not alter its own budget practices to incorporate PPBS. The Governmental Reorganization Act of 1969 required agencies to distinguish between requests: "To continue current programs," "To improve existing programs," and "For proposed new programs." This format which is in use today is designed to foster an incremental approach to budgeting, one in which attention is directed to the margins of change, but is not conducive to the comprehensive reviews that PPBS required.

The Department of Administration (DOA) did develop a program structure and, for a time, agencies were told to submit their budget requests according to the structure. Budget director Wallace Henderson, however, noted that the structure did not ". . . coincide with the points at which decisions are actually being made (Turnbull 1974, 2)." In retrospect, Florida's quest to relate planning to budgeting was harmed more than helped by the experiment with PPBS. Turnbull concluded that the effort created skepticism among state agencies. A substantial effort was required to produce analysis that many doubted was ever read, much less used. There was no incentive for agencies to do PPBS and they soon doubted that their efforts would lead to success in the competition for appropriations (Tin 1971).

State planning was begun in a state of flux and it has never found a stable locus or role since its inception in 1967. The planners sought to implement PPBS but they found that they were trying to impose an alien process upon established budgeting routines—routines that were well linked to time-honored modes of decision making in the political arena. The information that was generated through PPBS proved to be of limited value to newly elected Governor Askew when his staff prepared new initiatives in the governor's proposed budget for FY 1971. The failure of PPBS, coming at the very outset of state planning, caused a significant loss of identity among the state's planners (Haldi Associates 1973).

When the Florida State Comprehensive Planning Act (Chap. 72-295, Laws of Florida) was passed in 1972, planners began to turn their attention away from budget oriented planning. The DOA was instructed to prepare a comprehensive plan to guide most of the activities of the state, and the preparation of this plan dominated the agenda of the

Bureau of Comprehensive Planning for several years. Stresses remained, however, between planners and budgeters in the DOA. Policy formulation, broadly defined, became the focus of the planners. They developed an ambitious comprehensive plan that was submitted to the legislature in 1978. Senior officials in the DOA continued to reflect a budgeting oriented viewpoint, however, and were concerned that the plan could not be "costed out." Many of the plan's goals, they argued, were desirable to pursue but were too broad or amorphous to use as a basis for reliable cost projections.

The DOA recommended that the state comprehensive plan be advisory and the legislature concurred. Governor Askew's Executive Order 78-48, issued to implement the plan, indicated that the plan should guide all executive planning activities (Swanson and Tait 1978). There was little follow-up on the order. Incentives were not developed to induce agencies to use the plan, nor were sanctions threatened if they failed to do so. Most importantly, budgeters did not use the state plan as a guide to their review of agency budget requests. The budgeting activities of the DOA during the Askew administration enjoyed credibility and influence throughout state government, but its planning activities failed to take root, even within the DOA itself.

BOB GRAHAM VOWS TO PUT PLANNING IN THE DRIVER'S SEAT

When Bob Graham became governor in 1979, he brought several staff leaders who were committed to a radical restructuring of the planning and budgeting processes of the state. A decade earlier, Graham had written an article extolling the virtues of program budgeting, stating that the budget should be based upon long range planning (Graham 1969). Graham's staff believed that the failure of the Askew administration to integrate planning and budgeting was due to the organizational structure of the DOA. In that structure, the professional planners and budgeters were career civil servants who were "distanced" from the governor by intervening levels of supervision. In fact, the DOA did reflect Askew's preferences well and it conveyed his policy and budget initiatives to the legislature with both credibility and effect. Graham's staff, however, believed otherwise.

Graham's staff adopted a three pronged approach to link planning to budgeting (Polivka and Osterholt 1985). A planning document known as the governor's policies and priorities statement was used to provide policy guidance in each major area. Budget related performance measures that had been developed during the PPBS effort were reactivated, and efforts were again made to make these reflect outputs rather than inputs. Their most controversial change was to fundamentally alter the organizational structure for planning and budgeting.

Advisors to the governor were familiar with the budget system in the City of Tampa where a strong mayor form of governance existed. Efforts were made to incorporate elements of the Tampa system. What was proposed was a reorganization similar to earlier moves in the federal government. There, the Treasury Department's Bureau of the Budget had been moved to the Executive Office of the President and reconstituted into an Office of Management and Budget. In Florida's reorganization, (Chap. 79-190, Laws of Florida 1979), much of the DOA's planning activities were devolved to agencies. Land use oriented planning was moved to the Department of Community Affairs which was designated the state land planning agency. Statewide policy planning and the budget staff were placed in an Office of Planning and Budgeting (OPB) within a newly created Executive Office of the Governor (EOG). The newly aligned staff then embarked upon the development of a planning-budgeting-management system (Stryker 1979).

When budgeting was moved to the Executive Office of the President in the federal government, career service status was retained for professional staff. The Graham administration believed that career status had hampered both responsiveness and the integration of planning and budgeting in Askew's DOA, so career status was not retained in the Graham reorganization. Graham's incoming staff were highly critical of some of the top officials in the DOA, including some who had decades of experience in state government. A major staff turnover occurred, especially among leading budgeters, and much of the institutional memory that was a basis for credibility and influence in the Askew administration was lost in the Graham transition. Accounting ceased to be a preferred background, and general administrative and policy related backgrounds became favored for newly hired staff.

The legislature agreed to the reorganization because the Governor already headed the budget process when it resided in the DOA. It became increasingly uneasy, however, over the quality and nature of the budget products it received from Graham's new budget office. Errors were made in documents submitted to the legislature and the legislative staff complained that they were not receiving agency work papers as they had in the past. From the standpoint of the legislature, the playing field had been shifted. The older career budgeters in the executive branch had departed and been replaced by younger political appointees who were well educated but who were new to the job; documents the

PLANNING
AND
BUDGETING

legislature had grown to depend upon either were not credible or were not readily available.

The response of the legislature was to reassert the "status quo ante," the basic structure of the process that had preceded the reorganization. This process was specified in Chapter 80-45, Laws of Florida 1980. The legislative view was that the Constitution bestows sole authority for deciding appropriations upon the legislature and that the budget authority of the governor is dependent upon legislative authorization via statute. The act itself specified, among other things, that the budget instructions issued by the governor to the agencies had to be written in consultation with the appropriations committees. Further, the act required each agency to submit full copies of its budget requests directly to the legislature at the same time they are transmitted to the governor.

Section 2 (1) of the act required that agency requests be ". . . based on the agency's independent judgment of its needs." With this provision, the legislature effectively declared its independence from the governor's proposed budget. In some states, especially those which do not have independent legislative staffs, appropriations committees do not receive agency requests and use the governor's proposals as their starting point for deliberations. In such states, an executive budget process can truly be said to exist. In Florida, however, legislative staff begin to develop independent House and Senate versions of a budget as soon as agencies submit their requests.

Florida did have an executive budget process briefly during the Askew administration, one in which the chief executive's budget proposals served as the point of departure for legislative deliberations; but the seeds for weakening the executive budget were sown at the same time the governor was given authority to propose a budget. This occurred when the legislature decided to develop an independent staff. The growth of the seeds was speeded when Governor Graham sought to increase gubernatorial leadership but caused a legislative reaction that has lead to further fragmentation of the budget process and weakening of the governor's influence over appropriations.

THE CONSENSUS ESTIMATING CONFERENCE: FRAGMENTATION OVERCOME

Florida has not succeeded in developing a system wherein agency budget requests closely reflect directions established in plans. Florida has, however, succeeded in developing some important foresight mechanisms to guide the budgeting process—its estimating conferences. The conferences evolved from efforts to overcome fragmentation in the forecasting of state revenues. As recently as the 1960's, separate revenue forecasts were made on occasion by the staff of the Budget Commission, the Comptroller, and the legislature. When the forecasts, or "estimates" as they are called in Florida, were developed separately, pressures occasionally arose to adopt the higher estimate in order to justify spending increases.

One of the most influential budget officials in Florida's history, Joe Cresse, lead an effort beginning in the late 1960's to bring the separate forecasters together on an informal basis to prepare revenue estimates. The guiding principle that evolved in these informal sessions was one of consensus; participants continued to deliberate until an estimate was produced that was acceptable to all participants. Cresse and others felt that budget deliberations functioned best when something of a dichotomy existed between technical specialists and elected officials. It became the task of the specialists to produce their one best estimate. This estimate established the revenue parameters within which elected officials could decide spending priorities. With a consensus process, elected officials did not have to spend time arguing the merits of competing forecasts and were not tempted to adopt higher estimates.

Consensus estimating processes evolved steadily for more than a decade on a largely informal basis. In 1985, the processes were defined in statute (Chap. 85-286, Laws of Florida 1985). That law specified seven different estimating conferences and the number of conferences has subsequently expanded. Each estimating conference follows the same overall model. A conference is composed of expert participants from the governor's Office of Planning and Budgeting, staff members from the relevant legislative committees and the legislature's Demographic and Economic Research Unit and, in some conferences, staff from a state agency. Independent forecasts may be prepared by any participants, and both the governor's staff and the legislature have extensive, independent, computer-based forecasting capabilities.

Each conference has designated "principal" participants. Regular meeting dates are set for each conference to facilitate the initial preparation of budget proposals and final enactments of legislation. Any principal, however, may convene a conference meeting when they believe that a re-estimate may be needed. In the meetings, deliberations proceed until a consensus has been reached that is satisfactory to all participants. Conference estimates are generally binding upon all participants and other official users of the estimates. Conference estimates are not legally binding upon the legislature itself but it has, in fact, always used the results of the consensus forecasts since 1970.

The following topics are forecasted by the estimating conferences; U.S. and Florida economies, Florida's population size and characteristics, general revenue receipts, the gross receipts tax used to fund public education capital outlay, lottery revenues, local ad valorem taxes, corrections case loads, school enrollments, Medicaid and AFDC (Aid to Families with Dependent Children) caseloads, child welfare indicators, transportation revenues, state employees' health insurance, and state self-insured casualty insurance. The Economic Estimating Conference prepares official forecasts of the national and state economies. The staffs of the governor and legislature have independent econometric models and the forecasts of national economic forecasting organizations are used as well. In a similar vein, the Demographic Estimating Conference develops forecasts of Florida's rapidly growing population for the ensuing decade. The consensus estimates of the economic and demographic conferences are required inputs to the other conferences.

The Revenue Estimating Conference prepares the official forecasts of state revenues, including those for the general revenue fund. The conference distinguishes between recurring revenues that are the basis for operating budget commitments and non-recurring revenues. The latter are available on a one-time only basis; officials often look to these to fund capital projects such as buildings. In years when non-recurring revenues are meager, competition for favorite capital projects is intensified. Forecasts are made for each major revenue source and, in the case of the vitally important general retail sales tax, detailed forecasts are made of receipts from different categories of consumer purchases. Forecasts are also made of Florida's property tax base because the state oversees the assessment and collection of local property taxes. These local taxes are important factors in determining state policy for the revenues that it shares with local governments. Other revenue forecasting conferences exist for specific revenue sources such as transportation and the lottery.

Another set of conferences, the budget caseload conferences, forecast the number of persons who will need to be served by some of the largest programs in the state budget. The Education Estimating Conference has been underway since 1978 and incorporates a series of participative conferences to forecast enrollments for public schools, community colleges and universities. The Criminal Justice Estimating Conference develops five year forecasts of the number of incarcerated persons. The rapid growth in incarcerations that began in the mid-1980's caused corrections policy to become a dominant issue in capital programming and budgeting. Consequently, the estimates of offender populations attract much attention.

The Social Services Estimating Conference was originally established to forecast future caseloads for the Medicaid and Aid to Families with Dependent Children programs. It since has been expanded to include estimates of subsidized day care needs and estimates of persons infected with AIDS. In 1990, a related conference called the Child Welfare Estimating Conference was established to estimate the number of children who are in need of special protection and support services.

From a theoretical standpoint, the methods and deliberative processes of the conferences are well founded. Detailed computer models have been developed that enable forecasters to study the effects of a wide variety of changes in conditions or policy alternatives. Of particular importance is the way the conference process stimulates questioning of assumptions. In a landmark study of forecast accuracy, William Ascher (1978) found that clinging to outdated assumptions was a greater cause of inaccuracy than were the particular methods employed. Florida's conferences take advantage of the independence of the separate branches of government. Legislative and executive staff specialists develop independent forecasts and do not hesitate to question the underlying assumptions that others have used to generate their projections. The future is always uncertain, and Florida's forecasters will inevitably make errors, but the interactive processes that have been created in Florida are well designed to minimize error insofar as is humanly possible.

Florida's forecasters need to take care to assure that elected officials themselves also raise questions about the underlying assumptions of conference forecasts. Surveys of forecasting activities in other states (Klay 1985), indicate that elected officials learn more about their economies when they actively interrogate the forecasters. The quality of presentations made by Florida's forecasters to the state's elected officials is quite good. The consensus process, however, is designed to encourage elected officials to accept conference outcomes without deliberation. A task for Florida's forecasters, therefore, is to assure that the consensus process does not inhibit learning among elected officials. Because it is a process run by specialists, elected officials in the legislature have shown some signs of distrust of the consensus process.

The impact of the conferences upon Florida's budgeting system is considerable. Conference estimates define the revenue parameters within which the budget debate takes place. Budget caseload forecasts define levels of need for some of the state's largest expenditure programs. The consensus procedures of the conferences take advantage of natural rivalries between the different branches and organizations involved to assure that lively questioning and deliberation takes place among conference participants. Rivalries are harnessed, not ignored or suppressed.

Agreement on conference outputs enables policy debate to focus upon matters of substance regarding such matters as tax rates or expenditure levels for specific client groups. The consensus estimating process is a notable success, therefore, in developing a planning base for budgeting. Its success is due substantially to the fact that it is a process in which fragmentation has been overcome.

BUDGET AUTOMATION: A MAJOR IMPACT BUT NOT ALWAYS AS EXPECTED

Florida's budgeting process has become automated to a considerable degree. Agencies directly submit budget requests on-line via computer to both the governor's staff and the legislature simultaneously. When staff members have completed their inputs, documents such as the Governor's proposed budget and the separate versions of the House and Senate appropriations bills can be created automatically. Many bookkeeping calculations and postings from one document to create another are made automatically. No longer do officials have to wait for days for typing pools to prepare the documents. This extensive automation is due largely to a managerial structure that is designed to overcome fragmentation.

The computerization of the legislative appropriations system has been underway since 1971 (Johnson 1976). It began as a word processing operation that was intended to produce hard copies of the changes appropriations bills undergo in session. The next step was to develop a program that would facilitate comparisons between different versions of the bills. In legislative deliberations, comparisons must be made between the versions of the House and Senate as well as between these and the Governor's proposals. Within a few years, the General Appropriations Act could be written and printed automatically once agreement was reached.

During the past two decades, extensive efforts also have been made in the executive branch to develop a computer system to facilitate policy development and budgeting activities. Automation of routine budget functions was essential to the Graham administration's efforts to link planning and budgeting. Askew's DOA had separate staffs for planning and budgeting. Graham's reform effort, however, focused upon hiring staff members who could do both—planning oriented policy development and budgeting. These staff members, called "governmental analysts," were the key to achieving integration between planning and budgeting. If their time was dominated by the time consuming routines of budgeting, they would be unable to engage in policy development activities. Consequently, Graham's staff placed much emphasis upon developing its computerized Planning and Budgeting System (PBS).

For a time, development of the governor's system was entirely separate from the legislature's automation effort. It soon became clear, however, that the two efforts would have to be joined. The staffs of the House, Senate, and Governor each need access to a large, common data base. It was decided that there should be a single organizational unit of systems analysts and computer programmers who could write and operate integrated programs on behalf of both branches of government. The systems unit which houses these specialists is located within the Office of Planning and Budgeting in the Executive Office of the Governor. The unit, however, is jointly directed by the director of the OPB and the staff directors of the House and Senate appropriations committees.

When an agency directly inputs its budget request via computer, the request data is instantly available to analysts in the House, Senate, and OPB. The data that each of the three groups of analysts input, however, is maintained strictly confidential from one another. Such security over their inputs enables the three organizations to develop versions of the budget that are substantially independent. Premature disclosure of intentions could have serious political implications. Developing the Legislative Appropriations System/Planning and Budgeting System, or LAS/PBS as it is commonly called, has required a major commitment of resources. In 1979 the systems unit was authorized 7 positions, but by 1987 it had grown to 27.5 positions and in 1996 it included 44.

The legislature and the OPB also make extensive use of personal computers and related office automation technology. This automation has caused noticeable shifts in staffing patterns. Between 1979 and 1996, the OPB added a total of 55 professional positions while holding its clerical positions steady at 22. The ratio of professional to support staff changed from 2.8:1 to 5.3:1 in that time. Typing and bookkeeping oriented activities have been affected most by automation. Accountants who were once needed to perform calculations and reconciliations between documents are no longer needed in the OPB and have been replaced by staff analysts with a variety of administrative and substantive degrees.

Unfortunately, the automation of many of the time consuming routines of budget preparation and execution has not lead to an increase in planning by OPB's analysts (Klay and Yu 1988). Two-thirds of the additional staff of the OPB have been hired to make the computer systems work; they do not do planning or budgeting themselves. More time has been made available to the government analysts to do other things, but OPB's experience suggests that automation of routine activities alone is not sufficient to get a budgeting office to engage more in planning. What has happened is that management has called upon analysts to perform additional records management and control oriented activities. OPB's management has not taken the additional steps necessary to assure that the freed time is spent in the learning activities that are essential to policy development.

Reducing the effects of fragmentation through the arrangement for joint control over systems development has enabled much automation of the routine functions of budgeting to occur. The joint directors of the automation effort, however, have not yet made a commitment to use new technologies to incorporate planning oriented information in the LAS/PBS. Some analysts, however, are doing planning oriented analysis on their own with their personal computers. Computer software now exists that can be used to do such things as monitor performance measures and forecast trends. It is likely that a planning capacity will be increasingly become a part of Florida's computerized budgeting system. Improvements in information technology make it easier to do so, and many of the staff and numerous elected officials share a continuing desire to link planning and budgeting. The governance structure do so is in place. The rate at which the current system will be changed to incorporate a planning orientation is largely a matter of willpower and leadership.

A NEW PLANNING FRAMEWORK EMERGES IN THE 1980s

Legislation enacted in 1984 established a new planning framework for the state. The Florida State and Regional Planning Act (Chap. 84-257, Laws of Florida 1984) required the development of a statewide comprehensive plan and a plan for each state agency. The Capital Facilities Planning and Budgeting Act (Chap. 84-321) required each state agency to develop both long and short term plans for facilities maintenance and construction and the Local Government Comprehensive Planning and Land Development Regulation Act of 1985 (see Chap. 163, Florida Statutes) required each city and county to submit comprehensive plans for the state's approval. The language of these acts clearly called for links to budgeting but the links often remain incomplete or absent.

Significant advances have occurred in the area of capital programming and budgeting. A major step was taken when the legislature decided to establish the State Infrastructure Trust Fund to set aside money for capital projects. Prior to this action, capital facilities were often treated as afterthoughts and infrastructure investments were more likely to be neglected. In addition, the political attractiveness of new projects caused maintenance to be neglected. It will always be tempting to neglect infrastructure in favor of operating expenditures when revenues are scarce, and to favor highly visible construction over the less visible maintenance. The state's capital planning and budgeting process, however, has tempered these temptations to some degree.

In 1985, Governor Graham proposed a new state plan to the legislature. It was adopted after considerable revision. In reviewing the proposed plan, the legislature revealed its institutional weaknesses in dealing with matters that require comprehensive thinking about the future of Florida. The substantive committees of the legislature are designed to deal with matters only within specific functional policy areas, yet the state plan required reviews from a holistic perspective. It became apparent that only the appropriations committees deal with all of state government. The legislature undertook the task of deliberating a comprehensive plan for the entire state in the midst of a two month session when it also had to deal with appropriations. The House appropriations committee dealt with the plan in a single marathon session in which scores of amendments were considered, and nearly all that were not blatantly flawed or onerous were adopted.

Nevertheless a state plan was enacted and stands as a unique chapter in Florida law (Chapter 187, Florida Statutes). The plan is not restricted to an advisory role, as was its predecessor, but it does not give agencies the authority to act in the absence of regular statutory authority. Within the context of such authority, the state plan is intended to guide the actions of state agencies, regional districts and councils, and local governments. A few limited amendments have been made to the plan, but Florida has not developed a means to regularly reconsider and revise the plan in light of changing conditions and events. The 1984 planning act requires the governor to "identify and monitor on a continuing basis statewide conditions and trends which impact the state (Sec. 186.006 (1), Florida Statutes)." The Graham administration began trend monitoring and environmental scanning, but these were not continued in the Martinez administration. The monitoring of trends and conditions, which is essential to keep the state plan up to date in rapidly changing times, continues to be neglected.

The 1984 planning act required agencies to develop plans for their overall guidance. Unfortunately, agency level planning quickly deteriorated into a routine staff function that had little meaning to the agencies or to others. Agency functional plans, as they were called for several

PLANNING
AND
BUDGETING

years, were not being used to prepare and review agency budget requests. During 1989 and 1990, the agency planning process was reviewed by the House Strategic Budget Planning Committee. It concluded that agency planning had largely been a failure and nearly recommended an end to the agency level plans. Central to the committee's conclusion that agency planning was not succeeding was the fact that neither the staffs nor elected officials of either the governor's office or legislature were using the plans to guide considerations about resource allocations.

An effort to rescue agency planning began in the last years of the Martinez administration and continued in the Chiles administration. The OPB sought the help of staff members from the agencies and of others who had seen the problems with agency planning. What resulted was a successful effort to change agency planning to strategic planning. Strategic planning is built upon efforts to examine an agency's strengths and weaknesses and to study its environments to detect threats and opportunities. It seeks to focus the attention of all participants upon those things that most need doing in order to bring about needed change. Given flexibility by the OPB to do strategic planning to fit their own needs, some agencies (though certainly not all) responded with sincere efforts to do better planning.

Florida's laws call for linkages between agency planning and budgeting. Agencies' budget requests are supposed to be coordinated with their approved strategic plans. But if budgeters fail to use the strategic plans to guide their own reviews of the agencies' budget requests, a clear signal is sent that planning makes little difference to resource allocations. This is the current state of affairs. Believing that planning makes little difference to resource allocation decisions, some agencies continue to neglect planning. Statutory requirements for linking planning to budgeting already exist. What has been absent is a leadership commitment to use the state plan and the agency strategic plans. Legislative and gubernatorial staffs are highly responsive to their elected leaders. If our elected leaders will prompt (by example more than by edict) their staffs to use the state plan and the agency strategic plans to guide their budget reviews, the staffs will do so. Until the time that elected officials pay attention to the state plan and to the agency strategic plans in their own budget reviews, planning is likely to be neglected.

It is relatively easy for elected officials to take the lead in planning ahead. For example, legislators from the substantive and appropriations committees could meet annually with agency heads to review trends and conditions and discuss policy directions prior to the finalization of an agency's proposed strategic plan. The same legislators could then instruct their staff to use the approved agency strategic plans to guide reviews of agencies' requests for resources to assure that needed changes can be accomplished.

HEADING TOWARD THE 21ST CENTURY: CONSTITUTIONAL CHANGE AND A NEW LOOK AT WHAT ACCOUNTABILITY IS

In November 1994, the citizens of Florida adopted a constitutional amendment to limit the rate of growth in state revenues. The amendment was put on the ballot by the legislature in order to head off other amendments that were being circulated by a citizens group, amendments that were amateurishly written and that would have had several distorting effects. The adopted amendment requires that the rate of overall growth in state revenues cannot exceed the rate of growth in personal income in Florida. State revenues are defined as taxes, licenses, fees and charges for services imposed by the legislature on individuals, businesses or agencies outside of state government. Such charges as university tuition are included in the revenue cap. The rate of growth in personal income is determined by the average annual rate of growth over the previous five years. Any receipts in excess of the cap are to first go to a budget stabilization fund and, when that is fully funded, returned to the people. Thanks partly to low inflation in the mid-1990's the growth in Florida's revenues were well within the rate of growth in personal income.

If inflation rises again to the levels present in the late 1970's, it will be impossible to maintain state spending at a level equal to rising costs. When revenues reach the cap, any efforts by agencies to increase their revenue receipts, such as encouraging more people to use state parks, would generate more revenues and require such revenues to be given back to the public if the stabilization fund is fully funded. Under such constraints, efforts of universities to raise tuition, for example, could cause mandatory reductions in other sources of state revenues. The resulting effects upon state government are difficult to predict. Some agencies of the state might seek relative autonomy, with the right to set their own fees unfettered by the legislature, in order to escape the constitutional cap. If high inflation returns, it is almost certain that attention will be shifted from planning for the future toward managing a self imposed revenue crisis.

Also in 1994, the legislature enacted one of the most promising reforms of any state in the 20th century, the Government Performance and Accountability Act. The provisions of the act bear an uncanny resemblance to the recommendations of three experienced federal executives in a 1977 article with a memorable title, "How You Always Wanted to Manage But Were Not Allowed to Try" (Boynton, et al. 1977). They began with the "radical" assumption that agency managers are rational and dedicated to the accomplishment of their agencies' missions. Much of budget reform has assumed the opposite and has sought to constrain managers with close control of budget inputs and accompanying regulations to constrain managers.

Boynton, Medina and Covello recommended that agencies start by isolating problem areas that impede their accomplishment of their mission and that appropriate measures be developed to monitor the success of agencies in achieving that mission. They proposed an external review organization to evaluate agency performance. Agencies that perform well would be rewarded with a variety of incentives including freedom from detailed line item controls via lump sum appropriations, flexibility in personnel and pay systems, reduced regulatory controls and lesser reporting requirements, and the ability to retain some savings. If agencies perform less well, they should receive fewer rewards including less discretion. Agencies that perform poorly, they said should be the objects of intense consultation and possibly even placed under a form of "receivership." Where feasible, programs might be moved from poorly performing agencies to well managed ones.

Under the Government Performance and Accountability Act, Florida's agencies were offered many of the incentives suggested by Boynton, Medina and Covello. It called for performance based program budgets that incorporate approved performance measures for specific programs of agencies. It established an office called the Office of Program Policy Analysis and Accountability (OPPAGA) to conduct evaluations of agency performance. Furthermore, it called for a relatively slow, phased implementation strategy for the new performance based program budgeting. All agencies were not scheduled to be reviewed and included before Fiscal Year 2002. Incentives in the law include additional flexibility to line managers in managing their budgets to include lump sum appropriations, flexibility in salary rate and position management, and retention of productivity induced savings which may be used for bonuses, training, or other productivity enhancements.

In the initial years only some very small programs in agencies such as the Departments of Revenue and Law Enforcement were reviewed under the performance oriented procedures. They had just been rewarded with greater flexibility at the time this chapter was written, so the effects of this important reform are not included herein. Some conjectures, however, are possible. Some of the key supporters of the 1994 legislation have left the legislature and continued support might not be forthcoming. It remains to be seen whether legislators will learn how to focus their attention on performance measures to assure accountability from executive agencies. They might simply revert to their older habits of trying to manage agencies themselves through detailed inputs oriented controls. For that matter, it remains to be seen whether the legislature's staff will work hard to make the new law succeed or whether they, too, will stick to old habits. From the agencies' perspective, the incentives are attractive but it also remains to be seen whether agencies will make good use of the greater flexibility. Mistakes in the use of such discretion, as might occur if something like favoritism in procurement contracts emerges, will almost surely lead to efforts by the legislature to reassert the old forms of control.

The Government Performance and Accountability Act is a reform that is rooted in the ethos of the new post-industrial, knowledge based economy. It is now recognized that the form of budgeting that emerged to control the large government bureaucracies of the industrial era is counterproductive. The old habit of controlling agencies through detailed budget controls and complex overlays of regulations prevents government programs from achieving their potential for performance. Modern corporations have tended to decentralize and to build information systems to provide effective feedback about performance to top leaders. In a sense, that is what the 1994 act seeks to do in Florida. It seeks to shift the attention and deliberations of elected policy makers from their historical preoccupation with detailed budget controls. It seeks to have them focus, instead, on the trends in actual performance of the states program managers. The new reform is workable from the standpoint of its theoretical soundness. Its success rests mostly upon the willingness of elected officials and their top staff members to make it work.

LEADERSHIP AND FRAGMENTATION

Florida's budget process has always been an incremental one, but its outcomes are not always so. Easterling (1987) did a statistical analysis of outputs for selected programs of the state, and found much evidence of incremental outcomes. He also found, however, evidence of fundamental shifts in some priorities over time. About 15 percent of the cases of appropriations increases and decreases which he studied were decidedly nonincremental. He concluded, "The incremental nature of the process, therefore, does not dictate incremental outcomes (44)."

Florida's budgeting processes do not prevent leaders from accomplishing change if the will exists to do so. Leadership in our state, however, is diffuse—divided, scattered, and often transient. Empirical research underscores the fact that the ability of the executive to "steer" legislative budget deliberations in Florida is quite limited (Stanford 1989). Professional staffs have enabled the legislature to become more independent of the governor, and the two houses more independent from one another. The move of the governor's planning and budget staff from the career service in the Department of Administration to an unprotected status in the governor's office undercut its credibility with the legislature and heightened fragmentation in Florida's planning and budgeting. Governor Askew's considerable influence in budgeting came partly from the fact that his proposals were assembled by career employees and presented to the legislature by budget officials whose careers had been spent in state government and who were trusted by legislators.

What is most needed to link planning to budgeting in Florida is for leaders and their staffs to regularly use the planning process to inform their budget deliberations. Achieving regular use of plans is a difficult task even in highly centralized budgeting situations. Achieving such use in a fragmented system is doubly difficult. Consideration should be given, therefore to ways in which the fragmentation of Florida's budgeting process might be remedied. Consideration might be given, for example, to returning to the 1921 practice of holding joint meetings of the House and Senate appropriations committees. Legislative leaders could also review agency strategic plans, in the context of relevant trends and conditions, with agency leaders prior to the finalization of those plans and well before the agencies prepare their legislative budget requests.

Previous efforts to link planning and budgeting in Florida have been directed toward the behaviors of staff members. These have not succeeded. Bridging the gap requires much more than procedural requirements—e.g. that budget requests be cross referenced to plans or vice versa. It is the behaviors of political leaders which ultimately determine whether planning and budgeting are to be linked. What Florida needs is planning that will affect the way political leaders think about policy priorities. When planning affects the way leaders think, budgeting will follow.

There are some indications that such planning is possible. When Governor Graham prepared his proposed state plan in 1985, for example, the governor's staff had an environmental scanning operation underway and an extensive review of trends and conditions was conducted. A succession of Speaker's Advisory Committees on the Future advised the House leadership on emerging trends and conditions throughout much of the 1980's. Agencies are now mandated to do strategic planning, a form of planning that tries to help leaders selectively focus their attention on matters of greatest priority.

If policymakers become preoccupied with the procedural linkages between planning and budgeting, it is unlikely that sufficient attention will be given to the things that are needed to help political leaders to think about the future of Florida. Attention should first be given to such activities as trend monitoring systems and environmental scanning projects that can better inform leaders. Enormous gaps exist in Florida's foresight capabilities. No estimating conferences exist, for example, to forecast the future status of Florida's land, water, or economic competitiveness. When such learning mechanisms are in place, more informed plans can be written. Such plans need not be lengthy, but they must be used.

REFERENCES

Ascher, William (1978). *Forecasting: An appraisal for policy-makers and planners.* Baltimore: Johns-Hopkins University Press.

Boynton, Robert Paul, William A. Medina and Leonard S. Covello (1977). How you always wanted to manage but were not allowed to try. *The Bureaucrat,* 6(1): 131–151.

Dennis, James Milton (1974). *State executive branch reorganization: The case of Florida.* Ph. D. dissertation, University of Florida.

Doh, J. C. (1971). *The planning-programming-budgeting system in three federal agencies.* New York: Praeger.

Easterling, Claude Nelson (1987). *Budgeting in Florida: An analysis of the process and its effects on outcomes.* Master's thesis, Florida State University.

Graham, D. Robert (1969). The old myth and new reality. *Florida Planning and Development,* Florida Atlantic University (March/April): 1–7.

Haldi Associates (1973). *A survey of budgetary reform in five states.* Lexington: Council of State Governments.

Harper, Edwin L., Fred A. Kramer, and Andrew M. Rouse (1969). Implementation and use of PPB in sixteen federal agencies. *Public Administration Review,* 29 (November/December): 623–632.

Johnson, Dozier (1976). The Florida legislative appropriations system. *State Government,* 49 (Winter): 43–46.

Klay, William Earle (1985). The organizational dimension of budgetary forecasting. *International Journal of Public Administration,* 7(3): 241–265.

Klay, William Earle and Pyeong Yu. (1988). Constitutional and administrative implications of computers. *Public Productivity Review,* 12 (Winter): 193–203.

Kyle, Joseph F. (1975). Florida legislative budget review process. In Alan P. Balutis and Daron K. Butler (Eds.) *Political Pursestrings: The Role of the Legislature in the Budgetary Process.* New York: John Wiley and Sons, 69–80.

Stanford, Karen A. (1989). *State legislative appropriations committees: An exploration of factors that may influence the orientation of their deliberations.* Ph.D. dissertation, Florida State University.

Stryker, Laurey T. (1979). Planning and budgeting reunited: A contract marriage. *Florida Environmental and Urban Issues,* 7 (October): 12–13, 24.

Swanson, Helge and Jim Tait (1978). Adoption of the Florida state comprehensive plan. *Florida Environmental and Urban Issues,* 6 (December): 13–16.

Tin, Eastern W. (1971). *The Florida PPB experience: A case study.* Tallahassee: Department of Urban and Regional Planning, Florida State University (in FSU Archives).

Turnbull, Augustus B. III (1974). The Florida budget—the old reality and new myth. *Governmental Research Bulletin,* Florida State University, 2 (June): 1–4.

Waterman, A. J., Jr. (1949). Florida's budget system. *Studies in Florida Administration.* Gainesville: University of Florida.

CHAPTER

8

Fiscal Policy and the State's Financial Condition

Chapter 9

Gloria Grizzle

Fiscal policy deals with raising revenues and spending. Buried in decisions about who shall pay to support state programs and at what level are matters of equity and the future that the state's citizens will inherit. Florida's current tax structure taxes the poor at a higher rate than the rich and produces a revenue stream that is more volatile than is the economy as a whole. While its population growth has been close to three times the national average during the past two decades, its per capita spending during this period has been erratic and it has fallen further behind in building the infrastructure that its fast-growing population needs. The state's financial condition is deteriorating. This deterioration is fueled by a fiscal policy that both incurs long-term liabilities that will burden the next generation and underinvests in services for its children in order to maintain a low (albeit unstable and regressive) tax burden for the present generation.

Understanding how Florida's fiscal policy developed and how its revenue structure shapes its ability to serve its citizens is the purpose of this chapter. A historical review of taxation will precede an evaluation of the current revenue structure. These revenues, when combined with expenditure pressures, permit analyzing the state's financial condition. Other states provide the primary referent group for a comparative analysis of Florida's financial condition, presented in the final section of this chapter.

Historical Development of the Revenue Structure

Florida has opted to tax consumption rather than personal income and wealth. The reluctance to tax wealth is embodied in a constitutional prohibition against a personal income tax. Consumption, severance, and "sin" taxes on tobacco and alcoholic beverages are politically feasible in

215

the state. Consumption and severance taxes permit exporting a part of the burden. Tourists contribute a part of the state's sales, tobacco, and beverage tax revenues. Those who import phosphate and other minerals mined from the state bear much of the burden of the severance tax.

Sixty years ago the motor fuel and motor vehicle license taxes provided 72 percent of the state's total tax revenues. In 1931–32, the state turned over real property as a tax source to its local governments and adopted several new taxes for itself, including the documentary stamp tax, a gross receipts tax on public service firms, a tax on intangible instead of real property, and a tax on pari-mutuel betting. Later that same decade the state began taxing alcoholic beverages. During the 1940's the tax base was broadened to include a cigarette tax, a severance tax, and a sales tax (Cain 1979).

While there have been several changes in the rate and base of some of these taxes, this tax structure, with one addition, has persisted for fifty years. The citizens approved a constitutional amendment in 1971, authorizing a tax on corporate incomes. During the 1980's the legislature enacted but later repealed two other new taxes. A worldwide unitary apportionment approach for determining the tax on corporate income was levied in 1983 and repealed in 1984. A sales tax on services was levied in 1987 and repealed in 1988 (Florida Tax Handbook 1990). Chapter 14, on tax policy, will explain why the 1971 change, but not the two later efforts, was successful.

Until two decades ago, this tax structure was successful in providing a revenue base that grew at a rate that kept up with population growth. Although there are some aberrations, most notably during the recession of the early 1960s, state revenues (from all sources, including service charges and intergovernmental as well as taxes) grew at an average compound rate of 4.48 percent. Had this exponential trend continued, per capita revenues adjusted for inflation would have been about $800 by 1995. Figure 9-1 shows the actual revenues compared to (a) the projected revenues extrapolated from the trend established between 1950 and 1973 and, (b) the actual growth in population.

Since 1973 the revenue pattern has been erratic. Per capita revenues in dollars adjusted for inflation show two steep declines, from $346 in 1973 to $298 in 1977 and from $327 in 1979 to $284 in 1983. Economic recessions coupled with high inflation resulted in a substantial shrinkage in the state's resources available to serve its citizens.

Since 1951, the proportion of total state revenues coming from the federal government has fluctuated between 16 and 24 percent. The federal share peaked at 23 percent in 1960, at 24 percent in 1967, and at 24 percent in 1978. Since 1978, there has been a gradual decrease, with

Figure 9-1

FLORIDA PER CAPITA STATE REVENUES
COMPARED TO EARLY TREND AND POPULATION

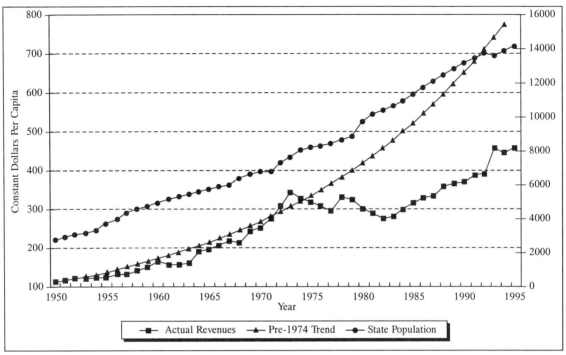

Data Sources: Dye, Thomas R. and Jesse B. Taintor. 1986. *States: The Fiscal Data Book.* Tallahassee: Policy Sciences Program, Florida State University.

Florida Tax Handbook. 1993. Tallahassee: Florida Legislature. Senate Finance, Taxation and Claims Committee. 1996. Tallahassee: Florida Legislature. Senate Ways and Means Committee.

State of Florida, *Florida Comprehensive Annual Financial Report.* Fiscal Year 1995. Tallahassee: Comptrollers Office.

U.S. Department of Commerce, Bureau of the Census. *State Government Finances,* GF84, No. 3 through GF92, No. 3 and 1992–94 data from Internet at http://www.census.gov/ftp/pub/govs.

federal aid appearing to stabilize in the 1980's at 19 percent (Figure 9-2). It is interesting to note that the primary fluctuation in year to year per capita revenues does not result from changes in federal aid but from the state's own volatile revenue base. Figure 9-2 shows that state revenues, net of federal aid, peak during periods of economic growth and bottom during economic recessions.

Some 61 percent of total revenues come from taxes. Federal aid is the second largest source, and fees and charges rank a distant third at 7 percent. The sales tax alone contributes 61 percent of all revenues raised by the state tax system (Florida Comprehensive Annual Financial Report 1995). Florida's sales tax is termed "narrow-based" because it exempts services and certain necessities, primarily food and drugs. The base that is exempted from the tax is the most stable in terms of declines

Figure 9-2
FLORIDA PER CAPITA REVENUES
IN CONSTANT DOLLARS (BASE = 1967)

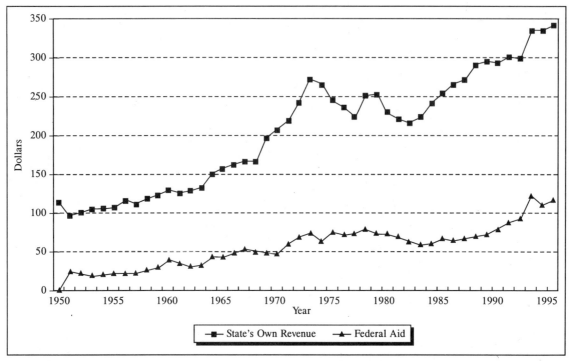

Data Sources: Dye, Thomas R. and Jesse B. Taintor. 1986. *States: The Fiscal Data Book*. Tallahassee: Policy Sciences Program, Florida State University.

Florida Tax Handbook. 1993. Tallahassee: Florida Legislature. Senate Finance, Taxation and Claims Committee. 1996. Tallahassee: Florida Legislature. Senate Ways and Means Committee.

State of Florida, *Florida Comprehensive Annual Financial Report.* Fiscal Year 1995. Tallahassee: Comptrollers Office.

U.S. Department of Commerce, Bureau of the Census. *State Government Finances,* GF84, No. 3 through GF92, No. 3 and 1992–94 data from Internet at http://www.census.gov/ftp/pub/govs.

during recessions. As a result, this narrow-based sales tax responds to economic changes by amplifying their effect on state spending rather than dampening the effect of economic down turns. Further, a narrow-based sales tax will grow slower than the growth in personal income, whereas a broad-based sales tax will grow at a rate that matches the growth in the state's economy (Hovey 1990; Zingale and Davies 1986). From 1970 to 1992, the percentage of personal income that Floridians spent on taxable sales fell from 76 to 55 percent (Florida's Tax Structure 1991).

Figure 9-3 shows the trend in tax burden. The revenues represent all sources, including state taxes, federal aid, and service charges. Revenues as a percentage of personal income of Floridians peaked in 1973, shortly after the state experienced the effects of adding the corporate income tax to it portfolio of tax sources. Since that time the burden

Figure 9-3
Florida Per Capita State Revenues
as a Percentage of Personal Income

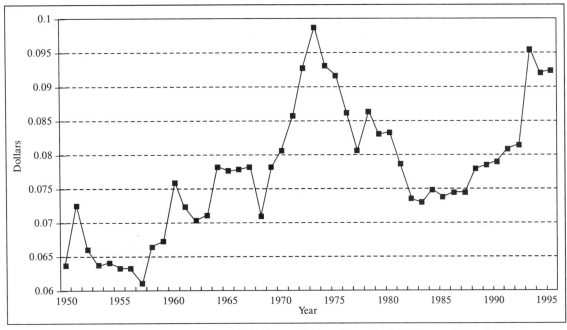

Data Sources: Dye, Thomas R. and Jesse B. Taintor. 1986. *States: The Fiscal Data Book.* Tallahassee: Policy Sciences Program, Florida State University.

Florida Tax Handbook. 1993. Tallahassee: Florida Legislature. Senate Finance, Taxation and Claims Committee. 1996. Tallahassee: Florida Legislature. Senate Ways and Means Committee.

State of Florida, *Florida Comprehensive Annual Financial Report.* Fiscal Year 1995. Tallahassee: Comptrollers Office.

U.S. Department of Commerce, Bureau of the Census. *State Government Finances,* GF84, No. 3 through GF92, No. 3 and 1992–94 data from Internet at http://www.census.gov/ftp/pub/govs.

has decreased from about 10 percent of personal income to about 9 percent. Thus, the revenue base is growing slower than personal income.

The volatility of the state's tax revenues creates an undesirable amplification of revenues and spending around this overall downward trend in tax burden. Given the state constitutional requirement of a balanced budget, the state's revenues set a ceiling on its capacity to provide services. Revenues fall off during recessions, but the demand for a number of services increases during recessions. Such services include unemployment compensation, increased caseloads for the criminal justice system, indigent care, and vocational education (Zingale and Davies 1986). Figure 9-4 and Table 9-1 show the year-to-year fluctuation in per capita spending, adjusted for inflation, in the five traditionally largest state functions.

A final unhappy twist is the difficulty of accurately forecasting revenues that are highly volatile relative to the economy. Table 9-2 shows

219

Figure 9-4

FLORIDA PER CAPITA STATE EXPENDITURES IN CONSTANT DOLLARS (BASE YEAR = 1967)

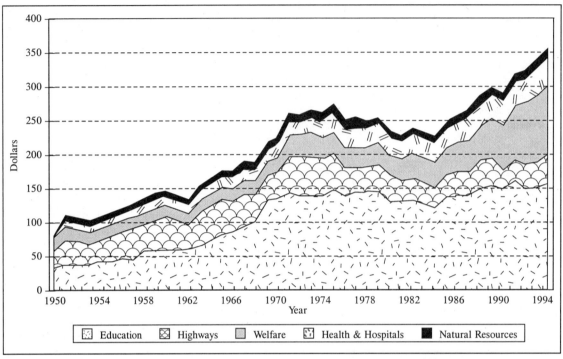

Data Sources: Dye, Thomas R. and Jesse B. Taintor. 1986. *States: The Fiscal Data Book*. Tallahassee: Policy Sciences Program, Florida State University.

Florida Tax Handbook. 1993. Tallahassee: Florida Legislature. Senate Finance, Taxation and Claims Committee. 1996. Tallahassee: Florida Legislature. Senate Ways and Means Committee.

State of Florida, *Florida Comprehensive Annual Financial Report*. Fiscal Year 1995. Tallahassee: Comptrollers Office.

U.S. Department of Commerce, Bureau of the Census. *State Government Finances,* GF84, No. 3 through GF92, No. 3 and 1992–94 data from Internet at http://www.census.gov/ftp/pub/govs.

that revenues tend to be overestimated during a recession. The resulting shortfall in revenues may require that in the middle of a fiscal year allotments to state programs be cut to withhold funds appropriated to agencies in order to avoid deficit spending. Such holdbacks occurred in the 1975, 1981, and 1989 recessions. In the 1989 recession, the state mandated seven rounds of budget cuts in order to cut spending back to the level required by the shortfall in revenues.

To recapitulate, per capita revenues and spending, measured in dollars adjusted for inflation, grew at a compound rate of over four percent during the 1950's and 1960's. After the addition of the corporate income tax in 1971 and the stagflation of the 1970's, the state's revenue and spending pattern has been erratic. The volatility of the revenue base and its inability to keep up with growth in population and personal

Table 9-1

PER CAPITA STATE SPENDING FOR MAJOR FUNCTIONS, 1950–1994, IN CONSTANT DOLLARS (BASE YEAR = 1967)

Year	Education	Highways	Welfare	Health and Hospitals	Natural Resources*
1950	$ 32	$23	$ 25	$ 0	$ 0
1951	37	34	23	8	8
1952	36	36	19	9	7
1953	37	30	19	8	8
1954	42	30	20	9	8
1955	42	36	19	10	9
1956	46	40	18	10	8
1957	44	46	17	10	9
1958	57	39	18	13	8
1959	57	47	18	14	8
1960	59	49	18	12	8
1961	58	43	17	13	7
1962	60	36	17	13	8
1963	64	49	19	13	8
1964	72	52	20	14	9
1965	81	52	20	14	9
1966	85	46	20	15	10
1967	93	47	21	16	12
1968	101	40	20	16	11
1969	132	36	21	16	12
1970	135	39	24	17	12
1971	143	54	32	19	13
1972	138	58	33	18	11
1973	138	57	37	21	11
1974	139	56	32	21	14
1975	146	55	32	25	17
1976	138	43	30	25	13
1977	143	38	29	27	17
1978	144	39	28	28	10
1979	145	40	32	28	10
1980	131	39	29	26	9
1981	130	32	32	25	8
1982	132	33	38	26	9
1983	128	30	36	28	11
1984	120	30	37	29	10
1985	136	33	42	26	11
1986	138	36	44	29	12
1987	139	36	46	33	13
1988	148	43	51	32	12
1989	153	41	58	35	11
1990	148	29	67	34	12
1991	160	31	80	34	12
1992	149	37	9	33	14
1993	151	38	99	39	16
1994	158	42	104	36	17

Includes agriculture.

Sources: Thomas R. Dye and Jesse B. Taintor (1986). *States: The Fiscal Data Book.* Tallahassee, FL: Policy Sciences Program, Florida State University.

U.S. Department of Commerce, Bureau of the Census. State Government Finances, GF84, No. 3, through GF92, No. 3, Table 11 and 1992–94 data from Internet at http://www.census.gov/ftp/pub/govs.

Table 9-2

ACCURACY OF FLORIDA'S CONSENSUS REVENUE ESTIMATES FOR GENERAL REVENUE COLLECTIONS

Year	Percent Error
1970	0.16
1971	12.72
1972	16.15
1973	8.18
1974	−10.02
1975	2.55
1976	0.76
1977	8.01
1978	12.91
1979	6.43
1980	4.95
1981	−6.49
1982	−4.41
1983	0.56
1984	−0.61
1985	2.27
1986	0.08
1987	0.70
1988	−0.97
1989	−4.39
1990	−8.21
1991	−5.55
1992	1.69
1993	0.55
1994	−1.60

Actual collection vs. original estimate used for General Appropriations Act.

Source: *Florida Monthly Economic Report,* 9:12 (August 3, 1989), 11:1 (July 1990), 12:1 (July 1991), 13:1 (July 1992), 14:1 (July 1993), 15:1 (July 1994), 16:2 (August 1995).

income have resulted in stop-and-go spending and have made it impossible to implement long-range planning to meet the citizens' needs for services the state provides.

EVALUATION OF THE CURRENT REVENUE STRUCTURE

Economists use several criteria to evaluate taxes. These criteria include equity, stability, efficiency, growth, and administrative cost (Mikesell 1991; Tuckman 1979).

Equity is determined by who pays and whether the distribution of the tax burden is fair. Generally, there are two bases for considering equity—the ability to pay and who benefits. Market equity prevails when those who benefit from a service pay for it. Florida's revenue structure does not attempt to achieve this form of equity. Service charges, licenses, and permits that directly link benefits and costs, all combined amount to only ten percent of total state revenues.

Equity as ability to pay in turn divides into two types—vertical equity and horizontal equity (See Table 9-3). Horizontal equity is achieved when people in equal income categories are taxed alike. Vertical equity is defined as falling into one of three categories—proportional, progressive, and regressive. It is this form of equity that receives the most attention when governmental revenue structures are evaluated. The type of vertical equity that one should favor depends upon how one wishes to redistribute wealth (Mikesell 1991, 222).

A tax structure is progressive when people with higher incomes pay a higher rate of tax and people with lower incomes pay a lower rate of tax. A tax structure is regressive when people with higher incomes pay a lower rate of tax and people with lower incomes pay a higher rate. A tax is said to be proportional when the same rate applies across all income levels. Judging which tax structure is fairest—the progressive, proportional, or regressive—is a matter of political ideology and values. The long-standing national political consensus that a progressive tax structure is fairest evaporated during the Reagan administration. Edwin Meese, Reagan's counselor in the White House, went so far as to call the progressive income tax "immoral" (Shuman 1988, 99).

No one disputes, however, that Florida's tax structure is in fact regressive. The Florida House Finance and Taxation Committee (1978) conducted an analysis of the vertical equity of Florida's taxes by tax source. It conducted a citizen survey in 1975 and combined that data with the United States Consumer Survey for 1972–73. Except for the tax on intangible wealth, such as stocks and bonds, the tax structure was regressive. The average tax burden (combining state and local taxes) as a percent of income was 11.37 for the lowest income group and 7.26 percent for the highest income group.

Table 9-3
DISTRIBUTION OF THE TAX BURDEN, BASED UPON DIFFERENT CONCEPTS OF EQUITY

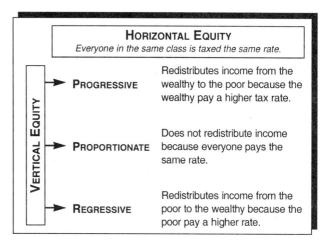

Florida has followed a policy of exempting some necessities from taxation, a practice that tends to reduce regressivity. Included in these exemptions are the first $25,000 of the assessed value of one's home exempted from the local property tax and the purchase of food and medicine exempted from the state sales tax. Even with these exemptions, however, these taxes are still regressive. The seven tax sources that yield the most state revenue are compared below in terms of their vertical equity. The incidence is listed for the lowest income group (incomes below $3000 in 1978 dollars) with the highest income group (incomes over $25,000).

TAX SOURCE	LOW INCOME	HIGH INCOME
Sales tax	2.66%	2.05%
Corporate income tax	.14	.12
Motor fuel tax	.75	.48
Documentary stamp tax	.37	.13
Alcoholic beverage/license	.42	.39
Gross receipts utility tax	.24	.07
Cigarette tax	.94	.21

A somewhat more recent study based upon 1980 United States Census and 1980–81 Consumer Expenditure Survey data shows a similar pattern for state and local taxes combined (Bell, Serow, and Shelley 1987). This study captures 85 percent of total state and local taxes in Florida. It shows that income, not age of taxpayer, is the more important issue in measuring the incidence of state and local taxes. While the tax burden for all households in Florida was 6.1 percent, the burden for non-elderly households ranged from 19.3 percent for households in the lowest income bracket to only 4.4 percent for those in the highest tax bracket. Figure 9-5 shows that this pattern of regressivity is similar for both elderly and nonelderly households.

A still more recent study, conducted by the Citizens for Tax Justice, estimates an even more regressive sales tax structure than the 1978 study. Listed below are estimated effective tax rates for a family of four at several income levels (Williams 1990b, 18):

Family Income	Percentage of Income Paid as Sales Tax
$ 12,000	5.6%
34,000	3.5
72,000	2.6
156,000	2.0

Figure 9-5
FLORIDA STATE AND LOCAL TAXES PAID
AS A PERCENTAGE OF HOUSEHOLD INCOME

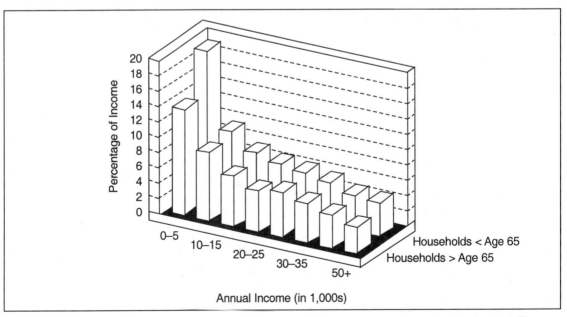

Data Source: Bell, William G., William J. Serow, and William J. Shelley, "Measuring the Economic Impact of a State's Tax Structure on an Elderly Population," *The Gerontologist,* 27:6 (1987), 804–808.

Stability of tax yield is another criterion by which tax structures are evaluated. The state's tax structure does not score well on this dimension because it is highly responsive to economic changes in a disruptive manner. During times of economic recession revenues decrease disproportionately, disrupting service delivery when citizens most need those services. Figure 9-2 shows the downturn in per capita state revenues after the 1974 and 1981 recessions.

Efficiency or neutrality means that a revenue structure does not affect economic decisions made by those paying the tax. Taxes may affect individuals' decisions about what to buy or how to allocate time between work and leisure. They may affect business decisions about where to locate or do business or what to produce or sell. Generally the aim is to achieve neutrality with the revenue structure, but sometimes taxes are justified on the basis of their ability to curtail some types of consumption, such as scarce resources and products whose consumption is believed harmful, like alcohol and tobacco. For example, Florida taxes the unlawful sale of drugs at 50% of the estimated retail price plus a 25% surcharge on the estimated retail price (Florida Tax Handbook 1990).

Growth in tax revenue in relation to economic growth is another criterion used to evaluate tax sources. The income elasticity of a tax refers to how much it changes in relation to a percentage change in income. Several national studies have estimated income elasticities for revenue sources important in Florida's revenue structure (Berne and Schramm 1986; Mikesell 1991). Table 9-4 shows that only the income tax revenue grows at a faster rate than income, and even then only slightly moreso. Gasoline, liquor, and tobacco tax revenues do not keep up with changes in income. Tobacco taxes are the most inelastic in the group, generating increased revenues of only 0.26 percent for each one percent increase in personal income.

As Florida exempts services from the sales tax, it excludes from its tax base the fastest growing sector in the economy. Coupled with its application of selective sales taxes to relatively inelastic goods and to its prohibition of a personal income tax, the state has developed a revenue structure that cannot keep pace with economic growth. During the decades of 1970-90, total personal

Table 9-4

THE ELASTICITY OF REVENUE SOURCES WITH RESPECT TO CHANGES IN INCOME

Revenue Source	Median Estimate	Range of Estimates	Number of Studies
General sales taxes	1.0	.8 – 1.3	10
Corporate income taxes	1.1	.7 – 1.4	9
Motor fuel taxes	.73	.4 – .8	10
Alcoholic beverage taxes	.5	.4 – .6	NA
Tobacco taxes	.26	.0 – .5	8

Sources: Berne, Robert and Richard Schramm, *The Financial Analysis of Governments.* Englewood Cliffs, N.J.: Prentice-Hall, 1986, p. 126. John L. Mikesell, *Fiscal Administration: Analysis and Applications for the Public Sector,* 3rd ed. Pacific Grove, CA: Brooks/Cole, 1991, p. 231.

income in Florida grew 657 percent, compared to a growth of only 544 percent in taxable sales (Williams 1990a, 16). Thus, the elasticity of sales tax revenue with respect to income during this period was only 83 percent, placing Florida's sales tax at the low end of the range reported in Table 9-4.

A final criterion is the cost of tax collection. The lottery is an example of a tax whose administrative cost is high relative to the amount of revenue it generates. Half of the collections are required by law to be distributed as prizes. Of the other half, at least 37.5 percent is distributed to education and 12.5 percent is placed in the administrative fund (Florida Tax Handbook 1990). The Department of the Lottery can therefore spend 25 percent of each dollar it collects for the state. This administrative cost is far higher than for other tax sources, such as the sales and corporate income taxes. Administrative cost estimates for sales tax collections in several states range from 0.37 percent to 0.81 percent; for the income tax, estimates range from 0.42 percent to 0.85 percent (Mikesell 1991, 329).

Table 9-5 summarizes by source the revenues that finance the state government. The lottery has become the fifth largest source of revenue, exceeded only by the sales tax, intergovernmental aid, the motor fuel tax, and the corporate income tax. Over half the revenues are earmarked for specific purposes and deposited into trust funds. The rest are deposited in the General Revenue Fund and are available to be appropriated as the legislature chooses.

We can use the per capita columns in this table to construct a profile of what the hypothetical "average" Floridian pays to support state government. Using per capita revenues to describe the average Floridian's burden ignores the fact that people's consumption patterns differ and that tourists pay some of these taxes. However, the profile that emerges is accurate enough to describe how money moves from the citizen to the state treasury.

First note that our citizen is not taxed on income, is barely taxed on property, and provides most support to the state treasury through consumption taxes. In a typical year this "average" Floridian will contribute $38 by buying alcoholic beverages, $32 by buying cigarettes, $68 by betting at the racetrack and playing the lottery, $157 by operating a motor vehicle, and $754 by purchasing items to which the general sales tax is applied. Although she pays no income tax directly to the state, she does pay a federal income tax, and the federal government in turn distributes $606 per capita in federal aid to the state. Finally, her tax on wealth consists of a tax on stocks and bonds amounting to $58 and a tax on the recording or transfer of real and intangible property amounting to $49.

In summary, Florida's revenue structure focuses on consumption, is regressive, volatile, and cannot keep pace with economic growth. Unless there is major reform in the tax base, the legislature will need to continually rachet up the rates simply to keep the revenue generated from declining as measured in constant per capita dollars. With the current revenue structure, revenue streams will also be unstable, making it difficult to sustain any long-range service delivery strategy, such as moving Florida into the top quartile of state governments in education spending.

THE STATE'S FINANCIAL CONDITION: A COMPARATIVE ANALYSIS

Financial condition may be defined as "the probability that a state will meet its financial obligations" (Berne and Schramm 1986, 70). Whether it can do so depends upon its available resources relative to spending pressures stemming from current demands or needs and from past commitments. To the extent that data availability allows, Florida's financial condition will be assessed relative to the other 49 states. This assessment will be organized within four major components—resource base, tax burden, financial management practices and needs.

Table 9-5

REVENUES THAT FINANCE STATE GOVERNMENT

	FISCAL YEAR 1994–1995 (THOUSANDS OF DOLLARS)			
	TOTAL		PER CAPITA	
REVENUE SOURCE	GENERAL REVENUE	TRUST	GENERAL REVENUE	TRUST
Auto Title & Lien	22,944	77,867	$ 1.62	$ 5.50
Beverage Licenses		17,332		1.22
Beverage Tax	522,267	17,398	36.91	1.23
Tobacco Tax	136,187	316,147	9.62	22.34
Citrus Tax		56,995		4.03
Corporate Fees	110,270	11,656	7.79	0.82
Corporate Income	1,063,455		75.16	
Documentary Stamp	359,288	335,955	25.39	23.74
Drivers Licenses	52,877	43,328	3.74	3.06
Health Care Assessment		239,651		16.94
Estate Tax	419,977		29.68	
Gross Receipts Utilities Tax		506,841		35.82
Hotels & Restaurants Licenses		17,447		1.23
Hunting and Fishing Licenses		29,968		2.12
Inspection Licenses		34,171		2.42
Insurance Licenses		26,470		1.87
Insurance Premium	234,407	52,068	16.57	3.68
Intangibles Tax	520,099	297,870	36.76	21.05
Interest	115,869	398,357	8.19	28.15
Intergovernmental Aid		8,569,016		605.61
Lottery		870,400		61.52
Motorboat Licenses		12,668		0.9
Motor & Special Fuel		1,417,884		100.21
Motor Vehicle Initial Reg. Fees	30,983	69,941	2.19	4.94
Motor Veh. & Mobile Home Lic.	550	498,262	0.04	35.21
Oil & Gas Production	7,196	1,148	0.51	0.08
Pari-mutuel Taxes	52,581	41,939	3.72	2.96
Prof. & Occup. Licenses & Fees		76,203		5.39
Pollutant & Environmental Taxes		246,507		17.42
Refunds	−184.900		−13.07	
Sales & Use Taxes	9,737,303	929,833	688.18	65.72
Securities Fees	8,909		0.63	
Service Charges	329,970	−329,970	23.32	−23.32
Solid Minerals Severance	16,228	35,019	1.15	2.47
Unemployment Compensation		714,764		50.52
Worker Comp. Tax		228,879		16.18
Miscellaneous Sources		2,500,363		176.71
Total Direct Revenue	**$13,806,000**	**$18,284,600**	**$975.74**	**$1,292.26**

Source: Senate Committee on Ways and Means, 1996.

RESOURCE BASE

Florida's capacity to generate taxes is somewhat above average for the states as a whole. Compared in terms of per capita income, the most widely used measure of fiscal capacity, Florida ranked twentieth in 1992 (Table 9-6).

The United States Advisory Commission on Intergovernmental Relations developed a tax capacity index in 1962. It estimates how much revenue each state, including its local governments, would raise "in a given year if it levied the national average tax rate for each of 26 commonly used state and local taxes" (Kincaid 1989, 10). During the period from 1967 to 1988, Florida's tax capacity ranged from one to five percent above the national average (ACIR 1985, 55; ACIR 1983, 29; Cohen 1989, 17; Cohen 1990, 17).

Florida experienced a high rate of growth in the number of jobs during the past decade. Jobs grew at a rate of 32.5% from 1980 to 1986 compared to the states' average of only 12.8%. Services, wholesale and retail trade, government, and finance, insurance and real estate employment grew faster than the other sectors between 1982 and 1994. Government employment grew slightly less than the rate of non-agricultural

Table 9-6
FLORIDA'S FINANCIAL CONDITION
RESOURCE BASE INDICATORS

INDICATOR	FLORIDA DATA	FLORIDA'S RANK*	STATES' AVERAGE	DATA YEAR
ACIR Tax Capacity Index[1]	104	16	100	1988
ACIR Revenue Capacity Index[1]	103	16	100	1988
Per Capita Income[7]	$20,133	20		1992
Sales Tax as a % of General Fund Revenue	69.1%	1	29.2%	1990
Federal Spending per Capita on Grants to State and Local Governments[9]		46		
Federal Expenditure per Tax Ratio[4]	$1.05	25	$1.00	1995
% of Population Over Age 25 with Education Level of 4 Years College or More[5]	14.7%	26	16.3%	1985
Unemployment Rate[3]	3.5%	42	6.7%	1986
Unemployment Rate[2]	5.6%	18	5.1%	1989
Per Capita Income Growth[6]	30.0%	16	35.0%	1980–84
Job Growth[3]	32.5%	2	12.8%	1980–86
Job Growth[2]	3.72%	29	4.1%	1988–90
Population Growth[3]	19.8%	4	6.4%	1980–86
Total Research and Development in Universities (dollars per capita)[5]	$16.0	44	$31.3	1986
Quality of Science and Engineering Faculty[5]	49.6	19	52.9	1986
Total Equity Capital in Commercial Banks (000's per capita)[5]	428.8	33	606.4	1986
Economic Momentum Index[8]		12		1995

*Rankings are from highest (= 1) to lowest (= 50).

Sources:
1. Carol E. Cohen, "State Fiscal Capacity and Effort: The 1988 Representative Tax System Estimates," *Intergovernmental Perspective,* 16:4 (Fall 1990), p. 18.
2. "The Fifty States," *City and State,* 7:9 (April 1990), pp. 11–40.
3. "The Fifty States," *City and State,* 4:4 (April 1987), pp. 14–47.
4. "Federal Tax Burdens Continue Steady Rise, But Many States Get Back More Than They Give," *Tax Features,* 40:6 (July 1996), 1–2, 6.
5. AmeriTrust Corporation and SRI International, *Indicators of Economic Capacity,* 1986, pp. 32–37.
6. "The Fifty States," *City and State,* 3:5 (May 1986), pp. 14–42.
7. "The Fifty States," *City and State,* 9:8 (April 1992), pp. 10–18.
8. "Hal Hovey's State Scoreboard," *Governing,* 10:2 (Nov. 1996), p. 53.
9. "Hal Hovey's State Scoreboard," *Governing,* 9:12 (Sept. 1996), p. 59.

employment as a whole for that same period. Mining employment actually declined by 27 percent. Three other sectors, manufacturing, construction, and transportation and public utilities, grew at a somewhat slower rate than did government employment (Table 9-7).

With jobs growing at a fast rate and government employment slightly declining as a proportion of total employment, one would expect Florida's long-term prospects for a healthy economic base to be rosy. The Economic Momentum Index ranks Florida twelfth in 1996 based upon changes in personal income, employment, and population. Other statistics, however, suggest reason for concern. Per capita income growth (30 percent) is slightly below the states' average (35 percent) for 1980–84 (Table 9-6). While Florida's unemployment rate was below average (3.5 percent) in 1986 compared to the states' average (6.7 percent), by 1989 unemployment had risen to 5.6 percent, changing its rank in unemployment from forty second to eighteenth. Similarly, its job growth rate, which was second fastest in the nation early in the past decade, slowed to 3.72 percent for 1988–90, placing it twenty ninth among the states, which averaged 4.1 percent. Other causes for concern include Florida's low investment in total research and development in universities and its below-average equity capital in commercial banks. Florida's high technology industry has the disadvantage of not being built upon a research base. Low per capita equity capital means that financial institutions have limited funds to loan businesses, making growth in the state's economy harder (AmeriTrust 1986, 10).

Florida's use of its resource base for supporting state government is not broad based. As mentioned before, it concentrates upon the sales tax rather than taxing income and property. As a result 69.1 percent of its General Fund revenues in 1990 came from the sales tax, the highest percentage in the nation.

Table 9-7

CHANGES IN FLORIDA NONAGRICULTURAL EMPLOYMENT BY INDUSTRY 1982 AND 1994

Industry	1982*	1994*	% Change	% of Total 1994	% of Total 1982
Mining	9.6	7.0	-27.08	0.12	0.26
Construction	256.6	297.5	15.94	5.13	6.82
Manufacturing	456.7	483.9	5.96	8.35	12.14
Transportation and Public Utilities	229.9	295.2	28.40	5.09	6.11
Wholesale and Retail Trade	995	1506.4	51.40	25.99	26.45
Finance, Insurance and Real Estate	276.6	376.0	35.94	6.49	7.35
Services	905	1923.9	112.59	33.19	24.06
Government	632.5	906.6	43.34	15.64	16.81
Total	3761.9	5796.5	54.08	100.00	100.00

*In 100,000s

Source: *Florida Comprehensive Annual Financial Report,* Fiscal Year 1995. Tallahassee, FL: Comptrollers Office, State of Florida.

Florida has tried to develop economically on the basis of cheap labor, physical resources, and low taxes. It has not made the investment necessary to attract businesses that produce high value-added goods and services. We have been warned that we are now moving into a global economy and cannot successfully compete globally on the basis of cheap resources (Zwick 1989).

TAX BURDEN

By any measure, Florida falls below the states' average in terms of total state and local tax burden. ACIR has developed two measures of fiscal effort—the tax effort index and the revenue effort index. Tax effort is calculated by "dividing each state's total tax collections by its estimated tax-capacity, and then multiplying by 100" (Kincaid 1989, 11). The revenue effort index captures the states' effort in collecting non-tax revenues (such as service charges) in addition to taxes. Florida in 1986 ranked forty seventh in revenue effort (84 on an index averaged at 100) and forty eighth on tax effort (77 on an index averaged at 100).

Table 9-8 furnishes several other indicators of relative tax burden. Florida ranks forty second in the ratio of 1993 total state and local taxes as a percentage of personal income. Florida ranks thirty second in the ratio of state government employees to total population. Its total government employment as a proportion of total nonagricultural employment decreased from 17.8 percent in 1979 to 15.6 percent in 1994. Because revenues are relatively low, spending is as well. Florida in 1989 ranked thirty ninth in terms of per capita state expenditures. It ranked forty fourth in per capita state and local spending on education in 1986.

Table 9-8
FLORIDA'S FINANCIAL CONDITION
TAX BURDEN INDICATORS

INDICATOR	FLORIDA DATA	FLORIDA'S RANK*	STATES' AVERAGE	DATA YEAR
ACIR Revenue Effort Index[1]	84	47	100	1988
ACIR Tax Effort Index[1]	74	48	100	1988
State Employees per 1,000 Population[2]	9.2	32	11.2	1990
Per Capita State Expenditures[2]	$1427	39	$1782	1989
State and Local Educational Expenditure Per Capita[3]	$527	44	$644	1986
Government Employment as a % of Total	17.8%			1979
Nonagricultural Employment[4]	15.6%			1994
State and Local Taxes as a % of Personal Income[5]		42		1993

Rankings are from highest (= 1) to lowest (= 50).

Sources:
1. Carol E. Cohen, "State Fiscal Capacity and Effort: The 1988 Representative Tax System Estimates," *Intergovernmental Perspective,* 16:4 (Fall 1990), p. 18.
2. "The Fifty States," *City and State,* 7:9 (April 1990), pp. 11–40.
3. AmeriTrust Corporation and SRI International, *Indicators of Economic Capacity,* 1986, pp. 32–37.
4. State of Florida, *Comprehensive Annual Financial Report,* Fiscal Year 1992, p. 139.
5. "Hal Hovey's State Scoreboard," *Governing,* 9:10 (July 1996), p. 53.

FINANCIAL MANAGEMENT PRACTICES

Major past commitments that affect Florida's

ability to meet its financial obligations in the future are pensions for its employees and bonded debt. Of the two commitments, pension liability is the larger. Each year the legislature appropriates funds to be set aside and paid out as benefits to retired state workers. Currently the pension trust fund receives, through appropriations and investment earnings, $3.70 in revenue for each dollar it spends. It is in no immediate danger of not mailing out retirement checks, but Florida has a large unfunded pension liability of $9.8 billion. This unfunded liability amounts to 21 percent of the total pension liability, or 63 percent of a year's payroll, or $687 for each person in the state (Table 9-9). It reflects the present value of estimated pension benefits that will be paid in future years for employee service to date (Florida Comprehensive Annual Report 1995).

The estimate of funds needed for pension benefits to be paid in the future is based upon assumptions about such factors as the rate at which people retire, how long they live after retiring, employee turnover, salary increases, growth in the workforce, and earnings from investing pension funds. One's confidence in the estimate is based upon an examination of the reasonableness of the assumptions made (Berne and Schram 1986, 298). Florida's estimate is based upon the assumption that investment earnings will average 8 percent, general wage increases will average 5.5 percent, salary increases due to promotion and longevity will average 2.0 percent, growth in workforce covered by the pension plan will average 1.5 percent, and annual benefit increases after retirement will average 3.0 percent a year (Florida Comprehensive Annual

Table 9-9

FLORIDA'S FINANCIAL CONDITION
FINANCIAL MANAGEMENT PRACTICES INDICATORS

INDICATOR	FLORIDA DATA	FLORIDA'S RANK*	STATES' AVERAGE	DATA YEAR
Bond Rating (Standard and Poor's)[1]	AA		AA	1993
Outstanding General Obligation Debt Per Capita[1]	$283	26	$433	1990
Long-term Debt as a % of General Fund Revenue[1]	30%	22	36%	1990
Per Capita Long-term Debt as a % of Per Capita Income[1]	2.0%	27	3.4%	1990
Unfunded Pension Liability (billions)[4]	$9.8			1995
% of Pension Liability Unfunded[4]	21%			1995
Unfunded Pension Liability Per Capita[4]	$687			1995
Ratio of Annual Pension Fund Receipts to Disbursements[4]	3.70:1			1995
Unfunded Pension Liability as a % of Payroll[4]	63%			1995
General Fund Revenue as a % of Total Revenue[5]	55%			1992
% of Tax Revenues Earmarked[3]	26%	16	23%	1988
General Fund Expenditures as a % of Revenues[1]	100.14%	35	102.05%	1990

*Rankings are from highest (= 1) to lowest (= 50).

Sources:

1. "The Fifty States," *City and State,* 7:9 (April 1990), pp. 11–40.
2. State of Florida, *Comprehensive Annual Financial Report,* Fiscal Year 1989, p. 131.
3. Ronald K. Snell, "Earmarking State Tax Revenues," Intergovernmental Perspective, 16:4 (Fall, 1990), p. 13.
4. State of Florida, *Comprehensive Annual Financial Report,* Fiscal Year 1995, pp. 168–9.
5. "The Fifty States," *City and State,* 10:9 (May 1993), pp. 8–18.

Financial Report 1990, 26). Overestimates in the first four percentages will produce annual contributions that are insufficient to cover future pension benefits.

Contribution rates are currently adjusted to eliminate the unfunded liabilities over a thirty-year period, and the funding ratio has improved from 40 percent in 1972 to 79 percent in 1995. This funding ratio is slightly below the 85 percent funding ratio for that half of the states that have unfunded liabilities in their public pension funds (McKinnon 1996). However, Florida's pension fund has the second largest deficit of assets compared to accumulated benefit obligations of all the state pension funds. Based upon an estimate by Wilshire Associates, its $3.5 billion deficit is second only to Massachusetts' $4.9 billion deficit (Zolkos 1990, 2).

On several indicators, Florida measures somewhat below average in terms of the size of bonded debt. Its outstanding general obligation bonded debt of $283 per capita places it twenty sixth among the states. It ranks twenty second in terms of long-term debt as a percentage of general fund revenue and twenty seventh in terms of per capita long-term debt as a percentage of per capita income (Table 9-9). The state's bond ratings, an indicator of its credit worthiness, are currently investment grade. Standard and Poor's bond rating for Florida is AA and Moody's is Aa. Fifteen states have the higher AAA or AA+ ratings and eleven have AA– or lower ratings. Half the states have the same AA rating as Florida.

Two thirds of the general long-term debt was used to finance education. About 24 percent was used for conservation and pollution control, and the remainder was used to finance roads and bridges. Revenue bonds outstanding make up slightly more than half the total bonds outstanding. Almost all these revenue bonds are for either toll roads or conservation and coastal preservation (Florida Comprehensive Annual Financial Report 1995).

Several other financial management practices merit at least a brief mention. First, some revenues are deposited in the general revenue fund and others in funds for which the revenues are earmarked for specific purposes. In terms of the proportion of funds from all sources available for general purposes, Florida ranks thirtieth, slightly below the states' average of 62 percent. In terms of the percentage of tax revenues earmarked for specific purposes, Florida ranks sixteenth, slightly above the states' average of 23 percent (Table 9-9). Earmarking serves to limit the legislature's ability to appropriate funds to those programs that best address current needs (Snell 1990). Particular programs, however, seek to have funds earmarked for them in order to remove themselves from the annual competition for general revenue funds (Rubin 1990). During the past 35 years, Florida has, as have states in general, significantly reduced the proportion of taxes that are earmarked—from 40 percent to 26 percent (Snell 1990, 13).

Second, Florida is one of twenty nine states reporting the use of a Rainy Day reserve fund. By law, this fund can amount to no more than ten percent of total general revenue. For the past ten years, the actual percentage has ranged between 2.7 and 1.0 percent. For fiscal year 1989-90, the first year of the last recession, the rainy day fund amounted to 1.4 percent of general revenue appropriations or, in case of a revenue shortfall, enough to run the general revenue budget for five days ("Florida's Current" 1989). Bond rating firms view this reserve as inadequate. Coupled with inadequate infrastructure funding, these inadequate reserves cause the bond firms to rate Florida AA. A higher rating would permit the state to issue bonds at a lower interest rate. It is estimated that the lower bond rating will cost Florida $100 million in additional interest payments during the 1990s (Williams 1990a, 14).

In some other respects, the state's financial management practices are noteworthy. In accordance with generally accepted accounting principles, Florida uses the modified accrual basis of accounting for revenues and expenditures. All state agencies use the State Automated Management Accounting Subsystem of the Florida Fiscal Accounting Management Information System. Florida published financial statements for the first time in 1984, but it was the first state to conform to the guidelines for the comprehensive annual financial report (McCall 1987).

NEEDS

Spending pressure resulting from current needs is the last component required to assess the state's financial condition. Describing need is more difficult than describing the state's resource base, tax burden, and financial management practices because (1) people disagree on what services government ought to provide and (2) not much comparative data documenting needs are available. Figure 9-6 shows the share of total state spending allocated to the state's five major functions over the past forty years.

In the decade of the eighties, the state's budget almost tripled. When the growth in the budget is adjusted for inflation, however, this increase falls to 82 percent. Most of the growth in the real output of the state is related to population increases, especially among children and the elderly. When the growth in the budget is adjusted for population growth, the ten-year growth falls to 35 percent. When adjusted for the growth in personal income, the residual increase in the budget over ten years is 12 percent (Bradley 1991). A part of this residual increase is due to rising expectations for service, particularly in the area of health care, where technological advances have raised the cost of care dramatically.

Figure 9-6
FLORIDA STATE EXPENDITURES BY FUNCTION
AS A PROPORTION OF TOTAL EXPENDITURES

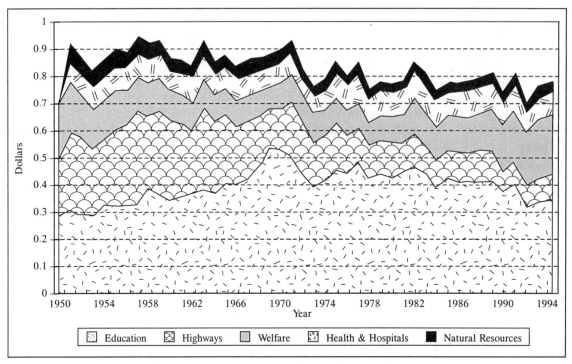

Data Sources: Dye, Thomas R. and Jesse B. Taintor. 1986. *States: The Fiscal Data Book.* Tallahassee: Policy Sciences Program, Florida State University.

Florida Tax Handbook. 1993. Tallahassee: Florida Legislature. Senate Finance, Taxation and Claims Committee. 1996. Tallahassee: Florida Legislature. Senate Ways and Means Committee.

State of Florida, *Florida Comprehensive Annual Financial Report.* Fiscal Year 1995. Tallahassee: Comptrollers Office.

U.S. Department of Commerce, Bureau of the Census. *State Government Finances,* GF84, No. 3 through GF92, No. 3 and 1992–94 data from Internet at http://www.census.gov/ftp/pub/govs.

One should also keep in mind those factors that may make services on a per capita basis more expensive in Florida than for the average state. These include a national policy to admit refugees but to leave serving them to the states; the services required for tourists, even though they are only temporary residents and therefore excluded from per capita calculations; a diversity of languages and cultures that complicate service delivery; and a population that is moving into areas that are more environmentally sensitive.

As Figure 9-4 suggests, the state has expanded services and improved their quality in some areas during the past 40 years. This expansion is typical of states as a whole and resulted from three factors—the states' policy choices, federal court orders, and federal standards (Hovey 1990). Florida's funding formula to equalize public

234

school spending is an example of a policy that the state's leadership chose to fund. Building more prisons to relieve overcrowding is an example of spending mandated by court order. Water supply and sewage treatment facilities, Medicare and Social Security taxes assessed on state payrolls are examples of spending required by federal standards.

The Advisory Commission on Intergovernmental Relations has developed an index of representative expenditures for the 50 states. This index estimates each state's workload by functional area and the costs to do the work (e.g., salaries, prices of commodities purchased). Workload is broken down into seven functional areas, such as highways, health and hospitals, police and corrections. For example, the workload for police and corrections is estimated as "the sum of the equally weighted percentage distributions of: (1) the population age 18–24, (2) the number of murders committed, and (3) the total population" (Rafuse 1990, 26). Each state's representative expenditures are then compared to what each state actually spends to estimate the extent to which spending is adequate to meet needs. Based upon this index, Florida ranked 29th in 1986-87, falling below the average of the fifty states in addressing needs for services (Table 9-10).

At current levels of service, most growth in spending during the next ten years will occur in services for school children and the elderly. The number of school-aged children (ages 5–19) in this decade is expected to grow by 24.8 percent. The number of elderly aged 70 and over is expected to grow by 48.4 percent (Zingale 1990, 1).

Table 9-10

FLORIDA'S FINANCIAL CONDITION
EXPENDITURE NEEDS INDICATORS

INDICATOR	FLORIDA DATA	FLORIDA'S RANK*	STATES' AVERAGE	DATA YEAR
ACIR Representative Expenditures Index[1]	95	29	100	1986–87
% of Population Aged 65 and Over[2]	18%	1	11%	1990
% of Population Aged Under 15[2]	19%	50	22%	1990
Median Age[2]	37.4			1990
% of Population over 25 with Education Level of Grade 8 or Less[3]	16.5%	22	18.4%	1986
Highway System Infrastructure Needs[4]	$16.2 billion			1987
Wastewater Treatment Infrastructure Needs[4]	$5.3 billion			1987
Stormwater Treatment Infrastructure Needs[4]	$17 billion			1987
Above Infrastructure Needs Per Capita[4]	$3,298			1987
% of State's Children Living in Poverty[4]	30%			1987
% of Children Without Safe Child Care[4]	50%			1987
% of Children without Preventive Health Care[4]	62%			1987
% of School-age Mothers in School[4]	10%			1987

*Rankings are from highest (= 1) to lowest (= 50).

Sources:
1. Robert W. Rafuse, Jr., "A Walk on the Expenditure Side: 'Needs' and Fiscal Capacity," *Intergovernmental Perspective*, 16:4 (Fall 1990), p. 27.
2. Stanley K. Smith, "Population Growth and Demographic Change in Florida." Paper presented to the Government Services Committee of the Taxation and Budget Reform Commission, Tallahassee, Florida, November 1990, p. 10.
3. AmeriTrust Corporation and SRI International, *Indicators of Economic Capacity*, pp. 32–37.
4. Speaker's Advisory Committee on the Future, Florida House of Representatives, The Sunrise Report, 1987.

However, the ratio of dependent-aged persons compared to working-aged persons (ages 15–64) will remain at about 37 to 63 (Smith 1990, 11).

About 67 percent of the general revenue budget funds programs that primarily serve dependent-aged persons. These are the public schools, colleges, and universities, Medicaid, and Aid to Families with Dependent Children programs. Adding the criminal justice system budget (including prisons) to these five programs accounts for about 80 percent of the general revenue budget (Zingale 1990, 1). In ten years, the workload growth in these programs alone will cause spending to exceed revenues by 17–36 percent ("Selected Highlights" 1991). Thus, there is a structural deficit built into Florida's revenue-expenditure equation.

Low tax burden in Florida has translated into a growing backlog of unmet needs. The state's tradition of underinvestment has created sizeable infrastructure needs that far outstrip its current revenues. As an example, an advisory group to the speaker of the House of Representatives in 1987 reported $16.2 billion was needed for expressway and arterial construction for additional highway system capacity, $5.3 billion for wastewater treatment, and $17 billion for stormwater treatment (Florida Legislature 1987, 38–39). As an example of needs unmet by social programs, the same report noted that 30 percent of the state's children live in poverty, 50 percent have no safe child care, 62 percent receive no preventive health care, and 90 percent of school-aged mothers are not in school (Florida Legislature 1987, 12). Further, the segments of the population that need the most services—children and the elderly—have been growing at a faster rate than the population as a whole.

Years ago Florida formed a fiscal policy to entice immigration. It was based on the promise of no income tax and low living costs (Koenig 1987). Now Florida has a population of over 14 million and its citizens face a deteriorating quality of life if these fiscal policies of low revenues and low spending continue. Since 1980 Florida "has averaged 893 new residents a day. . . . These newcomers bring dreams for a better future. What they do not bring are roads, bridges, schools, prisons, drinking water and all the vast and varied human services needed to realize their dreams and ours for a better Florida" (Gardner 1987, 2). Representative Gardner continues: "To provide for 893 new residents a day, the state should add each day: two miles of highway; one jail cell; two state prison beds; two police officers; two classrooms; two teachers; the resources to handle 38 more recipients of Medicaid, 79 more people in need of alcohol and drug abuse treatment, 13 more people who are mentally ill and 19 more applicants to Aid to Families with Dependent Children; over 111,000 more gallons of water and the ability to treat over 94,000 more gallons of wastewater, daily. And we are not even coming close" (1987, 2).

Charles J. Zwick, chief executive officer of Southeast Bank, echoes this theme: "Simply put, Florida urgently needs investments in its infrastructure to compete in the global world. . . . We have yet to accept that the way we finance state and local government in Florida is definitely broken and needs fixing" (Zwick 1989). He lays out four requirements for successful global competition:

1. A capable, motivated workforce produced by a top-notch educational system.
2. An adequate infrastructure (highways, hospitals, libraries, parks, utilities, and sewers).
3. An adequate environment (low crime; clean, well-managed environment; rich cultural climate).
4. Fiscal stability.

In summary, Florida's financial condition is deteriorating. Its tax structure does not provide the growth in revenues needed to match the growth in services required by its fast-growing population. Its failure to invest adequately in its human resources (through such programs as health and education for children) and in physical infrastructure will make it less competitive in the emerging global economy. This competitive disadvantage will in turn weaken the resource base and, thereby, the state's capacity to raise revenues in the future. Indeed, during the past decade, the state already evidences a deterioration of job growth and unemployment rates relative to the other American states. As if to underscore the state's condition, the cover page of the October 11, 1993, issue of *U.S. News and World Report* carried this headline: "Florida. Paradise Lost: The Sharp Decline of the Sunshine State."

This generation's low tax burden will translate into the next generation's lower quality of life. It is time for Floridians to rethink their responsibilities to their fellow citizens and to their children and grandchildren. Will we be remembered as the generation that took for our own personal gratification more than we gave back to the state and, in so doing, eroded the state's capacity to serve tomorrow's citizens?

CONCLUSION

Compared with the other forty nine states, Florida is below average in both total state and local tax burden and spending. Its revenue structure is regressive, volatile, and cannot keep pace with economic growth. The result is stop-and-go spending and the accumulation of unmet needs and increased long-term financial obligations in the form of bonded debt and unfunded pension liability. The state's financial condition severely limits the government's ability to develop and execute policies that will provide its citizens a future quality of life as good as the present.

REFERENCES

Advisory Commission on Intergovernmental Relations (1983). *1981 Tax capacity of the fifty states*. Washington, D.C.: the author.

Advisory Commission on Intergovernmental Relations (1985). *1982 Tax Capacity of the Fifty States*. Washington, D.C.: the author.

AmeriTrust Corporation and SRI International (1986). Indicators of economic capacity. *First Report* (December): 32–37.

Bill, William G., William J. Serow, and William J. Shelley (1987). Measuring the economic impact of a state's tax structure on an elderly population. *The Gerontologist,* 27:6, 804–808.

Berne, Robert and Richard Schramm (1986). *The financial analysis of governments*. Englewood Cliffs, N.J.: Prentice-Hall.

Bradley, Robert B. (1991). *Why is government growing and is there enough money to do everything we want to do?* Oral presentation made at the 1991 Florida Leadership Conference, February 12, 1991. Sponsored by the Florida Center for Public Management, Florida State University, Tallahassee.

Cain, Henry C. (1979). Financing Florida state government. *Financing Florida State Government*. Edited by Howard P. Tuckman. Tallahassee: Florida State University, 16–28.

Cohen, Carol E. (1989). State fiscal capacity and effort: An update. *Intergovernmental Perspective,* 15:2 (Spring): 15–20.

Cohen, Carol E. (1990). State fiscal capacity and effort: The 1988 representative tax system estimates. *Intergovernmental Perspective,* 16:4 (Fall): 17–22.

Dye, Thomas R. and Jesse B. Taintor (1986). *States: The fiscal data book*. Tallahassee: Policy Sciences Program, Florida State University.

Florida Governor's Office (1996). *Governor's budget recommendations summary 1996–97*. Internet document from http://www.dos.state.fl.us.

Florida Legislature. House Finance and Taxation Committee and Senate Finance, Taxation and Claims Committee (1991). *Florida's tax structure*. Tallahassee: the Committee.

Florida Legislature. Senate Finance, Taxation, and Claims Committee (1993). *Florida tax handbook*. Tallahassee: the Committee.

Florida Legislature. Senate Committee on Ways and Means (1996). *Florida tax handbook*. Tallahassee: the committee.

Florida Legislature. Speaker's Advisory Committee on the Future (1987). *The sunrise report*. Tallahassee: the Committee.

Florida Monthly Economic Report, 9:12 (August 3, 1989), 11:1 (July 1990), 12:1 (July 1991), 13:1 (July 1992), 14:1 (July 1993), 15:1 (July 1994), 16:2 (August 1995).

"General Revenue Collections for June." *Florida Monthly Economic Report,* 11:1 (July 1990), p. 1.

"Florida's Current Financial Outlook in Trouble?" *Dollars & Sense,* 1:3 (October 1989), p. 3.

Gardner, Bud. "Florida's New Sales Tax Law." *Florida Environmental & Urban Issues,* (October 1987), 2–3.

Hovey, Hal. "State and Local Tax Policy: Looking Ahead." *Intergovernmental Perspective,* 16:4 (Fall 1990), 5–8.

"Hal Hovey's State Scoreboard," *Governing,* 9:10 (July 1996), p. 53; 9:12 (Sept. 1996), p. 59; 10:2 (Nov. 1996), p. 53.

Koenig, John. "Putting Off the Inevitable." *Florida Trend,* 30:6 (October 1987), 61–66.

Kincaid, John. "Fiscal Capacity and Tax Effort of the American States: Trends and Issues." *Public Budgeting & Finance,* 9:3 (Autumn, 1989), 4–26.

McCall, Sam M. Deputy Auditor General, State of Florida. Reported in conversation in April 1987.

McKinnon, John D., "Backdoor Borrowing," *Florida Trend,* 39:1 (May 1996), 12–15.

Mikesell, John L. (1991). *Fiscal Administration: Analysis and Applications for the Public Sector.* 3rd Edition. Pacific Grove, Ca.: Brooks/Cole.

Rafuse, Robert W., Jr. "A Walk on the Expenditure Side: 'Needs' and Fiscal Capacity." *Intergovernmental Perspective,* 16:4 (Fall 1990), 25–30.

Rubin, Irene (1990). *The Politics of Public Budgeting.* Chatham, N.J.: Chatham House.

"Selected Highlights on the Demand for Services." Workshop material provided at the 1991 Florida Leadership Conference, February 12–13, 1991. Sponsored by the Florida Center for Public Management, Florida State University, Tallahassee, Fl.

Shuman, Howard E. (1988). *Politics and the Budget.* 2nd ed. Englewood Cliffs, N.J.

Smith, Stanley K. "Population Growth and Demographic Change in Florida." Paper presented to the Government Services Committee of the Taxation and Budget Reform Commission. November, 1990. Tallahassee, Florida.

Snell, Ronald K. "Earmarking State Tax Revenues." *Intergovernmental Perspective,* 16:4 (Fall 1990), 12–16.

State of Florida. Comptrollers Office (1993). *Florida Comprehensive Annual Financial Report.* Fiscal Year 1992. Tallahassee: the Office.

State of Florida. Comptroller's Office (1996). *Florida Comprehensive Annual Financial Report.* Fiscal Year 1995. Tallahassee: the Office.

"The 50 States." *City & State,* 3:5 (May 1986), pp. 14–42.

"The 50 States." *City & State,* 4:4 (April 1987), pp. 14–42.

"The 50 States." *City & State,* 7:9 (April 1990), pp.11–40.

Tuckman, Howard P. (1979). "The Criteria for Evaluating the Florida Tax Structure." *Financing Florida State Government.* Edited by Howard P. Tuckman. Tallahassee, Fl.: Florida State University, 1–15.

U.S. Department of Commerce, Bureau of the Census. *State Government Finances,* GF84, No. 3, through GF92, No. 3, Table 11. Washington: U. S. Government Printing Office.

S. Department of Commerce, Bureau of the Census. *State Government Tax Collections* (1992–1994) and *State Government Finances* (1992–1994). Internet documents from http://www.census.gov/ftp/pub/govs.

U. S. Department of Labor, Bureau of Labor Statistics (1991–1996). *CPI Detailed Report.* Washington: Government Printing Office.

Williams, David R. "No Shelter on a Rainy Day." *Florida Trend,* 32:11 (March 1990a), 13–14.

Williams, David R. "The Sales Tax Roller Coaster." *Florida Trend,* 33:3 (July 1990b), 15–18.

Zingale, James A. "Demographics and Florida's State Budget." *Fiscal Facts,* 1:2 (February, 1990), 1–2.

Zingale, James A. and Thomas R. Davies (1986). "Why Florida's Tax Revenues Go Boom or Bust, and Why We Can't Afford It Anymore." *Florida State University Law Review,* 14:433, 433–461.

Zolkos, Rodd. "State Pension Study Shows Funds 'in Good Fiscal Health.'" *City & State,* 7:25 (December 3, 1990), 2.

Zorn, Paul. "Public Pension Funding: Preliminary Results from a Survey of Current Practices." *Government Finance Review,* 3:4 (August 1987), 7–11.

Zwick, Charles J. "Growth Financing in the New Global Environment: Lessons from the Florida Experience." *Environmental and Urban Issues,* (Summer, 1989), 13–17.

PART IV

THE OTHER GOVERNMENTS

INTERGOVERNMENTAL RELATIONS IN FLORIDA: ISSUES AND ALTERNATIVES

ROBERT BRADLEY AND MARSHA HOSACK

A merican federalism began as an experiment. It gave substance to principles designed to shape the use of governmental power and the role of the citizenry in controlling the nation's destiny. For two centuries, the interpretation of these principles and their practical weight have been debated.

A dynamic federalism, working within broad contours, is necessary to the health of the Republic. But recognizing its significance for our democracy hardly solves the immediate problems before policy makers. How is the legacy of enduring principles to be applied to contemporary challenges? How is the State to order its relations with its local general purpose governments? What balance can be struck among the overlapping responsibilities and activities of counties and municipalities? What policies should be revised to ensure the cost-effective, efficient delivery of government services to the public?

These questions are of considerable concern in Florida. The relations among governments frame the possibility of action in many policy areas. This paper suggests such relations must be seen in the context of long standing arguments within the American experiment. It examines the three major intergovernmental challenges facing the state—the problem of legislative mandates, the absence of local government revenue flexibility, and the state of relations among local governments. This paper identifies evolving federal and state policies affecting these challenges—perhaps heightening them to a critical point—in areas including devolution, federal mandates, and the elimination of the federal deficit.

THE NATURE OF INTERGOVERNMENTAL RELATIONS

According to the Bureau of the Census, there were 85,006 governments of various types in the United States in 1992. The number has increased slightly in the last fifteen years after several decades of steady decline. The consolidation of school districts has slowed markedly; the creation of new Special districts continues (Census of Governments 1992, 7, Table 5).

There are hundreds of governments in Florida. The exact number is a matter of some controversy. The Census Bureau counted 1,014 local governments in 1992, including 67 counties, 390 municipalities, 95 school districts, and 462 special districts. State sources show a similar if somewhat different picture. The Department of Community Affairs, for example, counted 987 special districts in 1995; 452 of them independent.[1]

By any count, most states have more governments than Florida. This is particularly true of the largest states. California, for example, has 4,393 local governments; New York 3,299; Texas 4,792; Pennsylvania 5,159; Ohio 3,524 and Illinois 6,723 (Census of Governments 1992, 1, Table 1). Intergovernmental relations are, in this sense, less complex and confusing in Florida than elsewhere. Still, the scope and type of relations between and among governments is daunting.

The relations among these governments range from memoranda of understanding and informal agreements to compulsory orders and financial assistance. They embrace legal rules and functional arrangements for governance, fiscal relationships, and functional arrangements for the provision and production of public goods and services. In this Florida is a mirror of the nation. American federalism has been and continues to be multifaceted. Its hallmark has been experimentation. Its governmental structures and functions have been the subject of a changing series of innovations. In this context, the notion of a definitive, unambiguous theory or set of principles ordering the relationships among the various levels and types of government in the United States is illusory.

Still, the federal system is not without logic. The core of American federalism lies in its fusion of two basic principles—the principle of federation and principle of representation (Eulau 1978; Rees and Bradley 1988). In the United States, the areal division of power is coupled with geographical representation. What links state and nation, locality and state is the representation of people in complementary institutions. Differences among these institutions condition the possible policies that each level and type of government can typically pursue.

THE PLACE OF STATE AND LOCAL GOVERNMENTS: CONFLICTING VALUES

State and local governments are distinguished from the national government because they are relatively limited in the types of policies they can pursue. There are several dimensions to this limitation, but they are integral to the federal structure. From the perspective of economic theory, federation allows citizens to choose among alternative mixes of public goods and services offered by various governments. The options extended to capital and labor create choices unavailable in unitary, non-federal systems. In theory, at least, citizens can leave one jurisdiction for another relatively easily—the costs of leaving are relatively low when compared to those involved in leaving the country as might be necessary in a unitary system of government. This freedom enhances their voice in a system founded on geographical representation.

Another feature of federal systems is that policies of one jurisdiction that benefit another are discouraged. They are discouraged because taxpayers are not interested in providing benefits to non-tax paying citizens of other jurisdictions. As a consequence, policies which produce benefits that can be geographically limited are more likely to be adopted. Thus, federalism encourages some policies to the detriment of others. To an extent, states and localities are locked into inter-jurisdictional competition by the nature of their representational system and allocation of authority. State and local politicians may defy this logic by undertaking other sorts of policies, however, all things being equal, they will be punished by economic dislocations or by electoral defeat at the hands of those whose interests have not been given political voice.

National politicians face a similar calculus, but the situation is different in one crucial respect. Since few people are willing to leave the United States, the national government may, within certain bounds, assume responsibility for policies that at the state and local level would be difficult to enact. For example, the national government may play a role in redressing disparities among states and communities that might otherwise distort economic choices. From an economic perspective it may also assume responsibilities for redressing problems such as racial discrimination that, if left untended, might result in non-market incentives for migration which could reduce the productivity of the economy.

Overall, economic theory provides a powerful rationale for structuring the activities of government to the maximum extent possible on a decentralized federal basis. But it does not offer the last word. It entails a measure of autonomy for local governments. Yet local autonomy has at least two dimensions—the power of initiation and the power of immunity (Clark 1985, 68–70). Both depend in a crucial way upon the rights and privileges of local government vis-a-vis other tiers of government. Local governments, according to the economic design, can neither be wholly immune from imposed restrictions nor be perfectly free to initiate policy. The mix is crucially important. But the economic perspective does not allow the line to be drawn precisely.

Nowhere are the difficult choices confronting federalism more evident than in the treatment of the many forms of local government. The United States Constitution, of course, neglects local governments altogether. The history and status of municipalities, counties, special districts and school districts vary greatly from state to state and among one another, shaped as much by custom and tradition as by law and policy. Municipalities, for example, have a much different tradition than counties. Municipalities have a long history of independence from state authority based both on the participation of residents and their corporate status (Hartog 1983). Counties, for their part, evolved as subordinate local subdivisions of the state, created for the convenience of the state without any substantial popular consent, approval or solicitation. School districts and special districts, especially as they are established in Florida, spring from yet different roots. On the one hand they are limited and dependent partners in the federal system; on the other, they enjoy a measure of independence as the essential ingredients in a territorially based representative form of government. These characteristics stand in obvious opposition. Metaphorically, at least, local government was promoted as the best protection of individual rights by early theorists such as Jefferson. Relatively autonomous local governments, in this view, prevent the development of a centralized democratic despotism.

The federal design juxtaposed another principle to this one, however. Namely, representative structures and processes together with the division of power were tailored to ensure the opportunity for individual demands to be registered and responded to outside a locality. In James Madison's hands, this circumvention of local political processes was intended to ensure the individual protection from majorities. Individual rights are protected in the larger forums of the republic against local majorities.

Thus, in the American political system, two philosophical prejudices are woven into contemporary consideration of "local governments" broadly defined. In part, "local governments" are considered creations of the state, constrained for the protection of individuals. But they are also seen as local creations, arising from natural arenas of association in service of the individual. This tension is endemic to intergovernmental relations in the federal system (Thomas 1984). It stands apart from the sort of relations that would exist even among governments in a unitary system, revolving as they do around managerial concerns, collaborative actions and resource allocation. It colors the way in which local initiatives and state intrusion in such matters as land regulation and local planning are understood. It is this tension which stands at the center of disputes about such matters as home rule and legislative mandates.

The *Ultra Vires* rule is perhaps the most influential attempt to resolve this tension and establish the legal relationship between a state and its local governments (Alexander 1984). In its most well known form, Dillon's rule, local governments have only those powers expressly granted by state legislatures, those powers implied by others expressly granted, and those powers essential to the accomplishment of local objectives. Judge Dillon recognized in the 1860s, in the case of municipal corporations, that while they might be counted on as bulwarks against the state in protecting individual freedom, municipalities also possessed powers that could be deployed against the individual. Strictly followed, Dillon's rule reduces local government to little more than an appendage of the state with scarcely more discretion than an administrative agency.

The difficulties of Dillon's solution have long since become apparent. But the tension it sought to resolve remains. It galvanizes the debate on intergovernmental issues at any number of points. And despite the complexity of contemporary government, the rough outlines of the philosophical foundations behind the tension are still visible. They are still there for policy makers and the courts to draw upon.

Unfortunately, in a number of intergovernmental issues, the role of such basic design principles are not clear. In collaboration and disputes among local governments, for example, larger principles often get tangled in unexpected ways. Counties and municipalities overlap. Their practical roles, if not their constitutional positions, are in flux. Should the doctrine of local self-government be interpreted to insure that the smaller unit will prevail over the larger in intergovernmental disputes? Or, should primacy in such matters be given to units carrying out functions to which the state attaches the greatest significance? Where is the lodestar illuminating such relations?" Or, to take another example, where do school districts and independent special districts fit into the local pattern of governance? How are the interests of general purpose governments, which typically serve the general public, to be weighed in various disputes against those of special purpose governments, such as water districts or downtown improvement authorities, which answer to a public that is more narrowly defined? In all this the criteria are far from clear.

In the absence of well defined principles, design emerges from practice in an ad hoc way. The dynamic forces to which government must respond—changing demographics, economy and technology—assume greater importance, creating the circumstance in which governmental responses must be initiated . After all, the practical problems of everyday life must be addressed. And in the welter of everyday life, it is solutions and not design which is most valued.

INTERGOVERNMENTAL CHALLENGES IN FLORIDA

Intergovernmental relations in Florida have changed over the last fifteen years, perhaps spurred by changes in the federal system as a whole. Current initiatives at the federal level are likely to accelerate further changes to the intergovernmental dynamics in Florida, and in the nation generally.

NEW FEDERALISM—CHANGING THE BALANCE

A gradual but distinctive decline in federal funds to local governments beginning in the late 1970's was an initial indicator that the preeminence of the national government was no longer clear. Driven, by what John Shannon calls the three D's—defense spending, demographic fueled entitlements to the elderly, and deficit worries—federal spending is in eclipse (Shannon 1988, 16). Federal aid to state and local governments peaked in 1978, in inflation adjusted dollars. Local dependence on federal monies has returned to the levels registered in the late sixties. The structure of federal grant assistance has begun to resemble that which prevailed in the fifties. Over 60% of federal grants are now made as payments to individuals (U.S. ACIR 1994, Table C). In the mid-sixties, on the other hand, the largest share of federal grants were intended for capital investments. During the seventies, state and local governments received the largest portion.

Of course, the federal government still accounts for most governmental expenditures. Despite the change in the structure of federal assistance, the federal government expenditures still account for nearly 70% of all expenditures governments make from their own revenue sources. This percentage share has remained relatively stable for almost 40 years (U.S. Council of Economic Advisors, February 1996, 108). In fact, federal net interest payments on the debt alone amounted to more than 25% of the revenues raised by all the state and local governments in the country from their own sources in 1995 (U.S. Council of Economic Advisors, February 1996, Tables 80 and 81).

The size of federal transfers alone assures a continued influence for the federal government in state and local affairs. The number of federal grant programs remains high. And while literally thousands of local governments no longer receive any federal funds, federal assistance is still important in some areas, for certain activities and especially for state governments. Florida, for example, receives more than 25% of its state budget from federal sources even though it ranks near the bottom of all the states in per capita grants (U.S. ACIR 1992, Tables 22 and 80).

So, federal grants hold their importance, even if they promise to diminish in the years ahead.

Several significant developments have occurred recently at the federal level that suggest a new federalism may be developing. The 104th Congress approved, and President Clinton signed, federal welfare reform legislation which delegates primary responsibilities to state governments for administering welfare programs. The Congress continues to discuss administering other major programs like Medicaid and Workforce Development through decentralized flexible mechanisms such as block grants. These actions coincide with serious discussions on how best to balance the federal budget by 2002. Such developments, in the minds of many, are the beginnings of giving states greater authority, a "devolution revolution."

Arguably, the most significant aspect of the new devolution is welfare reform. The Personal Responsibility and Work Opportunity Reconciliation Act of 1996, combines a number of programs into single block of grants to states. The act alters the entitlement nature of welfare, institutes a five year lifetime limit on welfare assistance, and establishes certain work requirements for recipients. It also restricts the eligibility of certain groups, most notably for Florida, legal immigrants.

States generally seem to welcome the opportunity to administer their own welfare programs—if federal funding is maintained at adequate levels. Florida enacted a broad redesign of its welfare program in 1996. Like Florida, many states had sought waivers to implement their own programs prior to the passage of the reform act. The changes that affect eligibility of individuals to receive services, however, may have significant impacts on local governments. In the past, the costs of caring for indigents often has fallen to counties. With this in mind, the National Association of Counties opposed the welfare reform legislation and urged its veto, arguing that counties will ultimately be responsible for services not adequately supported by the states, shifting significant costs to local taxpayers (County News, Vol. 28, No. 14).

The policy shift in the welfare program is not alone. Other federal grant programs have also been affected. Examples include grant programs administered by the Housing and Urban Development Agency for housing and certain community projects, and modal transportation programs administered by the Department of Transportation. The Internodal Surface Transportation Efficiency Act of 1991 (ISTEA), an earlier initiative, provided both increased flexibility in administering grants for surface transportation, and recognized the importance of including state and local officials in the process of making long-term planning and funding decisions. State and local government are granted limited discretion in the Educate America Act, the Empowerment Zones and Enterprise Communities Program, among others. Delegating the responsibility and discretion to state and local governments to administer programs places additional emphasis on developing administrative capacity to deliver services.

The impact of devolution can also be seen in the enactment of the Unfunded Federal Mandates Act of 1995. The Act, is a variation of laws enacted in many states in the 1980's and 1990's aimed at curbing state imposition of costly programs on local governments but not providing funding. The act is applicable to federal mandates affecting state, local, and tribal governments, as well as the private sector. It is prospective and will not apply to past mandates. Several federal actions are excluded from the provisions of the act, however, including laws that protect constitutional or civil rights, conditions attached to most federal grant programs, auditing and accounting procedures, emergencies, national security, and Title II of the Social Security Act.

Essentially, the Unfunded Federal Mandates Act requires that legislation be reviewed to assess its costs to state and local government. Legislation that imposes intergovernmental mandates of more than $50 million per year, or private sector mandates of more than $100 million per year, is considered out of order unless funding is provided. The point of order, however, may be waived by a majority vote. It is too soon to assess the impact of the legislation on mandates. At a minimum, the act institutes a procedure to ensure visibility of legislation containing mandates, and necessitates that Congress assume political responsibility for imposing mandates on the state and local governments.

The concern for state and local sensibility has not been limited to Congressional action. Recent Supreme Court decisions also show a new respect for the states' constitutional sovereignty under the 10th Amendment. Throughout most of the period between 1964–1992, the Court's decisions generally preserved national perceptions. Recently this has changed. (State Legislatures, 51-52, July/August 1996). In *New York vs. United States,* the Court found a federal statute to constitute an unconstitutional "commandeering of the state." In *United States vs. Lopez,* the Court found that Congress had exceeded its authority under the Commerce Clause, and intruded into the states' police powers in enacting the Gun Free School Zone Act. The Court further found in *Seminole Tribe vs. Florida* that Congress violated the states' immunity from suit under the 11th amendment in authorizing tribes to sue states to enforce the Indian Gaming Regulatory Act. The extent to which this decision will protect states from lawsuits and policy intrusions in other areas is not yet clear.

Despite such developments, the federal regulatory apparatus is still largely in place. Federal courts have not broken decisively with the direction established in cases such as *South Carolina v. Baker* and *Garcia v. San Antonio Metropolitan Transit*. It continues to preserve substantial discretion in intergovernmental matters for the Congress (U.S. ACIR 1986).

For all the talk of New Federalism and devolution, the changes of this decade have not restored, what Edward Corwin once called, "dual federalism" (Corwin 1950). However, intergovernmental affairs have changed. In large measure, these changes have been induced by the fend-for-yourself fiscal environment that has prevailed in the eighties and nineties. State and local officials have begun to look to their own resources. There is a new found capacity in state governments and, by some indicators, a new sort of activism. State governments have assumed new roles in everything from antitrust and consumer regulation to education reform, economic development, and welfare reform. These changes have both reinforced the traditional roles of the state in intergovernmental relations and created new ones.

STATE/LOCAL RELATIONS

Devolving federal programs to state and local governments, and the possible strengthening of the federation through such measures as the Unfunded Mandates Act and court decisions affirming the states' sovereignty, places increased importance on the relations between the state and local, and interlocal government. Assuming added responsibilities and implementing programs will require a cooperative effort between the various levels and types of government. In the case of local governments especially, having sufficient resources and clearly delineating functional responsibilities is critically important in successfully taking on added responsibilities or, perhaps in many cases, doing more with less because of funding decreases. Existing constraints and obstacles in local governance will likely strain local governments efforts in accepting these challenges.

In Florida, despite constitutional guarantees of home rule for municipalities and counties, the state still often acts the part prescribed in Dillon's rule—it limits local initiative and overrules local immunity. The instances involved range from state policy towards local government pension funds to the regulation of vessels operating within local jurisdictions. But, they are probably most pronounced in fiscal matters. The discretion of cities and counties in financial matters is severely curtailed.

In fact, a study conducted by the U.S. ACIR in 1981 found Florida's cities and counties had relatively broad home rule powers in matters concerning their structure and delivery of services. However, in financial affairs, the same study determined Florida's cities and counties faced some of the most restrictive constitutional and statutory provisions in the country (U.S. ACIR 1981). Despite statutory changes granting greater local options during the eighties and nineties, this observation still has considerable weight.

The last major reform of the intergovernmental system in Florida was in the early 1970s, instigated by the 1968 constitutional revision. Since that time, Florida's population has nearly doubled, it has become more ethnically diverse, more urban, and its economy has diversified (Florida Institute of Government 1995).

In January 1995, a summit on intergovernmental relations was convened in Florida. Its participants included state legislators, local elected officials, and top administrators from state and local agencies. The summit participants recognized that many efforts have been made to deal with intergovernmental challenges—the adoption of a constitutional amendment to restrict unfunded mandates, revisions to growth management laws to improve intergovernmental coordination, adjustments to the state and local tax and revenue system, and legislation enacted to deal with unincorporated enclaves or to create special purpose districts. Despite the reforms and efforts of state and local officials, the summit participants concluded that intergovernmental conflict is common because authority, responsibility, and revenues are not adequately divided and aligned across governmental tiers and units. The state's intergovernmental system not only contains, but creates mandates, receives insufficient revenues to meet public expectations for services, and includes a considerable amount of duplication and overlapping of authority (Florida Institute of Government 1995).

State policy towards cities, counties, school boards and special districts inhibits local action and establishes an intergovernmental framework inadequate to ensure the effective delivery of services to its citizenry. The state plays several other roles, too broad for consideration here. In intergovernmental relations, it is at once a facilitator, an activator, and a moderator (Zimmerman 1984). Its policy towards cities and counties faces a number of significant challenges. As highlighted in the 1995 intergovernmental summit, three are especially important: legislative mandates, local revenue flexibility, and the effect of local government structure and function on interlocal relations.

LEGISLATIVE MANDATES

The single greatest source of friction between the state government and its municipalities and counties is the mandates enacted by the legislature requiring local units of government to perform various services without commensurate funding. This is true not only in Florida but across the country (Kelly 1992, 16).

In Florida, legislative mandates were a leading concern of the Florida League of Cities and the Florida Association of Counties throughout the eighties. Both associations worked to place on the ballot and then pass in 1990 an amendment to the Florida Constitution limiting the enactment of unfunded legislative mandates. Yet even the adoption of this amendment, has not eliminated the concern over unfunded mandates in Florida. The participants at the 1995 Florida Intergovernmental Summit ranked unfunded mandates as a top problem for local governments.

Definitions of Mandates. State mandates have been defined in a variety of ways. The U.S. ACIR, in its pathbreaking 1978 study, State Mandating of Local Expenditures, categorized a mandate as:

A legal requirement, constitutional provision, statutory provision, or administrative regulation that a local government undertake a specific activity or provide a service meeting minimum state standards (Zimmerman 1978).

This definition makes a distinction between state mandates and state constraints. Mandates, in this view, command action; constraints prevent action. Thus, the state requirement that municipalities and counties increase employer contributions to the Florida Retirement System must be considered a mandate. The state limitation on the fees that municipalities may charge for right-of-way use by telecommunication services is not.

This perspective occurs in another commonly held definition of state mandates. Namely, mandates arise in the marginal costs imposed on local governments. Specifically, they exist only when there is a difference between what a government is directed to spend on an activity and what it would have spent on the activity in the absence of some state directive. The state requirement that cities and counties make financial audits of their accounts would not be viewed as a mandate. Presumably, municipalities and counties would make provisions for such audits in the absence of state law.

Catherine Lovell has proposed yet another definition. In her view, mandates are "any responsibility, procedure or other activity that is imposed on one government by another by constitutional, legislative, administrative, executive or judicial action as a direct order, or as a condition of aid" (1981). This definition broadens the scope of mandates in two ways. First, it includes requirements that are imposed as conditions of aid. For example, as a condition for receiving revenue sharing, cities and counties must report their finances annually to the Department of Banking and Finance. Second, this definition includes constraints as well as requirements. Lovell suggests that state actions constraining local revenue bases, revenue rates and expenditures qualify as mandates.

Erosion of Home Rule. The concern among city and county officials in the mid-seventies over legislative mandates surfaced as a distinct issue in the wake of the seeming success of the Home Rule Movement. By 1977, the municipalities in virtually every state, and the counties in all but seven, had acquired the ability either to implement structural home rule authority or the power to adopt alternative forms of government by referenda (U.S. ACIR 1985, 294–296).

In Florida, the story was much of the same. For much of this century, Florida's municipalities had sought meaningful home rule. Despite many attempts, it was only with the passage of the 1968 constitution (Article VIII, s. 6, Fla. Const.) and the enactment of the Municipal Home Rule Powers Act in 1973 (s. 166.011, F.S.) that the goal was reached (Marsicano 1984). For counties, the effort began later and was realized in large measure through the 1968 constitution and judicial interpretation in *Speer v. Olson* where the Court held "The intent of the Legislature in enacting the recent amendment to Chapter 125, Florida Statutes, was to enlarge the powers of counties through home rule to govern themselves."

Home rule, in the minds of many local government officials, has long been thought synonymous with local autonomy. It has appeared in two basic forms in the United States: *imperium in imperio* (imperio) and devolution of powers (Zimmerman 1984). The imperio model insulates local government from the state by creating a distinct set of "municipal affairs." But in practice this approach has offered less autonomy than local officials hoped. It generally circumscribes local control quite narrowly, limiting it to a express set of powers, leaving the rest to the state. The devolution model, now nearly 40 years old, calls for all delegable powers to be passed back to local governments, subject to preemption by state general law. It also allows local autonomy to be compromised for compelling state purposes.

To its creator, Jefferson Fordham, and his patrons in the American Municipal Association, the devolution approach held great promise as a means of overcoming the limitations of the imperio model (Zimmerman 1984). And in fact, most state constitutions have adopted variants on this approach. Florida's constitution was clearly influenced by the devolutionary approach. The constitutional treatment of local taxing authority is the conspicuous exception.

Yet, by the mid-seventies, the form of the devolutionary approach favored in many states had come to be seen by many local observers as inadequate. It left the state too much latitude in its role as the arbiter of local government powers and, in doing so, reestablished a new tension between state sovereignty and local autonomy.

The proximate cause of concern was mandates. Mandates, of course, represent an intrusion of the state into local affairs, but they can often be justified and they need not be capricious. They are justifiable within the devolutionary model. They may be well founded, traced, in many instances, to the state's dramatic increase in population, to real worries over local fiscal emergencies, and calls for action in areas ranging from civil rights to the environment. State officials, through mandates, ensure that certain key functions are performed throughout the state with relatively similar levels of service.

Joseph Zimmerman has suggested a topology with 12 different types of mandates, including: due process mandates, entitlement mandates, equal treatment mandates, ethical mandates, good neighbor mandates, information mandates, membership mandates, personnel mandates, record-keeping mandates, service level mandates and tax base mandates (Zimmerman 1987, 78–84). In each of these areas, a good case can be made for state action. For many local observers, it was precisely this case that was missing in all too many instances. The compelling state purpose was often difficult to discern.

Financial Burdens. The local complaint against mandates, however, rests only partially with the intervention of the state into local matters. The crux of the issue, in the mid-seventies and today, lies in the financial burden state mandates impose on city and county governments. While a single mandate may have little effect, the cumulative effect of several mandates may be quite large. The discretionary revenues of most cities and counties are quite limited. Increasingly, local revenues come from user fees and charges dedicated to rather narrow purposes. Taxes, along with some intergovernmental revenues, constitute the major source of discretionary revenues. Federal payments have declined dramatically. State shared revenues have shown modest increases for counties in the past 10 years as a share of total revenues, and have maintained virtually the same share of revenues for cities. For most cities and counties in Florida, ad valorem property taxes are the primary if not sole remaining source of potential discretionary revenues. For several counties

(Calhoun, Dixie, Liberty, Glades, Jefferson, Hamilton, Hardee, Gadsden, Gilchrist, Lafayette, Madison, Sumter, Union and Washington), a few cities, and many school districts, this option is no longer practical, even if it were politically feasible: they already have reached, or are very near, their legal limit for property taxes (FACIR Profile 1996, 35–54, Table 1). Mandates, then, come at the expense of local priorities. Perversely, mandates not only intrude on local affairs, adding new substantive and procedural requirements, they also work against the pursuit of local goals.

Remedies. The remedy for mandates can take several forms, each differing in the degree to which it challenges the role of the state in local affairs. There are six major options which can be used to address mandates at the state level: monitoring programs, fiscal notes, sunset programs, sunrise programs, reimbursement policies, and prohibition. The first four involve increasing legislative scrutiny, designed to weed out mandates lacking a compelling state purpose. The fifth acknowledges the cost of mandates, if nothing else, and requires that it be factored into legislative decision making. The last seeks an outright ban on mandates.

Over the years, several of these options have been exercised in Florida. From 1978 to 1996, Florida law required the Legislature to provide funds or funding sources to pay for the cost of new mandates imposed on cities and counties (former s. 11.076, F.S.). However, the statutory reimbursement scheme found in the law failed to eliminate enactment of unfunded and under funded mandates for two reasons. First, the statute provided a partial exemption where the Legislature determines that a general law serves both state and local objectives. Second, and more importantly, it did not consider the prevailing Florida legal doctrine providing that later legislative enactments supersede previous ones in the event of a conflict (FACIR 1985). The legislature cannot pass general laws that legally bind future Legislatures. Consequently, the 1978 statute was ineffective in eliminating enactment of unfunded mandates. It was repealed by the 1996 Legislature (Ch. 96–311, L.O.F.) without fanfare or protest.

Prior to the enactment of the constitutional amendment in 1990, various alternatives to the statutory requirement for reimbursement were considered. For example, legislation to subject mandates to a "sunset process", establishing a timetable by which regulatory laws would be repealed unless explicitly reenacted, was filed in 1982 (S 795), and died in committee (FACIR 1985). Mandates frequently are permanent solutions to temporary problems (Kelly 1992, 16). The sunset review process serves to repeal mandated policies which have outlived their applicability.

The Florida Advisory Council on Intergovernmental Relations recommended a somewhat similar approach to the Legislature in 1982—a sunrise program (FACIR 1985). Sunrise proposals are designed to ensure more careful scrutiny of mandates prior to their enactment. The sunrise process generally requires proposals to meet a certain standard or criteria to merit enactment. In some variations, sunrise provisions may require extraordinary majorities either in committee, on the floor or in both to pass any bill that includes an unfunded mandate. The Florida Legislature did not adopt a statute with this approach.

The state did implement a formal monitoring program, however. In 1978, the Florida Advisory Council on Intergovernmental Relations published its first annual report of new legislative mandates on municipalities and counties as required by Chapter 163, *Florida Statutes* (FACIR 1980 and subsequent years).[2] The annual reports, together with periodic catalogs, offer some indication of the nature and magnitude of legislative mandates. They have been useful in reviewing the necessity of certain mandates and have led to the repeal of some mandates.

The Florida Legislature also employed fiscal notes as a means of ensuring adequate scrutiny of the fiscal impacts of legislation. Legislative staff prepare fiscal notes identifying the impact costs of legislation on the public or private sector. Section 11.076, *Florida Statutes,* prior to its repeal, had specifically required the economic impact statements to assess the costs of legislation on local governments.

The success of the ACIR monitoring program and legislative fiscal note process in limiting legislative mandates was mixed at best. In the first years after their implementation, mandates declined. They increased from 1982 to 1988 and declined thereafter. Overall, 362 legislative mandates were enacted between 1981 and 1990 (FACIR 1991b, Table 2). The increase was most dramatic in acts restricting local governments' revenues or revenue generating capacity. However, most mandates affected three substantive areas: public protection and judiciary, general government, and personnel. Unfortunately, the precise fiscal impact of the mandates is unknown. A significant number had substantial impact. However, there was a considerable increase in offsetting measures in the years following 1984: a greater percentage of the enacted bills containing mandates provide local governments with some means for partially recovering, through fees, taxes or appropriations, the costs imposed by the mandate. Still, the problem of mandates continued, culminating in the adoption of a constitutional amendment in 1990.

Table 10-1 offers a broad set of proposals advanced by Joseph Zimmerman. Perhaps the most obvious approach though entails a return to the solution proposed in 1978—reimbursement. Fourteen states,

Table 10-1

ALTERNATIVE STRATEGIES TO MANDATE REIMBURSEMENT

1. Constitutionally based prohibition of all statutory and administrative state mandates.

2. Constitutionally based prohibition of mandates in certain functional areas, or the employment of constitutional criteria to justify the mandates.

3. A default system, whereby local governments can decline responsibility for legislative mandates.

4. Permanent shift of program funding responsibility upward to the next highest level of government.

5. Increased grants-in-aid that support a myriad of locally provided services.

6. Increased reliance upon "fiscal notes" to inform legislators of the costs that will be imposed on local governments with the enactment of a proposed mandate.

7. A constitutional provision requiring a "Message of Necessity" from the governor and a super majority vote (two-thirds vote of both houses of the legislature) to enact a new mandate.

8. An increase in general purpose state aid whose use at the local level is unrestricted.

Source: Zimmerman 1987, 83.

including Florida, have either a statutory or constitutional mandate reimbursement provision (State Mandates 1992, 21). In seven states, the provision is constitutional. There is, however, considerable variation in the reimbursement schemes. Some states provide up-front funding, others reimburse actual costs. Some states pay only for increases in costs, other pay for increases in service levels. Some states permit local non-compliance when funds are not forthcoming, others do not. Perhaps most important, certain states allow for exemptions, others do not. In any event, for any reimbursement process to be workable, "significant support for it must exist within the legislature" (U.S. GAO 1988, 41).

Constitutional Amendment. In November of 1990, the electors of Florida approved Amendment 3, a constitutional amendment creating section 18 of Article VII of the state constitution. It has two major provisions. First, it exempts counties and municipalities from complying with laws requiring them to spend funds or to take an actions unless certain tests are met in enacting the law. Second, it places limited restrictions on the ability of the Legislature to reduce the authority of cities and counties to generate revenue or to change the level of state revenues shared with cities and counties.

Conceptually, the amendment represents a modification of the devolutionary model of Home Rule, not a wholesale rejection. Essentially it strengthens the devolutionary approach currently in the Constitution. Perhaps its most significant feature is the requirement for an extraordinary majority vote in favor of an unfunded mandate for enactment. Consonant with the devolutionary model of home rule, it still allows wide compass for state action. It rejects the retrospective reimbursement of mandates and exempts certain substantive matters of statewide concern (criminal and election laws and existing pension requirements).

This proposal, with a modified scheme for reimbursement, is a beneficial change in state-local relations. But the change has not been as great as some expected. Since 1990, laws containing 414 mandates have been enacted. Of those, most were exempt from the provisions of the amendment, either because funds were provided, the mandate affected a policy exempt from the amendment limitations, or the mandate did not have a significant statewide cost (FACIR Intergovernmental Impact Reports 1991–1996). Fundamentally, the amendment provisions merely alter the politics of the policy making process and help improve the information on which such decisions are made. After all, most mandates currently are enacted with the near unanimity of both chambers. The constitutional amendment does not alter state-local relations to the degree a total prohibition on unfunded mandates would. For example, in 1995 legislation was passed requiring that property owners be compensated for government actions that reduce the value of their property. This legislation may have significant fiscal consequences for cities and counties, but was passed by a 2/3 vote in both houses. The amendment still allows matters of compelling statewide interest to be enacted even if these fiscal implications for local governments is great.

Perhaps the most salutary aspect of the constitutional amendment is the manner in which it enhances legislative information. Before passage of the amendment, fiscal notes on legislative mandates were required, but they did not have to identify specific costs. The reimbursement provision of the amendment has a direct impact on state appropriations and, as a consequence, influences the legislative process in a tangible way that requires the development of specific cost estimates. The current House and Senate bill analyses specifically include a section that identifies whether legislation is subject to the constitutional amendment

There is evidence that fiscal information can deter the enactment of mandates. But accurate information can be relatively expensive and difficult to obtain (State Mandates 1992, v). The Florida legislature recognized this during the 1991 session in enacting SB 2000 which extended the fiscal note process only to those mandates having an impact greater than ten cents per capita. This procedure limited costs, but at the expense of reducing the number of mandates covered by the amendment. For this reason, among others, the Governor vetoed SB 2000. The provisions of Article VII, section 18 of the Florida Constitution have still not been executed in statutory law, although the legislature has implemented a detailed review process. Notably, the ten cents per capita criteria, or a $1.4 million impact implicated in SB 2000, is the standard under which the Legislature considers legislation to contain a mandate subject to the constitutional amendment provisions.

Florida's "mandate" amendment does help reduce unfunded mandates. Ultimately though, the amendment does not resolve the problem. There are many ways in which costs can be passed on to local governments by the state. They are difficult to regulate. However, the devolutionary aspects of the mandates amendment squares well with the most fundamental principles of our federalism. It assumes a stance, not unlike the one adopted by the U.S. Supreme Court in *Garcia*. That is, any fundamental restraint on state power is most appropriately obtained through state political processes.

The opposition of many local government officials to state mandates stems, in part, from a principled belief that local autonomy is a necessary condition for a vigorous and meaningful democracy. Mandates limit home rule however they are defined. Yet it is clear to most local officials that mandates are endemic to centralized federalism. They recognize the state's stake in ensuring the larger public interest, especially in such matters as the standards of "good government," nondiscrimination, and due process. The real difficulty lies in the costs that unfunded mandates impose.

LOCAL REVENUE FLEXIBILITY

Each year city and county officials must somehow fund new programs while also dealing with the cumulative effect of previous enactments. They must respond within a fiscal environment that is itself the subject of state policy. The Madisonian equation works doubly to the detriment of local interests. It allows state (and federal) officials to indulge the seemingly paradoxical public preference, uncovered in so many opinion polls, for more services and lower taxes.

A government's fiscal flexibility depends on the productivity, range and appropriateness of the revenue sources it is allowed to draw upon. Flexibility comes with authority over sources of considerable revenue generating potential that can be varied from year to year in response to changing demands for services and new circumstances. Flexibility is diminished by earmarked sources, whether taxes, charges or special assessment, and tightly drawn tax bases. For local officials, if not local taxpayers, increased fiscal flexibility is necessary to adjust to mandates and the coming changes in Florida. Local governments must find general revenue funds to provide a variety of services such as law enforcement, corrections, health care, and to perform a myriad of administrative functions.

Ad Valorem Taxes. Florida's constitution provides local government with one source of taxation, ad valorem property taxes. And notably, it limits their use (Article VII, Section 9). Article VII, section 1(a) insures "All other forms of taxation shall be preempted to the state except as provided by general law."

Over time, of course, the state policy has created taxing options for local governments. But they are capped, limited or rife with exemptions. For example, if property tax exemptions, exclusions, and value differentials allowed by the Constitution, state law, and administrative practices were eliminated, local property tax revenue raising authority would increase by over 65% (*Florida Tax Handbook* 1996). There is a ceiling on municipal utility tax rates; local occupational license taxes are constrained within certain limits; motor fuel taxes are earmarked; many local option taxes require a referendum (FACIR Handbook 1996). Cities and counties are even restricted in many of the fees they can charge.

Of course, it can be argued that most cities and counties have not exhausted the potential of the ad valorem tax, notwithstanding both constitutional and statutory limitations (FACIR Profile 1996, 36–54, Tables 7–9). Neglecting for a moment the political unpopularity of the property tax, this view overlooks both the diversity and circumstance of city and county government. Nearly half of the counties with a population of less than 50,000 were at their ad valorem cap of 10 mills in 1995 (FACIR Profile 1996, Table 7). Fewer municipalities find themselves in such circumstances, but cities such as Indian Creek Village, Islandia, Miami, Opa-locka, Zolfo Springs, Monticello, Greenville, Belle Glade, and South Bay, have an operating millage exceeding 9 mills (FACIR Profile 1996, Table 9). Clearly, the remaining potential of the property tax is not the same everywhere.

It is true that some counties levied less than 5 mills in 1995, and 34 municipalities levied no ad valorem tax at all: the average statewide municipal government operating millage rate was 4.95 mills (FACIR Profile 1996, Tables 7&9). But here the circumstance is crucial. Palm Beach County, for example, levied 4.217 mills in 1995. Yet, the county government is part of a web of other overlapping general purpose governments and special districts that limits what any single jurisdiction can do, first, by determining the overall burden on individual taxpayers, and second, by creating interjurisdictional competition for taxpaying residents and businesses. Residents in some areas of Palm Beach County now face nearly 30 mills of ad valorem taxation. (FACIR Profile 1996). This fact alone cautions county government against additional levies. County officials must also be concerned with emigration, prompted by tax differentials, especially to neighboring Martin and Broward Counties. In a similar way, policy makers in municipalities within Palm Beach County, such as Pahokee and Belle Glade, can scarcely afford the disincentives to businesses and residents that higher property taxes would mean. Increased reliance on user charges is an indicator of

pronounced interjurisdictional competition. In short, local governments are seldom free to consider their own level of property taxation in isolation from that of their neighbors. In the case of independent special districts, however, the governing boards are appointed rather than elected officials. Such appointed officers may not be attuned to the extent to which they are depleting a limited local tax base.

The formal restrictions on the ad valorem tax are also important. The Homestead Exemption of the first $2,000 of the assessed value of a primary residence results in a property tax loss equivalent to 15.5% of all ad valorem taxes collected (*Florida Tax Handbook* 1996). Over the long run, the constitutional amendment commonly called "Save Our Homes," which became effective in 1995, should constrain revenues by limiting the assessment increases on homesteaded property. Still, ad valorem taxes remain the single largest source of city and county taxes. Significantly, after a state-mandated rollback in the early eighties, average municipal and county millage rates have begun to rise. The increase has been particularly rapid in counties. In fact, Florida's cities and counties rely on ad valorem taxes in about the same way as cities and counties across the country. The per capita burden is about the same— $588 in Florida, $602 nationally in 1990 (FACIR 1989). Rather, it is the mix of available discretionary sources in Florida that limits local flexibility.

Nationally, per capita local revenues were $1400 in 1992; in Florida, it was $1601. (U.S. ACIR, *Significant Features of Fiscal Federalism,* September 1994, Tables 49, 50, 56, 57, and 63.) However, a substantial portion of local revenue in Florida cannot be used for general purposes. It is often earmarked for specific purposes. Less than 50% of local revenues in Florida come from taxes, traditionally the major source of considerable discretion. Nationally, the figure is over 63%. One example may put this lack of fiscal flexibility in perspective. Law enforcement typically is supported through discretionary revenues. It is not funded by fees, user charges or significant earmarked revenues. Yet, the expenditures of most municipalities on law enforcement activities now greatly exceeds their ad valorem tax revenues. Statewide, the ratio of municipal law enforcement operating expenditures to ad valorem revenues was .87 in FY 1993–94. For counties the ratio is lower, at 0.38.[3] Arguably, however, counties have been assigned a greater range of activities that are difficult to fund without discretionary revenues. For example, the county assumes major financial responsibility for the state's criminal justice system.

Essentially, there are three alternatives for the state to increase the revenue flexibility of its cities and counties. First, the state might change the level or pattern of intergovernmental assistance. Second, it can alter local tax options. Third, it can encourage or mandate a fundamental restructuring of the system of local governance.

State Shared Revenues. Both cities and counties became more reliant on state intergovernmental assistance in the eighties. For example, the portion of county governmental fund revenue attributable to State assistance grew from 12.3% to 15.6% between 1982 and 1994; for cities the increase was 2.0% (FACIR 1993). Virtually, all the increase came in state shared revenue programs. (FACIR Profile, February 1994, Table 6; FACIR Profile, May 1996, Table 3.)

Shared revenues are defined as "distributions from a portion or all of the revenue from a specific tax or taxes, levied by one government that are shared on a predetermined basis, often in proportion to the amount collected at the local level, with another government or class of governments." There are currently 15 shared revenue programs which provide various levels of funding to Florida's cities and counties (FACIR Profile 1996). The amount of state shared revenues distributed to counties and municipalities grew considerably following enactment in 1982 of the local government half-cent sales tax. Still, in real terms, growth has been less dramatic. Counties have benefited, but the growth in real revenues has slowed markedly in recent years. Municipalities, on the other hand, actually received less state shared revenues in 1993 than in 1973, when adjusting for inflation.

Florida's cities and counties would clearly benefit from more state assistance. But the evidence suggests a problem. State shared revenues are of greater importance in localities across the country than in Florida. The state would have to provide considerably more aid if Florida's cities and counties were to reach the national average. Relatively speaking though, Florida is fairly generous in the amount of its state budget shared with cities and counties. New York and California were the most generous states in 1990; Hawaii and New Hampshire are the least. Florida ranked 19th (U.S. ACIR 1992, Table 93).

The problem is clear. The state revenue base itself is relatively weak. The state makes a commitment to cities and counties, but this effort falls short of providing the sort of aid localities receive nationally. Florida is one of only a handful of states (Colorado, Texas, Nebraska, Kansas, New York and New Hampshire) whose state percentage of state-local general expenditures, from their own revenue sources, falls below 50% (U.S. ACIR 1992, Table 93). By virtually any measure, the state revenue system would be hard pressed to devote significantly greater resources to cities and counties.

Of course, the state might reconsider the pattern of its existing aid, if not the levels. The state shares revenues with cities and counties in order to:

   a. compensate for state restrictions on local government revenue raising capacity and to offset the impact of state mandates;
   b. redress differences in local government fiscal capacity and address specific needs; and
   c. provide general fiscal relief to local taxpayers (FACIR 1986).

The existing set of state shared revenue programs are generally intended to provide compensation or fiscal relief. Only a few programs such as Municipal Revenue Sharing and the Supplemental Distribution of the Local Government Half-Cent Sales Tax are designed to redress differences and address specific needs (FACIR 1996). It is possible though, within the constraints imposed by local bonding activity, to redesign the existing programs to provide more targeted financial assistance.

Such a redesign could be accomplished by changing either the distribution formulas or the conditions of assistance. Experience suggests either would be difficult; the former probably lies beyond the pale. Wholesale changes in the level and pattern of state aid are not likely given the significant fiscal pressures on state. Small changes are possible though and these can have major effects. The Municipal Revenue Sharing Program, for example, has long suffered a number of defects which limited its long term value to municipalities (FACIR 1987). In 1993, the Legislature enacted a change in the statutory formula that helps protect most municipalities against a gradual erosion of the funds they receive under the program.

In November 1994, however, a constitutional amendment was approved that may constrain state revenue streams to local governments. The amendment limits the growth in state revenues to no more than the growth rate of personal income in Florida. The cap does not directly apply to local government revenues, however, the revenues levied and collected by the state and shared with the local governments are subject to the limitation. As yet it is not clear what the impacts of the revenue cap will be on state shared revenues, but its ultimate effect on revenues distributed to local governments could be considerable.

Increased Taxing Authority/Local Option Taxes. The best prospect for greater local revenue flexibility lies in increased taxing authority. There are two ways in which taxing authority can be extended, through statutory or constitutional change. The latter is more squarely in keeping with the home rule premise of the constitution. It would extend the grant of taxing authority envisioned by the devolutionary model and retain for the state the role of watchdog. State policy makers would be able to redress abuses that fail local political resolution. Interjurisdictional issues, excessive compliance costs and economic distortions would be the explicit purview of the state. Ultimately, it would enlarge the role of cities and counties somewhat. Undoubtedly, it would also prove enormously controversial.

It is somewhat easier to provide flexibility statutorily. The legislature has enacted over a dozen local option taxes since 1967 (*FACIR Handbook* 1996). But recent experience with the statutory approach is not without its problems. Many of the taxes are narrowly drawn; they affect only a minority of all jurisdictions. Few local option taxes can be exercised in all 67 counties. With the exception of the infrastructure surtax, municipalities, as a group, do not have the authority to levy local option taxes. By and large, their participation in the local option fuel taxes and the tourist development taxes is dependent upon the participation of county government.

Local option taxes typically have been limited in a number of ways. Virtually all are earmarked for specific purposes. A voter referendum is generally required before they can be employed. Such considerations affect their use. The local option fuel taxes have been much more widely adopted than either the infrastructure surtax or the initial 2 percent tourist development tax, both of which must be approved by referenda. The creation of the small county surtax in 1992 to allow small counties to levy a local option sales surtax pursuant to an ordinance enacted by an extraordinary vote of the county commission provides a measure of flexibility unavailable in most local option taxes.

Limits on Local Discretion. The restraints placed on local taxation are symptomatic of the traditional relationship between state and local government based on the *Ultra Vires* Rule. They specify which jurisdictions can levy a tax, what the taxes may be used for, and how such levies are to occur. It is possible, of course, to uncover compelling state interests of the sort demanded by the devolution model in some of these conditions. For example, the concern for administrative feasibility, "tax exporting," compliance costs, and equity provides a basis for the state position on jurisdictional preferences. And there is in the referendum requirements and earmarking a sense of state priorities. Both, in their own way, are designed to protect local taxpayers. The enthusiasm for devolution must be viewed alongside substantial sentiments against additional taxation.

Yet such practices are inconsistent with the devolutionary intent of the Constitution. A meaningful devolutionary model should allow wide compass for local governmental processes and decision making. Instead,

265

the requirement for referendum actually bypasses local processes, altering the role of local taxpayers in one type of policy decision. However, the election of commissioners and council members (held in many jurisdictions every two years) already gives voters substantial control over local tax policy. Conceptually, referenda should be restricted to instances such as bonding where decisions are involved making long term commitments for the community that cannot be undone through regular elections. State policy departs from the devolutionary model to the extent it undermines and does not reinforce local governmental processes.

In a similar way, it makes little sense to earmark local revenues unless some larger public goal is involved and can be achieved in no other way. There is, as James Buchanan has noted, some danger that the movement away from earmarking to general fund financing will produce somewhat larger public expenditures (Buchanan 1967, ch. 6). Motor fuel taxes, for example, are used by the state for transportation purposes and are clearly identified in the public's mind with such purposes. Allowing local use for other purposes might encourage unnecessary expenditures and undermine the connection between tax and benefit crucial to public support. However, such connections are not always obvious. And state earmarking of local revenues does not necessarily serve fiscal responsibility nor is it a guarantee of results. By and large, state policy should recognize the premise of home rule and allow local processes to tailor the use of local taxes. If earmarking is needed, city and county officials are well positioned to arrange it. This is the direction promoted by the devolutionary model.

Other Approaches to Increasing Revenues. The lessons of the last fifteen years have shown that revenue flexibility is not always achieved directly. In pursuit of flexibility, cities and counties have sought to control fiscal stress through a number of non-revenue approaches. This approach has generally been supported in state policy. As a consequence, local investment possibilities have been broadened. The barriers to bond issuance have been eased somewhat. Good management practices have been encouraged. Various forms of "creative financing" have been sanctioned. With some notable exceptions, the state has acted well by not acting at all, giving free rein to local policy makers and managers across the state.

The range of such non-revenue solutions within the reach of city and county government is great. Across the state, they are being used. According to a study done for the state Chamber of Commerce, "most of Florida's cities and counties have had some experience with privatization" (FCC 1987). The evidence is that privatization increased in

Florida during the eighties. More specifically, in a sample of 169 cities and counties, the Chamber found:

> There were more than 1,200 instances of contracting out, 500 instances of franchising, and 250 instances of other forms of privatization, including the use of volunteers, self-help, regulatory incentives and subsidies. In addition, more than 300 services were shed to private firms and nonprofit organizations.

The most meaningful non-revenue alternatives deal with the very structure of local governance and taxation. These change the way in which the jurisdiction can approach situations where additional revenues are demanded. They shift the debate over revenues in a fundamental way. Invariably, they are controversial. They offer a different sort of challenge to state policy and implementation of the devolutionary model.

Three approaches exist. First, there are those that sever the intimate relationship between existing jurisdictions and their revenue base. Special districts, which usually perform single governmental functions, are the most obvious instance of this approach. The increasing number of municipal service taxing authorities and independent special districts also reflect alternative methods to fund the provision of services. In some cases, special districts merely serve the type of earmarking to which James Buchanan alluded. The Safe Neighborhood Districts created in 1987 are a case in point. But other districts, such as the Juvenile Welfare Boards enacted in 1988, provide for interjurisdictional tax base pooling, while also addressing other interjurisdictional issues.

There are several methods of pooling revenue bases, of course. The tax base sharing plan adopted for Minneapolis-St. Paul metropolitan area in 1971 is perhaps the most well known (Reschovsky 1980). Under the plan, all jurisdictions within the metropolitan area share 40 percent of the areawide tax base growth according to a formula based on each community's population and its fiscal capacity. Jurisdictions with less flexibility, receive a larger portion of the common base. This approach is designed to overcome fiscal disparities and locational inefficiencies that are the artifact of jurisdictional boundaries. For obvious political reasons, this model has not been widely emulated. It is nonetheless instructive.

A second non-revenue approach retains the relationship between a jurisdiction and its revenue base, but alters jurisdictional responsibilities. In various guises, privatization represents one form of this alternative. Article VIII, Section 4 of the Florida Constitution sanctions another form, transfer of powers from one jurisdiction to another. The Florida Interlocal Cooperation Act (Chapter 163, *Florida Statutes*) acts similarly. While transfer of powers is rare, interlocal agreements are used for a variety of purposes, ranging from fire protection to building inspections. They have proven enormously effective, but cumbersome and, in many instances, a source of friction.

Finally, the third approach actually modifies the jurisdiction's boundaries, enhancing the revenue base. Historically, municipal annexation of surrounding territory is the best example (FACIR 1984). While annexation serves a number of ends unrelated to revenues, it has been advocated as a means of insuring the financial integrity of municipalities and promoting equity in the finance of local services. More recently, various regional and metropolitan reform efforts including consolidation and charter counties have been advanced, in part, to resolve the fiscal problems of local government.

State policy, in Florida, allows variants of all three and favors none. Non-revenue approaches stumble on the absence of a coherent state policy guiding the relationship between and among governments at the local level. In such matters, the devolutionary metaphor is of little help. Without a clear sense of roles to be played by the various local governments, it is difficult to determine how they should be financed. But clarifying the roles has proven difficult, in no small measure, because in solving the very practical problems that have come with growth and change in this century cities and counties have developed their own expectations and approaches.

INTERLOCAL RELATIONS/STRUCTURE AND FUNCTION

In historical terms, Florida has only recently become a large state. In 1940, the state had 1.8 million residents and ranked 29th in total state population. Today, with estimated 14.5 million residents, Florida is the fourth largest state in the nation (Florida Consensus Estimating Conference 1996, 19, Table 5). It is difficult to catalog the consequences of such growth. But in Florida, the sweeping movements of people and economic activity across the urban landscape have had significant implications for local governance.

The participants at the 1995 Intergovernmental Summit generally concurred that the structure of Florida's government does not clearly assign responsibility for government functions. The division of responsibility among the state, cities, urban counties, rural counties, regional units of government, and special districts is ambiguous. This compromises the efficient delivery of services. Growth, especially sustained growth, accelerates the difficulties.

For local governments, many of the problems with growth lie in the way it manifests itself: as more people here rather than there; as demands for this service rather than that; as opposition for certain policies rather than support. It affects the delivery of services, the integrity of fiscal bases, the possibilities for social justice, the relations among governments, and the very nature of the problems which must be faced. As it changes the urban landscape, growth can complicate urban governance and administration, diminish public accountability and erode citizen confidence in the ability of government to handle problems for which it is improperly structured. Growth challenges the architecture of local governance.

Local Government Structure. Over the years, incorporation has been a favorite method for dealing with growth, providing urban services, and meeting the demands of the local citizenry for self-determination. But the incorporation practices of the Post-War period complicated the response to growth in many ways. As a result, state municipal incorporation laws were changed in the early seventies making it much more difficult to create a city (FACIR 1984). The formation of new municipalities has virtually stopped. In the fifties, 59 new municipalities were formed; during the sixties, 34 were created (FACIR 1984). Only three new cities were formed in the eighties (Jacob City, Destin, and Midway). While the number of municipal incorporations have increased thus far during the 1990s (seven as of 1995—Key Biscayne, DeBary, Aventura, Pine Crest, Ft. Myers Beach, Deltona, and Wellington) (Florida House of Representatives 1995).[4] Seven cities were actually dissolved during this same period. (Bithlo, Bayview, Munson Island, Pennsuco, Hacienda Village, Ward Ridge, and Painters Hill) (Florida House of Representatives 1995).

Most of the population no longer lives in municipalities. The percentage is down considerably from the level in 1970.[5] There are only 10 counties where the incorporated population exceeds the unincorporated population. The state's annexation procedures, strict by national standards, have not allowed municipalities to keep pace with population growth on their periphery. Non-voluntary and special act annexations have become relatively rare. Voluntary annexations account for most of municipal areal growth. In many places, annexation can no longer fully serve the ends for which it is intended. At times, existing voluntary procedures have actually exacerbated the response to growth.

There are mechanisms for responding to such growth. County governments, for example, may provide and fund municipal services in the unincorporated area through a Municipal Service Taxing Unit (MSTU), as authorized in Chapter 125, *Florida Statutes*. They also have recourse to mechanisms such as special assessments and dependent districts.

Alternatively, such services may be funded and provided by independent special districts. But these techniques have too often been unequal to the tasks. Demands have outstripped revenues. The physical infrastructure deficit facing cities and counties, for example, numbers in the billions of dollars (State of Florida 1987, Exhibit 54).

The search for ways to handle the problems of growth has led to a number of ad hoc solutions. Over the years, for example, the legislature has authorized a number of special districts to deal with pressing problems. In 1995, 922 active special districts existed, of which 452 were independent special districts and 469 were dependent special districts (Department of Community Affairs 1995). In 1990, there were 499 dependent districts and 314 independent districts. Significantly, while the number of dependent districts dropped slightly, the independent districts increased considerably—138 independent districts were created during that period. This likely is a result of the independent special districts authority to levy up to 10 mills ad valorem tax to fund their purposes, consequently providing an alternative method for funding service delivery. More than 30 types of special districts exist including fire control districts, hospital districts, water and sewer districts, community development districts, among many more created to provide numerous public services.

Absent a framework that can accommodate the demands of growth, most areas have proceeded obliquely. The increasing interdependence and specialization of urban areas have been met with a governmental response marked by complexity and improvisation. Interlocal agreements give testimony to ingenuity of local officials. But, such methods address problems as they arise, on a case-by-case basis. Some observers have advocated more sweeping solutions. State growth policy and the local planning process can be seen in this light. In fact, there have been several attempts to enact comprehensive solutions. For example, several jurisdictions have explored city/county consolidation since the successful Jacksonville-Duval effort in 1967. All have been rejected by the voters (Florida House of Representatives 1988). Charter counties have had a better run. There are now 15 in the state. By and large, though, they have yet to fulfill their potential.[6]

Function/Delivery of Services. In fact, despite the effort and energy of local officials across the state, jurisdictional conflict, especially between cities and counties, plagues the intergovernmental system. It occurs throughout the state and on virtually every imaginable issue. At times, naturally, the causes are personal or idiosyncratic. But state policy, or more specifically its ambiguity, must assume some of the blame.

Counties and cities both possess home rule powers under the Florida Constitution. Conflict arises when home rule powers overlap and aspirations clash. Florida's Constitution is largely silent on local government relations. State devolution governs; with respect to one another local governments act as *imperium in imperio*. There is, however, an instance in which the devolutionary model is extended to the local level. Article VIII, section 1(g) allows a county charter to prevail in the event of a conflict between a charter county ordinance and a municipal ordinance. However, the provisions of section 4 limit this authority. They establish the conditions for a transfer of powers by a local government. For the most part, local relations proceed in the absence of a governing set of principles or integrating metaphor. State policy is ad hoc, improvising solutions on a piecemeal basis.

Untangling the web of local governance is not easy. One school of thought suggests it may even be counterproductive. In this view the dynamics of urban growth and shifting public sentiments are such that structural solutions will always lag behind the realities they are designed to face. Thus, a certain tension is endemic and useful. Given time, local governments may sort out their roles. For Charles Tiebout and many scholars who have refined his position, metropolitan fragmentation is not, in itself, a problem (FACIR 1984, 68–69). It does not impede, for example, the efficient supply of services. In fact, many small local governments and contractors are capable of providing quite specialized services much more economically than those attempting to serve a broader, more diverse market. In addition, small, numerous and relatively homogeneous service areas may provide returns other than productive efficiency. They can allow for greater political accountability, through better access, control and citizen participation.

Unfortunately, the evidence for such a proposition is mixed. The US Advisory Commission on Intergovernmental Relations has conducted the most ambitious study of metropolitan organization from this perspective (U.S. Advisory Commission 1988). It argues the jurisdictional "patchwork" of St. Louis County works. Beneath the superficial fragmentation, the Commission finds a rich skein of coordination. The ACIR's study is a welcome corrective to the anemic literature on metropolitan organization. But, it would have been enormously surprising if the many local governments in St. Louis County had not worked out some form of accommodation in the interests of their residents. Throughout Florida, as in the St. Louis region, local officials have made government work.

A recent study of local government service delivery arrangements within four counties in Florida (Gadsden, Lee, Orange, and Palm Beach) identified substantial variation among local governments within and between the selected counties (FACIR 1995). The report also noted that while the majority of opportunities available for local government officials to address structural and functional arrangements reside in statutory law, others may be initiated through home rule powers granted to, and exercised by cities and counties.

Both the St. Louis County study and the four-county case study in Florida indicate that the extent and the scope of the problems between and among local jurisdictions varies from place to place. Clearly, the benefits of pursuing alternatives to the present situation would vary as well. But the festering conflicts and widely noted problems in coordination suggests alternatives are needed. There are two basic approaches to resolving the problems of local relations. One proceeds on a case-by-case basis; the other is more general.

Case-by-Case Approach. The case-by-case approach appears in several variations. The existing situation exemplifies one possibility. Here, jurisdictions work out arrangements much as sovereign nations might. Typically, agreements result from a form of bilateral diplomacy, unusually limited a narrow set of concerns. Occasionally, solutions can be forged within some other framework, but the efforts are not systematic or formal. A second model recognizes the existing ambiguities in the rules governing jurisdictional responsibilities and authority. It draws on the slack and opportunities of the existing intergovernmental system to create possibilities within a formal framework. This is the basis of exercises in conflict resolution and negotiated investment strategies. Such efforts typically require considerable time and energy, if they are to succeed. They are particularly difficult to implement in larger, more fragmented areas. The notable national examples of Columbus, Hartford, and Battle Creek, often involve the private sector. Such processes typically are not established or even encouraged by state policy; however, there are exceptions. The state has taken some limited steps in this direction through the creation of conflict resolution centers and the reinvigoration of the intergovernmental element of the local planning process enacted by the 1993 Legislature.

Charter counties provide another mechanism by which to order local relations on a case-by-case basis. Most of the state's densely populous areas are governed by charter counties. Still, the potential of charter counties is substantial. The Municipal Home Rule Powers Act (s. 166.021(3)(d), F.S.) prohibits municipalities from legislating on any subject preempted by a chartered county. In practice, of course, this provision has been a matter of considerable dispute. The Florida Supreme

Court narrowed the scope of charter county authority considerably in *Sarasota County v. Town of Longboat Key* (1978). More recently, it increased charter county authority, arguing section 1(g) of Article VIII permits preemption of regulatory activities, but not services (*Broward County v. City of Ft. Lauderdale* (1985)). The implications of this distinction remain to be seen. It is clear though that a large class of disputes (service areas) will remain even under the broadest possible interpretation. Moreover, relations within charter counties will still be confounded by the unsettled nature of relations among the municipalities themselves.

There is another model that works case-by-case. It plays to the very concerns addressed by Tiebout and his associates. Fragmentation, they argue, represents a choice for diversity based on well understood information about the performance of various governments. Perhaps, but citizen surveys as often as not reveal little understanding among the public about the responsibilities of local governments and the costs of the services they provide. Under full information, the jurisdictional preferences of the citizenry might change and create a working model of local relation. Under this model, market principles can be used, indirectly, to order local relations. Full cost marginal pricing and open disclosure can be employed usefully to this end. Market forces galvanized by a policy that requires Truth-In-Expenditures (TIE) statements might well encourage a local realignment of responsibilities. Full disclosure can provide a better foundation for local decision making and the key to improved relations. This approach was given limited expression in the solid waste management legislation enacted in 1988 (SB 1192).

The appeal of the case-by-case approach lies in its very limitations. It does not force uniformity where uniformity is uncomfortable. It does favor change in the face of custom and sentiment. It can be tailored to problems involving the overlap of service provision and production, or it can be limited to the overlap of governance and conflict resolution.

But these advantages exact a cost. First, they work slowly, requiring a commitment and sense of vision that can be all too easily lost. Second, they often misfire. Negotiation, electoral campaigns and even information can exacerbate conflict as well as mitigate it. Finally, to an extent, they miss the point. Even when local governments succeed in resolving their differences, their efforts can be undone by state policy.

State policy must explicitly recognize local arrangements. If state policy clarifies the relations among local governments it not only resolves local problems, it provides the basis for improved state-local relations in other area, as well. It provides a foundation for evaluating issues such as mandates and revenue flexibility that is now lacking.

General Approaches. The design of state policy towards local government must begin with a reassessment of the premises in the devolutionary model. Are all jurisdictions alike? Do they serve the same purposes? Must they all be treated alike? For school and special districts, the answer to such questions has long been clear. No! State policy has foundered on the treatment of general purpose governments that makes no distinctions when distinctions are needed.

A general redesign of state policy towards general purpose local government must be predicated on distinctions. It will call for distinctions that heretofore policy makers have been unwilling to make. It will not be easy or without controversy. As important, it requires criteria for making such distinctions and a sense of how competing priorities are to be evaluated. The redesign must recognize two sets of relations; those that exist between cities and counties, and those among cities. The first is conditioned by the second. City-county relations cannot be clarified until the roles of municipalities are understood.

There are examples of how this be done. Massachusetts, for example, has differentiated among its municipalities according to their functional responsibilities. Full service cities are treated differently than limited service cities. Several states categorize municipalities by size and extend, on that basis, varying degrees of home rule and extraterritorial authority. These approaches provide the basis for meaningful state policy, but they depend on substantive criteria. There is another method. It relies on procedural criteria. In Florida, for example, performance measures have been incorporated into a number of state-local relationships (i.e., environmental regulation, land use planning). These tools can be extended to differentiate among municipalities, allowing for the exercise of local preferences. The design principle would require greater local effort and commitment in exchange for a grant of greater autonomy. It would entail regulatory and service responsibilities and, in one conception, would result in various levels of autonomy within an *imperio* model.

A general policy towards city-county relations can be framed in similar fashion: directly, through substantive structural changes, or indirectly, through a procedural one. For example, it is possible, within bounds, to define the functional responsibilities of local government, working along the lines of the turn back strategies popular in New Federalism. In a sense, this would represent a return of the historic logic governing local relations, but it need not entail the historic distinctions. Such an approach need not be compulsory; the state has an array of incentives available to encourage such development. Even so, it would likely be controversial. Again, there is no readily available solution but procedural methods based on performance objectives offer an alternative. Counties can be made the default to municipalities whose citizens are committed to a limited set of responsibilities. Such governments would stand in different relation to the county and to municipalities assuming a broader range of functions. In this mix, the scope of major negotiations between city and county would be narrowed. Annexation laws, for example, would be shaped to the contours of local responsibility. Revenue sources and financing mechanisms would be tied to responsibilities. Counties and full service municipalities would stand in one relationship; counties and limited service municipalities in another.

Of course, it is in the details of such possibilities that policy is actually defined. Many alternatives within such a framework would be mutually unacceptable to all those involved. The existing policy of devolution, together with the exigencies of responding to growth and complexity, has produced an accommodation that may defy general redesign. But this can be determined only through a broad discussion of the possibilities.

Recent actions by the state indicate a new commitment to addressing state policies governing local governments, as well as soliciting local governments input in devising solutions. In recent years, the executive branch has established an unprecedented number of task forces and work groups comprised state and local officials to address the myriad of issues confronting state and local governments. In 1996, the Legislature enacted law changing the structure and name of the previous Advisory Council on Intergovernmental Relations to the Legislative Committee on Intergovernmental Relations, elevating its status and intergovernmental issues in the legislative arena.

Perhaps the best shot at resolving the jurisdictional and other problems of local governments is the creation of the Local Government Study Commission II. The commission, created by law for a two year duration, is comprised primarily of local officials, including representatives of the counties, cities, and special districts, as well as other interested state and private parties. Uniquely composed of local officials, this commission's ability to address and negotiate issues of service delivery, revenues, and government formation, may potentially result in a restructuring appropriate for modern Florida and its entry into the 21st century. It remains to be seen to what degree the local government entities will be able to put aside their parochial interests to achieve meaningful administrative and structural change.

CHAPTER 10

As the debate over federalism is renewed, the nation must focus on the critical role of cities and counties. It must find a meaningful way in which to realize a working partnership between the State and its local governments. Only such a discussion can sharpen the issues and focus on the need for a different conception of local governance and the means by which it can be realized.[7]

REFERENCES

Alexander, James (1984). "The Limits of Municipal Sovereignty: Legislative and Judicial Formulations Under Dillon's Rule." Paper prepared for the Annual Meeting of the American Political Science Association, Washington, D.C., August 30–September 2.

Bradley, Robert (1988). "Changes in the state-local-federal relationship." Paper prepared for the National Association of State Budget Officers (NASBO), St. Petersburg, Florida, July 20.

Buchanan, James (1967). *Public Finance in Democratic Process.* Chapel Hill: University of North Carolina Press.

Clark, Gordon (1985). *Judges and the Cities: Interpreting Local Autonomy.* Chicago: University of Chicago Press.

Corwin, Edward S. (1950). "The Passing of Dual Federalism." *Virginia Law Review,* 36 (February).

Division of Economic and Demographic Research (Summer 1996). *Florida Consensus Estimating Conference Book 3: State of Florida Population and Demographic Forecast.* Tallahassee, Florida Legislature.

Eulau, Heinz (1978). "Polarity in Representational Federalism: A Neglected Theme of Political Theory." In *The Politics of Representation,* edited by Heinz Eulau and John Wahlke, 91-106. Beverly Hills, CA: Sage Publications.

Florida Advisory Council on Intergovernmental Relations. 1980. *Catalogue of State Mandates.* Tallahassee: Florida ACIR.

———. (1983, January). "Legislative Mandates." In Florida ACIR Working Papers: Aspects of Fiscal Capacity. Tallahassee: Florida ACIR.

———. (1984, January). *Annexation in Florida: Issues and Options.* Tallahassee: Florida ACIR.

———. (1985, January). *Legislative Scrutiny and the Role of Fiscal Notes in the Enactment of Statutory Mandates.* Tallahassee: Florida ACIR.

———. (1986, September). *Catalogue of State Shared Revenues.* Tallahassee: Florida ACIR.

———. (1987, December). *Two State Shared Revenue Programs: Municipal Revenue Sharing and the Half-Cent Sales Tax Emergency Distribution.* Tallahassee: Florida ACIR.

———. (1991a, March). "Florida's Small Counties: A Profile of Service Demands and Revenues." Report-In-Brief.

———. (1991b, January). *1990 Report on Mandates and Measures Affecting Local Fiscal Capacity.* Tallahassee: Florida ACIR.

———. (1994). *A Profile of Local Government Revenues and Expenditures.* Tallahassee: Florida ACIR.

———. (1995, December). *Local Government Function and Formation in the Service Delivery Arena: Review of Relevant Research and Law.* Tallahassee: Florida ACIR.

———. (1996). *A Profile of Local Government Revenues and Expenditures.* Tallahassee: Florida ACIR.

———. (1996, July). *Local Government Financial Information Handbook,* Tallahassee, Florida ACIR.

Florida Chamber of Commerce (1987). *The Role of Privatization in Florida's Growth.* Law and Economics Center, University of Miami and Local Government Center, Reason Foundation.

Florida Department of Revenue (1988, October). *Florida Ad Valorem Valuations and Tax Data.* Tallahassee: the Department.

Florida House of Representatives (1988, March). *Getting Together: The Forming and Reshaping of Local Government in Florida.* Tallahassee: Committee on Community Affairs.

Florida Institute of Government (1996). *Summit on Intergovernmental Challenges in Florida: Summary Statement.* Tallahassee, co-authorized by Florida League of Cities, Florida Association of Counties, Florida Association of Special Districts, Executive Office of the Governor, Florida ACIR.

Florida Legislature (1988, March). *Florida Tax Sources: Fiscal Impact of Potential Changes, 1988–89.* Tallahassee: The Legislature.

———. (1991, March). *Florida Tax Sources: Fiscal Impact of Potential Changes, 1990–91.* Tallahassee: The Legislature.

———. (1996). *Florida Tax Handbook: Fiscal Impact of Potential Changes,* Tallahassee: The Legislature.

Francis, James (1988, September). "Florida vs. the Fifty States: Composition of Revenues and Selected Expenditures." Presentation to the Florida Crime Prevention and Law Enforcement Study Commission.

Hartog, Hendrik (1983). *Public Property and Private Power: The Corporation of the City of New York in American Law.* Chapel Hill: University of North Carolina Press.

Kelly, Janet (1992). *State Mandates: Fiscal Notes, Reimbursement, and Anti-Mandate Strategies,* National League of Cities.

Long, Norton (1978). "Federalism and Perverse Incentives: What Is Needed for a Workable Theory or Reorganization for Cities?" *Publius* (Spring): 87–92.

Lovell, Catherine (1981). "Mandating: Operationalizing Domination." *Publius* (Spring): 59–78.

Marsicano, Ralph (1984). "Development of Home Rule in Florida." *Florida Municipal Record* (April): 7+.

National Conference of State Legislatures (1986, August). "Recommendations of the Task Force on State-Local Relations." New Orleans: NCSL.

New York Commission on State-Local Relations (1988, October). "The State of State-Local Relations." The Nelson A. Rockefeller Institute of Government.

Rees, John and Robert Bradley (1988). "State Science Policy and Economic Development in the United States: A Critical Perspective." *Environment and Planning* A, 20: 990-1012.

Reschovsky, Andrew (1980). "An Evaluation of Metropolitan Area Tax Base Sheltering." *National Tax Journal,* 33: 55–66.

Sapolsky, Joann (1988, December). "Estimated FY1989 Federal Allocations to Florida Programs by the Percentage They Receive of the Total National Allocation and the Total Estimated Dollars Received." Florida ACIR Working Paper.

Shannon, John (1988). "The Faces of Fiscal Federalism." *Intergovernmental Perspective* 14 (Winter): 5–8.

State of Florida, State Comprehensive Plan Committee (1987, June). *Keys to Florida's Future: Winning in a Competitive World, Final Report,* Volume II.

Thomas, Robert D. (1984). "Cities as Partners in the Federal System." Paper prepared for the Annual Meeting of the American Political Science Association, Washington, D.C., August 30–September 2.

Thomas, Robert and Vincent Marando (1981). "Local Governmental Reform and Territorial Democracy: The Case of Florida." *Publius* (Winter): 49–63.

U.S. Advisory Commission on Intergovernmental Relations (1981, November). *Measuring Local Discretionary Authority.* Washington, D.C.: U.S. ACIR.

———. (1985, January). *The Question of State Capability.* Washington, D.C.: U.S. ACIR.

———. (1986, February). *Reflections on Garcia and Its Implications for Federalism.* Washington, D.C.: U.S. ACIR.

———. (1988, September). *Metropolitan Organization: The St. Louis Case.* Washington, D.C.: U.S. ACIR.

———. (1994). *Significant Features of Fiscal Federalism,* Volume II. Washington, D.C.: U.S. ACIR.

U.S. Council of Economic Advisors, *Economic Report of the President,* February 1996.

U.S. Department of Commerce, Bureau of the Census (1986). *State and Metropolitan Area Data Book, 1986.* Washington, D.C.: U.S. Government Printing Office.

———. (1988). *Statistical Abstract of the United States,* 108th edition. Washington, D.C.: U.S. Government Printing Office.

U.S. General Accounting Office (1988, September). "Legislative Mandates: State Experiences Offer Insight for Federal Action." Washington, D.C.: U.S. GAO.

University of Florida (1991, April). *Florida Population: Census Summary 1990.* Gainesville: Bureau of Economic and Business Research.

Walker, Rebecca (1987, December). Author's Communication with the Tax Assessor of Palm Beach County.

Warren, William T. (1996, July/August). "State Authority: A Rising or Setting Sun?" *State Legislatures.*

Zimmerman, Joseph (1978). *State Mandating of Local Expenditures.* Washington, D.C.: U.S. Advisory Commission on Intergovernmental Relations.

———. (1984). "State Response to Urban/Rural Problems." Paper prepared for the Annual Meeting of the American Political Science Association, Washington, D.C., August 30–September 2.

———. (1987). "The State Mandating Problem." *State and Local Government Review* (Spring): 78–84.

ENDNOTES

1. *The Official List of Special Districts,* 1995, Florida Department of Community Affairs.

2. The Florida Legislature enacted during the 1996 session, Ch. 311-96, Laws of Florida, which repeals provisions in Chapter 163, F.S., regarding the Florida Advisory Council on Intergovernmental Relations (FACIR) and recreates it in Chapter 11, F.S. as the Legislative Committee on Intergovernmental Relations. Thus, effective November 5, 1996, the provision requiring the legislative mandate report will be in Ch. 11, F.S.

3. Florida ACIR calculations using information derived from the State of Florida, Department of Banking and Finance, *Profile of Local Government Revenues and Expenditures,* May 1996.

4. Three of the incorporated municipalities required exemptions from one or more state standards regarding municipal formation (DeBary, Deltona, and Wellington) (Florida House of Representatives, 1996). Seven incorporation attempts failed to get approval from the voters between 1980 and 1995 (Deltona Lakes, 1987, Deltona, 1990, Ft. Myers Beach, 1982, 1986, Halifax, 1985, Marco Island, 1980, 1982, 1986, 1990, 1993, Spring Hill, 1986, Port LaBelle, 1994, Destiny, 1995. However, two were eventually approved by the voters in subsequent referendum elections (Deltona and Ft Myers Beach). Florida House of Representatives, Commission Community Affairs, *1995 Local Government Formation Manual,* 4th Edition, November 1995, 2–12. Florida House of Representatives, Committee on Community Affairs *Local Bill/Special Act Process: Time for Change?,* February, 1996, 16.

5. Florida ACIR calculation based on figures in University of Florida, Bureau of Economic and Business Research, *Local Government Financial Information Handbook,* July 1996, Table 11.1, pp. 287–302.

6. Florida Advisory Council on Intergovernmental Relations, *A Profile of Local Government Revenue and Expenditure,* 96-4, March 1996, Table 11, 63. See also Robert Thomas and Vincent Marando, "Local Governmental Reform and Territorial Democracy: The Case of Florida," *Publius,* Winter, 1981, 49–63; and Florida Advisory Council on Intergovernmental Relations, *Local Government Function and Formation in the Service Delivery Arena: Review of Relevant Research and Law,* 95-5, 66–69.

7. We would like to thank Joann Sapolsky, Beth Lines, David Cooper, and, of course, Dr. Carolyn Herrington for their assistance in piecing together this paper. We would also like to thank Chuck Hungerford, Steve O'Cain, and Stefanie Moran for their technical assistance. It should also be noted that the paper benefitted enormously from diligence and care of the editor.

CHAPTER

11

COUNTY GOVERNMENT

FRANK P. SHERWOOD AND VIVIAN ZARICKI

A merica's governance system has been characterized by a large and diverse number of institutions serving a wide range of areas, communities and interests. Florida is much like the rest of the nation in this respect. It has both general purpose governments, such as counties and cities, and special function governments, such as school districts, which take the responsibility for the great majority of governmental services directly to the state's citizens.

This chapter is concerned with a general purpose local government, the county, which has a broad mandate to exercise governmental responsibility within established geographical boundaries. While it enjoys substantial independence in the discharge of its local obligations, its ties to state government are very close. It is quite impossible to conceive of policy management in a large and complex society, like that of Florida, without an appreciation of the institutional character of the counties. The linkages between these general purpose local governments and the state are numerous and complex; they receive treatment in chapter 10.

Counties have been traditionally conceived as organizational subdivisions of state government, charged with performing services for citizens regardless of settlement pattern. Even in the most rural setting, there is need for law enforcement, a judiciary, for records that will support the orderly conduct of business, and for at least a minimum structure of transportation and public health services.

In the 19th and much of the 20th century in a large territory like Florida, it was impossible to conceive of performing these types of local government functions only in the state capital. There was a need to decentralize and to make it physically possible for people to get to a court, to register a birth, or to record a deed. Further, since a tax on property was the basic form of support for such local services, it was equally obvious that someone had to be close at hand to assign valuations and to see that taxes were collected. Thus the state was subdivided into counties to which the performance of such duties was assigned. The creation of counties to serve specific territorial areas generated a basic contradiction: the area orientation, i.e. the obligation to meet the needs of a specific community of people, argued for flexibility and discretion at the county level; but the functions involved, such as administration of justice, demanded a regularity and uniformity throughout the entire state. The accommodation that ensued was hailed for many years as a brilliant one. Local people were elected to manage county affairs in accord with detailed state laws that stressed uniformity and sharply limited local discretion.

As the U.S. population has become larger, more urban, and more complex, the contradiction between the responsibility of county elected officials to local constituencies and the demands for conformity from a growing state government has become increasingly apparent. Citizens have demanded that counties become more active and more effective in dealing with local problems, whereas traditionally the state has specified the activities in which counties might engage and the means of their finance. In Florida, as elsewhere, the counties have struggled to become responsive local governments.

In contrast, the municipalities started from quite a different base. They are artifacts of urban growth, which brings high interdependence to a society. People who live in close proximity are very much affected by the attitudes and behaviors of their neighbors. Collaterally, they can no longer act as independently. They cannot run a road wherever it suits their convenience; and the uses of one's neighboring property can quickly become a personal problem, which explains the more restrictive zoning requirements within cities. Sources of water also become more problematic; and the health of one's neighbor can quickly become a personal problem. Thus, urban growth brought urban problems, to be met through urban services. The traditional general purpose governments, the state and its subdivision counties, were established essentially to provide services required by everyone, either in the rural or the urban setting. To meet the special urban imperative, a new type of government emerged, the municipal corporation. In this case the citizens wanting urban services got together and incorporated. They formed a new government. Thus, today we speak of those residing in municipalities as in "incorporated" areas and those outside [even though urban] as in "unincorporated" areas.

The difference in the concept of jurisdictional boundaries between the counties and municipalities says a great deal about their characters. The shaping of the municipal jurisdiction has been determined by a need for urban services. Its boundaries have often been irregular, as has been urban demographic development. No one gets upset because all Floridians are not citizens of a municipality.

The basic imperative of a municipality is to be responsive to its citizenry. There is no requirement that all citizens of a state have access to a sanitary sewer system or a municipal recreation program. The cities have typically enjoyed greater autonomy, both in terms of the things that they do and also in terms of the means by which they finance those services.

Florida's great growth in the past half-century, and in particular its urbanization, has made these traditional orientations less realistic. By 1990 Florida was the third most urbanized state in the nation, behind only California and New York. As will be discussed later, the old rule that only the municipalities would serve urban needs has not applied for many years. Government boundaries were not redrawn to conform to new settlement patterns; and the counties, as the only general purpose local government available, were required to respond to a broader range of community needs and to provide urban services. Conversely, the urban growth outside the cities created new forms of interdependence. Municipal corporations had, in many cases in Florida, been created to serve local, highly parochial interests of some very small communities. Demographic shifts have required a change in the concept of community. The interrelationships are now much broader. The state government can no longer function as it did in the rural environment of 1900. Where Florida was only 20% urban in 1900, it was nearly 85% urban by 1980. In fact, growth rates in unincorporated areas have skyrocketed such that 51 percent of Florida's population lives outside its cities today. The predominantly urban character of the state has meant a far more activist state government. The municipalities have been subjected to more demands by the state; and the counties have been accorded somewhat greater freedoms. The institutional roles of the cities and the counties have thus been changing.

The Nature of Florida's Counties

Historical Evolution

Florida's counties were created much in the pattern of other states. General Andrew Jackson issued an order in July, 1821, which partitioned the Florida territory into two subordinate units, the counties of Escambia and of St. John's. Escambia encompassed all of the land lying between the Perdido and Suwannee rivers, roughly the Big Bend area;

and St. John's embraced everything else, essentially the whole of the peninsula. Territorially, St. John's was several times larger than Escambia but with fewer people.

The primary functions of the new counties were judicial, with five justices of the peace established in each. Other county officers were also established: clerk of the court and sheriff. In addition the two counties were empowered to grant and recall licenses or commissions for innkeepers, for retailers of liquor of every description, and for keepers of billiard tables. Within 20 years the original two counties had been expanded to 21, by which time such familiar names as Dade, Duval, Hillsborough, Alachua and Leon were on the map. Interestingly, the largest county in the state in 1840, Mosquito [covering the eastern portion of the state from Dade to St. John's] no longer exists. By 1925 the number of counties in Florida had expanded to today's 67, with the growth particularly rapid between 1920 and 1925, when 22 were created. The last county was Gilchrist, formed in 1925.

The four largest counties inevitably appear where Florida's population concentrates, in the south and central parts of the state. The two largest are in the Miami-Ft. Lauderdale area, Dade and Broward. Dade is also the greatest in terms of land area. The third and fourth most populated are Palm Beach and Hillsborough; and the smallest county is Lafayette, with a 1995 population of about 6,516. The difference between Lafayette and Dade, with a 1995 population of 2,013,821, emphasizes the important point that jurisdictions with similar designations are not at all the same kinds of governments. Lafayette, in the rural Big Bend area, is not only microscopic in terms of its share of the state's population but enjoys neither the economic wealth nor the cultural diversity of Dade.

As might be expected, the populations of the counties vary greatly in their ethnic composition. Gadsden county in the Panhandle is 59% Afro-American; Holmes and Pasco counties, on the other hand, possess little diversity, with respectively only 6% and 2% of the population Afro-American. Although Florida's Hispanic population (12.2% in 1990) is the fourth largest of the states and growing more rapidly than any other, it tends to be concentrated in the southern part of the state. Sixty percent of Florida's Hispanics reside in Dade. No other county approximates Dade in the percentage of Hispanics. The percentage in neighboring Broward, for example, is 8.6 (*Florida Statistical Abstract* 1995).

Florida's extremely rapid growth rate [over 33% in the 1980-90 period] poses inevitable problems for local government. There were 6.5 people to be served by local governments of Florida in 1990, as compared with 5 in 1980. U.S. Census Bureau statistics released in 1989, according to Mohl, revealed that seven of the nation's ten fastest growing metropolitan areas were located in Florida (Mohl 1990, 25).

More importantly, virtually all the increases occurred in urban settings. The Naples-Collier County metropolitan area recorded an increase of 48.8% in the 1980–87 period; and seven other areas had increases of over 30%. Further, these rates of increase are expected to continue to the end of the century, with Fort Myers-Lee projected to grow 50%; West Palm Beach-Palm Beach 40%; Orlando-Orange 32%; Broward 30%, with others not far behind.

Not only is most of the growth urban, but a major share of it is occurring outside municipal jurisdictions. People are increasingly moving to urban settlements in the "unincorporated" areas, where they do not have access to services from a city government. In the 1980-86 period the growth rate outside the cities was 30.6%, as contrasted with 23.6% inside the municipalities. Further, over half the people (51%) in this heavily urbanized state live outside the cities. This settlement pattern, a companion of increased urbanization, has been a major factor in reshaping the role of the counties in the major metropolitan areas. As the only general purpose governments in the unincorporated areas, the counties have increasingly expanded to meet urban service requirements. They function in many ways as cities. Their increasing population and expanding responsibilities have caused county expenditures to rise more rapidly than those of the cities.

The consequence has been to heighten the importance of counties as units of local government and to constrain the rise of very large cities in Florida. Miami continues to be the largest municipality in the state; but its population is less than one-third that of Dade County.

Not surprisingly, Florida possesses seven of the 50 largest counties in the United States, in terms of overall governmental revenues (*City and State* 1990, 13–14). Dade County is seventh in the nation (nearly $1.5 billions); and the others are Broward, Palm Beach, Jacksonville-Duval, Orange, Pinellas, and Hillsborough. Five of the seven also appear to have heavy operating responsibilities, as is to be seen in their numbers of employees per 1,000 population. The five, Dade (12.29), Jacksonville-Duval (11.4), Palm Beach (8.64), Orange (9.98) and Hillsborough (8.63), report figures higher than the average of 7.68 employees per 1,000 for the nation's top 50 counties. Only Broward (4.59) and Pinellas (5.76) are below the 50-county average. It is interesting to note that Florida is not represented in the top 50 cities in the United States.1

One area in which Florida's counties have a special national status is in their high percentage of elderly people. Four Florida counties (Pasco, Charlotte, Sarasota, and Citrus) are in the top five, according to

County News (1990, 10); and 1995 data reveal that Hernando and Highlands have replaced Sarasota and Pasco in the four "greyest" counties in Florida. The proportion of people over 65 in these counties comprised about one-third their total population (30 to 33%).

THE THREE ROLES OF THE COUNTIES

Demographic changes in Florida have caused the urban, metropolitan counties to assume three highly distinct roles. They are:

a. Traditional activities that have been a continuing part of their constitutional structure and which are directly related to their responsibility as a sub-unit of the state government. Examples include tax assessment and collection, vital records, elections, and court administration.

b. Area-wide services that have fallen to the counties because they are the local government unit with the broadest jurisdiction and therefore are most likely to have the capacity to deal with problems covering large geographic areas. Examples include animal control, natural resource protection, emergency management, and landfill operation.

c. Urban services to the unincorporated areas and also to small cities lacking capacity to engage in a full range of services. Examples include fire service, parks and recreation, land planning, and police protection.

While the urban service responsibilities are locally driven, county involvement in traditional and in area-wide, regional services necessitates a close involvement with state government; and the counties have become increasingly subject to state mandates. Thus, as citizens have demanded that counties have sufficient autonomy to respond to local needs, a contradictory trend has placed them in even more intimate interactions with the state government. They have been required to engage in a broader range of tasks, which have been mandated by both state and federal governments.

Traditional County Role. The counties are, as has already been emphasized, officially sub-divisions of the state, with an obligation to carry out certain state functions on a decentralized basis. All 67 counties engage in such functions as the maintenance of law and order, the operation of the justice system, and certain types of record keeping. The level and intensity of a particular service will, of course, vary greatly among the 67 counties.

For a variety of reasons involving policy choices at the federal and state levels, the counties have become important elements of a so-called "safety net," conceived as a basic support system for the less advantaged. Counties have been charged with administering some social programs particularly focused on the health. With the withdrawal of some federal funding, the counties have had to pick up much of the financial burden.

Another traditional function, public safety, has also demanded an increasing portion of county resources. The jails operated by the counties have posed particular difficulties as expanding numbers of people have been imprisoned. Federal standards, amplified and enforced by decisions of the courts, have required the replacement or upgrading of jails and improvements in their continuing operations. Essentially all the funding for construction and operation of jails comes from county sources.

Area-Wide, Regional Services. Because of their geographic size and reach, the urbanizing counties are increasingly assuming responsibilities as protector, provider, and advocate for the interests of the regional community which they encompass. This is undoubtedly the most ambiguous (and also ambitious) of the three prime roles in which the counties are involved. Its emergence is evidence of the way in which a rapidly changing society is forcing a transformation on governmental institutions.

The collection of solid waste, a typical urban function, is only a small piece of a much larger problem. As environmental hazards have been recognized and disposal sites have been filled, and new ones become more difficult and more expensive to acquire, regional responses have become imperative. The counties have become the general government jurisdiction responsible for handling solid waste disposal.

The situation in Palm Beach County typifies the underlying process that has led to regional responsibility. There are 37 municipalities in the county, the largest of which is West Palm Beach, but which contains less than 10% of the county's population. Further, the territory of the county covers 2,023 square miles. While the multiplicity of municipalities is one reason for the focus on the county as the regional unit, its size and special legal status provide other important advantages.

Besides solid waste disposal, the regional activities in which Florida counties may engage are: water quality control, air quality control, disaster management, emergency communication, emergency medical services, flood control, law enforcement, drug programs, transit, and growth management.

Urban/Municipal Services. In theory municipal governments are to provide those services that are required by people living in close proximity to each other, i.e. those residing in urban circumstances. But this requires governmental units to respond to rapidly changing demographic circumstances far more rapidly than is reasonable. Inclusion in a municipal corporation is a voluntary act, taken either through joining an existing unit or creating a new one. Many residents are unwilling to do either. Furthermore, municipal incorporation has been used as a form of protection and continued isolation from larger jurisdictions. Yet the need for urban services and controls remains.

It is within this context that certain of the larger, urbanizing counties have become providers of services to the unincorporated areas and to small municipalities. Unlike traditional and regional services, the triggering element is local demand. Although the list of possible activities in which a government may engage is very long, it is seldom that any two jurisdictions do exactly the same thing. Certainly this is true of Florida counties. It is not uncommon that urban counties will be involved in such disparate activities as communicable disease control, police patrol, fire protection, parks, libraries, water distribution, stadiums and arenas, family services, building control, subdivision control, zoning, environmental permitting, and soil conservation.

Even this brief list suggests how difficult it is to draw a tight distinction between urban and rural needs. Indeed, the differentiation probably has little operational utility. There are many functions classified as urban that the national and state governments have defined as obligations to all the people, without regard to settlement pattern. It is not surprising, then, that in Florida the Sheriff's road patrol is defined as both a municipal and traditional county function, depending on the distribution of the population. Everyone is entitled to protection on the roads. The function is defined as municipal when it occurs in an urban setting, traditional county in the less densely settled areas.

Even though it is established that a substantial number of counties are heavily engaged in urban responsibility, it has been difficult to change the political culture sufficiently to deal with the new reality. While the counties have been granted substantial freedom to engage in a variety of municipal/urban activities, traditional state control has not been relaxed sufficiently to permit their financing by the people who benefit from such services. The counties are therefore restricted in honoring the conventional norm that urban dwellers should pay fully for the urban services they receive. Financing, though, is simply the most evident of many ambiguities in the urban service role of the counties.

PROFILE OF COUNTY SERVICES

A catalog of services provided by county governments in Florida has been made by Donald C. Menzel and J. Edwin Benton of the

University of South Florida, with assistance from Charles Spindler of Auburn University (1990).

They studied 76 services characteristically provided by Florida counties and received data from 58. Despite their increased urban responsibilities, county governments continue to serve their total constituencies, those in the cities as well as those outside. Sixty-four percent of the 76 services studied were provided throughout the county area. It is also evident that the unincorporated areas have increasingly come to depend on the counties. Twenty-five percent of the 76 services were provided only in the unincorporated areas (Menzel et al. 1990, 2).

There is wide variation among Florida counties in the number of services they provide. They ranged from 12 in Liberty County to 62 in the consolidated Jacksonville-Duval area. Other findings were:

a. The typical county provides an average of 36 services.

b. The typical county delivers 48% of its services with its own employees.

c. Contracting and the award of franchises to private sector firms are commonly employed. The typical county has eight service contracts and three franchises.

d. A total of 606 intergovernmental agreements was reported by the 58 counties, with the typical county having 11. Forty percent of these agreements are with cities. The state is often a party to inter-governmental agreements for certain types of services (Menzel et al. 1990, 60).

e. Some services are provided by special districts or specially designated public agencies. There are 924 active special districts in Florida. Every Florida county has at least one dependent or independent taxing district.

f. While many sources of financing are used for county activities, the general fund (primarily derived from ad valorem taxation) remains the most common and is the source of money for 35% of the sampled services. User fees (8%) and enterprise operations income (7%) were other significant sources but lagged far behind the general fund. Menzel, Benton, and Spindler found that urban services[2] were financed much more significantly by their users. About two-thirds of such services were funded either by user fees or enterprise operations and slightly less than a third by county general revenue.

g. Traditional services were established and operating much earlier than were the municipal/urban. Fifty-three percent of urban services were launched in the typical county since 1970.

h. About the same proportion of urban and traditional services are delivered to incorporated and unincorporated areas in the typical county.

i. The typical county is apt to provide urban services to only a part of the unincorporated area (Menzel et al. 1990, 50).

SIGNIFICANT METROPOLITAN REFORMS IN FLORIDA

The great changes in role and responsibilities of county governments in Florida have created problems of organization and leadership, both external and internal. The external problems concern relationships with other governments operating within county territory. It is important to understand that a variety of public and private organizations serve citizen needs at the local level. How they work together will have major impact on the quality of community life.

Frequently the relationships between the county and its cities are severely strained; and proposals are made for radical reform of local government institutions. Propositions to consolidate all local governments into a single unit have reached the ballot in several Florida communities; but such a consolidation has been approved only in Jacksonville-Duval. Even there, existing municipalities and various services were not included in the consolidation.

While major changes in the structure of Florida local government have not accompanied the dramatic demographic movements, there have been two cases where Florida has been a leader in instituting reform in metropolitan areas. One is the Jacksonville-Duval consolidation, which occurred in 1968. The other was the introduction of "two-tier" government in Dade County [Miami] in 1957. Indeed, the two major reforms in Miami and Jacksonville have given Florida a special place in the literature on metropolitan government in North America. A 1977 book by Horan and Taylor, for example, treats five cases of major structural change, two of which (Miami and Jacksonville) were in Florida (Horon and Taylor 1977, vi).

METROPOLITAN DADE COUNTY'S "TWO-TIER" GOVERNMENT

The Miami area experienced a high degree of urbanization early. The drainage of wet lands and generous federal lending fueled a housing boom, particularly in the unincorporated areas of Dade County. The city of Miami had been incorporated in 1896; Homestead in 1913; Miami Beach in 1915; and Coral Gables in 1925. But the land was cheaper outside the cities and the population in the unincorporated areas zoomed from about 110,000 in 1950 to over 350,000 in 1960. By 1954 there were 26 cities in Dade County, and the state legislature said it would approve no more. Many communities were incorporated to serve diverse and special needs, resulting in great fragmentation and consequent difficulty in meeting area-wide needs.

Internally, Dade County was a conglomeration of officials elected under a commission form of government. There were 39 different public officers on whom citizens voted, including five commissioners, 10 heads of independent departments, and an assortment of judges. Surprisingly, the governor appointed a commission which set the budget for the county. Elections turned on individual personalities and past political experience. As early as 1945 a proposal to consolidate the cities and the county was brought before the Florida state legislature and defeated; other attempts were made in 1948 and 1953 (Hertz 1984, 10).

In 1954 the Public Administration Service (PAS), a nationally prominent public interest consulting organization, produced a study with sharp criticisms of current arrangements and included proposals for major reform. Services were pronounced inadequate in such areas as county-wide planning, law enforcement, fire protection (outside the city of Miami), traffic engineering, sewerage, and library services (PAS 1954, 194).

The multiplicity of governments also produced varying forms of inequity: divergent, uneven levels of service, extremely varied tax assessments, and the payment by city residents for services in the unincorporated areas. Finally, there were serious administrative problems in a county where the commissioners had no direct control over their own budgets and were dependent on a host of separately elected department heads.

Toronto Model Proposed. When the report on Miami was being prepared, major reform was under way in the Canadian metropolitan area of Toronto, culminating in the establishment of a "two-tier" government on January 1, 1954. In effect, municipalities were retained to perform local services and a superstructure, a metropolitan government, was created to perform region-wide services. At the time the Canadian solution seemed very clean, highly rational, and received a great deal of attention. The fact that the solution was imposed by the provincial government was reported but not emphasized (Rose 1972, 21).

The PAS report sought to transfer the Toronto solution to Dade County. Even in 1993 Miami-Dade stands as the only U.S. metropolitan area where the "two-tier" model has been formally instituted. Obviously, there are various types of metropolitan authorities throughout the nation but none was conceived as a comprehensive reform measure. Unfortunately, the proposal was not as daring as much of the publicity suggested at the time. It was formulated to fit a political circumstance in which the municipalities had already shown their prowess in defeating consolidation; and, while the state was a major actor, there was little likelihood of a reform imposed from Tallahassee. Thus the Miami-Dade two tier version retained the traditional county unit and a patchwork group of municipalities, with most of the county having no government to provide local services. Following developments in California, PAS proposed a dramatic reform of Dade County government and an expansion of its functions to include not only a regional role but one as a purveyor of municipal/urban services to the unincorporated area. Hertz, writing in 1984, observed: "What looked entirely workable in 1957, today has led to major overlap of services, jurisdictional conflicts, and citizen bewilderment over who is responsible and accountable for which services" (Hertz 1984, 10).

The record suggests that Professor Hertz may have been a bit optimistic in reporting a 1957 appraisal of the reforms. In fact, there was substantial controversy over the proposal; and the path to adoption was not an easy one. First, the people of Dade County had to be granted the freedom to decide how they wanted to be governed. Such autonomy was not in the Florida tradition. The first required step was legislation that would place a Dade County home rule provision on the ballot. The statute provided the general framework for a charter, permitted the abolition of certain elective offices, and specified that the school system could not be changed. It secured "grudging" approval according to Lotz, who commented further:

> [It was a] . . . dramatic departure from the tradition of state government in Florida. At the time roughly half the states had some form of constitutional or statutory home rule provision and 3,000 cities operated under home rule powers. So it was not a new concept; it was just new to Florida (Lotz 1984, 46).

New Charter Approved. The constitutional amendment providing home rule to Dade County was approved in November, 1956, 322,839 to 138,430. The following year, on May 21, 1957, a new charter was barely accepted by a small turnout of electors, 44,404 to 42,620. Lotz described the mandate of Dade County in the following terms:

> Essentially the Dade County government had been transformed from a limited purpose county government into one capable of performing most municipal type services and enacting regulations on a county-wide basis. In short, Dade County now served as the upper tier (or level) of government (Lotz 1984, 53).

The cities were the lower tier within a charter framework that did result in some diminution of their powers. Clearly, the county was to be the major unit of government and was to set uniform and minimum standards for all jurisdictions. It also had the power to create cities and, under some circumstances, to alter boundaries. In general, Dade became an urban county in much the same fashion that the approach had been pioneered in California.

Perhaps the most significant piece of the reform was the radical restructuring of the Dade County government. It became the first county in Florida to have a manager, not just in title but in real executive power. The governmental framework closely paralleled classic Council-Manager arrangements in municipal governments. Further, a very senior, highly respected city manager was recruited. O.W. Campbell had served in other cities, including San Diego, and brought a very considerable reputation as a top-notch, outside professional to the new government. Dade took top place among Florida's governments for the quality of its professional leadership, a status it held not only among counties but also municipalities for nearly three decades.

Criticisms of Reformed System. The two-tier approach brought many changes to the governance of the Miami metropolitan area. But it did little to reduce tensions in the system. Regularly, there have been efforts to create new reforms.

Part of the reason for continued dissatisfaction is the changing demographic composition of the area. It has been pointed out consistently that the Public Administration Service recommendations were designed for a homogeneous, relatively small population (about 80% non-Hispanic white), serving about 350,000 people in the unincorporated area, with a predominantly tourist-driven economy. By the 1980s these conditions were dramatically changed. The total population of nearly 2,000,000 was predominantly non-Anglo (35% Hispanic and 20% Afro-American); interest orientations were far more complex than racial statistics suggested;

the unincorporated area had grown to have a population that would make it the ninth largest city in the country (at about 865,000—roughly the same as the total population for all the cities in Dade); and the economy had become very much larger and far more diverse.

While there has been much criticism and many proposals for reform, the Metropolitan Dade government arrangements remained remarkably stable over three decades. The issues that have surfaced over the more than 30 years can be divided into two categories: (a) relations with the municipalities and arrangements for the provision of urban services and (b) the internal structure of the Dade County government.

As has already been noted, the tremendous urban development in the unincorporated area has raised basic questions about an appropriate municipal structure for the metropolis. An increasing number of people live outside the existing cities; and the county's status as the ninth largest municipal government in the nation imposes significant burdens on its policy and administrative structure. Its commission must deal with the most minute neighborhood problems and at the same time take leadership in resolving region-wide waste disposal problems. This overlap of responsibility has had its impact on the established municipalities, reducing the legitimacy of their claim to recognition as the urban service purveyors.

The other area prompting substantial reform proposals concerns the internal structure of the Dade County government and tends to involve issues of representation and articulation of the diverse ethnic and economic interests of Miami's heterogeneous population. It has been frequently argued that the Council-Manager plan does not fit the present circumstance; and an elective mayor with full executive powers should replace the county manager. The size and composition of the county commission have also come under considerable attack. Proposals have been made both to expand the size of the commission and also to provide for election by districts, in accord with a nationwide trend.

In May 1990 the Dade County electorate handed a 3-1 shellacking to two major proposals for internal change. One would have increased the number of commission members to eleven, with seven elected from districts and four by the county at large. The other would have expanded the power of the mayor by allowing him/her to hire and fire the county manager, who has traditionally been appointed and served at the pleasure of the commission. Another interesting proposition would have changed the name of Dade County to Metropolitan Miami–Dade County.

It was not an election that finally settled these issues. The turnout was very small, only 17%, and the propositions were phrased in ways which raised reservations even among those who favored change.

Meanwhile, minority interests in Miami had been pursuing reform through the federal courts, pursuing the argument that the structure of representation on the Dade County Commission, which typically resulted in the election of seven whites of the nine members, did not comply with one person, one vote principles. After six years of judicial activity, the federal court ruled in December, 1992, that the structure had to be changed. Indeed, it went further and determined a new one for the commission, providing for 13 members, elected by district. The court abolished the position of mayor but provided for its reinstatement in 1996.

Elections were held in March, 1993, with 91 candidates, half of them Hispanic, running for office. As expected, the minority became the majority, with African-Americans and Hispanics dominating. While turnouts were relatively small, it was significant that 29% of the eligible Hispanic voters appeared at the polls, compared to 17% of the Anglo community; 21% of African-Americans voted. In an earlier editorial, the Miami Herald commented, "This special election was hard-won by minority interests, who sued for fairer commission representation. The new election was challenged but affirmed on appeal. The delay has kept commission incumbents in office long past their terms" (*Miami Herald,* March 1993, 26A).

In the same election, voters rejected a proposal to create eight zoning boards, with seven members each, to operate in the unincorporated areas of the county. The margin was 2-1 and meant that the county commission would continue to rule on local zoning in the unincorporated neighborhoods. With the new commissioners elected from districts and yet making judgements on local matters outside those districts, much apprehension about the future was expressed by neighborhood groups (Tampani 1993, April 23, 1B).

On April 22, 1993, the 13 new commission members met and elected their new officers. A conservative African-American, a former member of the Reagan administration, was elected chairman after much maneuvering. His principal rival, an Hispanic, got no votes from Hispanic colleagues, indicating that ethnic interests play only a limited part in the political dynamics of Metro Dade (Filkins 1993, April 23, 1A).

It was apparent to all that much of the political machination was undertaken with a view to the mayoral election in 1996.

While the federal court resolved the immediate problem of more equitable representation on the Dade County commission, the broader issues of metropolitan "two tier" government remain. On the one hand, there is the question whether the new structure provides for the political leadership necessary to deal with metropolitan regional problems.

CHAPTER

11

Perversely, at the other end of the range of problems, it is not at all clear that anything has been done to enable local communities in the vast unincorporated area to deal with purely local problems.

THE JACKSONVILLE-DUVAL CONSOLIDATION

In October, 1956, a four-person delegation from Dade County visited Jacksonville. In many states the purpose of their visit would have seemed bizarre. They were seeking Jacksonville support for the constitutional amendment that would allow home rule and permit the creation of Metro Dade. As Richard Martin has put it, the amendment ". . . would make it possible for Miami-Dade to regulate local governmental affairs without having to petition a legislative delegation or wait on biennial legislative sessions to conduct routine county business" (Martin 1968, 50).

Duval County voted 2-1 in support of the Miami-Dade constitutional amendment, at least in part because of their own frustrations with an arcane, highly politicized process of reform. "Duval Countians," one newspaper editor wrote, "may well watch the Dade experiment in 'home rule' with more than passing interest because Florida's major urban areas have many problems in common. The handling of these through 'local bills' in the Legislature has presented legal, political, and other difficulties which proponents of the Dade amendment hope it will reduce if not entirely cure" (*JTU* 1956, October 16, 51).

The history of the Jacksonville-Duval consolidation, like that of Metro Dade, reveals the barriers imposed by the state government to major metropolitan reform. These hurdles remain for the most part; and it appears that only metropolitan communities facing total disaster are likely to mobilize sufficient support to secure major change.

Serious Governmental Problems and Needs for Change. Certainly Jacksonville had a history of very bad government since its incorporation in 1832. Until relatively recently Duval County essentially served a very large rural, sparsely populated area surrounding Jacksonville. A burst of reform in 1917 brought the city one of the strangest structures of government ever concocted in the United States. It was called a commission-council form, in which a nine-member elected council set policy and a five member elected commission executed it. The office of mayor was abolished and one of the commissioners served *ex-officio* in that role. The driving force for the reform was elimination of corruption through a system of checks and balances. As Martin observed, the system was termed ". . . unique by political scientists, and no wonder" (*JTU* 1956, October 16, 15).

Furthermore, it was corrupt. In 1931 the grand jury returned indictments against seventy five public officials, primarily in the schools and in the courts.

In these circumstances, consolidation has typically been a popular reform theme. When checks and balances seem neither to produce honesty nor effective performance, the solution is thought to lie in clear, unambiguous lines of accountability. David Hertz summarized the persistent, recurring appeal of consolidation in these terms:

> . . . Consolidation has a number of features that speak favorably of it. If all services, except those of a purely local nature, were provided through one central government, coordination and economies of scale would be noted benefits. At the same time, one county government would take much of the confusion out. . . . Consolidation would also eliminate the duplication of services at the municipal and county levels (Hertz 1984, 40).

It seems to be the conventional wisdom that dysfunctional conflict is much more likely among hierarchies than within them. Needless to say, experience has never verified the validity of such a proposition. Conflict goes on, regardless of the organizational setting; and there is mounting evidence that heightened scale may correlate negatively with efficiency.

Not surprisingly, movements in favor of consolidation are recorded in Jacksonville as far back as 1918. In 1924 an amendment to the Florida constitution would have permitted Jacksonville "to establish, change, and abolish a local government extending territorially throughout Duval County" (Hertz 1984, 16).

It was defeated both in the state at large and in Duval. Again, in 1934, a similar amendment was placed on the ballot and passed by a slimmer margin in the county than in the state as a whole. It appeared that consolidation was on its way; in reality, it was more than 30 years later that the amendment provided the authority for consolidation.

What happened in the 1930s revealed again how critical the state legislature has been to local government change. A citizens' charter group was formed at the time and proposed the substantial merging of city and county functions. The legislative delegation then intervened and ordered drastic changes, sufficient to gut the plan. The shell of consolidation was approved by the legislature and put on the ballot. But it was a bad scene. Many who had been for consolidation came out against the weakened proposal. Old-time politicos took advantage of the situation to launch a campaign against the gutted consolidation plan. There were many accusations of unfair campaign tactics by those in office. Not surprisingly the referendum was defeated, 9,499 against and 7,175 for. Outside the city of Jacksonville the vote was 3-1 against. The experience was so bad that the notion of consolidation was buried for three decades.

By 1965 Jacksonville appeared to be in a state of rapid deterioration. The city was still unique in its confused authority structure. Duval County was virtually a caricature of the problems of county government in the United States, with 74 elective offices and literally no one in a position of overall leadership responsibility. Jacksonville was suffering many central city problems in the metropolitan area; in 1962 leaders described it as having to provide services to half a million people with a tax base resting on fewer than 200,000.

Significant demographic changes were exacerbating the situation. In the period 1950–65, the city lost population; but the county had jumped from about 100,000 people to over 325,000. Where the city had twice as many inhabitants as the county in 1950, it had only about 60% as many in 1965. Further, its racial composition was changing; it was 41.2% Afro-American in 1960. Its costs were going up with a population less able to pay. Municipal government cost $116 per person in 1950; in 1965 the per capita cost had risen to $479, a growth of 300%. Increased expenditures did not halt declining service levels, and 80% of the city's industrial and residential waste was being dumped raw into the St. John's river.

In the suburbs the county was unable to cope. It had a poor tax base because of traditionally low assessments and because a major share of property was not on the tax rolls. There was no sewer system; more than 180 private utilities, most of them in poor condition, were operating; and police and fire protection was inadequate for urban communities. The most blatant problem, however, was in the school system, which served all of Duval county. An independent special district, it was crowded with elected officials and starved for funds. The schools were dependent on the county for the administration of their main source of revenue, the ad valorem tax. In 1964 it was estimated that property was being assessed at only about 30% of actual value, which deprived the schools as well as the general county government of very large amounts of revenue. Yet the elected tax assessor would not change the assessments and was returned to office in 1964. Following that election, the southern association discredited all 15 high schools in Duval.

Martin summarized the problems facing the metropolitan area:

Public education, pollution of air and water, sewers, lack of adequate police and fire protection in county areas outside the city, high costs of government and soaring taxes were among the problems which prepared the county for consolidation. There was also a rising crime rate, widespread and deteriorating slums in the city, population shifts tending to increase the Negro-to-white ratio in Jacksonville thereby threatening the political imbalance favoring whites, and then an economic slowdown (Hertz 1984, 39).

In appraising the possibility of transferring the Jacksonville experience to other metropolitan areas, analysts have been in consensus that the situation was particularly desperate. They express doubt that a similar level of breakdown was to be found in other metropolitan areas.

Annexation Efforts Fail. Before the move to consolidation, an effort was made to strengthen the city of Jacksonville through annexation of unincorporated territory in the county. Municipal growth had not, however, been favored in Duval County. Only nine annexations had been approved in Jacksonville history, the last in 1931. Since that time, six had been voted down. An ambitious plan to annex 66 square miles and 130,000 people was voted on in 1963. As is typically the case, it was approved by city voters and defeated by those in the affected areas. A similar plan was again defeated in 1964. Thus, annexation as a means of strengthening the central city and bringing needed services to the suburbs was no longer a viable alternative.

In 1965 new consolidation proposals were being made at about the same time fresh scandals were emerging. An investigative report on a TV station in 1966 revealed that the city was spending $1.3 million per year on insurance, more than the combined cost for the cities of Miami, Tampa, and St. Petersburg. Also, in 1966, a series of grand jury investigations resulted in the indictment of four of nine city councilmen, two of five commissioners, and two department heads. In a four year period the city bought 168 automobiles from one dealer, paying the maximum price. No other dealers received orders, and the grand jury concluded, "Political patronage controlled the purchase of these automobiles" (Martin 1968, 83).

A final report said there were people on the payroll who did no work and other employees who were used for private purposes, including political campaigns.

Consolidated Government Established in 1968. These scandals were said to have been a major factor in the 2-1 victory for consolidation in the referendum election of August 8, 1967. The densely populated urban fringe areas weighed in with 6-1 margin of support. Even though the Afro-Americans would have lessened clout in the larger government, they also were strong supporters. Lower income groups in the rural areas of the county were more negative, supporting the referendum by only a small majority. The unions were officially opposed because it was feared that more competitive bidding would bring in outside, non-union firms. Overall, the consolidation was regarded as a great victory and enthusiasts declared it the biggest reform event of the 20th century. The nearly 800 square miles involved did make it the largest consolidation on record in the U.S.

The new government took office on October 1, 1968, and rapidly proceeded to make major changes. However, the consolidation had not been total. The four cities outside of Jacksonville had not voted their abolition and were still in business. The school board remained independent, but with only the seven board members to be elected. A group of authorities, responsible for such functions as electricity, ports, hospital, and expressways, continued in existence. Internally, the changes were major. The mayor was to be chief executive, with substantial pay and significant appointive power. The city council was expanded to 19 members, 14 elected from districts and five at large. Councilmen were to be paid and had significant policy making responsibilities. The structure within the government deviated little from the traditional Strong Mayor form.

Appraisal of Consolidation Positive. There is high consensus among observers that the consolidated government has made a substantial difference in the governance of the metropolitan area. The new institution has brought substantial political leadership through the office of mayor; and the larger number of council members with district elections are felt to have made the system more representative and more accessible. The tax structure was significantly reformed, removing some of the confusion over responsibility and payment for services. Levies are made in support of a General Services District, which is obligated to provide services to the entire county; and other funds are collected in support of an Urban Services District, which essentially covers the old city of Jacksonville. A more integrated hierarchical system, with an infusion of professional staff, brought improved fiscal and management policies. Total ad valorem taxes increased 50% in three years, for example, as property was placed on the rolls and reassessed. Major infra-structure investments were made, and about 200 private utilities were acquired. Sewerage systems in both city and county were developed or rebuilt. The amount and quality of various services were particularly expanded in the urban areas outside the old city (Haron and Taylor 1977, 46ff).

In October, 1978, the *Jacksonville Times-Union* published a special supplement, entitled "Consolidation," in which an attempt was made to evaluate a decade of experience (*JTU* 1978, October 1).

The newspaper commissioned a poll which revealed a continuing, strong support for consolidation. Unfortunately, details of the poll procedure were not reported. Seventy-seven percent felt that services had improved with consolidation, rating fire protection the most improved; and 73% felt that the Jacksonville area was a better place in which to live because of consolidation. There was no agreement on whether taxes had gone up or down. People who had lived in Jacksonville before consolidation were less enthusiastic but they conceded that there was less corruption and more services. Although some Afro-American leaders were critical of the consolidation results, the poll showed 70% of them still supportive.

The consolidated police service, led by an elected sheriff, was seen as a top benefit of consolidation. It was agreed that people in the former county areas were getting better service, with no decline in the old city. Jurisdictional disputes, which had been a big problem, were obviously eliminated. There was the assertion that overlapping and wasted effort had been eliminated. On the other hand, there was significant dissatisfaction with the new government's performance in planning and zoning, labeled the "worst failure." While new purchasing processes had eliminated the insurance and automobile excesses of the old system, central services management was still a major problem 10 years later.

The least satisfaction with consolidation seemed to center in the four small municipalities. Their leaders were reported as saying they had gotten nothing from consolidation, had been neglected, and were taxed for services they did not get. Recently a movement has gotten under way to create "Ocean County," which would be carved out of the southern part of the consolidated government.

The problem conceptually has been more difficult than in Miami-Dade. There a two-tier system legitimated such local units; Jacksonville is a one-tier system in which there was presumably no place for other cities.

Questions were also raised about the continued existence of the special authorities. While consolidation had tied them more closely to the city through both appointive and budget controls, they were still seen as having a high degree of independence. It was observed that the question whether elected officials should have more control was "continually debated." The chairman of the Jacksonville Electric Authority declared that elected officials would (a) have difficulty making unpopular political decisions; (b) be unlikely to respond quickly to enterprise needs; and (c) not have the experience in technical matters. In an interview in 1988, a highly placed city official tended to reaffirm these views, noting that such enterprises must be run like businesses. The conclusion was that they were. "Thank God," he said, "they are free from politics to set rates." Other observers would disagree, however, with such a conclusion. The experience with the water utility, which is operated as a city department, has provided a marked contrast between the relatively free electrical operation and the tightly controlled water unit. There had been no increase in rates in the last "eight or nine" years, and the water utility "has to starve" before getting an increase. Clearly, there were problems in such an arrangement.

No Evidence of Savings in Jacksonville Consolidation. Benton and Gamble sought to test the hypothesis that a consolidated government will have lower property taxes and expenditures than if it had consolidated by examining data for Jacksonville-Duval during the period 1955–1981. They undertook to estimate the impact of consolidation in three areas: property tax revenues, total expenditures, and public safety expenditures. The findings proved to be discouraging for advocates of consolidation. Property tax revenues increased after consolidation; the rate of growth of expenditures over the long term went up, as did public safety expenditures. Commenting on their data, Benton and Gamble write:

> These findings demonstrate that city/county consolidation has produced no measurable impact on the taxing and spending policies of the consolidated government which was the focus of this study—Jacksonville, Florida. In fact, both taxes and expenditures increased as a result of consolidation, a finding completely opposite to the main reform hypothesis and other research (Benton and Gamble 1984, 196).

Major research questions, of course, remain. Given the chaotic state of Jacksonville-Duval public services, increases in taxes and costs may have been inevitable. Indeed, Benton and Gamble observe that the outgoing city council voted big salary increases for the fire service to take effect with consolidation. They called it an "obvious attempt" to embarrass the new government. There is the possibility, of course, that economy and efficiency are simply dogma, employed to overturn the old political order. Comprehensive consolidation, found very seldom in the

United States, does involve radical change in local political institutions. Commenting on the Jacksonville case, Rosenbaum and Kammerer wrote that it ". . . did significantly hasten the transformation in the socioeconomic base of the city's formal and informal political leadership" (Rosenbaum and Kammer 1974, 12).

Finally, one has always to consider the likelihood that the political structure has only a modest effect on taxes and expenditures.

The enthusiasm for consolidation had diminished considerably by 1996, even with the generally favorable view of the Jacksonville experience. Undoubtedly a major reason for the declining interest was a lack of success. An analysis of a reasonably short period of time, 1970–76, showed that there were five efforts at consolidation; and they all failed. Two involved Tampa-Hillsborough County; two Tallahassee-Leon County; and one Pensacola-Escambia County. The two efforts in Tampa-Hillsborough followed one in 1967, which was defeated by more than a 2-1 margin. In a highly interesting comparative study, Rosenbaum and Kammerer found that many of the forces driving consolidation in Jacksonville in 1967 were absent from the Tampa-Hillsborough effort in the same year (1974, 29ff).

Yet the hunger for consolidation does die hard. Several attempts have been made in Tallahassee-Leon County, the last in 1992, when a proposal to consolidate went down to defeat by a 3-1 margin.

ORGANIZATION ISSUES IN THE COUNTIES

CHARTERED AND GENERAL LAW COUNTIES

Both the Miami Dade and Jacksonville experiences suggest how important it is for a community to have the freedom to organize and tax itself as local imperatives and interests dictate. Yet both communities had to seek special permission to manage themselves in such basic ways. Both required approval in a statewide election before they could even begin the process of reform. Fortunately that situation was changed in the 1968 constitution, which substantially expanded the levels of local autonomy in Florida. Yet the counties still struggle with issues of state intervention into what appear to be local matters of organization and management.

Such problems have not, of course, been unique to Florida. They have been common throughout the nation for all local governments. As a result, the concept of chartering emerged. Originally applied to municipalities, the idea was to engage in a formal constitution-making process.

CHAPTER

11

Once approved by the local electorate, the constitution became the supreme law, much as occurs at the national and state level. The basic idea of the charter movement was to provide more home rule within a framework of local law and thus to limit the involvement of the state. That is generally the way the system has worked; but the states have varied tremendously in the level of local autonomy provided with charter status.

In the last decades the trend has been toward expanding the freedoms of the jurisdictions under the general laws of the state, thus making the charter less needed. Another trend has provided the opportunity for chartering to the counties. Both trends are found in Florida. The 1968 Florida constitution provided formal means by which the counties could obtain charters; at the same time it substantially broadened the freedom of counties operating under the state's general laws. The non-charter counties were permitted to do anything not prohibited by state law. Nevertheless, charter counties do have somewhat greater freedoms, largely in the areas of organization, taxation, salary setting, and in some relief from other state laws. Fifteen of the 67 counties have adopted charters, including all of the larger ones. In addition to Miami Dade and Jacksonville-Duval, Broward (pop. 1,364,170), Hillsborough (892,874), Orange (758,961), Palm Beach (962,802) and Pinellas (876,200) have charters. Smaller counties with charters include Alachua (198,261), Charlotte (127,646), Sarasota (301,528), Volusia (402,920), Seminole (324,130), Clay (120,896), and Osceola (136,627). Brevard (444,992) is the newest county to adopt a charter; and the largest county without a charter is Polk (405,400).

Charter adoptions are difficult to secure, and there seems to be little enthusiasm in Florida counties to engage in chartering efforts. Nationwide, the rate of failure is five out of six attempts.

LEADERSHIP STRUCTURE

One of the major incentives to secure a charter has been dissatisfaction with the traditional, pluralistic leadership structure of the counties. Three elements have been particularly subject to criticism: (a) the election of a substantial number of people who occupy essentially administrative roles; (b) a small commission which carries legislative and executive responsibilities but whose power is badly fragmented; and (c) the absence of a single leader who can function as a policy initiator and mobilizer of community resources. In Florida these issues have been very evident.

As occurs at the state level, there is a strong commitment in Florida to the election of people who occupy administrative roles. It is a system which has disappeared from the political landscape in much of America because of the need for technical competence in the management of increasingly complex functions.

Five Elective Officers. Florida's counties continue, however, to elect five important officials: sheriff, tax collector, property appraiser, supervisor of elections, and clerk of the court, who functions in many of the smaller counties as chief administrative and financial officer. Not only can questions be raised whether an election is the best way to get technically qualified people in these jobs, but also the independence of these officials raises difficulties in securing integrated, effective operations in the counties.

Criticisms of County Commissioners. Without control over some of the most important functions of the government, it is understandable that the board of county commissioners has been the object of much criticism. Such negative judgements seem to be exacerbated by a contradiction between expectations and reality. Formally the commissioners are in charge of the government. Except in certain of the charter counties, they have both legislative and executive authority. Thus there is essentially nothing that happens in county government in which the commissioners should not have a deep and direct interest. The reality is, however, that they have neither the resources nor the power to play such a pervasive role effectively. They are not in a position to manage substantial parts of county government, which are controlled instead by the independently elected Constitutional officers.

Attacks are also directed toward the commissions as policy bodies. Their involvement in administrative detail, for example, can rob them of valuable time which should be spent on policy questions. Increasingly, there are two charges: (a) they are insufficiently representative of the community to reflect its aspirations and to mediate among its interest groups; and (b) the small size and plural nature of the commissions do not provide the capacity to exercise political leadership, in initiating policies and mobilizing support for them.

The legitimacy of the commissions as representative institutions has been questioned primarily by minority groups who feel that elections at large provide no possibility of their being represented in the policy body. The courts have recognized this problem and have given support to elections by district as a means of guaranteeing fairer representation to minorities. Where candidates were previously nominated from districts and then elected at large, there is an increasing tendency, in accord with court rulings, to elect by district. Not only does the changed system make minority representation on governing boards more likely, it is also argued that the various geographic parts of a county will have stronger advocates of their interests. Election from a district requires that a commissioner be concerned with the welfare of his or her constituency, rather than the community as a whole; and, in this sense, the changes can lead to even greater fragmentation of the government as a whole.

The size of the commissions has been another object of criticism. As Florida's counties have grown larger and more urban, more discreet interests and needs have appeared. There is a heightening demand for more representatives to serve as advocates of such interests. Yet the county commissions remain small. In a few cases the size of the boards has been increased from five to seven, in order to provide a mix of district and at large members.

Interest in Strong, Elected Executives. As the counties have come to play increasingly significant roles in Florida's urban life political leadership has assumed greater significance. Leadership roles have characteristically been played by individuals—presidents, governors, mayors—in the U.S. political culture. The plural executive does not attract the enthusiasm and support of Americans. A strong executive, elected at large, has therefore become increasingly frequent on the agenda of county reform. However, the idea has not yet secured a substantial foothold in Florida, as in New York, New Jersey, and Maryland. The role has existed in Jacksonville-Duval, of course, for nearly 30 years; and, in 1988, Orange County voters decided to create such a position. The post of County Chairman became operative in 1990. As of November, 1996, Dade County also elected a chief executive.

While issues of representation and leadership have occupied the bulk of public attention, the expanding responsibilities of the counties have required an increasing number of employees. Scale and complexity have demanded more attention to management. To deal with this problem, county commissioners have appointed administrative officers with responsibility for such cross-cutting functions as budgeting, personnel, and purchasing. They serve at the pleasure of the commission and operate on the basis of authority delegated to them.

In 1996, 59 counties had some sort of administrative officer arrangement. However, there is much variation in the administrative role in the 59 counties. Names vary from County Manager to a passive Assistant to the Commissioners. In the smaller counties the frequently-used title is County Coordinator. In general the administrative officers are agents of the commissioners and do not possess power in their own right. In this sense they vary substantially from their professional colleagues operating under the Council-Manager plan, where certain authorities and responsibilities are assigned to the manager. Only three counties (Broward, Dade, and Volusia) have moved toward the Council-Manager plan.

FINANCIAL PROBLEMS OF THE COUNTIES

The increasing significance of the counties in Florida government has produced inevitable financial strains. Expenditures have continued to grow.

LIMITED REVENUE SOURCES

Yet the sources from which to draw these needed monies have remained extremely limited. Robert Bradley has commented on the problem,

> There is a range of needs which cannot be addressed well with the current revenue structures of city and county government. . . . Flexibility is diminished by the extensive use of earmarked sources, whether taxes, charges or special assessments, and tightly drawn tax bases" (Bradley 1989, 55).

Bradley reports that local governments were provided only "one source of taxation" by the Constitution. Others have subsequently been added but always with many limitations and exemptions. He observes that the homestead exemption is equivalent to 20% of all property taxes collected in the state (Bradley 1989, 56). The counties have been particularly hard hit because their dependence on the property tax has been considerably greater than the municipalities.

Compared to counties throughout the nation, Florida depends on the property tax in about the same degree as others. The ad valorem tax, which accounts for nearly one-third of all county revenue, is capped by the state and therefore is not a particularly flexible source of revenue. The average rate has hovered around 7.5 mills for the past 15 years, constrained not only by the Constitutional millage cap but by a review process which takes account of any increased property valuations in setting new tax rates.

As Florida counties have moved toward the delivery of an increased number of urban services, a distinctly different financing profile has emerged for such activities. They are supported in much greater degree from enterprise charges (32.9%) and from user fees (25.2%). In contrast only 3.5% of the financial support for the counties' traditional functions comes from enterprise charges and user fees.

EXPENDITURE PATTERNS

Expenditure analysis provides a revealing picture of the substance of programs and services in the counties and also suggests the reasons why their financial problems are so great. It is apparent that the large urban counties have the major needs for money. Dade, for example, annually spends $2,183 per capita as contrasted with $390 in Bradford, which is in rural North Florida and has a population of about 24,000.

Public Safety makes the greatest claim on county resources, taking about one out of every three dollars collected. The municipalities also spend a great deal on public safety; but their enterprise operations (electricity, gas, water, waste disposal, and sewers) yield substantial revenues from service charges and seldom constitute a tax drain. In some cases they produce handsome profits. The counties, on the other hand, tend to direct their expenditures toward functions for which charges for services cannot easily be made. Public safety, general government, and human services account for about 70 percent of county expenditures. Included in the general government category are substantial annual outlays for the court system. Corrections expenditures, for which counties pay nearly all local government costs, increased over 350 percent in the five year period, 1982-87 (Bradley 1989, 52).

THE ISSUE OF MANDATES

Financial problems have also been worsened by increasing numbers of demands made by the state and national government on localities to conduct certain services, maintain specific standards, provide varying kinds of benefits, and conduct business in approved ways. These are called *mandates,* and they very often end up costing money. An order from a higher level of government becomes a mandate when it requires a lower level to engage in a certain action. Bradley noted that the Florida state requirement that municipalities and counties increase their employer contributions to the Florida Retirement System was a mandate. It cost the local governments money, irrespective of their financial condition and their own local priorities. No money was provided by the state as an offset to these burdens. Bradley has observed,

> The local complaint against mandates . . . lies in the financial burden state mandates impose on city and county governments. While a single mandate may have little effect, the cumulative one

may be quite large. . . . Perversely, mandates not only intrude on local affairs, adding new substantive and procedural requirements, they also work against the pursuit of local goals.

CONCLUSION

The approximately 1,087,000 people living in the unincorporated area of the Miami metropolitan area can be considered the ninth largest city in the United States. They receive their most immediate urban services from Dade County, which also has responsibility for such traditional functions as the courts and the jails and is also the lead government in dealing with the area's larger regional problems, most notably indigent health care. While the scale of Dade's responsibility is dramatic, similar scenarios are to be found all over the state. As Florida is urbanizing, its county governments are a key element in meeting public needs.

It has been difficult, however, for the counties to make the organization changes and to secure the financing arrangements that will enable them fully to deal with their awesome challenges. These are not just Florida problems. They exist throughout the nation. Indeed, Florida has been a leader in pioneering new structures for metropolitan governance. The reforms in Miami Dade and in Jacksonville Duval continue to be hailed as among the most significant of the century.

The other 65 counties in Florida have proceeded more incrementally in coping with their new imperatives. Those in the rural north have made relatively few changes; but others, experiencing explosive urban growth, have undertaken a variety of changes. The 1968 Florida Constitution wisely provided for an enhanced level of county autonomy; and many changes have occurred without particular fanfare. Some reforms have already taken place at the policy and management levels of the counties; and more can be expected in the future. The size and composition of the Boards of County Commissioners are likely to change, with boards expanded and more commissioners elected by district. The move of Orange County to an elected executive is another significant development. Finally, it is important to recognize that 90 percent of the state's population is living in counties where an administrative officer has been appointed to coordinate managerial functions under the commissioners. In only a few cases has the idea of a county manager been fully embraced, but there is a clear trend in that direction.

The financing of their continually expanding operations is the challenge for Florida counties. Their most significant source of local revenue, the property tax, provides little possibility for expansion to meet increased spending needs. Twenty-one counties are at or near the Constitutional cap of 10 mills. Many other sources of income are earmarked and limited to specific purposes, for example the gas tax to transportation, bed taxes to tourist development). Tapping new sources of revenue has been substantially constrained by the state government. Further, it is proving difficult to secure the political leadership necessary to exploit fully those revenue resources that are currently available at the local level.

The expenditure profile does not offer promise that there can be belt-tightening sufficient to bring outlays into a rough balance with income. County expenses tend to be incurred for services for which charges and fees are not particularly appropriate. About 70 percent of total county monies goes to public safety, general government (including the courts), and human services. The cost of corrections services vaulted over 350 percent in a five year period; and it is likely there has been no slowing of that pace, particularly in light of devolution at the federal level, the expect move to sustain many services by using county revenues will impose an even greater burden.

The task for the future is relatively clear. The counties have already assumed major responsibilities in the state's communities; and they are likely to become even greater in the future. The need is to provide the freedom and support necessary to develop county governments which will be able to cope with a bewildering, complex range of societal demands.

REFERENCES

Benton, J. Edwin and Darwin F. Gamble (1984, March). City/county consolidation and economies of scale: Evidence from a time-series analysis in Jacksonville, Florida. *Social Science Quarterly.*

Bradley, Robert B. (1989). Intergovernmental design, legislative mandates, revenue flexibility and local relations. *Governor's conference on local government in the 1990s.* Gainesville: University of Florida, Center for Government Responsibility.

City and State, 1990, January 1.

County News, 1990, January 22.

Filkins, Dexter (1993, April 23). Metro: New faces, new feuds. *Miami Herald,* 1A.

Hertz, David Bendel (1984). *Governing dade county: A study of alternative structures.* Coral Gables: University of Miami.

Horan, James F. and G. Thomas Taylor, Jr. (1977). *Experiments in metropolitan government.* New York: Praeger Publishers.

Jacksonville Times-Union (JTU) (1956, October 16).

Jacksonville Times-Union (JTU) (1978, October 1).

Lotz, Aileen (1984). *Metropolitan Dade County: Two tier government in action.* Boston, MA: Allyn & Bacon.

Martin, Richard. 1968. *Consolidation: Jacksonville Duval County: The dynamics of urban political reform.* Jacksonville: Crawford Publishing Co.

Menzel, Donald C. and J. Edwin Benton (with Charles J. Spindler) (1990). *Identification of trends and practices in Florida county service delivery.* Tampa: Center for Public Affairs and Policy Management.

Miami Herald (1993, March 12).

Mohl, Raymond A.(1990). Florida's changing demography: Population growth, urbanization, and latinization. *Environmental and Urban Issues,* 17 (Winter).

Public Administration Service (PAS) (1954). *The government of metropolitan Miami.* Chicago: The Service.

Rose, Albert (1972). *Governing metropolitan Toronto: A social and political analysis, 1953–1971.* Berkeley: Institute of Governmental Studies, University of California Press.

Rosenbaum, Walter A. and Gladys M. Kammer (1974). *Against long odds: The theory and practice of successful governmental consolidation.* Beverly Hills: Sage Publications, series number 03-022.

Tampani, Joseph (1993, April 12). New commission: zoning friend, foe? *Miami Herald,* 1B.

ENDNOTES

1. Jacksonville is included in the *City & State* list Jacksonville City and Duval County are consolidated, however, and so the resulting unit, though identified as the City of Jacksonville, is more appropriately classified as a county.

2. Menzel and Benton use a substantially expanded definition of urban services and include all those defined in this chapter as regional/area-wide.

CHAPTER

11

POLICY ISSUES FOR FLORIDA CITIES

JACK M. SCHLUCKEBIER

T his chapter explores the nature and status of current public policy from the perspective of Florida cities. While some attention is given to structural issues such as organization and finance, the majority is focused upon policy issues of interest to municipal officials. These issues are: annexation, special districts, growth management and unfunded state mandates.

CITY ECOLOGY

Approximately 396 cities, towns and villages currently exist in Florida. This number is not static because at any given time cities may be in the process of incorporation or un-incorporation. Cities are organized and chartered under the *Florida State Constitution* and state statutes. The Constitution provides broad "home rule" power in Article VIII, Section 2(b), as supplemented by *Florida Statutes,* Chapter 166. State law also provides for incorporation by eligible population groups in *Florida Statutes* 165 061 (1)(e). Municipal annexation, merger, contraction, and dissolution are also provided for by Florida statutes.

Florida has few legal impediments to incorporation. It was not always easy however. Based on the 1885 constitution, Florida cities operated largely according to the provision of Dillon's rule. Dillon's rule provides the most strict and conservative construction of power to cities; generally, it provides that only authority precisely specified or deemed necessary by state law can be assumed or used by a municipality. After constitutional changes made in 1968, and as supplemented by Florida statutes, Florida became more of a "home rule" state. This means cities now have much wider operating flexibility than would be in case under Dillon's rule, at least in non-fiscal matters. In a home rule state, the city may unilaterally decide to join with another city, county or special district for joint service provision or production by mutual agreement, or with a private business firm for projects or services provision.

The criteria for incorporation require that a proposed charter meet two conditions. First, "that it prescribes the form of government and clearly defines the responsibility for legislative and executive functions." Second, that it "does not prohibit the legislative body of the municipality from exercising its power to levy any tax authorized by the constitution or general law." Municipal charters are adopted following a local referendum of the affected residents. The referendum must be authorized by a special act of the Legislature.

More than three quarters of Florida's cities have incorporated since 1900. The honor of being Florida's oldest incorporated municipality is shared by Tallahassee and Pensacola, each having been formally established as a municipal corporation in 1824. The most recent incorporations are Debary, Aventura, Deltona, Ft. Myers Beach and Wellington, which became cities in 1993, and 1996 (4) respectively.

Table 12-1 shows the distribution of population size for Florida cities. It is notable that roughly 70% of the cities are smaller than 10,000 and over half are smaller than 5,000. The fact there are not a larger number of small cities to some extent reflects enactment by the legislature in the early 1970's of minimum population limits to discourage small incorporations. The establishment of minimum population provisions makes it more difficult for small hamlets to incorporate.

It is instructive to compare the development of U.S. cities with other developed and less developed countries (Lineberry and Sharkansky 1978, 42–44). Compared to developed countries, Florida has a large number of general and special government units having relative autonomy and lacking in distinction between the urban and rural functions. Within the past decade there has been a movement to limit special districts in Florida. Aside from school districts, which are consolidated at the county level, the state has more than its share of special districts. Great Britain's recent example of merging local governments is the antithesis of the U.S. and Florida municipal experience. The Florida experience much

Table 12-1
FLORIDA MUNICIPALITIES BY SIZE GROUP

Size	Number	Percent of Total	Cumulative Percent
Less than 2,500	166	41.9	41.9
2,501 to 5,000	47	11.9	53.8
5,001 to 10,000	54	13.6	67.4
10,001 to 25,000	58	15.4	82.8
25,001 to 50,000	35	8.8	91.6
50,001 or Greater	33	8.4	100
TOTAL	**396**	**100**	

Source: *Florida Estimates of Population, 1995;* City estimates for newly incorporated cities of Aventura (21,000); Deltona (56,000); Ft. Myers Beach (6,700); and Wellington (30,000).[1]

more closely reflects the 'public choice' model of incorporation, and "service at-will" response to public demand (Bradley 1990, 46, 64).

Even with urban problems and the great in-migration to Florida, urbanization and city living continue to be the predominant choice. This is evident both in the fact that cities continue to accommodate 50% of the growing population and a proportionate share of growth in the state's six largest Metropolitan Statistical Areas (SMSAs) (70 percent of all SMSA growth over the past 25 years).[2] Given continuing importance of cities on the Florida landscape, the issues that confront them are important for the future of the state. In the following sections, discussion will focus on the important decision-making roles in cities, the adequacy and flexibility of their revenues, and other matters related to the growth and development of cities.

POLICY MANAGEMENT SYSTEM ACTORS AND LEADERSHIP STRUCTURE

Typically the elected officials comprising a city council are mayor and council members. Because each charter is locally drafted, the composition will vary by type of government. This section provides information about these and other important positions in the city policy management system.

Florida cities with a population greater than 10,000 elect the mayor at-large in 58 of the 71 reported cases.[3] In the remaining cases, the mayor is chosen by the council, typically from members of the council. For the mayor, selection and service period is established by the city charter. The mayor may serve for any set period, such as one, two, or four year terms. With few exceptions, mayor and council member elections are non-partisan. This is in keeping with municipal reform movements which have made local government elected officials non-partisan since the turn of the century.

Council members in 62 of 71 cities elect council members through the 'at large' election process for all seats (ICMA 1987).[4] Only nine elected some or all council members through geographic 'districts' or wards. In at-large elections all voters within the city may vote for the candidates. District elections restrict voting to those residing within a particular geographic area within the city and the elected official generally must reside in that district.

Appointed and administrative officials also vary depending on the form of government. While the form of government debate often focuses on the council-manager form versus the mayor-council form, for many

315

Florida governments this dichotomy is irrelevant. Based on general classifications, 210 of Florida cities can be classified as council-manager, 51 as mayor-council, and the remainder as council-mayor or commission.[5] Little is known of the arrangements for the last group, although at more than 140 they constitute a sizable number. In this group, it is probably safe to assume that the clerk is the chief administrative officer, but in many cases the arrangements are loose and not well defined.

Whether the government is headed by an appointed city manager, an elected mayor, or in some other way, a variety of administrative 'helpers' are essential to carry out city responsibilities. At the top of the governmental administrative system, directly beneath the elected officials, is either the city manager, or in the strong mayor form, a chief administrative officer. If it is a manager, the council appoints and holds her/him accountable for administrative performance. If it is a chief administrative officer, accountability is to the mayor. In the latter case, appointment is made by the mayor, although the council may reserve the power to confirm or ratify hiring and firing decisions. In terms of general management responsibilities, however, both systems are typically parallel. The manager or administrative officer takes care of day-to-day government operations including hiring, firing, and organizational policy development and implementation. Typically this person is appointed for an indefinite term, tenure ranging from a few years to decades. Tenure averages five to six years.

Two other positions which often are accountable directly to the full city council are the city clerk and the city attorney. The clerk is responsible for keeping records and minutes of official meetings, conducting municipal elections, and may also be in charge of financial record keeping and reporting. The attorney advises the council and staff in legal matters.

Other positions which are important in the conduct of city affairs are directors (department supervisors) in the following areas: finance, police, fire, parks and recreation, utilities, airport, sanitation and street maintenance, planning, zoning and building code services. The extent of a "policy management" role a departmental administrator may have varies considerably. However, in practical terms the importance of their roles and responsibilities, decisions, and recommendations should not be under emphasized. Because of the sheer vastness of local government services, and the inability of elected officials or managers to be omnipresent, the staff often plays an important policy management role. Further, when one considers that all but a few council members are part-time policy makers, the importance of the staff in resolving issues and implementing programs and policies should not be underestimated.

Across the country important differences in working styles between the city managers and executive mayors have been documented (Ammons and Newell 1989). No evidence suggests that Florida departs from the national pattern. However, there are differences of opinion regarding the likelihood of success and tenure of managers in Florida. In 1962, in a landmark study of managers in Florida, Kammerer described the manager's situation as hazardous duty (1962). In her detailed case reviews she concluded that the manager was a puppet of powerful community elites and that Florida was not going to evolve as a successful incubator for the council manager form.

By 1982, Benedetti concluded that this situation had changed dramatically (1982, 222). He noted that 76 percent of the cities with greater than 10,000 population had adopted the council-manager form. The scales seemed to have tipped from the manager being a 'puppet' to one in which there is perceived to be too much professional and managerial control of local government. Benedetti suggested two controls on the power of the executive, prior to the reformed model: political parties and ward elections. In Florida as elsewhere, these are limited in the classic council-manager form, although district electoral systems and mixed district/at large systems have been increasing since their inclusion as an option in the International City Management Association's *Model City Charter*. Constraint on governmental leaders is also exercised by groups such as taxpayers associations, civic leagues (i.e., The League of Women Voters), and neighborhood, condominium and mobile home park associations (1982, 223–225).

LOCAL GOVERNMENT REVENUE, EXPENDITURES AND FISCAL FLEXIBILITY

The sources of revenue and pattern of functional expenditure for Florida cities are summarized in the following two tables.

Table 12.2 indicates that the two biggest revenue sources are user fees (utilities, solid waste, recreation), and the property tax. Table 12-3 indicates that the two biggest expenditures areas are utilities (water/sewer) and law enforcement.

Take care not to consider the above 'typical' of any particular city. The variation in budgetary circumstances is probably the most important observation. Many of the largest cities operate utilities, including electric, as well as public safety functions such as police, fire, and emergency medical services, while the smallest cities operate only basic public works (street maintenance and trash collection). Obviously, revenue and expenditures will vary depending on the services offered.

Table 12-2

FLORIDA MUNICIPAL REVENUES

1993–94

	Amount	Percent
Charges for services	$3,325,946,059	40.5
Taxes	2,616,211,288	31.8
Intergovernmental	1,020,697,661	12.4
Miscellaneous	975,532,369	11.9
Licenses and Permits	184,425,194	2.2
Fines and Forfeitures	93,360,168	1.1
TOTAL REVENUES	$8,216,172,739	100.0

Source: A Profile of Local Government Revenues and Expenditures, 1996.

Growth is often perceived positively, yet it clearly does not pay for itself (SCPC 1987).[6] This is true not only for capital costs (roads, buildings, utilities, etc.), but also for long term operating costs which are required to support more population, commerce and industry. It is difficult for Florida local governments with the current set of rules, constraints, population growth and inflation to cope with continually changing needs.

The fiscal situation facing Florida local governments is described by Clark *et al* (1987, 71–81). They reviewed expenditure options with local government officials and concluded that expenditure options in the face of growth and inflation are:

1) Maintain status quo—cut services;
2) Transfer services to state or federal government;
3) Privatize and contract out services; and
4) Be more efficient by using management productivity tools such as zero based budgeting, sunset reviews, inter-local agreements and cost checks.

Some of these options undoubtedly are realistic. Even when taken collectively however, it is doubtful that they would suffice to meet the expected needs of the municipalities in the coming decades. Recognizing this, the study explored a fifth option, increasing revenues. The following provides a synopsis of revenue expansion possibilities:

1) Expand the use of impact fees for development;
2) Provide enhanced use of non-property tax sources by broadening the utility tax to include a sewer and cable TV tax. Another possibility they suggested, to lift statutory rate limits on occupational license fees, was partly accomplished in 1993.
3) Modify the state revenue sharing program. State revenue sharing is a state program which returns certain state collected taxes to cities and counties based on statutory formulas. The modifications might:
   —Change the sources of revenue sharing program to those which are more responsive to growth. One of the current main sources, cigarette taxes, provides declining revenue, particularly as higher rates of taxation are levied.
   —Target revenue sharing funds, through the disbursement formula, to the neediest cities.

318

4) Modify the property tax. Changes might include:

— Elimination of the 10 mill cap on property taxes and allowing local limits.

— Index the property tax to meet inflation and population growth without advertising and public hearing.

5) Provide cities the same or similar latitude as counties in setting up special service taxing units (Clark et al. 1987).

Table 12-3

FLORIDA MUNICIPAL EXPENDITURES
1993–94

	Amount	Percent
Utilities	$2,794,221,365	32.7
Public Safety	2,066,028,270	24.2
General Government Services	982,893,655	11.5
Debt Service	908,676,854	10.6
Culture/Recreation	749,436,409	8.8
Transportation	670,686,531	7.8
Economic Environment	292,329,287	3.4
Human Services	80,521,587	0.9
TOTAL EXPENDITURES	$8,544,793,958	100.0

Source: A Profile of Local Government Revenues and Expenditures, 1996.

The latter point reflects the small amount of flexibility cities have had relative to counties to establish fiscal home rule. This situation was modified in a significant way by the Florida legislature in 1996 when it added a major new tool to the cities fiscal toolbox. They did this by providing the county a tool similar to the Municipal Service Benefit Use (MSBU) effective in October, 1996 (Conn and Small 1966). It allows a uniform billing arrangement for virtually all municipal services. Further, it may greatly expand the fiscal capacity of cities, since many of the services which may be billed using this arrangement are now funded by revenue derived from the property tax or other limited revenue sources.

Other options are described by Montanaro (1990, 172–175). His analysis leads to the conclusion that the state's weak financial position, combined with its virtual monopoly on taxing sources, will continue to force local needs to take a back seat to state needs. He suggests that the state governments history of fiscal conservatism will continue to have negative effects on local government.

While offering some of the same suggestions outlined in the Clark report, Montanaro also makes some broader, more fundamental recommendations. In his view, for local governments to meet the fiscal needs prescribed in the Zwick Report (viz., an estimated annual operating and capital shortfall for cities of 2.5 billion per year through year 2000) constitutional modifications must occur (SCPC 1987, 20). He suggests repealing the constitutional preemption by the state of various taxes and replacing this with a preemption of major sources likely to be used by the state such as the local option sales tax, the motor fuel tax and corporate income tax. An exception would be allowed for the current levels of these taxes as authorized previously.

ANNEXATION, HOME RULE, GROWTH AND FLEXIBILITY

There are many views of the public interest surrounding municipal annexation. With the exceptional population growth in Florida, there are many demands upon cities for new services and for corporate boundary revisions to include newly developed areas. However, Florida's laws allowing annexation (boundary revision) limit and impede such changes.

Florida municipalities are allowed to annex in three primary ways: first, by voluntary agreement between the city and the affected land owner; second, by majority approval vote of (a) the group of residents affected in the area and (b) voters of the annexing municipality; and third, by special action of the legislature. The latter method occurs infrequently. It was not always this difficult to annex in Florida. Doyle, in an assessment of municipal government in the 1950's, noted that only one referendum, combining voters of the affected area with those of the existing city, was required for cities of over 10,000 population (1954, 394). The burdensome dual majority requirement was not a reality until 1975. The single (combined) referendum procedure in the 1950's provided a higher approval threshold of two-thirds, rather than the 50% plus one approval now required through dual majority votes. Nevertheless, the simplicity of returning to the earlier method would be a vast improvement.

Current policy emphasizes the interests of the neighborhood, or specific area to be considered for annexation, above all others. This is because the types and methods of annexation are limited. Many other needs receive a low priority as a result of existing annexation policy. For example, there is a need to have well considered municipal growth and some semblance of municipal planning rather than urban sprawl; a need to offer efficient and effective comprehensive services rather than responding piecemeal and engaging in "boundary bartering"; and a need of the neighborhood and community to receive public services without creating a special district. The dual majority referendum requirement allows a small minority in the community, the 'fringe dwellers,' to overturn the legitimate interest of cities to accommodate urban area growth needs.

Inadequacies of the current annexation laws are well documented in a report of the Florida Advisory Council on Intergovernmental Relations (FACIR 1987a). The report made two important suggestions: 1) Provide city reserve areas outside the current municipal boundaries which the city can more easily annex. For these areas the current dual majority referendum process would be eliminated; and 2) Provide immediate and simple annexation of isolated areas (enclaves) surrounded by cities. Unfortunately, neither idea is likely to be given the consideration the state experts have suggested.

Until 1993, the legislature expressed little interest in modifying the status quo on this topic. In 1993, the Florida Legislature provided modifications to rules concerning minor cases of enclaves, small scale annexations, and uninhabited but developed commercial properties. In all three cases the rules were changed to make annexations slightly less burdensome for cities. However, in practical terms the changes were not as far reaching as suggested earlier and will be practiced by only the few dozen cities who regularly make use of the boundary change provisions.

While Florida is one of the nation's leaders in total annexations, when measuring the area annexed and the affected *population* it significantly lags other high growth states such as Texas and North Carolina. The population of Florida cities has lagged, compared to the unincorporated areas, for the past two decades. This has occurred because people are locating where new housing is being built, which is primarily outside the old and relatively static city boundaries.

An effect of this condition is an increase in county government service expectations. Constrained municipal growth forces counties, the only other general purpose local government in Florida, to provide urban services rather than serve in their traditional role; and many do not have the fiscal or organizational resources to respond to urban service delivery needs. Further, particularly in the two dozen or so largely urbanized counties, the expansion of the county role as the lead urban service provider often leads to duplication, inconsistencies, confusion, inefficiencies, and intergovernmental conflict.

It is helpful to consider annexation from various perspectives however. When viewed outside the traditional view of the cities, annexation is not simply city versus county or incorporated area versus unincorporated area. Rather, it is an important local government event which should be considered and resolved on the merits of its service provision. One such alternative approach uses area wide long term planning agreements. Indeed, the process agreements the cities of Ocoee and Orlando have entered with Orange County are commendable models for other communities throughout the state (Yurko 1996).

CITIES AND SPECIAL DISTRICTS OF GOVERNMENT

Florida's increasing population and sprawling development have resulted in the creation of a large variety of specialized functional units of government. Nearly 700 special districts governments exist in Florida.

Many have had little documentation available at the state or local level until recently.

There has been an effort to establish uniformity in the impact of these units on local governments. The precursor to these reforms was a comprehensive study of special districts by the Florida Advisory Council on Intergovernmental Relations (1987; Falconer 1988). The FACIR review suggested that such a plethora of special districts is not good state policy. In the past few years, the Florida Department of Community Affairs has been empowered to coordinate information and to make better sense of the hundreds of units already in existence. The legislature also acted to limit special district growth and provide uniformity in reporting. It is likely that further efforts will be made toward these goals in the coming years.

Special districts in Florida are created for a myriad of public purposes. Typically they are chartered under the auspices of Chapter 165, *Laws of Florida.* Special districts are dependent or independent depending on the initial chartering arrangement. The accountability of the district to a city or county, and the degree of its authority to establish its own budget and taxes are the major determinants of the type. The Florida law can be ambiguous on these points because there are a wide variety of determinants which are situational. Based on the FACIR study, the following general classification scheme was developed regarding the various types of districts in Florida (FACIR 1987b, 8). (See Table 12-4.)

The proliferation of special districts in Florida, at the same time that the boundaries of general purpose local governments are exceptionally constrained, is short sighted and bad public policy for the state. In particular special districts pose threats because:

1) The complexity of service arrangements and fragmentation of service delivery units confuse voters;

2) They result in government by the unelected which leads to decreases in public accountability; and

3) They confound solutions to pressing area wide problems which often cross jurisdictional boundaries.

Table 12-4

SPECIAL DISTRICTS: NUMBER AND TYPE

Type	Number	Percent
Water Control	95	13.6
Housing Authority	84	12.1
Fire Control	72	10.3
Soil/Water Conservation	70	10.1
Hospital	51	7.3
Health	41	5.9
Development/Planning	32	4.6
Other Districts	251	36.1*
Total	696	

Other includes a wide variety of types such as port, library, utility, mosquito control, aviation, lighting, and various improvement districts.

Source: FACIR, 1987b.

Another approach attempts to place districts, the state and municipal interests in a comprehensive framework. Bradley offers a critique of the status quo regarding state-local relations and opportunities for improvement. He offers compelling arguments against case-by-case 'public choice' solutions for the complicated issue of intergovernmental design (Bradley 1990, 64). He suggests that the case by case approach may be too slow; may lack (or lose) a long term vision; may exacerbate conflict; and may further confound voters. To simply say it may work or has worked in a few select cases is hardly sufficient for broad based application. He recommends clarification regarding city/county roles, and small city/large city roles, as in California and Virginia.

Obviously, with so many districts having been created in the past several decades, it must be concluded they are serving legitimate public needs. They provide short term solutions to pressing urban problems which otherwise might result in decisions for incorporation or annexation of urban fringe dwellers. In many cases inhabitants of special districts have gained enough political strength to challenge general purpose local governments and impose functional services to the disadvantage of cities. Thus, the fact that special districts exist often impedes the ordinary growth, planning and service delivery of cities.

GROWTH MANAGEMENT

In 1985, the Florida legislature adopted landmark legislation to regulate growth, enhancing the ability of Florida cities and counties to control sprawling developments.[7] Each city and county is required to adopt a comprehensive plan embodying several specific elements. The adopted plans are to be submitted to the state Department of Community Affairs which reviews them for compliance with state standards. Following the adoption of comprehensive plans, and assurance they are consistent with regional and state agency plans, each city and county also must adopt land development regulations to enforce the main tenants of the plan.

In the mid-1980's, Charles Zwick was asked by the Governor to head a panel to forecast government needs for the next decade (SCPC 1987). The review resulted in some startling observations. The difference between revenues and expenditures necessary for Florida governments to meet expected growth approached seventeen billion dollars. As one reviewer succinctly observed, "Growth clearly does not pay for itself in most parts of Florida" (Clark 1987, 20).

In essence, the major objective of required city and county plans is to maintain the current level of local services while insuring that important and environmentally sensitive lands are not degraded. Other objectives are implied in the legislation and administrative rules adopted subsequently for statewide implementation. Examples are the principles that "growth should pay for itself," and that "urban sprawl should be discouraged." These ideas are not specifically addressed in the legislation, but are in the approach taken by the Florida Department of Community Affairs in its administrative reviews of local plans.

Local plans must be found to be consistent with the state and regional plans, or risk losing state revenue sharing entitlements. For most cities these represent a significant part, as much as 25%, of their annual budget. Clearly they have little choice but to comply.

Other than those elements specifically required by statute or administrative rule, no minimum community standards were established for levels of service. The specifics of the statutes and rules are much more pronounced in the related land development codes, also required, which are adopted subsequent to plan adoption by each city and county.

While the need to further regulate growth is understandable, the implementation methods remain the subject of frustration and debate at the local level. It is not clear that these regulations will prevent or even slow urban sprawl in any meaningful way, primarily because of 'grandfathering' vested rights of platted subdivisions and developments. In fact, the opposite may occur. As an example, rural areas often have undeveloped areas abutting state highways or other transportation corridors but with minimal (non-required) urban service availability. Downtown and existing urban areas are often deficient of required services, thus rural areas may be able to accommodate more of the growth more quickly and less expansively under the new service standards. The result is increased development at the fringe, along established transportation links, which is a consequence exactly the opposite of the intended objective.

The growth rules do not require cities or counties to provide service level minimums for police, fire, emergency medical services or school systems nor are there requirements for use of community wide utilities in defined urban areas. Simply put, the basic urban amenities are not required as part of a plan in most instances. Further, where such services exist, the growth plans are not likely to specify they be kept at current service levels.

Despite its limitations, the 1985 growth management legislation represented an important political agreement between local governments, environmentalists and developers. In the past significant developments received scrutiny only for transportation or environmental concerns. In the view of one public policy observer, the environmental degradation has been four fold and tremendous: 1) destruction of the natural water supply system; 2)water pollution because of expanded hazardous materials; 3)destruction of wildlife species and habitats and 4) destruction of intact ecosystems such as bays and lakes (deHaven-Smith 1995, 82). Under the regulations almost all new building and development will not be permitted in areas where it cannot be supported by existing infrastructure.

The 1985 Growth Management legislation was updated and revised in 1996 in some minor ways helpful to cities. The primary change of interest to cities was the exemption for small scale amendments (up to 10 acres at a time, up to 60 acres cumulatively annually, per city). Previously amendments of any size could not proceed except semiannually in any city, no matter what the level of impact or urgency of development (Salz 1996).

The remaining difficulty will be for planners, developers and regulators to make, and respond to, accurate assessments of the changes growth brings. To this point in time, many of these consequences continue to be unmeasured or measured only in their most unimportant respects.

UNFUNDED STATE MANDATES

The problem of unfunded state mandates occurs when the legislature, or state agencies, impose additional responsibilities on local governments without providing commensurate resources or the ability to secure them. Some examples are state mandated changes in pension provisions for firemen and policemen; additional insurance for municipal employees; and additional requirements for infrastructure.

There are excellent studies of how often the legislature has enacted such mandates as well as of the cost burden imposed upon local governments (FACIR 1988). The types of mandates imposed by the legislature from 1978–1987 are categorized in the following way (see Table 12-5):

In November, 1990, after years of lobbying by cities critical of mandating practices, the state legislature presented a constitutional amendment to the Florida voters to greatly restrict the practice. The amendment was approved in the general election. Nevertheless, for those who feel such practices will easily become a thing of the past, two concerns remain. First, the amendment did not retroactively undo past mandates. In other words, all the previous requirements continue, unaffected by the amendment and they are significant. Second, the amendment

Table 12-5

MANDATE TYPE AND FREQUENCY

Mandate Type	Frequency
Taxation/exemption	6
Public Protection/Judiciary	81
General government	63
Community Development	11
Health	18
Community Service	13
Environment	25
Personnel	45
Public Assistance	4
Recreation/Culture	1
Transportation	15

Source: FACIR, 1988.

may not fully restrict state agencies from imposing many of the same type of mandates. Instead, the imposition would occur by way of administrative rules, promulgated in accord with previously adopted legislation.

One veteran observer of state government has cautioned local governments that they should expect at least as much mandating in the future as in the past, if not more. He suggests that mandates will be more pronounced as the state faces greater fiscal pressure (Montanaro 1990, 170). Of course, the state also retains the option of wholesale transfers of functions to local government for which allocated revenue sources grow at a slower rate than expenditures. These options suggest there may not be a quick fix nor any significant change.

Mandates, both from the federal government to the states and from the states to local government, remain a paramount concern. Outside of the need for local governments to better coordinate, state/local relations must slow the train of state mandates. While ostensibly a concern only when the legislature is in session, in recent years state mandates have been worrisome on a year round basis because of the "power to legislate" invested in administrative rule making. At a minimum the growth of new mandates should be reduced until the following conditions are met:

1) A state-supported dialogue occurs which focuses on the roles and responsibilities of local governments to each other in the context of a much better defined home rule model.

2) The adoption of a state role model, such as California or Virginia, whereby local governments are endowed with sufficient home rule authority to avoid legislative usurpation in local matters.

3) The delegation of additional revenue sources by the state to local governments.

COMPREHENSIVE REFORMS ON THE HORIZON

Despite the great strides made by Florida in the past two decades to limit proliferation of new local units and special districts, much more must be accomplished. If growth is to continue, coordination between local units of government must be greatly enhanced. As examples, the processes and methods of city to city, city to county and city or county to special district mergers and functional service sharing must be clarified and simplified. Cities must have easier and more rational methods of natural growth and annexation, including establishment of urban growth reserve areas.

Growth continues to be a dominant factor for local governments. Florida cities continue to react to the growth occurring in ways which are highly constrained and inefficient compared to some other states. The state continues to reduce its assistance role in favor of more regulation.

What may have seemed only a bleak possibility for reform and improvement was greatly enhanced by action of the 1996 Florida Legislature in creation of the Commission on Local Government. The 21 member Commission, staffed by the Florida Institute of Government, had a two year mission to review many of the most pressing issues facing local government. Specifically, the tasks of the Commission were to recommend:

> appropriate reforms to the general laws, special acts, and constitutional provisions relating to organization, structure, powers, creation, duties, financing and service delivery capacity of county, municipal, and special district governments. The commission also is to recommend measures for elimination of overlapping jurisdictional responsibilities and duplication of costs among counties, municipalities, and special districts in the delivery of governmental services (Foster and Robinson 1996).

While it is lamentable that Floridians will have waited over two decades since the last such review, if this review is only half as successful as the earlier one, it will be monumental in its achievement and promise for enhanced intergovernmental designs to meet the 21st century.

REFERENCES

Ammons, Dave N. and C. Newell (1989). *City executives leadership roles, work characteristics and time management.* Albany: State University of New York Press.

Benedetti, Robert and Manning Dauer (1982). "Cities and counties." In *Florida's Politics and Government,* edited by Manning Dauer. Gainesville: University Presses of Florida.

Bradley, Robert P. (1990). "Intergovernmental Design, Legislative Mandates, Revenue Flexibility and Local Relations." In *Local Government in the 1990's: Proceedings of the Governor's Conference on Local Government.* Gainesville: Center for Government Responsibility, College of Law, University of Florida.

Bureau of Economic and Business Research (1996). Florida Estimates of Population, 1995. Gainesville: Bureau of Business Research, University of Florida.

Clark, Wayne A., J. Edwin Bentor, and Robert Kerstein (1987). *An Analysis of State-Local Relations in Florida. Monograph, Series One.* Tallahassee: Florida Institute of Government.

Conn, Kraig A., and Ken Small (1996). "Special Assessment Authority and Clarification of Land Use Quasi-judicial Proceedings." *Quality Cities,* Volume 70-1: 10–11. Tallahassee: Florida League of Cities.

deHaven-Smith, Lance (1995). *The Florida Voter.* Tallahassee: Florida Institute of Government.

Doyle, Wilson K., Angus M. Laird, and S. Sherman Weiss (1954). *The Government and Administration of Florida.* New York: T. Y. Crowell Company.

Falconer, Mary K. (1988–89). "Special Districts: The Other Local Governments— Definition, Creation and Dissolution." *Stetson Law Review* 18: 583–612.

Florida Advisory Council on Intergovernmental Relations (1987a). *Annexation in Florida: Issues and Options.* Report #94-2. Tallahassee: the Council.

———. (1987b). *Special District Accountability in Florida.* Report #87-5. Tallahassee: the Council.

———. (1988). *1988 Catalogue of State Mandates.* Report #88-5. Tallahassee: the Council.

———. (1996). *A Profile of Local Government Revenues and Expenditures.* Report #96-4. Tallahassee: the Council.

Foster, Darcy A. and Kelvin J. Robinson (1996). "Challenges for Local Governance in the 21st Century." *Quality Cities,* Volume 70-1: 6–7. Tallahassee: Florida League of Cities.

International City Management Association (1987). *1987 Municipal Yearbook.* Washington, D.C.: the Association.

Kammerer, Gladys M. et al. (1962). *City Managers in Politics: An Analysis of Manager Tenure and Terminations.* University of Florida Monographs, Social Sciences no. 13. Gainesville: University of Florida Press.

Lineberry, Robert and Ira Sharkansky (1978). *Urban Politics and Public Policy.* New York: Harper and Row.

Montanaro, Edward (1990). "Financing Local Government in the 1990's." In *Local Government in the 1990's: Proceedings of the Governor's Conference on Local Government.* Gainesville: Center for Government Responsibility, College of Law, University of Florida.

National Civic League (1989). *Model City Charter.* Seventh Edition. Denver: the League.

Salz, Diane (1996). "Local Government Comprehensive Plan Revisions." *Quality Cities,* Volume 70-1: 15–17. Tallahassee: Florida League of Cities.

State Comprehensive Plan Committee (SCPC) (1987). *The Final Report of the State Comprehensive Plan Committee to the State of Florida.* Tallahassee: the Committee.

Yurko, Allison (1996). "A Practical Perspective About Annexation in Florida." *Stetson Law Review*. Volume XXV. No.3. St.Petersburg: College of Law, Stetson University.

ENDNOTES

1. Data compiled by the author. *Florida Estimate of Population: 1995,* Bureau of Business Research, University of Florida, April 1995, 8–27.

2. Data compiled by the author. *Florida Estimate of Population: 1995,* 32–33.

3. Data compiled by the author. International City Management Association (ICMA), *1987 Municipal Yearbook,* Washington, D.C.: ICMA, 1987. Based on cities with greater than 10,000 population.

4. Data compiled by the author. International City Management Association (ICMA), *1987 Municipal Yearbook,* Washington, D.C.: ICMA, 1987. Based on cities with greater than 10,000 population.

5. Based on communication from Ken Small, Florida League of Cities.

6. The interplay between growth and revenues is discussed further in Chapter 13.

7. Growth management policy is discussed further in Chapter 13.

CHAPTER

12

PART V

POLICY MANAGEMENT ISSUES

LINKING GROWTH MANAGEMENT AND ECONOMIC DEVELOPMENT
FLORIDA'S DEVELOPMENT MANAGEMENT SYSTEM

BENJAMIN "WOODY" PRICE AND RICHARD FEIOCK

INTRODUCTION

O ver twenty years ago Florida joined the quiet revolution in land use control (Bosselman and Callies 1971). Since then Florida's quiet revolution in growth policy has become increasingly noisy. This revolution has shifted much of the responsibility for fostering and managing growth from local government to the state. Florida has been a pioneer in the effort to develop a management system to take greater control of development at the state level. The concept of a "development management system" as we use it connotes both economic development activities to encourage and direct growth as well as growth control policies designed to limit and redirect growth. A natural tension exists between these two dimensions.

Public economic development efforts are consistent with a reliance on market forces to allocate resources. Since the beginning of the Republic, government actions which promote or accommodate growth have been accepted practice. Only recently has limiting and controlling economic growth been added to the role of government. Not only do governments have little experience in this role, but it is a role which brings into conflict some of the most fundamental values of American society. To protect the public interest in clean water and air, to provide affordable housing, and to do so without burdensome taxation often requires restricting individual rights, especially property rights.

Florida's experience with growth management is relatively short. Not until the 1970s did Florida government acknowledge a need to protect the natural and built environment from the most severe impacts of economic growth. Over the following decades the development of the state growth policy system has had significant implications for economic development, public/private relationships, and the relationship between the state and local governments.

While promoting and facilitating economic development is carried out effectively by local government, the state has become more active in coordinating local economic development activities by creating a more centralized economic development policy apparatus. Local governments have been less successful at controlling growth without the state as a guiding partner. As the Florida development management system has evolved it has required periodic adjustments when experience indicated that previous steps were inadequate. Not surprisingly considerable conflict and disagreement have accompanied each change.

This chapter considers the relationship between economic development and growth management in Florida within the development management framework. After discussing the allocation of government authority for development management between state and local government, we describe the dramatic changes in the relationship between public and private interests in growth policy that have occurred over the last four decades. We then examine the implications that the concurrency and compact development requirements of recent growth management legislation have had for public administration and intergovernmental relationships in Florida.

THE DEVELOPMENT MANAGEMENT SYSTEM

In the last half-century Florida has experienced growth far beyond anything that could have been imagined just fifty years ago. In 1950 there were fewer than 3 million permanent residents in the state. The population grew by over 2 million in each of the following decades. By 1980 the population had increased to almost 10 million. The 1990 Census reported more than 12 million residents; making Florida the fourth largest state in the country.

Until the 1970s this growth was viewed by most observers as desirable for the state and the economy. Florida rode a wave of new jobs, new development, and economic prosperity. In recent years there has been increased recognition that growth can be a mixed blessing. Concerns about the environment, congestion, and public services have created pressure to limit or control growth and development.

Florida is a large and diverse state. While some areas of the state have grappled with ways to manage and control rapid growth, other less rapidly growing areas actively encouraged development. Even in areas with high growth there have been locations which were deteriorating economically. Growth management is appropriate when redirecting the pattern or extent of growth promotes the public interest, but when the economic base of an area is not growing, economic development public policy tools may be necessary. Growth management and economic development can be seen as parts of a larger government responsibility to manage and direct local markets. This broader view of governmental responsibility has been called development management.[1] Development management includes choices to either induce, accommodate, or restrain development.

Growth policy in Florida has expanded to include controlling, not just promoting, growth. This shift has greatly complicated the relationship between governments and economic interests in Florida. Not only is there a potential conflict between business and labor interests in economic growth and the government's interest in trying to deal with the consequences of that growth, there is also the problem of protecting individual rights against abuse from improper exercise of governmental authority. This is particularly relevant to land use controls and private property rights.

Traditionally, citizens' concerns about the potential abuse of individual rights by government has led to constitutional and structural limits on public authority. The tradition of "home rule" places the responsibility for development management with local governments. Local governments have had less extensive authority than state or national governments yet are most accessible to citizens and private interests.[2] These conditions contribute to a bias in the balance of authority between public and private sector interests favoring the market and unrestrained economic growth. Florida's tax structure also contributes to the bias toward the market by economic development to increase local revenues.

In the following sections we will explore some of the conflicts between government, the market, and individual rights and how these conflicts have been exacerbated as policy has shifted from an emphasis on growth promotion to an emphasis on growth management. We also consider how this shift in emphasis has made the state more active in traditionally local affairs but without yet fully addressing state responsibilities in development management. Further, we speculate on how the shift in development management challenges both scholars and practitioners of public administration.

THE ALLOCATION OF GOVERNMENT AUTHORITY FOR DEVELOPMENT MANAGEMENT RESPONSIBILITIES

Narrow and limited authority, separation of powers, and checks and balances all serve as constraints on governmental authority (Dye

1991; Lindblom 1977) and are formalized in the U.S. and Florida constitutions (Zimmerman 1992). These constraints on authority have the purpose of protecting the citizens from abusive government actions. The Bill of Rights defines the most fundamental protections, including property rights. A fundamental condition for both personal liberty and an effective market is the right to privately own property.[3] When the exercise of government authority literally extends into regulating the use of private property (land use regulation) the conflict between the market and political authority is pronounced. Land use regulation is a key element of growth management and challenges the constitutionally protected right to private property (Pelham 1995; Stroud and Wright 1996).

Florida state government has relied on consumption taxes for revenue, while local revenue has been derived primarily from property taxes. The Florida Constitution prohibits a state income tax, setting the stage for continuing struggle between state and local governments over revenue sources. The state, exercising its greater legal authority, limits the discretion of local governments in levying taxes and fees (Florida Advisory Council on Intergovernmental Relations 1991).

A consequence of the tax structure is to bias state and local growth policies toward promoting economic growth. Without a personal income tax, growth in tax revenues occurs primarily through economic expansion and enlarging the property tax base, therefore, new tax producing development is a prized commodity for which governments compete. While Florida competes with other states, local governments compete with other local jurisdictions for revenue producing development. Such competition provides an incentive for the state to minimize its direct role in many state-wide and regional growth management issues and to rely on local governments to control growth. By delegating responsibility for development management to local governments and avoiding important, but politically difficult, policy options, the state allows the process to be shaped primarily by market interests (Lindblom 1982; Molotch 1976; Peterson 1981).

In the following sections we review the evolution of Florida growth policy from the 1950s and 60s to identify the relationship between public and private authority and between levels of government. This review provides a context for understanding current constraints on development management in Florida.

LOCAL GOVERNMENT ENTREPRENEURSHIP: 1950S AND 60S

Before the 1970s development management in Florida was characterized by two outstanding features: the delegation of responsibility for growth to local governments and the dominance of the promotion of economic development over growth management. Prior to 1970 Florida's cities provided a wide array of incentives to developers virtually without restraint. These included financial inducements as well as the manipulation of land use and zoning.

Before 1972 state government played a minor role in regulating local land use and generally supported local sponsorship of growth (DeGrove 1984). In addition, state provided economic incentives reinforced local development efforts. *Industrial Development Magazine's,* "Annual Survey of the Fifty Legislative Climates," shows that during this period Florida was a leader in providing tax exemptions and development incentives.

Delegating development policy to local governments and reinforcing it with state incentives encouraged a frenzy of development subsidies as local governments pursued population, employment, and tax base growth. Local governments in Florida often responded to developers' demands with subsidies, concessions and lax land regulation which promoted private interests to the neglect of any larger public interest. These events fit a pattern of growth politics described by Robyn Turner:

> The growth politics scenario assumes a decentralized political process without standards or guides. Policy is a product of interest group influence with local government as the willing facilitator of articulated demands. Each city is thus up for grabs to the highest political bidder with political influence and organization (1990, 37).

The result of unrestrained competition between localities for development and growth has been uneven development. While some areas of the state, particularly in the north and panhandle, received little investment and suffered from persistent economic problems, other areas, particularly along the coasts and in South Florida, developed at a break-neck pace.

THE 1970'S: A PROCEDURAL REVOLUTION

The 1970s was the beginning of a broader state development management system. The state took initial steps toward creating a more centralized structure of control both for economic development and growth management. Economic development policy was characterized by two new approaches in this decade. First, the role of the state as facilitator and director of local action was enhanced. Second, the state actively encouraged public/private partnerships. Growth management policy began to acknowledge state responsibility for greater-than-local resources (both built and natural) and established requirements for local government planning.

ECONOMIC DEVELOPMENT

The centerpiece of economic development policy in the 1970's was the Community Redevelopment Act of 1969. This act authorized the creation of community development agencies. The scope of the act is broad as it directs redevelopment of slum areas, blighted areas, and areas with housing shortages. The Act also provides for the implementation of traditional local economic development incentives in combination with public/private cooperation.

The Redevelopment Act specifies a series of steps a county or municipal governing body must take to initiate redevelopment. An area must be designated a slum, blighted area, or area of housing shortage. Second, the governing body must establish that development of the area is in the interest of public health, safety, and welfare of community residents. Third, the governing body must appoint a board of commissioners to oversee redevelopment actions. Fourth, a community redevelopment plan must be prepared and approved by the governing body after recommendations are received from the local planning agency and a public hearing is held. When the approval process is complete, the act gives these community redevelopment agencies authority to make contracts with public or private entities, invest money from the redevelopment trust fund, acquire and dispose of property, issue revenue bonds, and implement tax increment financing for development projects.

GROWTH MANAGEMENT

As with economic development, the 1970s saw the state taking more control over procedures in growth management. There were two thrusts to the more activist state role. The first was the initiation of a mandatory vertically integrated planning process. Laws mandating the preparation of a state comprehensive plan and local government comprehensive plans were adopted. The second thrust was direct state involvement in regulating and managing development activities in areas of greater-than-local significance. The state created legal mechanisms for intervening 1) when proposed development projects had multi-jurisdictional impacts, and 2) when an area of regional or state significance was particularly vulnerable to growth impacts (Finnell 1985; Siemon 1992). Governor Askew provided leadership in the first stage of growth management in the 1970s (DeGrove 1989; Siemon 1992, 36). A task force appointed by Askew presented the 1972 legislature legislation which constituted the state's first effort to balance growth and environmental interests. Four key laws were passed in 1972.

The Florida State Comprehensive Planning Act of 1972 established a formal role for sub-state regional planning councils. It also called for the governor to submit a state comprehensive plan to the legislature. The Water Resources Act of 1972 established five Water Management Districts with planning, management and regulatory powers. The water management districts were granted taxing authority by a statewide constitutional amendment referendum. The Land Conservation Act of 1972 permitted the State to issue bonds to acquire environmentally sensitive lands.

Another particularly significant law adopted in 1972 was the Environmental Land and Water Management Act. This legislation, while keeping most land use decisions at the local level, defined a "development of regional impact" (DRI) as projects whose size or character would impact a greater-than-local area. These developments would be subject to state review. The Act also created the Area of Critical State Concern program (ACSC) (DeGrove 1984 and 1988; Pelham 1979). Areas possessing resources of particular significance on a regional or statewide basis could be designated as critical areas. The local governments in the critical area were required to revise their local plans to meet state guidelines and development orders were subject to appeal to the Florida Land and Water Adjudicatory Commission (FLWAC), the governor and elected cabinet. While limited to no more than 5% of the state's land area, the critical state concern program represented a major intrusion into historically local prerogatives and, taken with the DRI provisions, constituted a major shift of responsibility for growth policy to the state level. The legislation also established the Environmental Land Management Study (ELMS) committee for land and water management issues and to recommend appropriate legislation. One of the ELMS committee recommendations was the requirement for local governments to prepare and implement comprehensive plans.

Three years later the legislature passed the Local Government Comprehensive Planning Act (LGCPA) of 1975, which required the adoption of a comprehensive plan by every general purpose local government in the state and congealed the centralized approach to land use planning. While this legislation specified the topics that must be addressed, the content, quality, and rigor of the local plans were left up to local governments. Even though local governments retained the authority to amend their plans to facilitate development, the Act mandated a standardized professional planning process at the local level. Moreover, this act set up an institutional framework that would serve as the mechanism for a more centralized approach in the future.

The impact of the LGCPA was limited by the lack of substantial new funding to support local planning efforts, numerous difficulties in implementation, inadequate vertical integration, and the lack of enforcement mechanisms to assure local compliance. At the state level the comprehensive plan proved to be of little practical consequence and the regional planning councils' role was limited primarily to DRIs. Despite this weakness, this legislation put in place the initial pieces of an integrated policy framework for managing growth and economic development.

THE 1980S: ENHANCED STATE CONTROL

The 1980s extended the revolution in growth policy as the state assumed more control over the substance of growth in addition to control over procedures. There was a dramatic effort to centralize development management. Enterprise zones were designated by the state as a primary tool for promoting economic development. Growth management was enhanced by strengthening the vertical integration of the planning framework, mandating local plan provisions, and requiring adequate public facilities for new development. By the end of the decade the state had also engaged the issue of preventing sprawl.

ECONOMIC DEVELOPMENT

In economic development there was continued encouragement of public/private cooperation and state level efforts to direct growth. The major development policy innovation of the 1980s was the implementation of a state enterprise zone program. In response to the Miami riots of 1980, the legislature passed a package of incentives for redevelopment. Two years later the Florida Enterprise Zone Act, which organized and modified the 1980 legislation, was passed. The Act attempted to centralize development programs at the state level of government. The intention of the Act was to increase economic development within enterprise zones by providing state and local incentives for private investments. The state provides a number of development incentives to zone employers. These include tax credits, corporate and sales tax exemption and other development support. Local governments may provide a number of incentives to augment the state tax breaks including tax and license exemptions, tax increment financing, and industrial revenue bonds.

The Department of Community Affairs (DCA), responsible for enterprise zone implementation, selected thirty enterprise zones on a competitive basis. DCA made these decisions based upon economic conditions and local participation. In 1988 the legislature amended the Act to designate an additional twenty zones. This program provided a way to coordinate state and local actions and centralized the authority for the designation of enterprise zones at the state level.

GROWTH MANAGEMENT

Despite the centralized growth management process set up by the Local Government Comprehensive Planning Act of 1975 (LGCPA), several problems remained. The LGCPA offered no means of gauging the quality of local plans and the required state reviews proved ineffective. Further, no means were provided for assuring the local plans were implemented through local enactment of land development regulations. The courts limited the standing of citizens to challenge local government actions inconsistent with the adopted plans. In addition, local governments still retained authority to determine their growth plan independently of neighboring jurisdictions as long as procedural requirements were met. Local plans also were not required to be consistent with state and regional plans (Pelham, Hyde, and Banks 1985).

Governor Bob Graham became the *entrepreneur* for modifying the approach to growth management strengthening the framework of an integrated system for growth management (Pelham, Hyde, and Banks 1985). In 1982 Graham appointed the Second Environmental Land Management Study (ELMS II) committee. The ELMS II committee recommended a "statewide planning framework" that included a state plan, regional and local plans that "achieve the goals" of the state plan, and "a continuing effort to communicate, coordinate, and mediate differences" among those engaged in the planning process.[4] The State and Regional Planning Act of 1984 and the Growth Management Act of 1985 (GMA) addressed these issues. The ELMS II committee recommended that no land use map be included in the state plan to prevent allegations that the plan would lead to a statewide zoning map (Rhodes and Apgar 1984).

The State and Regional Planning Act of 1984 required the Governor to prepare a state plan and present it to the legislature in the next (1985) session (Rhodes and Apgar 1984). The State and Regional Planning Act of 1984 acknowledged the importance of a state level planning policy framework for local planning and the failure of the state planning process initiated by the 1972 law. The state plan was adopted by the legislature in 1985. Unlike the much more detailed and extensive version prepared in the 1970s and never accorded more than "advisory only" status,[5] the adopted 1985 version included goal and policy statements to guide state actions.

The policy provisions of the state plan were made more specific in agency functional plans and adapted to sub-state areas by comprehensive regional policy plans. The regional plans provided a link between the state and local plans. The agency functional plans and regional policy plans were required to be consistent with the state plan. While expressly rejecting a goal of compact development patterns that discouraged urban sprawl, the adopted state plan included numerous policies with that effect. For example, it included incentives to separate urban and rural land uses and for private investment in downtowns.[6] In 1985 the legislature also adopted the Omnibus Growth Management Act of 1985.

The Growth Management Act of 1985 centralized comprehensive planning at the state level through a top-down decision process (DeGrove and Juergensmeyer 1986). The integrated policy framework placed into law by the 1985 legislature involved a vertical integration of goals, policies and implementation strategies (see Figure 13-1). The GMA responded to each of the weaknesses identified in the local comprehensive planning process established by the 1975 act. It also incorporated language to assure that adequate public facilities would be available to support new development and provided the foundation needed by the DCA to address urban sprawl.

The GMA directed the DCA to prepare minimum criteria for local comprehensive plans which the Department adopted as Rule 9J-5, F.A.C. A schedule for local plan submission was prepared pursuant to the GMA. If the DCA found a local plan to not be in compliance with the minimum criteria, sanctions were authorized by the new statute including withholding of certain state revenues. Local land development regulations were required by the GMA to be consistent with the local comprehensive plan. The GMA significantly broadened the standing of citizens to challenge the actions of local governments believed to not be consistent with the local plan (Morrell 1989; Pelham 1986, in DeGrove and Juergensmeyer 1986; Siemon and Kendig 1996).

The ability of local governments to amend their plans, once adopted under the GMA requirements, was also severely restricted. The economic feasibility of the local plans was furthered by more demanding provisions for the capital improvements element (McKay and Shoemyen 1988). Further, the intergovernmental coordination element received more emphasis. As part of the vertically integrated planning framework, the DCA compliance review procedures were especially effective at identifying potential local, regional, and state interjurisdictional

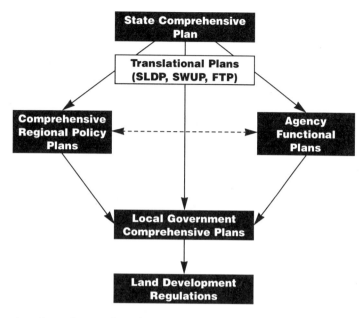

Figure 13-1
ELMS POLICY FRAMEWORK: I

conflicts. The 1985 GMA also provided the framework and basis for one of the most important, far reaching, and controversial provisions of Florida's development management system: concurrency.

Adopted in 1986 as amendments to the 1985 GMA, concurrency is a simple concept that becomes complex when put into practice (Boggs and Apgar 1991; DeGrove and Miness 1992). Concurrency is a doctrine requiring that adequate public facilities be available "concurrent with the impacts" of new development.[7] One of the most controversial provisions of Florida's growth management system, concurrency became pivotal in implementing the GMA and a key test of the entire top down, vertically integrated planning framework.[8]

Controversy surrounded implementation of the concurrency requirement. DCA opted for a strict interpretation but as a planning concept, thereby according sufficient flexibility to prevent concurrency from being unworkable (Pelham 1992b, 1011–1012). Concurrency placed the planning process, and its attendant controversy, squarely in the traditional domain of public administration: capital improvements budgeting and public facilities management. As concurrency was implemented the controversy shifted to the impact of concurrency on the economy.

Concurrency was criticized for creating dislocations in the market (Holcombe 1990; Feiock 1994), for infringing on private property rights by increasing regulatory takings (Mele 1989) and for contributing to urban sprawl by encouraging development to locate in areas with excess facility capacity, typically the urban fringe or rural areas rather than downtowns (Siemon 1992, 51; 1996). The concern with market dislocations have been met with calls for increased funding for public facilities (Boggs and Apgar 1991; Mele 1989; Pelham 1992b; Siemon 1992) and increased regulatory and funding support for affordable housing (Pelham 1992b). The state addressed the issue of urban sprawl with a major policy initiative in the late 1980s (DeGrove and Miness 1992, 17–21).

Governor Bob Martinez appointed a task force on urban growth patterns in 1988 with representation from a cross section of the potentially affected interests as well as subject matter experts. Among the conclusions and recommendations of the task force were the following:[9]

- Prevent urban sprawl through a combination of planned urban service areas, land development regulations, and incentives (economic and regulatory) for compact development.
- Guide public investments and urban form with a strategic state urban policy.
- Improve intergovernmental coordination to better integrate planning efforts, especially transportation, to resist urban sprawl.

The legislature's 1985 rejection of a state plan goal for compact development created a degree of policy ambiguity about preventing urban sprawl. To overcome uncertainty the Department of Community Affairs crafted a clearly articulated state policy for compact development patterns from provisions in the state plan, Chapter 163 (local government comprehensive planning requirements) and Rule 9J-5, F.A.C., which implements Chapter 163 (Florida Department of Community Affairs, vol. 4, no. 4, undated, issued in 1989; Pelham 1992a; 1992b; 1009–1011). The policy was applied to local government comprehensive plans and has been sustained against legal challenges in administrative hearings and in at least one judicial appeal.[10]

Compact development, however, poses complex policy issues that will continue to challenge the Florida development management system (Dubbink 1984; Murley 1996; Siemon 1996). And while the premises for opposing sprawl are appealing (DeGrove 1989; Pelham 1992a; 1992b) the research findings so far, are less than compelling (Audirac, Shermyen, and Smith 1990; Frank 1989).

The state virtually completed construction of a top down, vertically integrated planning framework for local comprehensive plans with the compact development/anti-sprawl policy. By strengthening the vertically integrated planning framework more of the responsibility for managing greater-than-local resources could be shifted to the planning process with a commensurate lessening of reliance on the Development of Regional Impact process. This trend continued into the 1990s.

1990s: MANAGING DEVELOPMENT MANAGEMENT

To balance the increasing influence of growth controls on the private sector, the state 1) opened selected public growth promotion activities to greater involvement by the private sector and 2) created a public-private forum for resolving conflicts between environmental protection and economic development policies.

Particularly bothersome to business was the Development of Regional Impact (DRI) process. Since its creation in 1972 the DRI process had been one of Florida's most conspicuous growth control mechanisms. It continued to operate through the period when the vertically integrated planning framework was constructed. With the addition of concurrency management systems and urban service areas, the role of the DRI process became an issue. The Third Environmental Land Management Study committee (ELMS III) examined this and other issues emerging from experience with development management in the late 1980s and early 1990s.

ECONOMIC DEVELOPMENT

The movement toward public private partnerships in economic development continued in the 1990s. At the state level public private partnerships were institutionalized through the Enterprise Florida program. Enterprise Florida is a public-private nonprofit corporation supported by industry and state government to provide economic development information and services to promote growth. The Enterprise Florida Board of Directors oversees economic development in Florida and is responsible for implementing a strategic development plan, formulating policy, and assessing performance of economic development efforts. A bill, backed by Governor Chiles, to eliminate the Department of Commerce and turn most of its functions over to Enterprise Florida passed the House in 1995 but was blocked in the Senate because of concerns with public accountability. After accountability provisions were added the bill passed both chambers and was signed into law in 1996.

Enterprise Florida now has primary responsibility for economic development in Florida. In addition to promotion and incentives, Enterprise Florida works with state and local agencies to coordinate development permitting for new business.

The legislature also approved the "Partners for a Better Florida" program in 1992. While this initiative has received far less attention than Enterprise Florida, it provides the means by which state agencies, business and industry groups, and environmental interests to better reconcile environmental protection and economic development. A key provision in the legislation creates a one-stop permitting system.

GROWTH MANAGEMENT

Florida's initial growth management effort in 1972 pursued two parallel tracks: 1) integrated vertical planning, and 2) state management of greater-than-local resources. While much of the legislative effort in the '70s and '80s focused on constructing the planning framework, the other growth management track was also being traveled. The second track was intended to deal with development impacts in greater-than-local arenas where plans and regulations were, or were anticipated to be, ineffective in protecting and managing resources of regional or state significance. The Development of Regional Impact and Area of Critical State Concern were the growth management programs on the greater-than-local track.

DRIs required the developer to submit a detailed analysis of proposed projects, including an assessment of market need, an analysis of its impact on the host community and potentially affected jurisdictions, and to identify community needs such as schools, public safety, roadways, and parks. The cost of preparing the DRI application could range from $250,000 to millions of dollars but left the applicant with no assurance of development approval. The DRI process also consumed large amounts of time ranging from months to years (Siemon 1992, 47). The DRI application was submitted to the regional planning council. The development order and implementing development permits were issued, or denied, by the host local government. The regional planning council and Department of Community Affairs had authority to appeal the development order action to the FLWAC, the governor and elected cabinet, for final action.

To receive approval, developers would routinely agree to satisfy community needs identified in the DRI applications even if they were not directly attributable to the proposed DRIs. The costs of preparing the application, the time required for the DRI process, and the payments for needed community facilities imposed significant costs on DRI projects that were not generally applied to other developments in the same area. This caused significant differences in costs between DRI and non-DRI projects and thereby influenced local real estate markets.

Similarly, the Area of Critical State Concern program was used when the growth controls in an area of regional or state significance were deemed inadequate. The ACSC provided a topdown vertically integrated planning process for selected areas of the state before the mandatory local planning laws were adopted in 1975 and 1985. In designated critical areas, local governments were required to adopt land development regulations which were consistent with "principles" approved by the state for that critical area.[11] Development approvals and permits granted by the local government were subject to appeal by the DCA to the FLWAC which could modify or overturn local action (DeGrove 1984; 1988; Pelham 1979).

The changes to the Florida development management system made by the LGCPA in 1975 and the GMA in 1985–6 allowed the state to shift more of the responsibilities for management of greater-than-local resources (DRIs and ACSC) to the integrated vertical planning process. These changes in the planning statutes helped relieve the DRI process of much of the burden of preparing applications for projects in communities that previously had weak local comprehensive plans. Regional policy plans prepared in the 1980s helped make the review of DRI applications more routine because regional issues and concerns were addressed in adopted policies.

The requirements of a capital improvements element that supported plan financial feasibility and concurrency in local comprehensive plans helped erase many of the market dislocations attributable to the DRI process. The playing field was leveled substantially for DRI projects because the planning framework provided a basis for determining the pro rata share of facilities required to support projects. The planning framework helped reduce the pressure on DRIs to fix pre-existing facility deficiencies, thus avoiding subsidizing current users. In addition, the local comprehensive plans also provided DRI developers greater assurance that public facilities would be provided by local governments as promised. In many respects the top down, vertically integrated planning framework eliminated many of the conditions that led to direct state intervention in local affairs.

Another prominent consequence of the strengthened planning framework was the need to integrate growth management issues into local government operations, particularly Concurrency Management Systems (CMS). DCA required local governments to establish concurrency management systems in local government comprehensive plans so they would appropriately apportion the costs of facility capacity.

Concurrency management systems combined financial management systems and land development regulation systems of a local government into a framework capable of assuring that when new development was authorized adequate facilities would be available. The amount of development that could be approved by a local government was dependent on the availability of adequate public facility capacity. The timing of the construction or expansion of public facilities would be crucial then in considering development management actions. A system for allocating facility capacity was required; commitments to new development of facility capacity had to be tracked; and, actual available facility capacity had to be monitored (Young 1988). Fiscal planning and management, and land use planning and regulation have always been difficult to manage as largely independent subjects. Since their management has been integrated and their functions made to overlap, they have become even more problematic for public administrators.

Concurrency management systems, like concurrency generally, had few statutory guides for implementation. The Department of Community Affairs used its administrative rulemaking and local plan compliance review processes, albeit with considerable consultation with the Florida Legislature to make concurrency operational (Pelham 1992b, 1011). Relying on these two levers caused the implementation of the planning framework to focus almost exclusively on local government planning. State planning efforts were largely outside the authority of the DCA. Because of the wide variety of circumstances found among the more than 400 local governments, implementing the 1985 GMA took time and fostered controversy. Governor Lawton Chiles in 1991 appointed the Third Environmental Land Management Study committee (ELMS III) in part to address these controversies as part of the effort to "re-invent" government.

The ELMS III committee made 174 recommendations in their final report issued in late 1992. A substantial number of the recommendations were adopted by the legislature in 1993. Among the recommendations adopted were those which strengthened the vertically integrated planning process; shifted some of the reliance on the direct state management of significant state and regional areas to the planning process; fine tuned the implementation of the local comprehensive planning process; and, increased funding options for local governments.

The planning process received attention at the top as well; the state comprehensive plan became part of a strategic planning process. Agency functional plans required by the State and Regional Planning Act of 1984 were designated state agency strategic plans. (See Figure 13-2.) The comprehensive regional policy plan was designated the strategic regional policy plan. The law called for the growth management strategic plan to be prepared first and for it to consider land development, water resources, air quality, transportation and related issues. The growth management strategic plan was required by the law to be approved by the legislature. Similarly, the state comprehensive plan was subjected to biennial review and revision, as appropriate and necessary, presumably to better integrate the state planning and budgeting processes.

The improvement in the structure and performance of the planning process allowed state management of significant state and regional areas to be even more narrowly specified. The thresholds for DRIs were increased and subjected to an expedited review if determined to be consistent with the local comprehensive plan. Review criteria for DRIs were restricted to proposed projects which were multi-jurisdictional or of state or regional significance. Importantly for the DRI process, the regional planning councils were prohibited from permitting or

Figure 13-2
ELMS Policy Framework: II

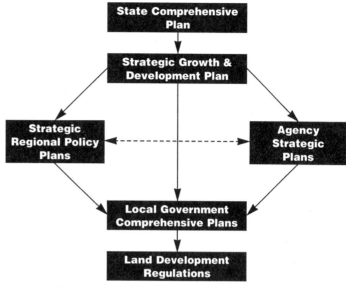

Source: ELMS Committee 1992.

regulating, an action which significantly limited the uncertainties facing the applicant for a DRI class project. And when taken with the designation of the regional planning councils as the sole multi-purpose planning agency at the regional level, demonstrated the shift in emphasis toward the planning process.

Further evidence of the increasing reliance on the top down planning process was the stipulation of a schedule and conditions for terminating the DRI process in certain counties contingent on intergovernmental coordination provisions being adopted although the 1996 Legislature dropped this link between DRIs and intergovernmental coordination elements (ICE) (Florida Chapter of the American Planning Association 1996). In an effort to get intergovernmental coordination to work more effectively, the law required local governments include processes for identifying and mitigating potential conflicts with other local jurisdictions and regional or state resources or facilities. Intergovernmental coordination was also required to include provisions for dispute resolution as a means for resolving conflicts.

Funding for local governments was also significantly broadened for plan implementation. The ninth cent gas tax was authorized subject to an extraordinary vote of the local governing body rather than by referendum. An additional tax of between 1 and 5 cents per gallon of gas was authorized for local governments with a requirement for a majority-plus-one vote of the governing body or, optionally, a referendum.

FUTURE OF FLORIDA'S DEVELOPMENT MANAGEMENT POLICY

Development management is a diverse set of programs including economic development and growth management (Kelly 1993). In the absence of a national development policy states have become the focal point of growth policy formulation activities. Florida is clearly a leader in growth policy in the 1990s and is likely to maintain a leadership role out of both virtue and necessity. The innovativeness of Florida growth policy and the institutional structures set up for its implementation provide a basis for continued activism. The continuation of location specific development problems and continued population growth make development management initiatives a necessity (Grosso 1996).

ECONOMIC DEVELOPMENT

In addition to direct economic development programs, state growth policy is likely to continue to facilitate economic development within the planning framework, directly by requiring plans to address growth promotion activities and indirectly by lessening the inadvertent impacts of growth management activities on the market. An example of direct growth promotion is the ELMS III proposal that incentives be provided for local governments to prepare economic development elements as part of their comprehensive plans (Florida Environmental Land Management Study Committee 1992, 37). An example of indirect facilitation of growth is the additional flexibility for administering transportation concurrency provided by the 1993 ELMS legislation.

The trend over the last 20 years has been to blend the planning framework and the state and regional management tracks. Relying on the top down, vertically integrated planning framework to meet the needs of managing greater-than-local issue areas helps minimize market dislocations attributable to state intervention in traditionally local affairs. The redefinition of the role of the DRI and Areas of Critical State Concern programs is likely to continue as the planning framework becomes more mature and effective. For example, ELMS III recommended that as the ACSC is better integrated with the planning process, it be considered the state's action of last resort for use by the state with local governments that refused to comply with planning mandates. The threat of direct state management of development reinforces the fiscal sanctions available.

As growth management programs become more effective, economic development is less likely to be in conflict in ways that the market cannot accommodate. The emerging strategic character of the state and regional planning process promotes a development management system that more effectively promotes the public interest by applying public policies to induce and restrain growth, as appropriate, based on the conditions in particular locations. The strategic approach to development management should help with the trade-off decisions confronting the state. Opportunities for reconciling the environment and growth are available within the strategic planning framework.

Focusing on infrastructure provides policy instruments that can facilitate and encourage development where it is desirable as well as manage and limit development where it is less desirable. Policies promoting intergovernmental coordination and the use of conflict resolution are also important for reconciling environmental protection and economic development. The development management system has committed these policy tools to supporting compact development patterns that prevent urban sprawl.

GROWTH MANAGEMENT

Florida's strategic planning system highlights the need for intergovernmental coordination (Bryson and Einsweiler 1988). The institutional structure of public organizations may be modified to formally acknowledge and institutionalize these emerging intergovernmental relationships. Someone at each level of the development management framework and in each agency would need to be charged with the "care and feeding" of these relationships if they are to be effective (Bryson and Einsweiler 1988, 2). Those assigned intergovernmental management responsibilities will find it requires more than spare time and incidental attention. It is likely to become an even more integral part of the public administrator's domain, a strategic and tactical component in managing public agencies (Agranoff 1989).

Through intergovernmental coordination and conflict resolution, the strategic planning framework provides an excellent mechanism for overcoming the competition among governments for economic development and growth, competition encouraged by the dispositions and biases created by tax policies and government structures.

Reducing intergovernmental conflicts can also help resolve many of the conflicts between public and private interests. Reducing inefficient and counterproductive interjurisdictional competition is consistent with the tradition, and builds on the practice, of public administration (Bidol-Padva and Stroud 1990). The development management framework relies on information being provided to the public about policy alternatives and the implications for the community for each of the alternatives.

In this "market place of ideas" citizens may assess their personal and community interests and "purchase" with their votes those policies they favor. An antidote to both fiscal illusion and public avoidance (Tyer 1989) is substantive community participation (Florida Office of the Attorney General 1992) and aggressive intergovernmental coordination as part of normal agency operations (Wright 1990, 173). A systematic approach is required if coordination with potentially affected interests is to become almost second nature for an organization (Anton 1989; Wright 1988). The Institute for Participatory Management and Planning, for example, offers a compendium of methods for analyzing coordination needs and selecting the appropriate coordination methods (Bleiker and Bleiker 1986; Thomas 1990).

The Florida development management system has been extended and refined in the '90s. Balancing public and private interests continues to be particularly contentious as demonstrated by efforts to broaden property rights through changes to the statutes and Florida constitution (Stroud and Wright 1996; Pelham 1995). In addition, the emergence of "strategic lawsuits against public participation" (SLAPP suits) poses a direct threat to effective citizen participation (Cook and Merriam 1996a and 1996b).

INTEGRATION OF GROWTH POLICIES

The 1993 ELMS legislation and subsequent legislative actions contribute to the continued emergence of an effective development management system and strengthen the link between economic development and growth management by refining the strategic planning process for growth management, promoting intergovernmental coordination and conflict resolution, and tailoring the application of concurrency.[12] The Florida development management system has critics (Siemon 1996) and advocates (Murley 1996). The Florida strategic planning framework provides virtually all of the elements necessary for effective development management programs. Concurrency, compact development patterns, internal consistency, financial feasibility, intergovernmental coordination, and public participation are in the statutes and rules. The continuing challenge is to improve them in practice.

The ELMS III recommended that the planning process could benefit from increased emphasis on vision to guide plans at every level (Florida Environmental Land Management Study Committee 1992, 16–18, 35–36). A vision for a plan is long range (20 to 30 or more years) and describes the type of community (state, regional, or local) that is desired (Bryson 1988, 184–196). The vision provides a clearer basis for planning by making trade-off decisions more explicit: this community rather than that one, this approach rather than another.

The call for a vision for the state's planning framework, in part, acknowledges that effective development management cannot be achieved by minimum criteria and mandates. The ELMS III recommendation implies an increasing awareness that the state must provide guidance to local governments by better articulating state plans. With state strategic plans for transportation, water use, economic development, and environmental protection integrated by a strategic growth management plan and guided by a vision, then the top down, vertically integrated planning process could begin to accommodate more bottom up, vertically integrated planning (Siemon 1992). The state level plans would reinforce bottom up planning to strengthen top down planning. The visions of local plans could blend into regional plans that fit into, while helping to define, the state plan. In this way economic development and growth management could be integrated synergistically, each reinforcing the other, one drawing strength from the other.

It is much too early to declare the Florida development management system a success; too many fundamental questions remain unanswered. For example, are economic development initiatives and growth management effective? Global and national economic conditions make this issue difficult to assess. But research is beginning to indicate that growth management is affecting growth (Feiock 1994). What is unknown is whether the effects will be confirmed by other research and, if so, whether the effects are in the locations and of the type intended. The funding question continues to aggravate development management efforts, complicate intergovernmental relationships, and unsettle the relationship between political and market forces. Regulations are an inadequate substitute for infrastructure funding. The questions of development patterns and the related costs of growth are of particular concern because of the implications of the remedies. Development regulations boost the costs of housing even while housing affordability remains a pressing problem. Are the benefits derived from the regulations worth the costs incurred? And what is the obligation of the larger community to offset the impacts of growth regulations on those residents least able to afford decent housing? These are appropriate questions for research, but definitive answers are unlikely soon.

REFERENCES

Agranoff, Robert (1989). Managing intergovernmental processes. in James Perry, ed., *Handbook of Public Administration.* San Francisco, CA: Jossey-Bass Publishers, 131–147.

Anton, Thomas J. (1989). *American federalism & public policy: How the system works.* New York: Random House.

CHAPTER

13

Audirac, Ivonne, Anne H. Shermyen, and Marc T. Smith (1990). Ideal urban form and visions of the good life: Florida's growth management dilemma. *Journal of the American Planning Association* 56(4) (Autumn): 470–482.

Bidol-Padva, Patricia and Nancy E. Stroud (1990). *Managing public conflicts in Florida: A guide to collaborative approaches. sponsored by Palm Beach Countywide Planning Council and Florida Growth Management Conflict Resolution Consortium.* Tallahassee, FL: Florida Center for Public Management.

Bleiker, Hans and Annemarie Bleiker (1986). *Citizen participation handbook for public officials and other professionals serving the public.* 5th edition. Laramie, Wyoming: Institute for Participatory Management and Planning.

Boggs, H. Glenn and Robert C. Apgar (1991). Concurrency and growth management: A lawyer's primer. *Journal of Land Use and Environmental Law* 7:1–27.

Bosselman, Fred and David Callies (1971). *The quiet revolution in land use controls.* Washington: Council on Environmental Quality.

Bryson, John M. (1988). *Strategic planning for public and nonprofit organizations: A guide to strengthening and sustaining organizational achievement.* San Francisco, CA: Jossey-Bass Publishers.

———— and Robert C. Einsweiler, editors (1988). *Strategic planning: Threats and opportunities for planners.* Chicago, IL: Planners Press, American Planning Association.

Cook, Darrell F. and Merriam, Dwight H. (1996a). Recognizing a SLAPP suit and understanding its consequences part 1. *Florida Planning* 8 (5) (June): 11.

————. (1996b). Recognizing a SLAPP suit and understanding its consequences part 2. *Florida Planning* 8 (6) (August): 3.

DeGrove, John M. (1984). *Land, growth and politics.* Chicago: Planners Press, American Planning Association.

————. (1988). Critical area programs in Florida: Creative balancing of growth and the environment. *Washington University Journal of Urban and Contemporary Law* 34 (Fall): 51–97.

————. (1989). Consistent, concurrent, compact: Florida's search for a rational growth management system. *The Political Chronicle,* September: 32–38.

———— and Deborah A. Miness (1992). *Planning and growth management in the states: The new frontier for land policy.* Cambridge, MA: Lincoln Institute for Land Policy.

———— and Juergensmeyer, Julian Conrad, eds. (1986). *Perspectives on Florida's Growth Management Act of 1985.* Lincoln Institute Monograph #86-5. Cambridge, MA: Lincoln Institute of Land Policy.

Dubbink, David (1984). I'll have my town medium rural, please. *Journal of the American Planning Association* 50: 406–418.

Dye, Thomas R. (1991). *American federalism: Competition among governments.* Boston: Lexington Books.

Einsweiler, Robert C. (1980). Goals and objectives of growth management programs—federal, state, and local. In *Proceedings of the National Land Use Conference on Growth Management,* San Francisco, California, March 14–17, 1979, by the Golden Gate University. San Francisco, CA: Golden Gate University, 15-37-A.

Finnell, Gilbert L. (1985). Keynote address for the Conference on Managing Megagrowth: Florida's new mandate. *Journal of Land Use and Environmental Law* 1: 189–200.

Feiock, Richard (1994). The Political Economy of Growth Management: Local Impacts of the Florida Growth Management Act. *American Politics Quarterly* 22: 208–220.

Florida Advisory Council on Intergovernmental Relations (1991). *1991 Report on mandates and measures affecting local government fiscal capacity.* (September) Tallahassee, FL: Florida Advisory Council on Intergovernmental Relations.

Florida Chapter of the American Planning Association (1996). Growth management bill clears '96 Legislature. *Florida Planning* 8(5) (June): 9.

Florida Department of Community Affairs (1989). Discouraging urban sprawl in local government comprehensive plans. *Technical Memo* 4(4). undated.

Florida Environmental Land Management Study Committee (1992). *Building successful communities. Environmental Land Management Study Committee final report.* unpublished. (December) Tallahassee, FL: Florida Environmental Land Management Study Committee.

Florida Governor's Task Force on Urban Growth Patterns (1989). *Governor's task force on urban growth patterns, final report.* (June) Tallahassee, FL: Florida Governor's Task Force on Urban Growth Patterns.

Florida Office of the Attorney General (1992). *Government-in-the-sunshine manual.* Tallahassee, FL: First Amendment Foundation.

Frank, James E. (1989). *The costs of alternative development patterns: A review of the literature.* Washington, D.C.: ULI- the Urban Land Institute.

Grosso, Richard (1996). Florida's growth management act: How far we have come, how far we have to go. *Nova Law Review* 20(2) (Winter): 589–659.

Holcombe, Randall G. (1990). Growth management and land use planning in Florida. *Florida Policy Review:* 6–12.

Joint Select Committee on Growth Management Implementation (JSC) (1989). Urban sprawl: A term of art? Appendix. *Oversight Advisory: Staff Report* October 1989: 5.

Kelly, Eric Damian (1993). *Managing community growth: Policies, techniques, and impacts.* Westport, CT: Praeger Publishers.

Lindblom, Charles E. (1977). *Politics and markets: The world's political-economic systems.* New York: Basic Books, Inc.

———. (1982). The market as prison. *The Journal of Politics* 44: 324–335.

McKay, Patricia L. and Shoemyen, Anne H. (1988). *Preparing the capital improvements element.* Gainesville, FL: Bureau of Economic and Business Research, University of Florida.

Mele, Dennis (1989). Temporary regulatory taking under the Florida Local Government Comprehensive Planning and Land Development Regulation Act. *University of Miami Law Review* 43: 1203–1227.

Molotch, Harvey L. (1976). The city as a growth machine: Toward a political economy of place. *American Journal of Sociology* 86: 1387–1400.

Morrell, Michael Wm. (1989). Third party standing and the "fairly debatable" rule: Is GMA litigation "easy in, easy to win"? in Joint Select Committee on Growth Management Implementation, *Oversight Advisory: Memorandum* September 1, 1989: 7–8.

Murley, James F. (1996). DCA Report. *Florida Planning* 8(5) (June): 7.

Pelham, Thomas G. (1979). *State land use planning and regulation: Florida, the model code, and beyond.* Lexington, MA: Lexington Books.

———. (1986). Litigating under DCA's minimum criteria rule: Easy in difficult to win. in John M. DeGrove and Julian Conrad Juergensmeyer, eds., *Perspectives on Florida's Growth Management Act of 1985.* Lincoln Institute Monograph #86-5, Cambridge, MA: Lincoln Institute of Land Policy, 83–100.

———. (1992a). Shaping Florida's future: Toward more compact, efficient, and livable development patterns. *Journal of Land Use and Environmental Law* 7(2) (Spring): 321–332.

———. (1992b). Adequate public facilities requirements: Reflections on Florida's concurrency system for managing growth. *Florida State University Law Review,* 19(4): 973–1052.

———. (1995). Coping with the private property rights protection act. *Florida Planning* 7(6) (July/August): 1 and 15.

———, William L. Hyde, and Robert P. Banks (1985). Managing Florida's growth: Toward an integrated state, regional, and local comprehensive planning process. *Florida State University Law Review,* 13: 515–598.

Peterson, Paul (1981). *City limits.* Chicago, IL: University of Chicago Press.

Porter, Douglas R. (1992). Issues in state and regional growth management. in Douglas R. Porter, ed., *State and regional initiatives for managing development.* Washington, D.C.: ULI- the Urban Land Institute, 157–211.

Rhodes, Robert M. and Robert C. Apgar (1984). Charting Florida's course: The State and Regional Planning Act of 1984. *Florida State University Law Review* 12: 583–606.

Solnit, Albert (1987). *The job of the planning commissioner.* 3rd edition revised. Washington, D.C.: Planners Press, American Planning Association.

Siemon, Charles L. (1992). Growth management in Florida: An overview and brief critique. in Douglas R. Porter, ed., *State and regional initiatives for managing development*. Washington, D.C.: ULI- the Urban Land Institute, 35–56.

————. (1996). Viewpoint: Try again, Florida. *Planning* 62(3) (March): 50.

———— and Kendig, Julie P. (1996). Judicial review of local government decisions: "Midnight in the garden of good and evil." *Nova Law Review* 20(2) (Winter): 707–741.

Stroud, Nancy E. and Wright, Thomas G. (1996). Florida's private property rights act— What will it mean for Florida's future? *Nova Law Review* 20(2) (Winter): 683–706.

Thomas, John Clayton (1990). Public involvement in public management: Adapting and testing a borrowed theory. *Public Administration Review* 50(4) (July/August): 435–445.

Turner, Robyn (1990). New rules for the growth game: The use of rational state standards in land use policy. *Journal of Urban Affairs* 12: 35–47.

Tyer, Charlie B. (1989). Municipal enterprises and taxing and spending policies: Public avoidance and fiscal illusions. *Public Administration Review* 49(3) (May/June): 249-256.

Wright, Deil S. (1988). *Understanding intergovernmental relations*. 3rd edition. Pacific Grove, CA: Brooks/Cole Publishing Company.

————. (1990). Federalism, intergovernmental relations, and intergovernmental management: Historical reflections and conceptual comparisons. *Public Administration Review* 50(2): 168–178.

Young, Randall L. (1988). Concurrency: Matching facilities and development. Subchapter in *Florida Planning Commissioner Handbook*. Price, Woody. compiler and editor. Tallahassee, FL: Florida Center for Public Management, Institute of Science and Public Affairs, the Florida State University: 7–40.

Zimmerman, Joseph F. (1992). *Contemporary American federalism: The growth of national power*. New York: Praeger Publishers.

ENDNOTES

1. "[D]evelopment management . . . is not implementing a physical plan. It is not a correlate to the construction of a building from a blueprint. Rather development management is managing a market. It is the public manipulation of private development and we should admit that. . . . I think that it's false for planners, managers and lawyers to declare otherwise. . . . [Every government manages development. It may do it consciously or not; it may do it in a centralized fashion or decentralized; it may do it efficiently or inefficiently. But if a government has a property tax, zoning, a capital improvement program, charge fees for development or any similar activity— actions that affect the market and the act of development by the developer—we would argue that it is managing development. . . . What we are really talking about . . . is private sector investment and public sector investment and the leveraging or influencing effect of all kinds of public controls on that private sector investment. That is what we mean by managing a market" (Einsweiler 1980, 17–18).

2. "Americans believe in a series of little governments. We have been increasingly put off with big government in recent years, especially its bureaucratic complexity. We favor diversity in the establishment of local standards and a homegrown flavor in our communities. We also cherish the opportunity to fight city hall when it might choose a flavor we don't like" (Solnit 1987, viii).

3. "The tie between market and liberalism [liberty] is tightly knotted in Locke, the principal source of American revolutionary thought. For Locke, the foundation of the liberal constitutional state was property. The function of the state was protection of property, including property rights in one's own body, a set of rights that consequently subsumes liberty under property. And property is one of the foundations of market exchange, since people cannot exchange assets or money for assets or services if they do not 'own' the assets and money. . . . The liberal notion of freedom was freedom from government's many interventions, and for that kind of freedom markets are indeed indispensable" (Lindblom 1977, 164).

4. Environmental Land Management Study Committee Final Report (February 1984) as quoted in Pelham, Hyde, and Banks (1985).

5. See *Florida Statutes* section 23.0114(1) (1983).

6. Joint Select Committee on Growth Management Implementation, 1989. Urban sprawl: A term of art? Appendix. *Oversight Advisory: Staff Report,* October 1989: 5.

7. *Florida Statutes* section 163.3177(10)(h) (1989).

8. "[T]he concurrency requirement is the teeth of the 1985 Growth Management Act." Letter from Thomas G. Pelham, Secretary of the Florida Department of Community Affairs to Senator Gwen Margolis, Democrat North Miami Beach, pg. 1 (March 7, 1988) as quoted in Boggs and Apgar, 1991, 1.

9. See Florida Governor's Task Force on Urban Growth Patterns. 1989. *Governor's Task Force on Urban Growth Patterns, Final Report.* (June) Tallahassee, FL: Florida Governor's Task Force on Urban Growth Patterns.

10. Home Builders & Contractors Association of Brevard County v. Department of Community Affairs, 585 So. 2d 965, 968 (Fla. 1st DCA 1991) as cited in Pelham, 1992, 1011, footnote 259.

11. Five areas have received the critical area designation: Florida Keys, City of Key West, Big Cypress Swamp (in the Everglades area), Green Swamp (in central Florida), and Apalachicola/Franklin County (in the Panhandle, Gulf coast area).

12. The 1993 ELMS legislation made numerous changes to the various planning and growth management statutes. Adopted as CS/CS/HB 2315, summaries of the ELMS bill were prepared by the Florida Senate Committee on Community Affairs and the Florida Chapter of the American Planning Association.

TAX POLICY: FACTORS RELATED TO SUCCESS AND FAILURE

WILLIAM EARLE KLAY, JOANNE R. SNAIR
AND GLORIA A. GRIZZLE

T he tax structure of Florida's state government is inadequate and unfair. The state places a greater tax burden upon persons of modest income than it does upon those who are affluent. In addition, the tax structure consistently fails to keep abreast of the growth in Florida's economy. Forced to keep pace with the needs of a growing population, elected officials are repeatedly pressed to raise tax rates, but the increases fail to remedy underlying problems. These problems are well understood by many of the state's leaders, but efforts during the past decade to reform the tax policies of the state have met with failure.

Chapter Nine discusses the inadequacies of Florida's tax structure with respect to both incidence and elasticities in some detail. Another excellent analysis of these inadequacies is that of Zingale and Davies (1986). To summarize, the combined incidence of all state taxes is such that a greater burden is placed upon poorer Floridians than upon wealthier ones. Exemptions of food and drugs from the sales tax has a moderating effect, but the overall burden is still regressive. In addition, Florida faces two problems related to the elasticity of its taxes relative to changes in the overall economy. The first problem is that the state's tax base is quite narrow, causing growth in revenue receipts to continuously lag behind growth in the economy.

Grizzle's analysis (Chapter Nine) shows that the state's revenues as measured in real per capita revenue (the inflation adjusted dollars collected per person) has remained about the same for the past two decades. This failure to grow has occurred in spite of the adoption of new revenue sources and numerous increases in tax rates. Simply put, the state is on a fiscal treadmill; its political leaders must repeatedly increase tax rates just to avoid falling behind in real (viz. inflation adjusted) expenditures per person. The primary reason the state is on the treadmill, the reason that its revenues fail to keep pace with growth in personal incomes, is that Florida has chosen not to tax personal income directly. Instead, the state relies mostly on taxing the consumption of things that people are buying relatively less of (durable goods) and incomes increase, but it does not tax the consumption of the things they are buying more of (services).

The second problem of elasticity is that the narrow tax base is quite volatile, causing receipts to fluctuate more than changes in the overall economy. This means that when a recession creates new demands for state services, Florida's revenues are in the process of rapidly shrinking. Volatility is present in the state's sales and income taxes alike. Personal incomes are less volatile than corporate incomes, yet Florida taxes the latter while exempting the former. Purchases of services are more stable than purchases of such things as consumer goods, yet Florida taxes the latter while exempting the former. Purchases of food and drugs are relatively stable, but to tax these would greatly worsen regressivity.

Many of the state's leaders believe that the inadequacies of Florida's revenue structure are endangering the future of the state. In 1985, for example, the Florida Council of 100 reviewed the state's actions and concluded that the future economic competitiveness of the state was imperiled. Noting inadequacies in roads, schools, water and sewer systems, parks, and so on, this group of prestigious business leaders recommended major changes, including the elimination of many exemptions to the sales tax. In 1987 the State Comprehensive Plan Committee—a group of elected and other leaders from across Florida who were appointed to review the state's capacity to implement the state plan that was adopted in 1985—came to a similar conclusion.

Noting such things as the vulnerability of our natural environment, the fragility of our social structure, and the increasingly competitive world within which Floridians must compete, the State Comprehensive Plan Committee issued a warning, "Our failure to provide the transportation, wastewater, solid waste, corrections, schools, and other public facilities we need threatens to have a chilling effect on Florida's economy." It also concluded, "And our low tax rates and our undue reliance on a narrow-based sales tax keep us from having the stable and reliable flow of governmental revenues that is needed to attract and accommodate quality growth" (SCPC 1987, 2).

The revenue structure of Florida is not just inadequate, it is also unique and highly resistant to fundamental change. Forty states have a broad-based personal income tax and at least four others have more narrowly defined personal income taxes. The only other large and rapidly growing state that has no personal income tax is Texas, a state that has enjoyed the fruits (and instability) of oil and gas taxes. Other than the sun and sand to attract tourists, Florida lacks such natural resources upon which to base its tax policy. Why has Florida become an outlier, the only large, rapidly growing state with neither oil nor an income tax in its revenue structure?

The answer lies in the nature of Florida's natural amenities and the impact these have had upon plans and aspirations for economic development. For most of its history, Florida could not offer such things as proximity to large markets or to the resources needed for manufacturing, and so it could not adopt economic development strategies similar to those of the industrial states. What it could offer was plentiful sun, sand, water, vast stretches of vacant land, and a cheap labor force. Its economic development policies, therefore, sought to attract tourists, retirees, and employers who wanted cheap labor and low business costs.

Tourists might venture a visit to a high tax state, but back in 1923 law makers decided that the retirees and employers of the state sought something more—the inducement of a constitutional prohibition to taxes upon incomes. The rationale behind the prohibition was clearly stated by Senator John Stokes of Pensacola, the principal author of the joint resolution to amend the constitution. "Hundreds will be attracted to this state from the states which have income and inheritance taxes," said Stokes, "and the state will gain greatly increased ad valorem taxes. It will bring wealth, industry and commerce to the state." Leading the small opposition to the prohibition was Senator James Caulkins of Fernandina. He argued that the state would attract growth and wealth without a prohibition on income taxes and that such an amendment would bring "tax dodgers" to the state (both quotes, *Florida Times Union,* May 10, 1923, 8).

The constitutional prohibition against income taxes is now a longstanding cornerstone of Florida's policy framework to attract growth. It is an ingrained element of the political culture, and it seems to be viewed by inmigrants as something of a social contract. After nearly seven decades, Florida's tax policy is still based upon Senator Stokes' assumptions. Tax effort in Florida, the proportion of our wealth that is taxed, is among the lowest in the nation. Was Senator Caulkins' prediction accurate?

Florida is no longer the impoverished, nearly vacant state that it once was. It must compete in a global economy while protecting its delicate ecosystems and fragile social structure. Doing so successfully requires adequate resources which, in turn, requires tax reform. Such reform, however, must be achieved in the context of a political culture that was shaped by the tax policies of an earlier era.

In this chapter, we will look at four major efforts to significantly alter Florida's tax base. Two of these, the adoption of the general retail sales tax in 1949 and the corporate income tax in 1971, were successes that were achieved in the face of substantial political opposition. The other two efforts, the attempts to adopt the "unitary tax" on corporate incomes in 1983 and to adopt a broad-based tax on the sale of services in 1987, were failures. Both reforms were enacted into law, but political willpower evaporated and the reforms were rescinded. The story of each reform effort is unique. Viewing them together, however, reveals several factors that seem to be associated with success and failure in reforming Florida's tax structure.

ADOPTING A RETAIL SALES TAX

When Fuller Warren was elected governor in November of 1948, his platform included such items as the creation of a civil service, a central state purchasing agency, and banning livestock from the roadways of the state. He was apparently unaware of the state's growing financial problems and was opposed to new taxes. Shortly after taking office, however, he was confronted with the reality that the state's revenue base was grossly inadequate. During World War II, the nation's manpower and other resources had been shifted to defense and the state accumulated a substantial revenue surplus. When peace came, citizens expressed pent up demands for new domestic spending. The 1947 legislature responded by spending far more on operating costs than the state collected in taxes. When Warren took office, the state had been running in the red for two years.

One of the most memorable orators in Florida's history, Warren passionately declared in his opening address to the 1949 legislature that the state was approaching bankruptcy.

> There is a strange paradox, a striking contradiction about the prosperity which pervades Florida's economy. In the midst of the abundant prosperity which permeates nearly every segment of business in Florida, the State government stands strapped financially, and indeed it is almost insolvent (*Journal of the House of Representatives,* April 5, 1949, 6).

In 1949 the state depended on a wide variety of excise taxes and fees, but it levied neither an income tax nor a general sales tax, although both were then common in other states. In the midst of a revenue crisis created by the great depression of the 1930s, Governor Dave Sholtz and a special committee recommended a personal income tax, but to no avail

(Special Committee 1935). Governor Sholtz and the committee recommended against a general sales tax, saying that it would be regressive and that an income tax was the only equitable alternative. Warren, too, had reservations about the regressivity of a general sales tax. The governor's populist tendencies evoked his strong opposition to a general sales tax.

Instead, Warren presented the legislature with seventeen separate revenue proposals. Saying that business was undertaxed in Florida, he argued that new revenues should be directed mostly toward business. Among his proposals were: severance taxes on phosphate and petroleum, taxes on commercial lodging, forest products, amusements, tobacco, and a tax of 0.5 percent on gross receipts of all retail sales. The gross receipts tax, he claimed, was a tax on business and not a general sales tax. In this era of government in the sunshine, it is interesting to note that Governor Warren first discussed these taxes with the cabinet in a closed executive session in January, 1949. He said that airing his proposals in public would give those from whom the revenues would be raised a head start with the legislature.

They got a head start in spite of the governor's efforts. In the ensuing legislative session, none of Warren's tax proposals passed. It was not a good session for the governor; his proposals for a central purchasing agency and state civil service also were defeated. The legislature, though, did end the practice of allowing hundreds of continuing or automatic appropriations which had greatly confounded budget making.

Opposition to the governor's revenue proposals came from several camps. First were the many lobbyists who represented the businesses that would be affected by the governor's proposals. Throughout the session, the governor decried their influence, but the fact that he had offered so many distinct proposals allowed his opponents to defeat them one by one. Second, a so-called "economy bloc" which included representative Ferris Bryant, who later became governor, argued that greater economy and efficiency would eliminate the need for additional taxes. Third, a minority of legislators supported the passage of a major new revenue source, a broad-based sales tax, rather than the multifaceted approach of the governor.

The Florida Chamber of Commerce opposed the governor's proposals but left the door open to a retail sales tax. The Florida State Hotel Association advocated a three percent general sales tax while opposing the governor's seventeen point program, one of which was directed at commercial lodgings. An informal poll of legislators in April 1949 indicated a substantial majority opposed any form of sales tax, and that the governor's proposal of a tax on gross receipts from retail sales was the least popular form of such taxation. Governor Warren, on the other hand, steadfastly argued that he would veto a retail sales tax that "would have the effect of cutting the wages and salaries of every employed person in Florida" (*Florida Times Union,* April 22, 1949, 10).

The stage was set for an impasse in the 1949 legislative session. One by one the governor's proposals went down to defeat. Senator John Matthews of Duval County, a legislative confidant and floor leader for the governor, proposed a constitutional amendment to allow an individual income tax. Statements made by Governor Warren indicated he was philosophically inclined toward an income tax but he did not explicitly propose one and Matthews' proposal was promptly defeated.

On May 16th, with time running out on the deadlocked session, Governor Warren invited legislative leaders to dinner at the mansion. Following the dinner, the governor said he would accept any tax except a general sales tax "on the necessities of life." With this phrase, the governor had opened the door for a retail sales tax with some populist features. The "necessities of life" were subsequently defined as food, medicines, rent, and inexpensive clothing. A committee of legislative leaders was announced to develop a tax program in collaboration with the governor.

Senator LeRoy Collins, chairman of the Senate Appropriations Committee, announced support for a three percent general sales tax. He also called for an amendment to allow individual or corporate income taxes with the proviso that the adoption of an income tax would trigger a reduction of the sales tax to two percent. The income tax would apply only to high incomes. Said Collins, "It will give the people the right to decide whether they will wish to continue the entire three percent sales tax in effect or reduce it by one-third and take on the income tax" (*Florida Times Union,* May 18, 1949, 8). The Senate adopted a resolution calling for an income tax amendment to be placed on the ballot, but the House failed to act on the matter.

On May 23, 1949, the committee of legislative leaders proposed a three percent sales tax on retail transactions, exempting food, cotton clothing, medicines, and rentals up to $50 per month. Taxation of retail sales of services was included in the committee's proposal. On May 27, Governor Warren sent both houses a letter urging prompt action to fulfill their constitutional obligation to appropriate needed revenues. The governor also announced he would not give the legislature additional time by calling a special session. Neither the governor nor the legislative leadership, however, were able to break the impasse. On June 3, the legislature approved a conference report for general appropriations of some $240 million, far more than projected revenues, and then adjourned.

What followed was an "interesting" summer for the governor and cabinet. On June 8, Warren announced his engagement for his third marriage to a 24 year-old California "socialite." On June 17, the governor and cabinet, sitting as the State Budget Commission, voted to cut twenty-five percent from the appropriations of every agency for three months. Warren announced that he would postpone drawing any salary for three months; that he would borrow money to live on; and that his top assistants would be paid seventy-five percent of their salaries. He later announced that he would not claim all of the travel reimbursements that were due to him.

Superintendent of Public Instruction, Thomas D. Bailey claimed that Florida schools would be able to operate only seven months during 1949-50 and the Florida Council for the Blind announced a twenty-five percent cut. In the weeks that followed, Warren disclosed that he was cutting short his honeymoon to deal with the state's crisis. He also convinced the Cabinet to ban all pay raises for state employees in the belief that doing so would undercut public support for new taxes. Said Warren, "We may lose some professors, but we are reduced to this stark and almost desperate position" (*Florida Times Union,* July 29, 1949, 9). Layoffs and dire predictions were announced by various agency heads and, on July 7, notice was given that the state was withdrawing the last of its wartime surplus from the banks to pay pending bills. The comptroller said a deficit was near.

Although opposition continued from various business interests, support grew for a sales tax. A special conference of legislators was held on July 23 at Wakulla Springs. Before this group, the governor pleaded the case for additional revenues and announced he would call a special session in September. A joint legislative committee was established to hold a series of hearings around the state and to draft legislation. Members of Florida's school boards, the Florida League of Municipalities, and the League of Women Voters called for a sales tax. The joint legislative committee responded with a recommendation to adopt a three percent sales tax that exempted "the necessities of life."

In a statewide radio address prior to the special session, Warren said the hearings had demonstrated public support for the level of spending that had been appropriated and that it was clear that new revenues were needed to overcome a $55 million deficit. In his opening address to the session on September 7, Warren made an impassioned plea for "vision" and new revenues as an investment in Florida's future. He did not explicitly endorse a limited sales tax, however, and dogged infighting and parliamentary maneuvering ensued. The "economy bloc" tried but failed to cut appropriations while supporters of a broad-based sales tax, one that did not have extensive exemptions but which would be a two percent levy, were also stymied. On September 16, a divided Senate voted 22-16 to support a limited three percent sales tax. Finally, on September 21 following eight hours of debate and amidst a gallery packed with opponents to a sales tax, the House voted for the tax 56 to 39.

By a vote of 24-12, the Senate again approved a resolution to place an amendment before the people to allow income taxation. On September 24, this measure died in the House when time ran out on the special session. On September 29, the governor announced that he would sign the sales tax bill and he accompanied this announcement with a call for a resolution to allow an income tax. "An income tax," said Warren, "is the only means by which the soundest and fairest of all principles of taxation—ability to pay—can be applied" (*Florida Times Union,* September 30, 1949, 43). The opportunity for an income tax was gone, however, and the fiscal crisis of 1949 had yielded instead the sales tax that remains the primary source of state revenue today.

ADOPTING A CORPORATE INCOME TAX

In the 1970 gubernatorial primaries, Reuben Askew began as a rather obscure state legislator from Pensacola who was little known in other parts of the state. One of the things that began to cast attention upon him was his steadfast advocacy of a tax on the incomes of corporations. Askew, however, was not the first to raise the possibility of taxing some form of income. Most other states already had income taxes, so their effects were generally well known. In April 1970 the Florida Education Association endorsed both corporate and personal income taxes and called for a referendum to enable the people to vote on the matter. A subsequent resolution was introduced in the House of Representatives to authorize such a referendum. In May the Senate Ways and Means Committee passed a bill calling for a two percent tax on corporate incomes to enable debate on the floor of the Senate. Nothing came of these legislative efforts, but deliberations in the state had begun to occur about the possibilities of income taxation.

It is important to remember that the years immediately preceding and following 1970 were a time of great change in Florida. In 1966 the state had elected its first Republican governor since Reconstruction, Claude Kirk, who had run on a pledge of no new taxes. Kirk subsequently supported some tax increases, but he vowed to oppose any income taxes. A new constitution had been adopted in 1968, but it had retained the old prohibition against both individual and corporate income taxes. The legislature had been recently reapportioned under court orders and it began to reform both itself and the executive branch of state government.

The needs of a rapidly growing population and those of a newly energized state government required an expanded tax base. Numerous state leaders, including House Republican Leader Donald Reed, predicted that the 1971 legislative session would adopt major tax increases. Gubernatorial candidates, however, were not anxious to endorse new taxes. On August 6, Askew separated himself from other candidates with an announcement that he would seek a tax on corporate incomes. He claimed that the no-tax pledges of other candidates were actually efforts to shield special interests from taxes while paving the way for increases in taxes upon average citizens. If elected, he said, he would persuade the legislature to approve a special referendum that would enable the people to change the constitution. At the same time, he strongly disavowed any tax on personal income.

Askew offered business something in return. He pointed out that businesses could deduct the tax from their federal income taxes, and he promised to fight for repeal of the corporate stock tax if the income tax was adopted. Declaring that tax reform was the most important issue of the campaign, Askew spoke often about his proposal. He repeatedly framed the proposal in populist terms, stating that low and middle income persons would suffer if any of his opponents were elected. To make his proposal even more attractive to persons with moderate incomes, Askew promised to fight for repeal of the sales tax on household utilities.

Some opponents, on the other hand, suggested that the corporate income tax would be passed on to the consumer. Askew himself said that he had opposed a corporate income tax as recently as 1968 when he believed that it would be passed on to the consumer. Subsequent studies, he maintained, showed that it would not be passed on. Most of the tax revenues, he said, were going to be paid by large multistate corporations who set prices according to nationwide criteria. These prices, he said, were such that Floridians were already paying for corporate income taxes to other states but that the additional taxes Florida would impose would not be so large as to have any appreciable effect on prices in Florida. Some objected to the tax on the basis of horizontal equity, saying that a tax upon corporations but not upon partnerships or sole proprietorships was unfair, but this argument failed to gain momentum.

Askew continued to stress tax reform through his solid runoff victory over Attorney General Earl Faircloth and overwhelming victory over Governor Kirk in the general election. Kirk's supporters waged what some called the "rattlesnake campaign," placing advertisements showing a coiled snake and the message that the corporate tax would lead to a personal income tax. Askew's subsequent electoral margin was widely interpreted as a mandate for tax reform and for putting the corporate income tax question before the voters. Nevertheless, winning support and final approval of the tax required a major leadership effort from the newly elected governor during the following year. A few days after the general election, the chairman of the House Select Revenue Study Committee announced that improvements in tax administration would produce a windfall that would preclude the necessity of any new taxes. Representative Richard Pettigrew, a strong Askew supporter, accused lobbyists who were opposed to the corporate income tax of trying to prevent his election as speaker-designate.

Pettigrew won the election 80-36 and played a key role in subsequent legislative battles. Other key supporters of a corporate income tax included Ralph Turlington, chairman of the House Committee on Finance and Taxation, and Marshall Harris, chairman of the House Appropriations Committee. Senate Ways and Means Committee Chairman Louis de la Parte became a supporter, but Senate President Jerry Thomas never supported the tax. Thomas, however, said the governor's proposal deserved a "speedy trial" and he did not obstruct Askew's efforts to get the legislature to approve a special referendum.

Askew faced a troublesome procedural obstacle. A three-fifths vote of each house is needed to place a proposed amendment before the people in a general election, but a three-fourths vote is needed to hold a special election. Hoping to sustain his electoral momentum, Askew claimed that the additional revenue was needed as soon as possible and he sought to obtain a special election as early as possible in 1971, rather than waiting until the general election in 1972. The three-fourths requirement gave additional leverage to Republicans, most of whom opposed Askew's effort, and to the dissident Democrats who also sought to delay a vote. After failing in a special session, proponents eventually managed in the final days of the regular 1971 legislative session to place the question before the voters in November 1971.

The governor pushed hard for an earlier referendum, but compromised on the November date. Lobbying against any 1971 referendum was intense, and legislative approval was obtained only after similarly intense pressure by Askew and his legislative allies. Delays on the Senate vote were common and it was noted that the governor's wife was present whenever a vote on the tax was scheduled. Said one senator, "If we don't hurry up and take a vote, we're going to wear Donna Lou out going up and down the stairs" (*Florida Times Union,* April 29, 1971, B-2). She said that she merely enjoyed the debates.

Askew personally led the campaign to secure voter approval of the proposed constitutional amendment. Promising to be "available Askew" during the critical months of the campaign, Askew's strategy was to utilize the campaign network that had served him the previous year. County level committees were set up and "good government" groups around the state were relied upon extensively. The strategy was to spend as little as possible while anticipating well-financed opposition and scare tactics. These anticipated threats did come to pass. Modest sums were spent by Askew's organization, but the governor did not hesitate to use state transportation or his ability to gain free media exposure to conduct his campaign.

Askew sought support from the state's business leaders. He appointed several key business leaders to his campaign organization, called the Citizens for Tax Reform. Former state senator and citrus magnate Ben Hill Griffin was its chairman. Members included top executives of leading industries and financial institutions (Deltona, Arvida, Jim Walter Corporation, Florida Home Builders Association, Gulf Life, Stockton-Whatley-Davin, Florida Farm Bureau, Southeast Bank, General Motors Acceptance Corporation, Monsanto, Continental Oil, Seaboard Coastline, etc.). Other members included state and local elected officials and civic leaders including the NAACP, AFL-CIO, Congress of Senior Citizens, and Florida Association for Retarded Children.

Opposition to the tax seems to have been centered in Florida, rather than among the multistate corporations. Leading the opposition was the Associated Industries of Florida; its member employers contributed money and circulated messages opposed to the tax among their employees. Efforts were made to take advantage of national economic woes, especially President Nixon's wage-price freeze; the message was conveyed that a new tax on business in Florida would be both inflationary and destructive of jobs. Other opponents included the Winn-Dixie food store, which was identified by Askew as his main source of opposition, the Florida Bankers Association, a bank holding company headed by the powerful Ed Ball, and several utility companies.

Brochures opposing the tax were inserted in numerous bank statements and utility bills. Television time was purchased on numerous stations to convey the opponents' message. Askew called for equal time under federal communications policy and some stations granted his request. Others refused and claimed that equal time had been provided through the governor's appearances on news and public interest programs. James E. Davis, chairman of Winn-Dixie, was quoted as saying that Askew was a "nut with a Huey Long outlook" who would "ruin" a favorable business climate (*Wall Street Journal,* November 1, 1971, 1).

369

Askew replied, "I'm doing exactly like I said I would during the campaign. If it's populism, I assume I'm a populist" (*Florida Times Union,* October 31, 1971, B-2).

The governor delivered his message intensively to groups across the state during the final two months of the campaign. His message was carefully tailored to each group. When addressing a meeting of circuit court judges, Askew said the tax would enable judicial reform. To members of the Florida Public Health Association, he promised health expenditures. Addressing the homecoming banquet at Florida State University, he said the tax was needed to support higher education. To the Florida Fruit and Vegetable Association he offered the prospect of better agricultural research, law enforcement protection against pilfering in groves, and less pressure on property taxes for schools. On the same day that the Florida Bankers Association announced its open opposition, Askew gained headlines by telling the Dade County Bankers Association that they were among the state's most protected and least taxed businesses.

Askew was so closely involved with the campaign that the press regularly referred to the proposal as "Askew's tax." His campaign gained momentum as time passed. On October 12, the cabinet adopted a resolution endorsing the tax. Only the comptroller, who was also the banking commissioner, abstained. In the November ballot, seventy percent of those voting supported the proposal. Askew promptly called a special session of the legislature to pass enabling legislation, but the battle continued in spite of the electoral mandate. In the session, legislators debated day and night for ten days and numerous attempts were made to grant exemptions, especially for utilities. The legislature eventually passed a bill that was nearly identical to that proposed by Askew. In keeping with the governor's promises, sales taxes on household utilities and apartment rents were repealed. An Associated Press poll of editors ranked Askew's "personal battle" and victory as the top news story of the year (*Florida Times Union,* December 20, 1971).

ABOUT FACE: ADOPTION AND REPEAL OF THE UNITARY TAX

In 1983 the Florida legislature made a significant change to the state's tax structure by enacting the Unitary Tax Act. Prior to that time, Florida's corporate income tax was levied against income earned only within the State of Florida. Rather than a new tax on corporate income, the unitary tax represented an alternative method of calculating corporate income subject to state taxation.

Simply stated, the unitary tax allows a jurisdiction to levy taxes on a proportion of all of a business' income regardless of where it is earned. The purpose of the tax is to prevent multinational (or multistate) companies from escaping taxation by allocating income to other jurisdictions where tax rates are lower. The worldwide unitary tax method adopted by Florida required corporations to report on all of their operations wherever located, while the domestic unitary method (also called the "water's edge" method) would have only covered operations in the United States.

The impetus for passage of Florida's unitary tax came from two separate events. First, Governor Bob Graham had identified improvements in the state's educational system as the number one priority in his 1983–85 biennial budget recommendations. As an important financing source for these improvements, Governor Graham proposed a one percent increase in the corporate income tax rate, a measure supported by the state's business community in exchange for a complete revamping of the personnel process in public education. The merit pay plan subsequently offered by Governor Graham, however, fell short of their demands and they withdrew support for the tax increase. As a result, the House and Senate could not agree on funding measures during the regular 1983 legislative session and adjourned in June, deadlocked over the issue of education funding. Second, in late June 1983, the U.S. Supreme Court upheld California's "unitary business" concept in the case of *Container Corporation of America v. Franchise Tax Board* (77 L. Ed. 2d 54 (1983)).

Seizing this opportunity, the governor and legislative leaders called a special legislative session in early July 1983 to consider unitary taxation as a way out of the educational funding deadlock. The governor and legislative leaders drafted proposed changes to the tax code on the weekend prior to the convening of the special session on July 12th. Key provisions of the draft included the definition of a unitary business group and the formula used to apportion business income among the jurisdictions where the unitary business groups were located.

A business was defined as unitary if it met either one of two tests: the "three unities" test, requiring unity of ownership, operation, and use; or the contribution/dependency test as to whether members of a group were integrated with, dependent upon, or contributed to each other in the operations of the business group as a whole (Zuckerman and Hochman 1984). The apportionment formula consisted of the ratio of sales, property, and payroll within Florida to total sales, property, and payroll located everywhere. The sales ratio was weighted at fifty percent, and the property and payroll ratios were weighted at twenty-five percent each.[1] Several other changes pertinent to corporate taxation were

371

also included in the Unitary Tax Act: non-business income used in a corporation's trade or business was considered business income and thereby subject to Florida tax; the foreign-source income exclusion was repealed, thus subjecting worldwide income to Florida tax; and a throwback rule was enacted requiring that sales made by a Florida taxpayer not taxed or counted as income in the state to which the property was shipped were considered a Florida sale for tax purposes. According to Governor Graham, these measures were expected to raise $95 million in revenues during the first year and to affect about 18,000 of the state's 180,000 businesses.

The breathtaking speed of passage of the tax laid the groundwork for subsequent criticism and ultimate repeal of the unitary tax. The House and Senate passed the measure on July 12th, the first day of the special session, with the required three hearings in each house compressed into less than twenty-four hours. Despite the remarkable speed with which the tax bill was handled, numerous corporate representatives appeared to testify against the bill. The list of corporate lobbyists testifying before the Senate Finance and Taxation Committee, for example, reads like a Fortune 500 sampler. Among those represented were Coca-Cola, Proctor and Gamble, IBM, Motorola, Anheuser-Busch, Texaco, and Shell Oil. The legislature passed the tax bill, and within twelve hours of its passage enacted a $210 million education spending bill.

Reaction to the unitary tax law was swift and intense. Associated Industries, a powerful business lobbying group, immediately began to lobby legislators to revise or repeal the tax law. A group of twenty-nine multinational corporations (including Alcoa, Gulf Oil, Honeywell, IBM, Motorola, Sony, Texaco, Westinghouse, Xerox, Colgate, Bristol-Meyers, and Sears) hired former Florida Chief Justice Arthur England, a primary author of the corporate income tax, to represent them in their fight against the unitary tax. According to a Palm Beach newspaper, England said "The business climate in Florida has changed from the most hospitable, fair, and accommodating in the United States to the most hostile, unfair, and greedy" (*The Post,* September 25, 1983). The London (England) Chamber of Commerce dropped plans to visit Florida on an investment scouting trip, and a member of the British Parliament demanded retaliatory action against any state applying such a tax to British multinational subsidiaries. The deputy consul general for the West German government said he "deplored the production of the unitary tax system in Florida" (*Miami Herald,* October 19, 1983) and the Sony Corporation threatened to relocate a recently acquired Florida company to South Carolina. The Florida Economic Development Advisory Council voted unanimously to recommend the immediate repeal of the unitary tax and further urged Governor Graham to appoint a long-range tax planning commission.

The business community was not alone in its opposition. In a poll sponsored by three newspapers in October 1983, a majority of legislators reported that they favored repeal of the unitary tax, saying that they had not been informed of and did not understand the full impact of the law they had passed barely three months earlier. Two cabinet members, Comptroller Gerald Lewis and Secretary of State George Firestone, publicly urged changes in the tax law. While Governor Graham was in Japan seeking foreign investment, Lieutenant Governor Wayne Mixson, who also served as the Secretary of the Department of Commerce, publicly called for repeal of the unitary tax because it was discouraging businesses from locating or expanding operations in Florida. Although Mixson recanted his call for repeal after Governor Graham returned to Florida, much damage had been done.

In spite of the growing pressure for repeal or revision, some political leaders stood firm. Senate President Harry Johnston and House Speaker Lee Moffitt reaffirmed their opposition to a special legislative session to deal with the unitary tax. Governor Graham had his budget director outline the reasons why Florida's business climate was better than ever before, and in late 1983 Graham created the Governor's Unitary Tax Study Commission in response to the mounting uproar from politicians and big business interests. In February 1984 the commission unanimously approved draft legislation to repeal the unitary tax; Governor Graham indicated that he was looking for recommendations but was not wedded to them.

Prior to and during the regular legislative session in the spring of 1984, Governor Graham made it clear that he would veto repeal of the unitary tax unless revenues were fully replaced. Both the House and the Senate seemed willing to amend the unitary tax or to repeal it and replace it with other tax revenues. Last minute indecision, however, stymied repeal and replacement, so the legislative session ended before an acceptable bill could be framed.

Adding to the furor over the tax was an announcement by U.S. Treasury Secretary Donald Regan in August 1984 giving states with worldwide unitary tax systems (a total of ten) a deadline of July 31, 1985, to drop the unitary tax or he would recommend that the administration propose federal legislation to eliminate it. Regan, speaking as the chair of a twenty-member working group concluding a ten-month study of the unitary tax, indicated that he would support the "water's edge" method of unitary taxation, but that the worldwide unitary tax interfered with the ability of the United States to speak "with one voice in dealing with its foreign-trading partners" (*Miami Herald,* August 1, 1984). Governor Graham responded that unitary taxation should be state policy rather than a federal preemptive action, and that he did not expect the announcement to have any effect on the Florida legislature.

Nevertheless, in September 1984 legislative leaders called for a special session to deal with the unitary tax. Governor Graham continued to declare that repealing the unitary tax was possible only if revenues were replaced by other business taxes. The legislature repealed the unitary tax in a December 1984 special session and replaced it with an increase in the corporate income tax from five percent to five and one-half percent, thus shifting the increased tax burden away from the multinational corporations to all Florida corporations. Early estimates indicated that these changes would cost the state $9.9 million over the two subsequent budget years.

ABOUT FACE AGAIN: ADOPTION AND REPEAL OF THE SALES TAX ON SERVICES

Florida has had a general sales tax since 1949, when it was three cents. It was not until 1968 that the tax was increased to four cents. In 1982 the tax was again increased to five cents, but growth pressures mounted and lawmakers soon had to search for a way to raise more funds. Legislative leaders were reluctant to increase the sales tax rate still further, but the constitutional prohibitions against state levies of real property taxes or personal income taxes limited policy choices to an expansion of taxes on consumption.

In the early 1980s concern mounted across the nation about inadequate public infrastructure and the influential Council of 100 recommended in March 1986 that the state eliminate many of the exemptions in the sales tax to provide infrastructure. In 1985 the legislature adopted the State Comprehensive Plan (*Florida Statutes,* Ch. 187). Adoption of the plan required the appointment of a "blue ribbon" group called the State Comprehensive Plan Committee to estimate the cost of accomplishing the plan and the means for financing. Known as the Zwick Commission after its chairman Charles Zwick, a leading banker and former federal budget director, this group also gave a strong endorsement to taxing services.

Thanks to research that had been conducted by staff members, the state's leaders were aware that the economy was undergoing a long-term shift away from the purchase of manufactured goods and toward the purchase of services. The existing narrow-base sales tax, which excludes the sale of most services, taps a relatively declining portion of purchases. Some lawmakers were also concerned about the regressivity of the sales tax, and staff analysis showed that services tend to be purchased more by people as their income increases. Broadening the sales tax base to include most services, therefore, would enable the tax base to keep more abreast of economic growth and lessen regressivity.

Legislative leaders were concerned about the intensity of lobbying efforts that would emerge if they sought to eliminate exemptions to the sales tax on a case-by-case basis. The result of a piecemeal strategy would be unfair; services with strong lobbies would remain exempt while those with less influence would become taxed. Proponents of a services tax, most notable of whom was Senate President Harry Johnston, decided to adopt an inclusive strategy. On June 6, 1986, the legislature passed a bill repealing more than one hundred exemptions to the sales tax, including those for virtually all service transactions in Florida. It was called a "sunset" bill because all repeals were to take effect on July 1, 1987, unless specific legislation was enacted to reinstate an exemption. A Sales Tax Exemption Study Commission, with membership from both business and government, was appointed to make final recommendations regarding exemptions and implementing legislation to the 1987 legislative session.

There was surprisingly little political resistance to the bill. The sunset provision seemed to be a procedural master stroke. It enabled each legislator to resist pressure from any one special interest. "After all," staff economist James Francis (1988, 130) observed, "how could he make their case for exclusion to his peers when they too were accountable to certain groups whose exempt status was subject to sunset?" Under normal procedure, if a special interest group wishes to block legislation, it needs only persuade a committee of the House or Senate, or the governor, any of whom can block new bills. The sunset procedure, however, removed nearly all exemptions and reinstating any would require the support of the House, Senate, *and* governor.

Extensive research was conducted between the 1986 and 1987 sessions and the enabling legislation was enacted early in the 1987 session. The final law taxed less than half of the potential service tax base (Francis 1988), but its scope was broader than in any other state. A shortcoming of the inclusive sunsetting strategy was that it created public confusion. Critical to understanding the debacle that followed is that the state itself does not collect sales taxes from consumers; sellers of goods (and services, if taxed) collect the tax and convey it to the state.

It was estimated that the Department of Revenue would have to begin collecting the services tax from 120,000 to 140,000 businesses and individuals who sold services but who did not sell goods (Ross and Valente 1987). These persons were ignorant of collection procedures. Widespread confusion existed about what constituted a taxable service. The tax involved some highly technical matters such as "pyramiding" (which occurs when various transactions among businesses are taxed before final retail sale which is also taxed) and the status of transactions involving interstate activities.[2] Many small service providers mistakenly thought the tax was a tax on their income. Few knew that they could keep a small portion of the taxes as compensation for their time and effort. The Department of Revenue and some senior legislative staff members advised a delay in the effective date of the tax, but legislators were anxious to appropriate the new revenues and refused to delay the July 1, 1987, starting date. The Department of Revenue was not well prepared to explain the new tax. Written instructions were complex, and simple brochures, tailored to each major category of service provider, were needed but not written.

Probably the greatest contributing factor leading to the subsequent repeal of the services tax was the vacillation of the governor. The actions of Bob Martinez were never easy to predict. After rising to prominence as a labor leader, one of his first actions as mayor of Tampa was to break a garbage workers strike; a prominent Democrat in a city that is staunchly Democratic, he switched to the Republican party to run for governor. His gubernatorial campaign consistently conveyed an anti-tax message, but he did leave open the possibility of taxes on services. He played no role in the enactment of the 1986 sunset legislation, but after his election, Governor Martinez was confronted with a fiscal dilemma created by an inadequate tax base and he decided to support the services tax as the best remedy.

His support was announced in February, 1987, and his proposed budget called for ending exemptions except those on medical services, day care, interest on banking accounts, and certain agricultural products. Martinez also called for cutting the sales tax rate from five to 4.5 percent. In April the Sales Tax Exemption Study Commission issued its recommendations and the full legislature approved a service tax package that was expected to generate $761 million the first year and more than $1.2 billion in the second. The sales tax rate stayed at five percent. Approval was by a wide margin, 28-12 in the Senate and 84-35 in the House.

Opposition to the new tax quickly emerged at a national level as well as within the state. National advertisers and media companies feared that if Florida sustained its innovative, broad-based tax on services, other states would follow. Threats were issued that conventions would be cancelled. NBC television, for example, announced withdrawal of its 1988 affiliates' convention in Orlando. The Florida Association of Broadcasters began an advertising campaign in opposition to the new tax, and a coalition of advertisers and other groups formed an organization called Sales Taxes Oppressing People (STOP) to conduct a petition drive to amend the constitution to prohibit the new taxes. The Florida Bar sued the state on the grounds that the law unconstitutionally interfered with the right to legal counsel. A subsequent advisory opinion from the Florida Supreme Court indicated that most of the new tax was constitutional.

There is an adage in politics—never argue with people who buy ink by the barrel or video tape by the mile. Inclusion of advertising services turned media companies, many of whom had editorialized on the need to reform Florida's tax base, into self-serving propagandists. There were indications, however, that advertisers' opposition might fade. On July 29, Johnson and Johnson, one of the nation's largest advertisers, ended its boycott on advertising in Florida. Florida's markets were too large for advertisers to boycott for long. At first the governor stood firm, announcing on July 23 that he would veto any legislation that tried to repeal the services tax.

The mass advertising campaign took advantage of the public's widespread confusion about the new tax. Polls showed extensive disapproval of both the tax and the governor. Governor Martinez proposed a March, 1988 referendum to let the people decide the fate of the services tax, and he called a special session in September, 1987 to authorize it. In the midst of the session, Standard and Poor's bond rating company announced that it was putting Florida on a "credit watch" due to growing uncertainty about the willingness of state leaders to maintain adequate revenues. Prior to the first of a series of special sessions which began on September 21, Martinez called for repeal of the services tax. On October 8, the legislature passed a compromise bill that simplified the services tax and that called for a referendum to ask the voters whether they preferred the services tax or an increase in the narrow-base sales tax. Martinez vetoed the bill.

In a second special session in October, the legislature remained deadlocked and adjourned with the services tax still in effect. House Speaker John Mills and Senate President John Vogt, both supporters of services taxation, conducted a thirteen-city campaign to save the tax, but met with orchestrated opposition. In a third special session that convened on December 8, the legislature voted to repeal the services tax and to replace it with a one cent increase in the narrow-base sales tax. The governor signed the bill.

FACTORS ASSOCIATED WITH SUCCESS AND FAILURE TO REFORM TAX POLICY

The most striking fact about tax reform in Florida is that failure is common. Successful reform, on the other hand, is very hard to achieve. This section draws upon what we have learned from reviewing four reform attempts in Florida to assess the prospects for future tax reform.

Several factors have been found to be important in successful reforms in Florida and elsewhere. These include: *sustained leadership* in making the case for tax reform, the presence of a *fiscal crisis,* a promise to *distribute the benefits* across many interest groups and geographic areas, *coupling a new tax with an offset* on an existing tax, and *gaining the support of the news media* (Lemov 1990; Koenig 1987). In Florida, *the public's perception of a tax reform is a crucial factor.* It is not enough that leaders understand a fiscal problem and enact legislation that provides a fairer and more adequate tax structure. The unitary and service tax cases have shown that a reform cannot be sustained unless the public also understands the fiscal problem and supports the tax.

During the past half century in Florida, taxes on consumption have been the easiest to justify. Consumption taxes and the relatively minor severance taxes are attractive, in part, because they permit exporting some of the tax burden to tourists and users of exported products. Taxes on drinking and smoking have been justified on the basis that they discourage bad behaviors, while the gasoline tax is justified as a fee for the use of roads. Floridians continue to believe that their consumption taxes are fair, but among these only the general sales tax and gasoline tax can generate sizeable revenues relative to the needs of the state. As rates on these narrowly based consumption taxes rise, it seems likely that the public will increasingly question the fairness of Florida's taxes.

Across the nation, a variety of new consumption taxes have been suggested for states to fill gaps between revenues and spending. These include a value added tax and a tax on the consumption of each BTU of energy (Rivlin 1990). For Florida, the personal income tax has been advocated (Koenig 1987; Khan and Escobar 1988). It seems more likely, however, that we will continue to search for answers in the realm of consumption taxation.

A SERVICES TAX FOR FLORIDA?

Floridians still prefer the sales tax to a personal income tax. According to the 1989 Florida Annual Policy Survey, thirty-seven percent of the public believe increasing the sales tax is the best way to raise more revenues and thirty-two percent believe extending the sales tax to services is best, while only nineteen percent believe the personal income tax is best (Parker 1990). Associated Industries, one of the opponents of the sales tax on services in 1987, three years later reversed its position and proposed to the Tax and Budget Reform Commission that a modified version of the sales tax on services be enacted.

It appears, then, that expansion of the sales tax base into the realm of services is likely. Given the climate that led to the repeal of the services tax only a few years ago, how is it possible to achieve successful reform of the sales tax?

First, the public must clearly understand the need for more state revenues. This need was not clearly and forcefully communicated to the public in the cases of the two taxes enacted and later repealed in the 1980s. It was communicated in the cases of the two successful reforms—the original sales tax enactment and the corporate income tax. Governors Warren and Askew persistently and dramatically conveyed a message of need for additional revenues. For tax reform to be successful *in Florida, any new tax must be justified in terms of fairness* in distributing the burden (Herbers 1990). It should also be *linked to a clear articulation of the need* for the public services that will be provided.

Need can be justified on two grounds. First, the state is moving toward a fiscal crisis. Florida's tax base is built upon the taxation of durable goods, but the economy is growing more in the area of services. Increasing tax rates on a tax base that is a shrinking portion of the total state economy, as is Florida's habit, is the fiscal equivalent of treading water in an ever-widening ocean. Recessions have underscored the inadequacies of our tax base. Today, the state has no rainy day fund of any size to fall back upon. The federal government, rather than helping the state, compounded the problem with enactment of the 1990 Revenue Reconciliation Act. This act mandated more state spending for Medicaid, Medicare, and Social Security payroll taxes and weakened the state's potential revenue base by raising the federal government's own taxes on gasoline, alcohol, and tobacco products. It is estimated that this legislation alone will cost Florida $250.4 million during 1991-95 (Perlman 1990).

A second argument for justifying need is that rapid growth requires increased spending and investment in such things as education and infrastructure to avert worse situations in the future. We do not live in isolation. The state must spend to protect our quality of life and to make us competitive in a world economy. State government is seen as the institution that must meet our infrastructure needs in the form of good schools, transportation, and a clean and pleasant environment. This theme is one of growing importance (Sunrise Report 1987; Zwick 1989). It will gain

more momentum as the European Community becomes a single unified market and as American firms face intensified competition from both Europe and the Pacific rim (Roberts 1990; Lemov 1991).

LEADERSHIP: AN ESSENTIAL BUT OFTEN MISSING INGREDIENT

Leadership that informs the public of the need for state tax reform in the 1990s must come from three sources working together: the governor, the legislature, and the business community. Given the opposition from business that resulted in the repeal of both the unitary tax and the extension of the sales tax to services, it is unlikely that elected officials will expose their political necks again without a commitment from prominent business interests. As then Senate President John Vogt was quoted as saying after the repeal of the services tax, "Any movement . . . would have to be generated by the business community" (Koenig 1987, 66).

The single *most important factor* in the four cases studied here has been *the role of the governor.* The governor can take the lead for a specific tax reform as Askew did on the corporate income tax, or he can articulate the need and let the legislature choose the tax reform as Warren did on the sales tax, but he cannot vacillate as Martinez did on the services tax issue. The corporate income tax would not have been enacted if Askew had not persistently advocated its cause and taken the issue directly to the people. The original sales tax was not what Warren preferred, but his dramatic efforts to publicize the plight of the state and the pressures he placed upon the legislature were essential to its passage. Moreover, his insistence that it not be too regressive—exempting food and medicines—remains a hallmark of the sales tax today.

Some political observers believe that the opposition to the services tax had peaked and was beginning to ebb when Governor Martinez abandoned the tax. Whether this observation is correct or not, the fate of the services tax was sealed when the governor abandoned it. For Governor Graham, the unitary tax was a convenient target of opportunity for new revenues rather than something in which he steadfastly believed. When he removed his opposition to its repeal, its fate, too, was sealed.

There should also be *a gestation period* during which the public is informed and comes to understand the need and the fairness of the distribution of the tax burden. This gestation period should precede, not follow, legislation. When state leaders propose a tax policy that is nationally innovative, they should anticipate that interests outside Florida who stand to bear the burden of the tax, should it spread to other states, will invest heavily in defeating the tax reform in Florida. Such was the state's experience with opposition from multinational corporations to the unitary tax and with opposition from national media companies who conducted a mass advertising campaign against extending the sales tax to include services.

Leaders who build support for tax reform must be clear in the message delivered to the public in order to overcome opposition from special interests. Moreover, when reform proponents *successfully convey a populist message,* the chances of success are enhanced, but when the opposition can effectively appeal to populist instincts, reforms are more likely to fail in Florida. The sales tax on services, for example, was actually a less regressive tax than the tax that replaced it—an increase in the sales tax rate on the previous tax base. Yet the campaign that the advertising media waged against the tax on services succeeded in convincing the public that what was in the interest of the advertising media, the more regressive tax, was actually in the public's interest. In the corporate income tax case, on the other hand, Askew successfully conveyed the populist message that low and middle income people would be the gainers. The leadership could have framed and communicated a similarly strong argument for the services tax in 1987 but did not.

Another factor that has facilitated past reforms has been to *couple a new tax with an offset or repeal of an existing tax.* New Jersey voters, for example, approved a personal income tax in 1976 when that tax was coupled with a partial offset in property taxes (Koening 1987). In 1991, Canadians replaced a 13.5 percent manufacturers sales tax with a much broader seven percent goods and services tax. Askew promised Floridians that he would work to repeal the corporate stock tax and the sales tax on household utilities in order to build support for the corporate income tax. Martinez tried to couple the sales tax on services with a half percent reduction in the sales tax rate, but the legislature did not reduce the tax rate. Such offsets may be important in convincing the public that the tax reform will increase the fairness of the tax system.

It is our expectation that any future individual income tax in Florida is likely to be the result of a tradeoff, one with populist overtones, that is effectively advocated by a persistent governor and other leaders. The income tax proposal made by former Governor LeRoy Collins when he headed the Senate Appropriations Committee in 1949 included both a tradeoff and a populist dimension. His proposal called for a major reduction in a regressive retail sales tax in favor of an income tax from which persons of low and middle incomes would be exempt.

CHAPTER

14

ISSUES MANAGEMENT NEEDED

Leadership for tax reform in the 1980s was opportunistic and ultimately reactive, rather than anticipatory. Twice, Florida enacted innovative legislation that was subsequently repealed due to an unanticipated backlash. Leaders who propose future tax reforms should follow the lead of corporate strategists and others who engage in issues management (Renfro 1982).

Issues management requires thinking about the future of an issue, particularly the political and perceptual dimensions of it, as early as possible. Its practice requires leaders to anticipate how the public might perceive an issue and take steps to see that the issue is framed in a way that will influence the public's perceptions of it. Such thinking was notably absent in the service tax case, where legislative leaders equated success with the passage of a piece of legislation, but gave little thought to its future implementation. If successful implementation of a tax requires the cooperation and understanding of tens of thousands of Floridians, as does a tax on services, it is only prudent to try to anticipate the public's perceptions and inform them as well as is possible before they are subjected to the disinformation of special interests.

Issues management to gain public support for tax reform was proposed by the Speaker's Advisory Committee on the Future in 1987 (Sunrise Report 1987). In a sense, Reubin Askew practiced a form of issues management in his persistent advocacy of the corporate income tax. He anticipated that there would be opposition and carefully devised a strategy to deal with it. He tailored his addresses to each audience, describing how their interests would be better served by enactment of the tax. Such tailoring of messages and conveying of information to the public was mostly absent in the unitary and service tax incidents.

Issues management is essentially a way of harnessing political common sense. As we approach the end of this century, Florida is badly in need of fundamental tax reform, but the necessary leadership has not yet emerged. There are no panaceas for Florida's financial dilemma. If tax reform is to occur, political common sense must be accompanied by both political courage and persistence. These have been the ingredients of successful reforms in the past and they will be needed in the future.

REFERENCES

(Note: Numerous news articles appearing in several of the state's newspapers, including especially the *Florida Times Union, Saint Petersburg Times,* and *Miami Herald* were used in assembling the case studies in this chapter.)

Florida Council of 100 (1985). *Financing Florida's Future Growth.* Tallahassee: the Council.

Francis, James (1988). "The Florida Sales Tax on Services: What Really Went Wrong?" In *Unfinished Agenda for State Tax Reform,* edited by Steven D. Gold. Denver: National Conference of State Legislatures.

Herbers, John (1990). "Read My Lips: The Tax Revolt Hasn't Had All That Much Impact." *Governing* 3 (April): 11.

Kahn, M. Aman and B. J. Escobar (1988). "Florida's Need for New Sources of Revenue: State Income Tax May Be the Only Choice." *Florida Environmental and Urban Issues* 15 (July): 18–25.

Koenig, John (1987). "Putting Off the Inevitable: Florida Faces a Catastrophic Revenue Shortfall If It Doesn't Find New Sources of Funding." *Florida Trend* 30 (October): 61–66.

Lemov, Penelope (1990). "How to Win (or Lose) a Bond Referendum," *Governing* 3 (February): 34–40.

———. (1991). "Europe and the States: Free Trade, but No Free Lunch." *Governing* 4 (January): 49–52.

Parker, Suzanne L. (1990). "Florida: Out of the 80s and Into the 90s." *Governing Florida* 1 (Winter): 12–24.

Perlman, Ellen (1990). "Budget Fisticuffs KO States." *City & State* 7 (November 5–18): 1, 37.

Renfro, William L. (1982). "Managing the Issues of the 1980s." *The Futurist* 16 (August): 61–66.

Rivlin, Alice (1990). "Wanted: A New State-Level Tax to Prepare Us for the 21st Century." *Governing* 3 (April): 74.

Roberts, Brandon (1990). "EC 1992: Opportunities and Challenges for State and Local Governments." *Government Finance Review* 6 (December): 11–14.

Ross, Jim and Michie Valente (1987). "Frustration Reigns in Tax Reversal." *Tampa Tribune* (December 11): 1.

Special Committee (1935). *Report of the Special Committee on Taxation and Public Debt in Florida.* Tallahassee: the Special Committee, May 20. With preface and endorsement by Governor Dave Sholtz.

State Comprehensive Plan Committee (SCPC) (1987). *Keys to Florida's Future: Winning in a Competitive World.* Final Report of the Committee. Tallahassee: SCPC, February.

The Sunrise Report (1987). Tallahassee: The Speaker's Advisory Committee on the Future, Florida House of Representatives.

Zingale, James A. and Thomas R. Davies (1986). "Why Florida's Revenues Go Boom or Bust, and Why We Can't Afford It Anymore." *Florida State University Law Review* 14 (Fall): 433–61.

CHAPTER

14

Zuckerman, I. L. and E. F. Hochman (1984). "The Unitary Tax: Florida Style." *Tax Executive* 36 (April): 211–21.

Zwick, Charles J. (1989). "Growth Financing in the New Global Environment: Lessons from the Florida Experience." *Environmental and Urban Issues* (Summer): 13–17.

ENDNOTES

1. See Zuckerman and Hochman, 1984, for an excellent, detailed discussion.

2. For an excellent discussion of these matters see Francis, 1988.

FLORIDA PRIVATIZATION IN THE MID-1990S
A FOCUS ON CONTRACTING

WILLIAM B. TANKERSLEY AND RICHARD CHACKERIAN

The trend in the United States toward utilization of the private sector for the delivery of government services attained a large measure of popular support in the early 1980s and continues today as a serious policy alternative at all levels of government. In this respect, Florida is no exception. Both the 1995 and the 1996 sessions of the Florida Legislature saw several proposals introduced that would privatize programs and services previously delivered by Florida state agencies.

From the prevalence and qualitative significance of the 1995 proposals emerged the general presumption that 1996 would see continued, and perhaps expanded, interest in exploring private sector delivery of public services by legislative decision makers. So prevalent was this view that the Florida House of Representatives Committee on Governmental Operations undertook a descriptive study of privatization for the purpose of providing guidelines for the analysis of privatization proposals (Committee on Governmental Operations 1995).

A generic, and very useful, definition of privatization emerged from this study. After an extensive review of extant literature on the subject, the Committee determined that, "Authors have used the terms 'privatization,' 'alternative service delivery,' and 'entrepreneurial government' interchangeably (9)." Noting that the literature defines privatization in a variety of ways, the Committee concluded that a standard definition is needed to facilitate the discussion of these concepts; consequently it adopted the following from Chi (1988):

> Privatization means the use of the private sector in government management and delivery of public services (10).

This working definition was felt to be broad enough to include most of the privatization concepts and modes found in the literature, and in this conclusion, we concur. Thus, we borrow the definition to facilitate the present discussion of privatization, alternative service delivery and entrepreneurial government. The focus here, however, is on contracting out as one of the most important alternative modes of public service delivery.

It is important to note the significant differences between these alternatives and traditional governmental delivery. Rather than utilizing government employees and agency resources *directly,* non-public agents are utilized including for-profit as well as not-for-profit entities. And, in these relationships, contracting is only one of a number of important modes utilized to control results. Major alternatives include:[1]

1. franchise agreements,
2. grants and subsidies,
3. vouchers,
4. sale of publicly owned assets,
5. deregulation and tax incentives,
6. volunteers, and
7. user fees and demarketing.

In the following sections each of these methods will be discussed briefly. This will be followed by a detailed discussion of contracting, the policy environment out of which this practice has developed, the contexts within which it is likely to be most effective, and finally, the extent of its implementation in Florida.

FRANCHISE AGREEMENTS

Franchising as a form of privatization is the award to a private entity of the governmentally granted right to provide a service within a specified geographical area. After the award of a franchise, the government role generally is restricted to regulation, with citizens dealing directly with the franchisee and paying it for services received.

The use of a franchise for service delivery is based on the assumption that private entities operate more efficiently than government. The savings from franchise operations must outweigh required government oversight and monitoring costs. In some instances, franchise fees are charged to cover these expenses. Typical franchised services are electric power, gas and water utilities, cable television, taxi and bus services, concessions at government owned parks and book stores and cafeterias at public universities.

Among the regulations imposed by the government are price controls and service standards, including in some cases, the requirement that the franchisee offer service to all potential customers whether or not it is economically justifiable.

The franchise may be exclusive or nonexclusive, a decision that probably should be made on the basis of significant economies of scale. The franchisee with a nonexclusive franchise may be faced with competition from other private (or public) entities. Nonexclusive franchises provide the benefits thought to accompany competitive markets. Exclusive franchises, that is where other providers are not allowed, tend to offer free market benefits only if they are renewed frequently and competitively.

GRANTS AND SUBSIDIES

Government grants and subsidies may sustain a program without assuming the entire responsibility for the service. Grants and subsidies are particularly appropriate where there are high costs incurred in starting a program or where it is important to reduce user fees because some citizens cannot afford the service. The first case may call for a one-time start-up grant; the second may be addressed by annual subsidies to help meet recurring costs. The subsidy may be in the form of money, but it may also be in the form of equipment loans, office space, or other in-kind contributions. Government grants and subsidies are used extensively in health care provision, research and development projects, low-cost housing, and cultural and art projects, among many others. Grants and subsidies also are useful in supporting services which are unique or poorly understood with respect to how service requirement can be met. Accountability for these ill defined services is established by earmarking funds for specific projects, requiring periodic reports and independent audits, and relying upon trustworthy relationships and professional standards of the grantee.

VOUCHERS

Grants and subsidies are made directly to service producers. Vouchers, on the other hand, are government subsidies made directly to service consumers. Voucher systems have been used by public agencies primarily in health care, food distribution, and higher education. The government provides citizens coupons that can be used as currency to purchase only specified goods or services. The coupons are collected by the supplier and later redeemed for cash from the government.

Vouchers enable participating consumers to obtain specified goods or services from a relatively wide selection of suppliers. Within the constraints imposed upon the use of the voucher, the system assumes voucher holders are informed and capable of making rational marketplace choices. If there is a large number of suppliers active in the market, voucher holders will reap the benefits of market competition. It is also assumed that suppliers who provide poor quality goods or services will be spurned. Rational behavior on the part of both suppliers and consumers is thought to produce efficient and responsive service delivery.

SALE OF PUBLICLY OWNED ASSETS

Outside the United States, a significant method of privatization involves the transfer of title, primarily through a sale, of state-owned enterprises (SOEs) to individuals, corporations, or other forms of private ownership. In recent years some 7,000 SOEs have been privatized through sales bringing in upwards of $250 billion in revenues to governments around the world. Interest in this privatization alternative has been more prevalent in other countries because of the relatively larger concentration of SOEs overseas. Examples from the United States include the transfer of the National Consumer Cooperative Bank to the private sector in 1982, the sale of Conrail in 1987, and the on-going sale of obsolete military bases and equipment. There continues to be debate at the national level about the sale of the Amtrak railway system, the Tennessee Valley Authority, the Postal Service, the National Weather Service and mapping activities of the U. S. Geological Survey. President George Bush issued an Executive Order in 1992 "encouraging state and local governments to sell their assets—in an effort to balance their budgets and increase efficiency" (Henry 1995, 323). It is not unusual for state governments to sell surplus furniture and equipment. Medical facilities and nursing homes are among the types of enterprises that have been transferred to private interests by local governments.

DEREGULATION AND TAX INCENTIVES

Government regulation or deregulation of the private and nonprofit sectors and tax policy can provide incentives to meet community needs. The possibilities range from complete deregulation and elimination of taxation relying solely on free market dynamics to imposing high levels of governmental taxation and regulation. Deregulation remains of great interest to policy makers in the United States at all levels of government; and, there is much discussion of the value added tax and flat tax as alternative modes of taxation which may have fewer negative effects on incentives.

Examples of regulatory control at the state and local level include zoning of land, vocational and professional licensing requirements, adoptive parent eligibility requirements, and fire and safety codes. At the national level, trucking and airline transportation have seen significant relaxation of regulatory control in recent years. And, with respect to the process of regulation itself, Congress continues to focus attention on the need for benefit/cost analysis of regulatory changes. Clearly, caution and balanced judgments are imperative here. Deregulation may result in exposure to hazards or other undesirable conditions, but regulation may result in excessive costs and inconvenience. In some regulatory areas complete avoidance of hazards may be extremely costly to accomplish (Miller, Benjamin, and North 1996). The goal of regulation should be to enhance service delivery by reaching an optimal balance between under-protection and overprotection. This is an area calling for special care in policy design when privatization has been newly instituted. It is imperative that regulatory policy be carefully crafted to match new service delivery modes. For example, there has been the tendency for govern-ments to reduce control by contracting services with other entities, while at the same time greatly increasing rules and regulations over service provision. The net effect of these countervailing behaviors may be little change in either the effectiveness or efficiency of service delivery.

The concept of tax incentives is fairly straightforward: tax credits, exemptions, deferrals, and deductions encourage specified behaviors; tax penalties along with disallowance of exemptions, deferrals, and deductions act as disincentives. Unfortunately tax incentives tend to become complex very quickly, seemingly at an exponential rate. This is partly due to the complexity of the tax structure within which new incentives must operate and partly due to the fact that tax changes have important budgetary implications which reach far beyond the specific service delivery of concern. Tax incentives came under increased scrutiny because of federal deficit spending and the negative view of tax-ation. Nonetheless, tax incentives have been used effectively to encour-age private organizations and individuals to make capital investments, expand research and energy conservation efforts, employ new workers, and to provide health care, day care, and dial-a-ride programs.

VOLUNTEERS

Volunteerism is a prevalent form of privatization. Individuals, char-itable associations and other voluntary associations provide, for example, "recreation programs, street cleaning, protective patrol, and fire protec-tion" (Savas 1987, 90). Adopt-A-Mile highway programs and Neighborhood Watch Groups are commonplace. Many hours of service were volunteered during the 1996 Summer Olympics. Local school dis-tricts are also major beneficiaries. "A majority of states now have volun-teer offices to coordinate volunteer action programs. These programs provide a variety of services: tutors, interpreters, drivers, shopping assistants, adoption, state parks, and geological studies" (Committee on Governmental Operations 1995, 14). Surprisingly, volunteer fire departments constitute more than 90 percent of all fire departments in the United States (Savas 1987, 81).

USER FEES AND DEMARKETING

User fees can have at least two purposes: (1) to raise revenue and (2) to adjust the demand for services. Fees give an indication of the level of demand for the service rendered; and, if the fee approximates at least the cost of production, continued demand indicates that expansion of the service should be considered. Likewise, since users incur costs under this method of service delivery, they can be expected to adjust their demand for the service to match the value they set on the service. When user fees replace financing from general revenues, individuals tend to reduce usage. This affords government the opportunity to reduce costs by reducing service delivery.

In demarketing, the government simply attempts to lower the demand for a service. User fees may be combined with public education campaigns and other information programs to encourage citizens to reduce their demand. Demand adjustment can be particularly useful in public transportation, and electric and water utilities to reduce consumer demand during peak load periods. Finally, demarketing, even without user fees, can reduce government costs by encouraging carpooling, health maintenance, and reduction in careless and wasteful use of government provided services.

Each of these methods is widely used by the governments of Florida. At the local level, franchises, regulation, and contracting are widely used. The state government depends less heavily on franchises, but uses regulation, contracting, and tax incentives extensively. Contracting out is especially prevalent in transportation, health care, and social services. (Committee on Governmental Operations 1995)

THE POLICY ENVIRONMENT, PRIVATIZATION, AND CONTRACTING OUT

Government contracting has a long history in construction, maintenance and repair of roads, building construction, weapons manufacture, aircraft and shipbuilding, activities that typically require heavy capital investment. The practice is ubiquitous. As reported by Henry (1995), "It has been estimated that there are some three million indirect federal employees in the private sector working for the government under contracts with corporations and other organizations. The federal government lets, on the average about 17 million contracts a year to private enterprise" (322). Most of these contracts have been in the form of procurement contracts, that is, contracts for the purchase of goods and commodities rather than services.

Since the early 1980s however, contracting has received growing attention, particularly in widely expanded human service areas largely because it is seen as a way to reduce the growth in government spending on social services. Contracting now reaches far beyond the traditional areas of building and road construction or the acquisition of tangible goods and commodities. The privatization debate within the State of Florida emerges from the public demand that government costs be stabilized without compromising service quality. These demands originated in the stagflation of the 1970s and have been reinforced by supply side economics, supply side management, and austere fiscal conditions (Chackerian 1990). This was clearly evident in 1990 when the Chiles campaign for governor made it a centerpiece. The state budget adopted in early 1991 was the leanest since the early recession budgets of the 1970s; by the 1993 legislative session, cuts in real state government purchasing power continued. These forces continue in the late 1990s. In 1994, the Florida legislature adopted the following policy statement.

> It is the policy of this state that all state services be performed in the most effective and efficient manner in order to provide the best value to the citizens of the state. The state also recognizes that competition among service providers may improve the quality of services provided, and that competition, innovation, and creativity among service providers should be encouraged. (*Florida Statutes,* Ch. 14.203)

With this action, three Florida state agencies including 1) the State Council on Competitive Government, 2) the Commission on Government Accountability to the People and 3) the newly created Office of Program Policy Analysis and Government Accountability were to:

> . . . identify commercial activities currently being performed by state agencies and, if it is determined that such services may be better provided by requiring competition with private sources or other state agency service providers, they may recommend that a state agency engage in any process including competitive bidding, that creates competition with private sources or other state agency service providers. (*Florida Statutes,* Ch. 14.203)

Pressure to privatize state agency functions continued throughout 1995. *PRIVATIZATION* (Committee on Governmental Operations 1995) reports:

> In January 1995, the Chair of the Ways and Means Committee of the Florida Senate asked all Florida state agency heads to submit plans to reduce each agency's budget by 25%. He specified that the plans should cut costs by:
>
> - eliminating low priority programs;
> - increasing the efficiency of existing high-priority programs;
> - reducing the size and cost of government; and
> - eliminating duplication of effort between state government and the private sector.
>
> The Florida Board of Regents proposed extensive privatization in its response to this request. In September 1995, the Chair again asked agencies to submit a 25% budget-reduction plan. Agency efforts to meet these requests could lead to a renewed focus on privatization (57).

"Supply side management," the other force driving the interest in privatization, emerges rather directly from the assumptions supporting supply side economics (Chackerian 1990). The supply side manager has been described as:

1. more interested in line or operating activities than in staff functions;
2. more likely to view government service as a temporary tour of duty or as a stage in a career than as a lifetime profession;
3. more interested in "bottom line" tangible programmatic results than in process or system maintenance values; and
4. more executive centered than congressionally oriented or clientele focused (Carroll 1985).

"Demand side" managers, on the other hand, tend to be:

1. more interested in program design, policy analysis, and broad policy formulation and often attracted to staff rather than line function;
2. more concerned with process values and consensus building and risk aversion; and
3. comfortable with direct contacts with congressional staff and interest groups (Carroll 1985).

"The [Reagan] administration's supply-side management strategy [was] . . . particularly pronounced in intergovernmental relations. The primary objective [was] . . . to reduce the financial and programmatic

dependency of state and local governments on the federal government . . ."
(Carroll 1985, 805). This thrust was accompanied by a shift of regulatory authority to state and local government entities, by an emphasis on
block grants in place of categorical grants, and by attempts at systematic reduction in federal aid.[2] Although seeming to produce somewhat
of a "Catch-22" bind for state and local governments by saddling them
with more responsibility while removing financial support, the supply-
side management argument is that reduced federal regulations allow
more efficient, results-oriented state and local management which may
lead to private sector initiatives (Chackerian 1990). The fundamental
tenants of supply-side economics provided grounding for the
Republican Contract With America around which Republican candidates successfully rallied in the November 1994 Congressional elections. Bob Dole and Jack Kemp, the Republican nominees in the 1996
presidential campaign, appeared to be continuing this policy position.
Dole proposed a $548 billion tax cut package while indicating, "that he
could achieve a balanced budget by the congressional target of 2002
while at the same time providing tax relief" (*Pensacola News Journal,*
August 6, 1996, 2a). Kemp, of course, is well known as a champion of
supply side economics.

In summary, beginning with the stagflation of the 1970s, the impact
and continuing effect of the political and management orientation of the
Reagan administration, the 1994 Republican Contract With America and
the policy position expressed by the major Republican candidates in the
1996 campaign all have contributed to a continued interest in privatization. Likewise the political impact of national budget deficits have led, not
only Republican administrations, but the Clinton administration as well,
to lean toward the favorable treatment of privatization.

CONTRACTING AND PRIVATIZATION: CLARIFICATION OF THE DISTINCTION

Kolderie (1986) suggested that privatization in the United States
has simply become a new name for contracting. But, privatization, as
defined by the Florida Committee on Governmental Operations, is a
much broader concept. As noted above, the Committee adopted the following definition:

Privatization means the use of the private sector in government
management and delivery of public services (10).

To more clearly see the distinction between privatization and contracting using this definition, it is helpful to consider the roles that government may take. We begin by distinguishing *provision* of a service from *production* of a service:

> One distinct activity of government is to *provide* for its people. In other words: policy making, deciding, buying, requiring, regulating, franchising, financing, subsidizing.
> A . . . distinctly separate activity of government may be to *produce* the services it decides should be provided. In other words: operating, delivering, running, doing, selling, administering (Kolderie 1986, 286).

While production is a fairly straightforward term, provision needs amplification:

> A service is publicly or socially *provided* (a) where the decision whether to have it ... is a political decision, (b) when government arranges for the recipients not to have to pay directly for the service themselves, and (c) when the government selects the producer that will serve them.
> . . . service is privately *provided* (a) where individuals and nongovernmental organizations make their own decisions whether or not to have it, (b) where, if they choose to have it, they pay for it in full out of their own resources, . . . and (c) where they select the producer themselves (Kolderie 1986, 286).

Service provision relates to policy decisions about the service itself: Is the service needed? Will the market allocate resources to it effectively without government intervention? Will there be fair distribution among citizens, etc. On the other hand, service production implies the actual work involved in delivering the service. When policy makers consider privatizing, it is important that they distinguish options for the *provision* of the service from options for the *production* of that service.

The alternative to government provision and production is private sector provision and production. There are, however, intermediary cases: (1) government provision and private sector production, and (2) private sector provision and government production (Kolderie 1986, 286).

Some forms of contracting by governments may not involve privatization at all. Government agencies may enter into contracts for the delivery of services with other government agencies acting as the provider. Henry (1995) reports, "More than half—52 percent—of cities and counties have entered into intergovernmental service contracts. Cities and counties contract most frequently with each other for jails, sewage disposal, animal control and tax assessing" (391). *Florida Statutes,* Ch. 14.203 authorizing the State Council on Competitive Government recognizes this facet of contracting at the state level also:

> In performing its duties under this section, the [State Council on Competitive Government] may:(f) Require that an identified state service be submitted to competitive bidding or another process that creates competition with private sources *or other governmental entities. (Florida Statutes,* Ch. 14.203(3)(f)) [Italics added.]

It is not uncommon to find that reported "privatization" of a government service is an *intergovernmental* contract. Contracting in this respect at least, is a concept somewhat broader in meaning than privatization, just as privatization can have meaning beyond contracting out. Yet, under the proper circumstances, contracting between public sector organizations, just as with private sector organizations, offers competitive benefits often attributed to market competition. A question remaining is, how prevalent is contracting out as a distinct form of service delivery?

THE TRANSFORMATION OF SERVICE DELIVERY IN THE NATION AND IN FLORIDA

IN THE NATION

More than one hundred services have been reported across the nation as being provided by private organizations under contract to municipalities (Savas 1990). The variety of these services is wide, ranging from child care to weed control. Included, among others, are adoption services, animal control, day care, family counseling, juvenile delinquency programs, management consulting, mosquito control, public relations, planning, and training of municipal employees. The possibilities seem endless, particularly as general governmental programs are disaggregated into functional specialties which are more amenable to contractual service delivery. Contracts for specialized support services include data processing, keypunching, microfilming, parking meter collections, and payroll processing.

The International City/County Management Association (ICMA) conducted a series of surveys to determine both the extent and the trend in privatization by municipalities and counties in the United States. The first survey occurred in 1982 and the most recent in 1992. Table 15-1 reports selected statistics for health and human services. The table indicates the extent of activity with both for profit and nonprofit organizations. Clearly, contracting has become an important delivery alternative across many programmatic areas.

Table 15-1

USE OF PRIVATE AND NONPROFIT CONTRACTING BY LOCAL GOVERNMENT FOR SELECTED HEALTH AND HUMAN SERVICES DELIVERY

| | Percent of City and County Responses | | | |
| | For Profit | | Nonprofit | |
Service Contracted For	1982	1992	1982	1992
Animal shelter operation	13	11	17	23
Daycare facility operation	33	54	34	35
Child welfare programs	5	4	22	13
Programs for the elderly	4	6	28	24
Operation/management of hospitals	0	31	0	30
Public health programs	7	5	25	8
Drug/alcohol treatment programs	6	20	38	34
Mental health/retardation programs/ facilities	6	15	38	29
Operation of homeless shelters	0	5	0	54

Adapted from Miranda and Andersen, 1994.

IN FLORIDA CITIES AND COUNTIES

Political subdivisions within Florida also are transforming how services are delivered through contracting. A 1986 survey of Florida's cities and counties indicates that most have had some experience with privatization (Law and Economics Center 1987). Respondents reported more than 1,200 cases of private sector contracting. Based on data from 163 Florida cities and counties, a tabulation summarizing results from this survey is displayed in Table 15-2. The table shows the total frequency of contractual arrangements reported in each major functional service area. This total is disaggregated to show the number of contractual arrangements with private and intergovernmental units. Clearly, contracting out is an important alternative in the State of Florida.

A more recent nationwide study of cities and counties and their usage of alternative delivery methods was conducted in 1988 (Kirchner and Karas 1989). A summary of Florida responses dealing with the delivery of cultural, recreational, and health services is presented in Table 15-3. Again, reported contractual arrangements are disaggregated to show private sector and intergovernmental arrangements.

IN FLORIDA STATE GOVERNMENT

Contracting at the state level is also an important service delivery alternative in Florida. The Florida Department of Health and Rehabilitative Services (DHRS) during the 1987–88 fiscal year entered into 6,642 contracts with outside parties costing approximately $1.15

Table 15-2

CONTRACTUAL ARRANGEMENTS FOR SERVICE DELIVERY BY FLORIDA CITIES AND COUNTIES

1986

billion (Auditor General 1990a). By 1993, HRS contracts reached 2.037 billion dollars (DHRS 1993). Although DHRS has been significantly restructured since 1993, with responsibility for many services previously performed by the department being transferred to Health Care Administration, Child Support Enforcement and Juvenile Justice, during the 1994–1995 fiscal year there were still some 3,800 contracts initiated which, in the aggregate, amounted to roughly $1.171 billion (DHRS staff, personal communication, May 17, 1995).

Service Area	Total Contractual Arrangements	Inter-governmental	Private Sector
Physical Environment/ Public Works	502	134	368
Transportation	394	96	298
Public Safety	357	208	149
Health and Human Services	323	161	162
Parks and Recreation	123	36	87
General/Support Services	383	105	278

Source: Law and Economics Center, 1987.

The state has also used contracting for service delivery for corrections. The Department of Corrections has established contracts with private providers for health care, food, and other services, but it was not until October, 1985, that the first contract for the private management of a state correctional facility was written. The department contracted for the management of one of its thirty-seven community correctional centers and one of its eleven probation and restitution centers. "In response to the slow pace of privatization, the Florida Legislature created the Correctional Privatization Commission in 1993" (Committee on Governmental Operations 1995, 63). Legislation for the commission provides the following:

> The Correctional Privatization commission is created for the purpose of entering into contracts with contractors for the designing, financing, acquiring, leasing, constructing, and operating of private correctional facilities. . . . (*Florida Statutes,* Ch. 957.03(1)).
>
> The commission may not enter into a contract . . . for the designing, financing, acquiring, leasing, constructing, and operating of a private correctional facility unless the commission determines that the contract ... in total for the facility will result in a cost savings to the state of at least 7 percent over the public provision of a similar facility (*Florida Statutes,* Ch. 957.07).

Chapter 957 includes a detailed listing of some twenty contract and contractor requirements that must be met in an effort to attain cost savings

Table 15-3

CONTRACTUAL ARRANGEMENTS BY FLORIDA CITIES AND COUNTIES FOR THE DELIVERY OF CULTURE, RECREATION AND HEALTH SERVICES

1988

Contractual Service Area	Total Inter-Arrangements*	Private governmental	Sector
Mental health/retardation	8	7	2
Public health programs	17	16	4
Drug/alcohol treatment	14	12	5
Programs for elderly	19	16	7
Sanitary inspection	8	8	0
Insect/rodent control	9	8	1
Animal control	14	12	2
Homeless shelters	5	3	2
Food programs for homeless	8	6	3
Recreation services	12	7	6
Recreation facilities	12	6	7
Parks landscaping/maintenance	10	3	7
Cultural/arts programs	15	9	10
Libraries	9	8	1

*The number of cities and counties reporting contractual arrangements does not equal the sum of intergovernmental and private sector arrangements because some reporting entities report both arrangements. Only cities and counties are included.

Source: Krichner and Karas 1989.

while maintaining quality standards. "Thomas indicates that the statute which created Florida's Correctional Privatization Commission may provide model legislation for other jurisdictions" (Thomas 1994, quoted in Committee on Governmental Operations 1995).

In an effort to determine the extent of privatized state services, the Committee on Governmental Operations conducted a 1995 survey of all state agencies which asked them to indicate the percentage of programs or services privatized. Contracting out was defined in the survey as, "the state entering into agreements to pay private providers to manage state programs, provide services, or conduct public projects with state funds" (Committee on Governmental Operations 1995, 185). Administrative, support services and direct client services were included within this definition. Statutorily created not-for-profit corporations were explicitly excluded from the count. Results indicate that contracting out is the most prevalent form of privatization utilized by the State of Florida agencies. The following administrative and support services were reported as being frequently provided through this method (Committee on Governmental Operations 1995, 186):

- computer maintenance
- printing
- consulting
- employee training and development
- computer system design
- custodial service
- court reporting
- mail/courier services, and
- moving services

Table 15-4 displays services and programs reported by the Florida Department of Corrections, Department of Elderly Affairs, Department of Health & Rehabilitative Services and the Department of Juvenile Justice where at least fifty percent of the program or service activities were contracted out. The list is extensive; the array of contracts is comprised of nearly sixty different categories of programs and services.

ISSUES INVOLVED IN THE DECISION TO CONTRACT

There are, of course, many issues that must be resolved in the decision to contract. For present purposes, four classes of factors will be considered. First, consideration is given to the legal constraints that must be faced; second, characteristics of the administrative infrastructure itself are discussed; third, microeconomic factors are considered. Finally, program technology and monitoring are discussed.

LEGAL CONSTRAINTS

Compliance with all laws and regulations relating to the contracting of an activity is of primary importance.

Table 15-4

SELECTED STATE OF FLORIDA SERVICES AND PROGRAMS: PERCENT REPORTED AS CONTRACTED OUT

1995

Function	Department*			
	DCOR	DOEA	DHRS	DJJ
Air Quality	80			
Alcohol/Drug Treatment	77–95			
Architectural Service			90	
Asbestos Removal	100		95	
Auditing	100	100		
Building Construction	60	100		100
Building Inspection	100	100		
Building Maintenance				55
Claims Payment Processing	100			
Client Assessment & Evaluation		100		100
Community Living Support Service		100	90	
Computer Maintenance		100	100	
Computer System Design	60		90	
Consulting			80	
Foster Care			62	
Halfway House				85
Health/Dental				100
Employee Health Screening	100			
HMO			70	
Immigration Services			99	
Information Systems		80	80	
Lab Testing & Services	60–100			
Landscaping			65	100
Laundry			60	85
Mail/Courier			95	100
Medicaid Processing		100		
Mental Health Care Service	75	100		100
Moving		100	65	100
Pest Control	10–100		100	
Pharmacy			100	
Correctional Facility Construction	60			100
Correctional Facility Operations				85
Counselors/Psychologists/Social Workers	100	100		59
Court-Ordered Electronic Monitoring	50		100	100
Custodial Service			95	100
Data Collection			80	
Data Processing			40–50	
Daycare Programs		100	100	
Domestic Violence Services	50–100		100	
Education, Special	100			
Employee Assistance Program		100		100
Employee Training & Development		90		
Engineering			90	
Environmental Inspections	95		95	
Fleet O & M			90	
Food Service			84	
Printing		100	90	
Program Evaluation			70	
Road Construction	90			
Road Design	100			
Security	100		85	
Sign Manufacturing	95			
Telecommunications		100	95	
Transportation			80	
Waste Cleanup			95	
Waste Disposal	100		95	
Waste Water Treatment	70			
Work Release				100

*DCOR = Florida Department of Corrections
*DOEA = Florida Department of Elderly Affairs
*DHRS = Florida Department of Health & Rehabilitative Services
*DJJ = Florida Department of Juvenile Justice

"During 1995 The Florida House of Representatives Committee on Governmental Operations surveyed 24 departments of Florida state government collecting information on the extent of privatization of State of Florida programs and services. Table 4 displays the responses of the Department of Corrections, Department of Elderly Affairs, Department of Health & Rehabilitative Services and the Department of Juvenile Justice for those program or service areas where at least fifty percent of the activities were reported as contracted out. Some of the larger organizations surveyed distributed the survey instrument to various divisions within the organization. As a result, some cell entries contain a range of percentages which reflect the minimum and maximum percentages reported" (Committee on Governmental Operations 1995, 185).

Adapted from *Privatization,* Florida House of Representatives, Committee on Governmental Operations, Table 2-A, pp. 188–191.

CHAPTER

15

Unfortunately, whether at the state, county, or municipal level, contracting exists in a complex morass of legal restrictions. The present discussion does not address specific questions of law and only attempts to illustrate the administrative impact of legal constraints on privatization and contracting.[3]

In the first instance, the *emerging nature* of these legal requirements must be recognized. This is perhaps best illustrated in a statement issued as recently as 1987 in *The Role of Privatization in Florida's Growth* published by the Law and Economics Center, University of Miami, and the Local Government Center, Reason Foundation:

> At present there are no explicit constitutional or statutory privatization provisions in Florida. Moreover, many relevant provisions are ambiguous, posing potential obstacles to privatization (Law and Economics Center 1987, 395).

Further, the review of legal considerations included in *Privatization,* the 1995 report issued by the Florida House of Representatives Committee on Governmental Operations, prominently displayed the following caveat:

> . . . privatization efforts should always incorporate a thorough legal review. As public and private roles blur, courts face the unenviable task of determining when public-sector restrictions and immunities apply to private and quasi-public organizations. Due to the elusive nature of such distinctions, the law remains in a state of continual flux. Resulting complexities and uncertainties veil the legal ramifications of privatization. Consequently, public officials considering privatization should obtain legal assistance during the *earliest stages of the planning process* (Committee on Governmental Operations 1995, 131). [Emphasis added.]

Because of the complexities involved in this administrative area, the Committee notes that while its discussion of the legal considerations related to privatization may provide "a broad perspective on some legal issues it [that is, the Committee Report] cannot substitute for competent legal advice" (131). This is, of course, equally true in the case of the present writing.

Not only does the dynamic, emerging nature of law relative to privatization result in contractual issues that are difficult to negotiate, the complexity is exacerbated by the layering of restrictions at different jurisdictional levels. These layers can be found at least at seven levels including: the federal constitution, federal statutes and regulations, federal court decisions, the state constitution, state statutes and regulations, and finally, state court decisions. With respect to the federal constitution, the Committee Report highlights the Supremacy Clause of Article Six of the Constitution, the Eleventh Amendment, the Fourteenth Amendment, and the Establishment Clause of the First Amendment as "provisions that warrant special attention" by officials who are considering privatization (Committee on Governmental Operations 1995, 132).

Some federal statutes and related regulations can be seen as hindering privatization while others encourage the practice. Among the former are the Urban Mass Transit Act of 1964, the Securities Acts of 1933 and 1934, The Tax Reform Act of 1986 and the Federal Bankruptcy Code. On the other hand, provisions of the Intermodal Surface Transportation Efficiency Act of 1991 and the Fair Labor Standards Act, for example, are reported to positively affect privatization efforts (Committee on Governmental Operations 1995).

From these few federal examples it becomes clear that privatization does indeed exist, as above, "in a complex morass of legal restrictions." The Committee Report concludes its consideration of federal statutes and regulations with the following:

> Of course, a variety of other federal laws could affect state privatization efforts. These include the Americans with Disabilities Act, the Parental Home Leave Act, and the Clayton Antitrust Act. A comprehensive inventory of federal legislation, however, falls beyond the scope of this report (142).

Development of a complete, yet static, inventory of federal statutes, regulations and court interpretations that might have an important impact on state and local privatization efforts in Florida seems to be an important, but perhaps impracticable, task.

The Florida Constitution also includes a number of provisions that can impact the privatization movement both at level of state government activity as well as at the level of the various government subdivisions within the state. The Committee specifically mentions constitutional provisions that:

- limit the delegation of powers by government
- limit the mixture of public and private business
- affect financial aspects of privatization
- impact employee relations
- grant sovereign immunity and reduce liability, and
- provide for public access to records and meetings.

Although numerous Florida laws impact the privatization enterprise both by and within the state, Chapter 287, *Florida Statutes,* has been called "the centerpiece of legislative efforts to regulate the process of bidding and awarding contracts" by the State (Committee on Governmental Operations 1995, 168). This Chapter and Chapter 13A-1, *Florida Administrative Code,* have provided many legal conditions for government contracts (Department of HRS 1990, 2-1). The underlying framework upon which state agency contracting is to be carried out is expressed in the statement of legislative intent included in Chapter 287. A careful reading of this portion of the statute suggests the types and extent of the requirements imposed upon government agencies:

> The Legislature recognizes that fair and open competition is a basic tenet of public procurement; that such competition reduces the appearance and opportunity for favoritism and inspires public confidence that contracts are awarded equitably and economically; and that documentation of the acts taken and effective monitoring mechanisms are important means of curbing any improprieties and establishing public confidence in the process by which commodities and services are procured. It is essential to the effective and ethical procurement of commodities and contractual services that there be a system of uniform procedures to be utilized by state agencies in managing and procuring commodities and contractual services; that detailed justification of agency decisions in the procurement of commodities and contractual services be maintained; and that adherence by the agency and the contractor to specific ethical considerations be required (*Florida Statutes,* Ch. 287.001).

Chapter 287 then defines commodities and contractual services, provides for and prescribes competitive bidding procedures, and indicates circumstances when competitive bidding shall, or shall not, be required.

In cases where contracts are funded by federal grants, they become subject to even more requirements. For example, contracts issued in the past by the Florida Department of Health and Rehabilitative Services and funded by the U.S. Department of Health and Human Services contained provisions relating to compliance with Executive Order 11246, Equal Employment Opportunity, the Copeland Anti-Kickback Act, and the Davis-Bacon Act, along with relevant Department of Labor regulations. Additionally, provision for compliance with standards promulgated by the Office of Management and Budget included in Attachment O, Procurement Standards, OMB Circulars A-102 and A-110 have been required (Department of HRS 1990, 9–12—9–13). And, it is important to recognize that these requirements, just as others mentioned, are in a continual state of flux.

It is not surprising, given this complexity and the related uncertainty, that the implementation of contracts, especially in the face of disappointed bidders, is often a long and litigious process. This condition suggests that the true cost of contracted services must take into account the possibility of legal delays and associated legal costs.

ADMINISTRATIVE INFRASTRUCTURE

Chackerian (1990) has noted elsewhere the irony of government contracting is that while it usually is seen as an instrument for circumventing bureaucratic failures of incompetence, underfunding, inefficiency, corruption, etc., success depends on having a competent bureaucracy. The reason for this is clear. Contracting for the delivery of government services does not remove the administrator from the chain of responsibility and accountability; it simply imposes different, and perhaps additional responsibilities:

> Most critics believe that the proper relationship between the government and its contractors depends on the government agency clearly being in control of the service and the private supplier. The government agency should set goals, draw up the proper procedures to encourage competition, and make careful performance evaluations in an objective manner (DeHoog 1984, 13).

Kettl in *Sharing Power* (1993), describes this relationship succinctly:

> The expansion of government's partnership with private suppliers...has created a new kind of management. . . . government's role has changed. In public-private partnerships, contracts replace hierarchy. Instead of a chain of authority from policy to product, there is a negotiated document that separates policymaker from policy output. Top officials cannot give orders to contractors . . . they can only shape the incentives to which the contractors respond. There is a gap in the chain of authority, which the contract fills. . . . The argument here is not that the contractual relationship, which lies at the core of the competition prescription, is prone to breakdown, but that it entails a *different kind* of public management. And that raises the central question: What role must government play to fill the competition prescription? (21 and 22) [Italics in original.]

Increasingly, governments are involved with *administered* contracts, which require a high level of administrative capacity. In earlier periods, government contracts were primarily for infrastructure and equipment of various sorts. These are often items that are produced in competitive markets and for which clear performance objectives can be specified. Administered contracts are those where there must be continual involvement of the government with the contractor because of non-competitive markets, legal complexity, and the ambiguous technologies of service delivery. There must be a governmental capacity to specify program requirements, monitor contract performance, encourage the development of competitive markets, and assure the fiscal integrity of operations. Governments must be able to shift focus from hierarchical control to contract control; to shift from bureaucratic failure to competence (Chackerian 1990).

One reason often cited for shifting from government to contract provision is the lack of expertise in the government. The lack of such expertise was one of the reasons frequently mentioned in the past by Florida's Department of Health and Rehabilitative Services to explain contracting for human service delivery (Chackerian 1990). Unfortunately, the austerity that is usually the reason for the lack of government expertise almost necessarily means that it will be very difficult to hire the new competencies necessary for expanded contract planning and monitoring (DeHoog 1984, 20 & 32).

Another reason for contracting is corruption. Certainly contracting changes the pattern of control and accountability, and thereby affects opportunities for public administrators to engage in corrupt practices (Chackerian 1990). While some argue that contracting out under open competition will cure corrupt practices, others argue that contracts are one of the most common and lucrative sources of corruption in government. Probably neither is entirely correct. What both sides fail to understand is that the problem lies with administrative incentives and values, not the method of service delivery. If bureaucrats do indeed act solely in their own interests, introduction of contracting will be seen by them as simply presenting new opportunities for self-aggrandizement. It follows that if contracting is to produce efficient and effective delivery of services, the administrative infrastructure must be comprised of administrators who value efficiency and effectiveness.

Contracting is often ostensibly undertaken to overcome low motivation and incompetence in public organizations. These administrative faults are generally attributed to the lack of incentive pay for public employees as well as the lack of managerial discretion in compensation, budget, and personnel decisions (Chackerian 1990). The prospect of market provision implies all these positive incentives for performance. This result, however, is grounded upon the rather important assumptions that, first, providers are operating in competitive markets and, second, as noted earlier, the government is, in fact, able to administer the contractual relationship competently.

MICROECONOMIC CHARACTERISTICS

The public justification of contracting often involves the assertion of economic efficiency. This efficiency is said to be the direct result of operating in a competitive market place. Kettl (1993) notes, however, "The fundamental irony of the competition prescription is that practice has galloped madly ahead of theory. The government's reliance upon the private sector has grown faster than its ability to manage it" (20). It is important to examine the competition/efficiency argument closely and from all sides before making the decision to contract out. Kettl does this noting, among other things, that the agency must be certain that a market actually exists in which contracts can be negotiated. A pre-existing market as opposed to a market that government creates to provide a particular good or service reflects two very different sets of institutional arrangements with very different competitive dynamics. Additionally, in either case, the level of competition may vary from highly competitive on the one hand to monopolistic on the other. Finally, any market may "be affected by externalities, that is, by costs and benefits that the market does not capture" (Kettl 1993, 32). Kettl's analysis of market theory leads him to assert:

> Privatization works best where markets are lively, where information is abundant, where decisions are not irretrievable, and where externalities are limited. It works worst where externalities and monopolies are abundant, where competition is limited, and where efficiency is not the main public interest (39).

There are other economic considerations that must be taken into account when making the contracting decision. One particularly important variable is the potential for increased efficiencies due to large purchasing arrangements or scale economies. Scale economies can result from at least two different sources: (1) savings on the elements that go into a good or service (viz., input prices) and (2) minimizing the effective variance in levels of demand or capacity utilization (Farris and Graddy 1986). Volume discounts for purchasing in large quantities may result in lower input prices (i.e., costs) for materials and equipment. Contract arrangements allow smaller communities to band together and acquire large quantities of inputs, but it may also help large programs such as might be seen at the state level. With the privatization of state correctional facilities a growing trend in Florida, it would not be unreasonable to expect corporations such as Wackenhut or Corrections Corporation of America to enjoy enhanced purchasing power by the enlarging scope of their activities. As this national market grows, Florida may be able to reap benefits from economies of scale by contracting with entities such as these.

Similarly, in cases where peak service load demands are dramatically higher than normal loads, or where there are wide variances in load levels over time, labor and equipment may be underutilized during low demand periods. This is particularly true where manpower or equipment is required to be kept on reserve and called to service upon the occurrence of random events such as an equipment failure or a natural crisis. Larger organizations, because they are exposed to a wider distribution of such events, should be more flexible in managing inputs, thus avoiding costly underutilization. Contracting may allow smaller units to share equipment and services and to spread uncertainties.

Other economic characteristics which may affect the method of service delivery are the size of the initial capital investment and the continuing operating capital requirements. In the current period of governmental austerity, private organizations may have more investment capital than the government. Utilization of the capital base of private organizations can offer financial leverage to government entities through contracting arrangements such as leases, lease-purchases, or similarly structured agreements. Just prior to contracting with Bay County, Florida, for the construction and operation of jail facilities in 1985 Corrections Corporation of America (CCA) had recently gone public and issued some $30 million worth of shares of capital stock (Law and Economics Center 1987).

Even if the government has adequate capital, its application of those resources may be restricted. One important restriction may occur with respect to employee compensation.

> There is fairly good evidence that some wanted to contract educational services in Florida's Department of Corrections because it was the only way to increase salaries for inmate educators. As long as educators were paid by the Department of Corrections, it would be difficult to raise salaries above prison guards. Since teachers working for school districts and community colleges are paid higher salaries, contracting the inmate teaching function with school districts would bring prison teachers into these more generously paid positions (Chackerian 1986).

Interestingly, in this case, "contracting inmate education was not based primarily on a desire to reduce costs, but to make better use of funds and perhaps to increase resources to the program" (Chackerian 1986).

PROGRAM TECHNOLOGIES, OUTPUTS, AND MONITORING

It has been noted that for government agencies to successfully contract, it is necessary that the agency be able to properly monitor contract performance. This entails setting program goals as well as performing meaningful performance measurement and program evaluation. In this connection, it has been argued that "the more complex the product, the better suited it is to public production. Historically governments have been more likely to contract services that can be easily monitored, such as, services that have tangible and simple outputs" (Farris and Graddy 1986, 333). Farris and Graddy focus on measurable program outputs as the key to program evaluation and monitoring. This implies that contracting is less appropriate for those service areas which tend to produce intangible, difficult, perhaps even unmeasurable, outputs. However, these are the characteristics of social services such as health and human services, correctional programs and many other professional services. Is contracting patently inappropriate here? Not necessarily.

At least two approaches can be suggested. In resonance with the current resurgence of interest in performance based budgeting and service efforts and accomplishment reporting at all levels of government, Harvey (1996) addresses the issue of intangible outputs. She suggests, "understanding the determinants of productivity in complex professional services and developing tools to improve it is a clear research priority" (Harvey, 188). The object of this research should be to develop productivity indices for these intangible areas. Harvey concludes:

> Unless information systems are in place, and being gradually improved, there are no systematic feedback mechanisms that allow professionals to learn from the system and thus find ways to improve delivery processes. Unless some kind of proxy measurement is available for the results the organization is seeking to achieve, it cannot focus on the customer (197–198).

On the other hand, the exclusive focus on measurable program outputs when designing methods of evaluation for contracted service delivery ignores the wide area of *action* or *process controls* in monitoring. Process controls allow monitoring of programs which do not have tangible, simple outputs; and, since this is the case with many government

services, policy makers who consider contracting as an alternative delivery mode should be alert to the usefulness of these controls and their application to contracting situations. William Ouchi provided an insight into these alternative controls:

> If we understand the technology (that is the means-ends relationships involved in the basic production or service activities) perfectly, . . . then we can achieve effective control simply by having someone watch the behavior of the employees and the workings of the machines: if all behaviors and processes conform to our desired transformation steps, then we know with certainty that proper [products or services] are coming out the other end. . . . By specifying the *rules of behavior* and of *process,* we could create an effective bureaucratic control mechanism . . . (Ouchi 1979).

These process controls can take many forms, ranging from levels of professionalization to time and budget allocations. Where contracting seems compelling, effective government monitoring may be achieved even in the presence of intangible, perhaps even unmeasurable, outputs. The optimal approach in such situations would seem to include dual accountability tracks where Harvey's emphasis on research to develop output measures is combined with Ouchi's concepts regarding the potential for effective process control. When contractual outputs are difficult to measure, the two approaches compliment each other.

CONCLUSION

"More steering and less rowing." That was a phrase heard frequently during the 1990 campaign for the Florida governorship. The phrase was seen by political commentators as the wave of the future if Lawton Chiles was elected governor. It should be clear, however, that state government rowing was a sport in precipitous decline much before the election. As we have shown, contracting and other forms of government action which place emphasis on non-government providers now accounts for much of what governments provide. The Chiles campaign phrase was forward looking, however, with respect to steering. While governments in Florida have embraced alternative production, they have been less able to steer and control. Perhaps the management rationality demonstrated in the institutional initiatives recently undertaken by the State of Florida will provide the requisite guidance. Examples include The State Council on Competitive Government, The Office of Program

Policy Analysis and Government Accountability, The Commission on Government Accountability to the People and The Correctional Privatization Commission. Hopefully these initiatives will provide models for the development of the bureaucratic competency required to reap the benefits of alternative production methods at both state and local levels throughout the State of Florida.

REFERENCES

Auditor General (1990a). *Operational performance audit of the Florida Department of Health and Rehabilitative Services*. Tallahassee: State of Florida, Office of the Auditor General.

Auditor General (1990b). *Performance audit of the Department of Corrections' management of its contract with National Corrections Management, Inc.* Tallahassee: State of Florida, Office of the Auditor General.

Bowsher, Charles A. (1990). Budget reform for the federal government. In Frederick S. Lane (Ed.), *Current Issues in Public Administration*. New York: St. Martin's Press.

Carroll, James et al (1985). "Supply side management on the Reagan Administration." *Public Administration Review* (November/December): 805–14.

Committee on Governmental Operations, Florida House of Representatives (1995). *Privatization*. Tallahassee: State of Florida.

Chackerian, Richard(1986). "From hierarchy to market and back again." *Florida Policy Review* 1:26–29.

Chackerian, Richard (1990). *Contracting public services: Ways of thinking about the decision to buy or make*. Tallahassee: Florida State University, Florida Center for Public Management.

Chi, Keon S. (1988). "Privatization and contracting for state services: A guide." *Innovations* (April).

DeHoog, Ruth Hoogland (1984). *Contracting out for human services*. Albany: State University of New York Press.

Department of Health and Rehabilitative Services (DHRS) (1990). *Procurement and contract management: Contract management system for contractual services*. Tallahassee: State of Florida, the Department.

Department of Health and Rehabilitative Services (DHRS) (1993). Interoffice memo. Processed (September 10).

Doyle, Richard and Jerry McCaffery (1991). The budget enforcement act of 1990: The path to no fault budgeting. *Public Budgeting and Finance* (Spring): 25–40.

Farris, James and Elizabeth Graddy (1986). Contracting out: For what? With whom? *Public Administration Review* (July/August): 332–44.

Harvey, Jean (1996). Productivity in professional services: To measure or not to measure. In Arie Halachmi and Geert Bouckaert (Eds.), *Organizational Performance and Measurement in the Public Sector: Toward Service, Effort and Accomplishment Reporting*. Westport, Conn: Quorum.

Hatry, Harry P. (1983). *A Review of Private Approaches for Delivery of Public Services*. Washington, D.C.: The Urban Institute Press.

Havens, Harry S. (1986). Gramm-Rudman-Hollings: Origins and implementation. *Public Budgeting and Finance* 6 (Autumn): 4–24.

Henry, Nicholas (1995). *Public Administration and Public Affairs*. Englewood Cliffs: Prentice Hall.

International City Management Association (1989). *Service Delivery in the 90s: Alternative Approaches for Local Governments*. Washington, D.C.: ICMA.

Kettl, Donald F. (1993). Sharing power: Public Governance and Private Markets. Washington, D.C.: The Brookings Institution.

Kirchner, Geraldene and Kathy Karas (1989). *Culture, recreation and health—ensuring the quality of life*. Special Data Issue Number 12. Washington, D.C.: International City Management Association.

Kolderie, Ted (1986). The two different concepts of privatization. *Public Administration Review* (July/August): 285–91.

Law and Economics Center, University of Miami, and Local Government Center, Reason Foundation (1987). *The role of privatization in Florida's growth*. Tallahassee: Florida Chamber of Commerce Foundation.

Leloup, Lance T., Barbara Luck Graham, and Stacey Barwick (1987). Deficit politics and constitutional government: The impact of Gramm-Rudman-Hollings. *Public Budgeting and Finance* 7 (Spring): 83–103.

Miller Roger, LeRoy, Daniel K. Benjamin and Douglass C. North (1996). *The economics of public issues*. (10th ed.). New York: Harper Collins.

Miranda, Rowan and Karlyn Andersen (1994). Alternative service delivery in local government, 1982–1992. In *The Municipal Year Book 1994*. Washington, D.C.: International City Management Association.

Nathan, Richard P. and John R. Lago (1988). Intergovernmental relations in the Reagan era. *Public Budgeting and Finance* 8 (Autumn): 15–29.

Ouchi, William (1979). A conceptual framework for the design of organizational control mechanisms. *Management Science* 25:833–48.

Pensacola News Journal (August 6, 1996). Pensacola, Florida.

Rehfuss, John A. (1989). *Contracting out in government*. San Francisco: Jossey-Bass.

Rosenfeld, Raymond A. (1989). Federal grants and local capital improvements: The impact of Reagan budgets. *Public Budgeting and Finance* 9 (Spring): 74–84.

Salamon, Lester (1989). *Beyond privatization: The tools of government action*. Washington, D.C.: The Urban Institute.

Savas, E. S. (1987). *Privatization: The key to better government*. Chatham, New Jersey: Chatham House.

Savas, E.S. (1990). On privatization. In Frederick S. Lane (Ed.), *Current Issues in Public Administration*. New York: St. Martin's Press.

Shuman, Howard E. (1984). *Politics and the budget*. Englewood Cliffs, NJ: Prentice Hall.

Tankersley, William B. and Alfred G. Cuzan (1996). Privatization and decentralization in the United States and Chile. *Journal of Developing Societies,* 12:104.

Thomas, Charles W. (1994). *Private adult correctional facility census* (7th ed.). Gainesville, FL: University of Florida, Center for Studies in Criminology & Law.

ENDNOTES

1. Discussion of these alternative service delivery modes is based substantially on Committee on Governmental Operations, 1995; Hatry, 1983; ICMA, 1989; Law and Economics Center, 1987; Salamon, 1989; Savas, 1987; Tankersley and Cuzan, 1996.

2. For interesting studies of these trends, see Nathan and Lago, 1988 and Rosenfeld, 1989.

3. Much of what follows is based on Chapter VII, "Legal Aspects of Privatization," Law and Economics Center, 1987, and Chapter VI, "Legal Considerations: Constitutional Provisions, Legislation, and Court Decisions Affecting Privatization," *Privatization:* Final Report, Florida House of Representatives Committee on Governmental Operations, 1995.

CHAPTER

15

CONSTITUTION REVISION IN FLORIDA

LANCE deHAVEN-SMITH

Imagine a state where it is almost impossible to make meaningful political reforms except every twenty years, when for a brief period of less than twelve month the most radical options imaginable are open for consideration and adoption. In such a state, pressure for change would build and build, until finally the brief window for reform would swing open and proposals would rush in like winter air into heated room. Clearly, a community characterized by years of relative calm punctuated suddenly by moments of upheaval would be rather wild.

Welcome to Florida! It is the only state in the nation with a regular constitution revision process that empowers a citizens commission to place wholesale constitutional changes directly before the voters. Every twenty years, a Constitution Revision Commission is appointed to review the Florida Constitution as a totality and recommend changes to the electorate. The Commission has complete authority to offer whatever revisions it deems appropriate, including constructing an entirely new constitution. A Commission was formed in 1997, and its recommendations will be voted on in November 1998. History suggests that, while many of the proposals may be rejected by the electorate, this constitution revision process will set the agenda of political reform in Florida for the next twenty years.

CONSTITUTIONAL POLITICS

Understanding the issues surrounding constitution revision requires knowledge of Florida's current political challenges along with insight into the workings of its constitutional framework. Constitution revision tends to focus on fundamentals—notably the rights of citizens, the balance between the branches of state government, the system of taxation and public finance, and the powers of cities and counties. Both the state of Florida and its constitution have some special characteristics that repeatedly place certain issues at the top of the reform agenda.

One of the most important and controversial features of Florida's constitution is its cabinet system of executive governance. Unlike all other states, Florida has a quasi-legislative body overseeing its executive branch. This body consists of the Governor plus a cabinet of six public officials also elected statewide. Although other states often have executive branch officials in addition to the Governor who are elected by statewide vote—such as elected secretaries of education, of agriculture, etc.—few vest power as extensively as Florida in a system of collective decision-making.

Florida politics is also special because of the state's extreme diversity. Most states have one, two or a few large cities that dominate state policy making. For example, Georgia is dominated by Atlanta; New York by New York City; California by Los Angeles; and so on. In contrast, Florida is a state of relatively small cities and regions. Most of the largest cities have populations of 500,000 or less. Rather than one large urban powerhouse, Florida has Jacksonville, Orlando, Tampa, Miami, Ft. Lauderdale, West Palm Beach, Daytona Beach, Tallahassee, and other medium-sized metropolitan centers, all vying for control.

This geographic dispersion makes for rapidly shifting political coalitions and constant change. On the surface, Florida voters seem to be unified around a conservative, "if ain't broke, don't fix it" philosophy, but this appearance is misleading. Actually, Florida is deeply divided into three main voting blocks: Republicans in southwest and central Florida; liberal Democrats in southeast Florida; and conservative "Dixiecrats" or "Reagan Democrats" in the rural areas. The state seems moderately conservative only because conservative Democrats hold the balance of power between the liberal Democrats on the left and the Republicans on the right. State politics swings like a pendulum between the left and the right as the Dixiecrats vote one year for Republicans and the next year for Democrats (deHaven-Smith 1995).

Still a third special feature of Florida politics is its mix of old and new. The political roots of Florida extend deep into history. They include a native American era plus periods of rule by both Spain and Britain. One has merely to look at the names of Florida's cities and counties to see the influence of these earlier times. Similarly, during the 19th Century, Florida was part of the Deep South, and even now the state retains a strong southern culture, especially in its rural areas. These holdovers from times past are entwined with modern urbanization. For most of this century, people have been pouring into Florida from the Northeast and the Midwest, and from other nations. With perhaps the exception of California, no other state contains such a complex combination of historical influences.

These characteristics combine to make Florida politics colorful and dramatic. Because the state is geographically large and fragmented, no single region is able to dominate state politics. Each region produces its own brand of leader, and unstable coalitions between regions form and reform as problems and conditions shift. The whole process looks something like a kaleidoscope, which produces a new configuration with each twist of the lens.

However, while Florida politics is exciting and interesting, it is also characterized by certain fundamental problems. The cabinet system causes Florida to have a weak executive branch, because the Governor shares power with six other officials, some of which are often from a different political party. Until recently, the weakness of Florida's executive branch did not create an imbalance in state government, because the legislative branch was equally weak. The latter met only once every two years, and it did not have a professional staff. However, under a revised Constitution drafted in 1968, the Legislature was greatly strengthened. It now meets annually, has a large staff, and oversees the executive budget in exacting detail.

Florida's constitutional structure leaves the state unable to overcome its inner divisions and forge a strong civic culture. Florida is run largely by a legislative process which is inherently fragmented. Without a strong executive to unify the electorate, the state's deep political conflicts remain unresolved from year to year. Elected officials focus on the near term, intergovernmental gridlock is common, and concern for the state's future is a rare commodity.

The political fragmentation of Florida government leaves the state poorly equipped to meet the challenges confronting it. The main problem Florida faces is rapid population growth, which is harming the state's fragile natural environment, overwhelming its public facilities, and steadily eroding the quality of life. Despite many efforts to resolve these problems, the state experiences recurring fiscal and ecological crises.

FLORIDA'S CONSTITUTIONS

Florida is operating under its sixth state constitution.[1] The first constitution was drafted 1838, when a convention was held to prepare for statehood. The 1838 Constitution provided for a one-term Governor, a bicameral legislature, and departmental officers elected by a joint vote of the two houses of the Legislature. The departmental officers—Secretary of State, Treasurer, Comptroller, and Attorney General—served four-year terms and were eligible for reelection.

This group of departmental officers gradually evolved into today's Cabinet. In the year of statehood, 1845, the Legislature created within the executive branch the office of Registrar of Public Lands. In 1851, the Legislature mandated the appointment of the Board of Agriculture. The Registrar and the Agriculture Board became the basis for the Office of Commissioner of Agriculture (which was created by the Constitution of 1868). In 1855, the Legislature named the Governor and four "departmental officers" as the Board of Trustees of the Internal Improvement Trust Fund.

A second constitution was adopted in 1861 when Florida joined other southern states in seceding from the union. The 1861 Constitution reduced the terms of the Governor and the departmental administrators from 4 years to 2. This constitution became void with the collapse of the Confederacy.

The third constitution was drafted in 1868. It provided for a strong office of governor, but it was unpopular because it was adopted during the period when Union troops occupied the South. It is referred to as the "Carpetbag" or "Reconstruction" Constitution of 1868. It was the first state constitution to use the term "cabinet" in describing the departmental officers. Under the 1868 Constitution, however, cabinet members were not separately elected but instead were appointed by the Governor and confirmed by the Senate, as they are in the federal government. This gave the Governor control over the executive branch.

After union troops were withdrawn from the South, Florida abandoned the "Carpetbag Constitution" and adopted the Constitution of 1885. Drafted in reaction to the politics of the Reconstruction era, it was designed specifically to weaken the office of the Governor. White Floridians' were trying to reassert control over their political institutions and purge everything associated with Reconstruction. The 1885 Constitution did not recognize the Cabinet's official status, but it did establish six administrative offices with the intention of fragmenting the executive branch. The Governor was limited to one four-year term, and the office of Lieutenant Governor was eliminated. The six administrative offices were elected by a statewide vote, and officeholders were eligible for an indefinite number of reelections.

Florida's state government evolved in a predictable direction under the 1885 Constitution. The six administrative officials began to be repeatedly reelected, and each one accumulated considerable power, whereas the Governor's office remained a position with constant turnover and hence less real clout. Furthermore, the Legislature began assigning the administrative officers with duties beyond those enumerated in the Constitution and began collectivizing responsibilities. By the mid-1960s, this arrangement had become so unmanageable that the reorganization of the executive branch became a priority. Also, reapportionment shifted power from the rural areas to the urban areas, and the latter were inclined toward political modernization.

Florida's sixth and current constitution—the Constitution of 1968—was written over a period of two years. In 1966, the Legislature established a 37 member Constitution Revision Commission. The latter was required to submit its product to the Legislature before its proposals could be placed before the voters, and the Legislature revised the Commission's draft four times in special sessions. In the 1968 Constitution, the word "Cabinet" was reinstated, and certain specific line responsibilities were assigned to Cabinet officers. However, no collegial responsibilities of the Governor and Cabinet were mandated. Instead, the Constitution defined the members of the Cabinet, the State Board of Education, and the State Board of Administration, and it left the responsibilities of all of these collegial bodies to be designated by statute. The 1968 Constitution also required the executive branch to be consolidated into no more than twenty-five departments.

THE BALANCE TODAY

Florida's cabinet system has not functioned as intended by the designers of the 1968 Constitution.[2] The intent of the designers was to strengthen the executive branch by clarifying the role of the cabinet officers and creating a single point of decision-making. The 1968 Constitution envisioned the Governor and Cabinet as virtually the sole executive body to make decisions that in most other states are handled by a variety of separate and independently staff decision-making bodies. The aim in Florida was to avoid the fragmentation, duplication, and lack of coordination associated with independently functioning siting boards, boards of education, state land use boards of appeal, pardon and parole boards, etc. In Florida all of these functions were to be handled by the Governor and Cabinet meeting collegially, thus providing for unified decision making, better coordination, and clearer accountability.

In practice, however, the Governor and Cabinet system became so overloaded with responsibilities that it could not work as envisioned. Rather than providing a clear forum for accountability, the Governor and Cabinet had to delegate much of their workload to their cabinet aides.

For reasons of efficiency, chief cabinet aides to the Governor and the cabinet officers began to meet in advance of the Governor and Cabinet meetings to work out agreements and resolve issues among themselves, so that recommended decisions could be presented to their principles at the public meetings. The cabinet aides accumulated almost as much power as the Cabinet itself, and their meetings became the forum in which many executive branch decisions were made.

The issues that now make it through the gauntlet of cabinet aides to reach the real Governor and Cabinet—the elected officials—are those that tend to spark public attention. These include, among other things, controversial local land-use decisions that the Governor and Cabinet review on appeal, the hiring of agency heads, and discipline problems in schools. The public visibility of these and similar issues tend to turn out a crowd, and the Governor and Cabinet meetings are at times quite raucous. In this highly visible and politicized setting, the Governor and Cabinet are motivated to compromise between the audience and the executive administration, even though the administrative recommendations may be sound and lawful. Of course, in some instances the Governor and Cabinet forum make it possible for legitimate concerns to be factored into otherwise narrowly bureaucratic decisions. But such instances are rare, and, in most cases, the Governor and Cabinet system simply inserts unpredictability into issues that should be decided on principle and law.

It was probably unavoidable that the Governor and Cabinet system evolved as it did. The elected officials had no other choice but to delegate authority to the maximum extent possible. This was because the number of decisions and their complexity precluded the ability of any single individual to absorb and resolve them. A single development order on a land-use decision could easily run hundreds of pages. Each packet of reports and other items for every Governor and Cabinet meeting were several inches thick. The Governor and Cabinet had to ask their staffs to handle routine matters and bring only pressing problems to the elected officials' attention.

The devolution of authority from the Cabinet to the cabinet aides had several unfortunate side effects in addition to removing decisions from public awareness and accountability. First, it resulted in an unnecessarily redundant administrative structure. Rather than one or a few members of the executive branch focusing on particular issues, such as environmental questions or transportation, each cabinet officer and the Governor had to appoint his or her own expert on every issue. Therefore, in addition to the seven chief cabinet aides, the Governor and Cabinet also came to have aides for dealing with specialized topics. This staff is many times larger than would be necessary if executive branch decisions were handled in a more traditional structure. In effect, the citizens are paying for more government than is really needed.

Second, the role of the cabinet aides complicated rather than simplified many decisions. This was because the cabinet aides came to think that they should fine-tune many negotiated decisions that reached them for review. Issues that would not have sparked much interest among the elected officials therefore came to be unnecessarily modified in the final step of the review process. In turn, this reality led lobbyists and others to view the cabinet aides as a panel requiring some sort of chit, so in negotiating with administrative agencies they often held back concessions to give to the cabinet aides.

Third, the Governor and Cabinet system created false expectations among affected publics. Citizens in administrative processes are told that they have a chance to take their case to the highest officials in the land if they are dissatisfied. However, citizens subsequently find themselves dealing with a group of appointed administrators who for all practical purposes have the final say. When the issue reaches the elected officials, the latter almost invariably simply accept the staff report. The exceptions are not always when the citizens have good arguments but rather when they can generate media attention.

With the executive branch splintered and its attention diverted to decisions involving rather small stakes, the legislative branch has become the center of power in Florida politics. The legislative branch gains its strength from a large professional staff and from its extensive control over the state budget. Reflecting this legislative dominance, state agencies are required to submit their proposed annual budgets directly to the Legislature at the same time that their budgets are given to the Governor's office for preparation of the Governor's budget request.

The dominance of Florida's legislative branch over its executive inevitably leads to parochialism and a short-term focus. Two of the three most important members of the state government—the President of the Senate and the Speaker of the House, both of whom have enormous power—are elected by small (sub-state) jurisdictions and remain in their positions for only two years. Despite a strong commitment to statewide leadership, these officers are usually preoccupied with legislative coalition-building, temporary crisis solving, and bringing home benefits to their local constituents. The one political officer who might be expected to take the long view and speak for the state as a whole— the Governor—can be effective only by working within this narrow political context.

LOCAL GOVERNMENT

Another significant defect in the 1968 Constitution relates to local government. Florida has been undergoing extremely rapid population growth for over three decades, and high growth is expected to continue for the foreseeable future. In an effort to manage this growth, the 1968 Constitution established a system of limited "home rule," allowing cities and counties some flexibility in their political structure and in how they raise and spend public monies. Home rule included the option for counties to adopt their own charters, which are like local government constitutions, and thereby to choose their own form of representation and administration. Trying to assure that local governments respected regional and state concerns in local land use planning and regulation, the legislature subsequently augmented home rule with requirements for local and regional land use planning.

However, while local governments have modernized and have made many strides in intergovernmental cooperation, they have not been able to keep pace structurally with urbanization. Rather than establish or expand municipalities to serve the urban areas, Florida has responded to urban development with a patchwork of special districts, interlocal service agreements, and municipal service districts of county governments. Whereas in 1970 almost two-thirds of the state's population lived in municipalities, most residents today live in unincorporated areas served by a combination of special districts and county and municipal government woven together locally in unpredictable, ad hoc patterns. The ability to adopt local county charters has been somewhat helpful in putting sound local government atop the state's urbanization, but other mechanisms have proven to be less effective. For both legal and political reasons, few new municipalities have been formed, and the borders of existing municipalities have seldom been significantly expanded. Likewise, city-county consolidation has been achieved in only one case, despite numerous consolidation drives around the state. Today, local governments grapple with service delivery, annexation, and land use issues. Conflict is common, and progress in resolving disputes is sometimes hampered by lack a of clear guidelines and positive incentives for cooperation and reform.

Probably the biggest problem in Florida local government is duplication and fragmentation. Over the past 25 years, the number of local service providers has expanded greatly. Most of this growth has been in the form of dependent and independent districts to serve residents in unincorporated areas. In part, the proliferation of districts has been a response to citizen preferences for governmental units with narrowly focused missions and clearly earmarked funding, but it has also been stimulated by tax limitations placed on municipalities and counties in the 1968 Constitution and by the State Legislature. Because the taxes of independent districts are not counted in the mileage rates of cities and counties, districts have been used as a means to increase the overall tax capacity of local government.

Another factor contributing to duplication in the delivery of local government services has been the movement of counties into urban services without a commensurate reorganization of service responsibilities among other providers. The urbanization of county governments was in line with state policy, but the state failed to fully anticipate the implications of this trend. The state policy in support of county governments delivering urban services emerged in response to problems with the 1968 Constitution. In the early 1960's, some counties began delivering urban-level services in the unincorporated areas. They paid for these services by levying taxes county wide, which meant that they subsidized services in the unincorporated areas with revenues from their underlying cities. The 1968 Constitution sought to end this practice by prohibiting such "dual taxation" of city residents, but judicial rulings largely nullified the dual taxation prohibition. Consequently, the Local Government Commission of 1972 recommended, and the Legislature enacted, a law aimed at requiring counties to finance urban services with special taxes in the unincorporated areas. Specifically, the legislature authorized counties to levy an additional 10 mills in "municipal service taxing units" in the unincorporated area in addition to the 10 mills counties can levy county wide. In effect, this gave counties the equivalent of municipal taxing power and therefore enabled them to finance an intense city-level of public services. Many counties began to do just that.

Although this solved or at least mitigated the equity issue surrounding city and county taxes, it did not address the problems of service duplication and intergovernmental conflict. Delivering urban services via counties or special districts rather than cities would have been fine if service responsibilities had been divided up in a rational, orderly fashion, but no mechanism was established for choosing among service providers as more of them came on the scene. Instead, each area usually had its own set of service deliverers depending on history and happenstance. In one area, a special district might gradually expand its functions until it was a quasi-city. In another area, services might be provided by the county and financed by MSTUs. Elsewhere, cities might have contracts to provide services to an unincorporated area, or, conversely, the county might have contracts to deliver services to various cities. In the end, duplication became not merely normal, but virtually unavoidable.

Today, the disorder among Florida's local governments is of special concern because of the changes occurring within the federal system. Many governmental responsibilities are being shifted from the national government to the states and localities. In some cases, programs are being transferred directly to counties, municipalities, and other local units. In other instances, changes in federal programs will result indirectly in additional burdens on local government. For example, welfare term limits will probably expand the need for indigent health care in local public hospitals. Together, this direct and indirect devolution will pose a great challenge to counties, cities, and special districts throughout the nation. Local government in Florida is not well structured to accommodate this fundamental reallocation of governmental responsibilities.

REVISING THE CONSTITUTION

Under Florida's current constitution, the constitution can be amended or revised in four ways.[3] The most common approach is initiated by the state Legislature. A joint resolution containing the proposed amendment must be passed by a three-fifths vote of the membership of each house. Usually, the amendment is then submitted to the voters at the next general election occurring at least 90 days after the amendment has been legislatively endorsed. General elections are held in November of each even numbered year. To place a proposed amendment before the voters at a time other than the general election, each house of the Legislature must call for a special election by a three-fourths vote of its members.

A second way to amend the constitution is by popular initiative. A petition must be circulated which describes the proposed amendment. To be placed on the ballot, the petitioners must obtain signatures from at least eight percent of the voters in each of at least one half of the state's congressional districts and of the state as a whole. The number on which the eight percent figure is applied is the number of votes cast statewide and in the congressional districts in the most recent Presidential election. For the statewide elections this is a little under six million voters, which means that the petition must be signed by almost 500,000 registered voters. After sufficient signatures are gathered, the item is placed on the ballot at the next general election.

A third way to revise the constitution is through a constitutional convention. A petition is circulated stating the call for a convention. Signatures must be obtained from at least 15 percent of the registered voters in at least half of the congressional districts and of the state at large. As before, the 15 percent figure is applied to the number of votes cast in the most recent presidential election. The final decision to hold a convention is made by the electorate. If a convention is endorsed by the electorate, convention delegates are selected at the next general election. One delegate is selected from each district of the Florida House of Representatives. The convention is organized three weeks later in Tallahassee, and the convention's product is placed before the voters at the next general election (a little less than two years later).

The fourth and most important way in which the Florida Constitution can be revised is through a Constitution Revision Commission. The Commission is composed of: the Attorney General; fifteen members selected by the Governor; nine members selected by the House Speaker; nine members selected by the Senate President; and three members selected by the State Supreme Court. The Chair of the Constitution Revision Commission is designated by the Governor. The Constitution Revision Commission is authorized to place any number of amendments, in any form, including an entirely new constitution, directly to the voters without going through the state Legislature. The first Constitution Revision Commission authorized by the 1968 Constitution met in 1977. The second commission was organized in the spring of 1997, and will submit its proposed revisions in November of 1998. The Constitution Revision Commissions are slated to meet every twenty years unless the constitutional arrangements for this are themselves revised through one of the four methods of constitutional reform discussed above.

Incidentally, the idea for a recurring Constitution Revision Commission came from Thomas Jefferson. In a letter he wrote to Samuel Kercheval, Jefferson expressed concern that the Founding Fathers were becoming too sacralized by the populace. He argued that the Founders had feet of clay and that every political constitution should be overhauled every 20 years. The designers of Florida's 1968 Constitution followed Jefferson's advice.

CONSTITUTIONAL AMENDMENTS SINCE 1969

Between 1968 and 1996, 105 proposed amendments have been put before the Florida voters.[4] Most of these were initiated by the state Legislature. The 1977 Constitution Revision Commission placed eight propositions on the ballot. All eight were rejected.

The failure of the propositions from the 1977 Constitution Revision Commission is attributable to several factors. One reason was the large number of proposals and their complexity. Many of the amendments included multiple subjects, some of which were controversial. Second, the amendments were on the ballot at the same time as a proposal to legalize casino gambling in Florida. Reubin Askew, who was then Governor, devoted most of his time to campaigning against the gambling proposal and therefore was not very active on the other amendments. Third and perhaps most important, the 1977 Commission made at least one radical proposal, which was to eliminate the elected cabinet. Many voters might have been willing to relinquish their ability to vote for a few officials, but most were unwilling to forego voting on all of them.

The events surrounding the recommendation to eliminate the Cabinet are worth recounting, because they provide a glimpse into the politics of constitutional reform. The 1977 Constitution Revision Commission was chaired by Sandy D'Alemberte. Before the Commission's work began, another Commission member, Senator Dempsey Barron, a renowned power broker and strategist in state politics, approached D'Alemberte with a request. He told D'Alemberte that he might be willing to support eliminating the Cabinet but he wanted to make sure that D'Alemberte would side with him if he went out on this limb. D'Alemberte thought he had secured a key ally for something many state leaders wanted to do; he did not realize that Barron was laying a trap.

As the Revision Commission undertook its deliberations, three proposals related to the Cabinet were put forth. On one extreme, some members preferred to make no changes to the Cabinet at all. At the other extreme was Barron's proposal to eliminate the Cabinet altogether. The position in the middle was staked out by former Governor Leroy Collins, who advocated eliminating just a few of the Cabinet offices.

A vote was taken to decide between Barron's approach and the more moderate proposal by Collins. Barron's proposal was supported by exactly half of the members, and Collins' proposal was supported by the other half. The tie had to be broken by the Chair. D'Alemberte was torn, because he knew that Barron's proposal would probably be too extreme for the voters, but he had given Barron his word and had to fulfill his pledge.

The unpopularity of the radical proposal to eliminate the Cabinet may have doomed the rest of the slate of items developed by the 1977 Commission. This is because past voting on constitutional amendments shows that voting tends to be generally positive or generally negative in a given year. In other words, one bad item can turn the electorate against all of the items on the ballot for that year. Figure 16-1 shows the number of amendments on the ballot each year. In general, Presidential election years tend to attract a greater number of amendments than other years.

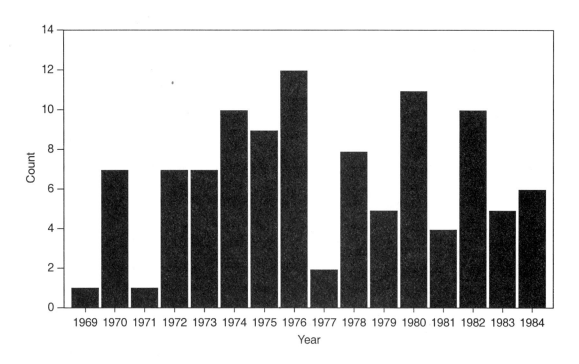

Figure 16-1
TOTAL PROPOSPITIONS PER YEAR

In part this is because political activists sometimes place items on the ballot in an attempt to influence turnout and thereby affect the Presidential vote. Because Florida is almost evenly split between Republicans and Democrats, a small increase in turnout, especially among voters from one party or the other, can have a big impact on the outcome of an election. Figure 16-2 provides of yearly breakdown of the amendments in terms of whether they were endorsed or rejected. Usually, proposed amendments are supported; of the 105 amendments dealt with since 1969, almost 80 were enacted and fewer than 30 were rejected. However, some years were very bad for propositions. A large number of proposed amendments failed in 1970, 1976, and 1978.

Of course, the topics addressed by proposed amendments also makes a difference. Figure 16-3 displays the breakdown of amendments since 1969 with respect to their subject matters. The most common issues are state government procedures. Other issues frequently put before the voters include state finances, the rights of citizens, and local government finance. Figure 16-4 shows the number of amendments that passed and failed within each subject matter area. The highest success rate has been for state tax and finance issues. Most of these propositions placed limits on the ability of state government to tax the citizenry. The voters have been least likely to support propositions that limited government personnel or that altered the rights of citizens.

425

Figure 16-2

Total Number of Amendments Passing and Failing, by Year

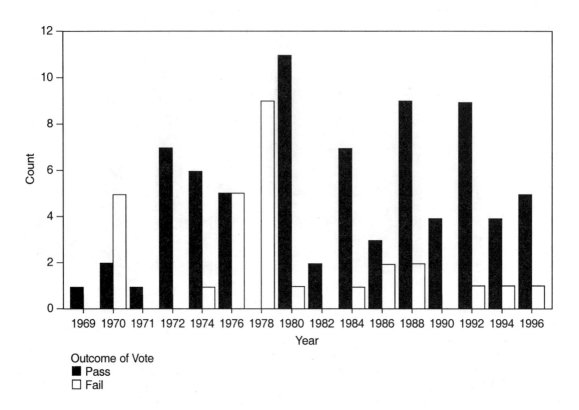

The Electoral Politics of Constitutional Reform

THE ELECTORAL POLITICS OF
CONSTITUTIONAL REFORM

Like other political issues in Florida, proposed constitutional amendments tend to divide voters along geographic lines. A typical split is between urban and rural areas. This was the main division surrounding the proposals from the 1977 Constitution Revision Commission. Figure 16-5 is a map showing the average level of support in Florida counties for all eight propositions. The greatest support was in urban areas, regardless of whether they were predominantly Republican, as in southwest Florida, or predominantly democratic, as in southeast Florida. The least support was in the rural counties of central Florida and the Panhandle. The geographic differences were especially sharp on the issue of the Cabinet. The rural areas probably did not like the idea of eliminating the elected Commissioner of Agriculture.

Geographic divisions more complex than urban-rural are also common, especially if a proposed amendment has the potential to hurt or help some areas much more than others. A good example here is the voting pattern in November, 1996, on the proposed constitutional

Figure 16-3

PROPOSITIONS BROKEN DOWN BY SUBJECT MATTER

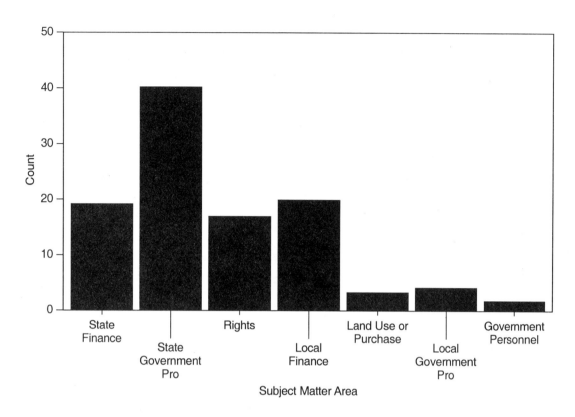

amendments about Everglades pollution. Several propositions related to Everglades cleanup:[5]

- A one cent per pound fee on raw sugar grown in the Everglades to be used for conservation, preservation, and pollution abatement in the Everglades;
- A requirement that those responsible for polluting the Everglades should pay for cleanup; and
- A limitation on voter initiatives to require taxes and fees to be adopted by a two-thirds vote.

The latter amendment was placed on the ballot by supporters of the sugar industry, who opposed the fee on sugar. If enacted, the requirement for a two-thirds majority on new taxes and fees would apply to the sugar fee and therefore would nullify the fee unless it was supported by at least 66 percent of the voters. Analysts doubted that voters would see the connection between the sugar fee and the tax and fee limitation, because it was not obvious that the latter applied to fees and taxes adopted alongside it in the same election. But most observers expected individual citizens to vote consistently either for or against the sugar fee

Figure 16-4
AMENDMENTS PASSING AND FAILING, BY TOPIC

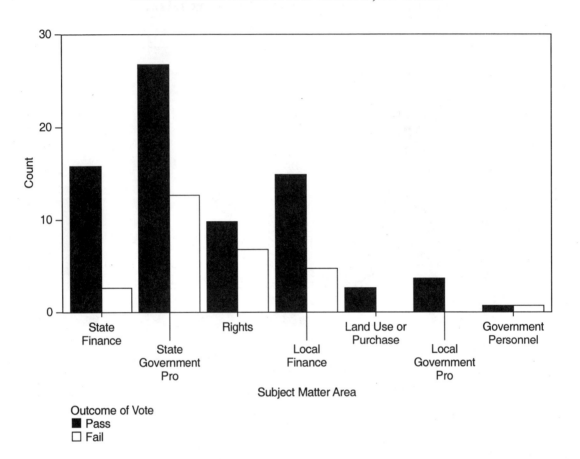

Outcome of Vote
■ Pass
□ Fail

and the mandate to make polluters pay, because both issues clearly applied to the Everglades, and both had similar aims.

In actuality, most voters found a third logic. As anticipated, the tax and fee limitation passed by a wide margin (69.3% yes; 30.7% no).[6] Support was greatest in the Panhandle, around Jacksonville, and in rural central Florida, but the tax and fee limitation was popular everywhere. A majority of voters in each of Florida's sixty-seven counties favored requiring a two-thirds vote on any new taxes and fees placed on the ballot by initiative.

However, voters were less consistent when it came to the propositions on Everglades cleanup. Some voted the same way on both amendments, but a great many voted against one and for the other. The sugar fee failed (45.6% to 54.4%), while the proposal to make polluters pay for cleanup passed (68.1% to 31.9%).

The logic of the voters can be gleaned from the geographic pattern of voting. The map in Figure 16-6 breaks down counties in terms of how they reacted to the two Everglades amendments. The lightest shade is

Figure 16-5
AVERAGE PERCENT SUPPORT FOR 1978 PROPOSITIONS
(The darker the more support; no counties had majority average)

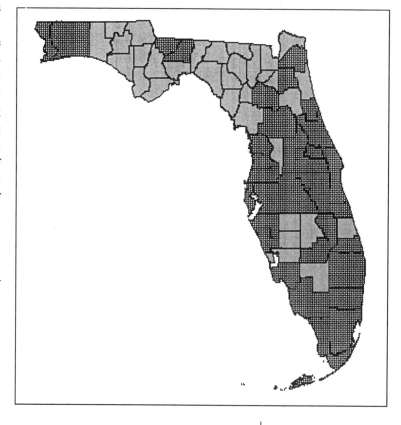

assigned to those counties that voted in favor of both. Note that many of these counties are on the Everglades' periphery. They would not been harmed very much by the sugar fee, but they have been experiencing the problems of Everglades pollution. Hence residents of these counties were more supportive than others of tough cleanup policies, even if such policies hurt agriculture.

At the other extreme are counties where a majority of voters opposed both amendments. These counties have a medium level of shading. As might be expected, counties in opposition to the amendments were those directly in the Everglades and in the most rural parts of the Panhandle and the Big Bend. These are the agricultural centers of the state, and the areas with the least urbanization.

Voters elsewhere appear to have had mixed feelings. The most darkly shaded counties voted against the sugar fee but in favor of making polluters pay. The residents of these counties appear to want the Everglades protected and cleaned up, but they are nevertheless sympathetic to the plight of Everglades farmers.

ISSUES FOR CONSTITUTION REVISION

The issues dominating the constitution revision process of 1997–98 include: the Cabinet system; the initiative process; tax and budget issues; and local government home rule.

The Florida Cabinet. As we have seen, the Constitution Revision Commission of 1977 put an item before the voters to abolish the Cabinet. The 1997 Commission is revisiting this issue. A Citizens

Figure 16-6

ALTERNATIVE APPROACHES TO POLLUTION CLEANUP

(Lightest Shade = Sugar Fee; Medium Shade = Don't Tax the Polluters;
Darkest Shade = Don't Impose Sugar Fee, but Do Make
Polluters Pay for Cleanup)

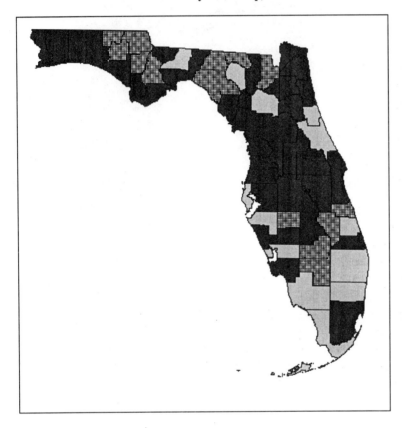

Commission on Cabinet Reform, appointed the Governor and each member of the Cabinet plus the House Speaker and Senate President, met in 1994 and 1995 to review the statutory responsibilities of the Governor and Cabinet and to recommend changes. This was seen as a precursor to examining the Cabinet system from a constitutional, as opposed to a statutory, perspective.

Unfortunately, the issue of the plural executive tends to be treated in fairly narrow, political terms. Those who oppose the Cabinet believe that it costs too much, makes it difficult for the Governor to exert true leadership, and causes inordinate political power to be vested in the non-elected administrators who support the Cabinet officers. Those who support the Cabinet system believe it offers access to the public, assures that any given issue is looked at from many perspectives, and provides a check on potential gubernatorial abuses.

While these are important considerations, the crucial issue from a constitutional perspective concerns the balance between the legislative and executive branches. The Cabinet system is problematic because it weakens the executive branch and tilts the political balance too much toward the legislature. The key to devising reforms to the Cabinet system that will be both salubrious and politically popular is to leave the Cabinet intact but alter its functioning so as to strengthen the executive branch relative to the Legislature.

Several rather minor amendments might do this. One would be to give the Governor veto power over all Cabinet decisions. Currently, statutes allow the Governor a veto in some areas but not others. A second amendment that would help concentrate power in the executive branch would be to constitutionally define the Cabinet's role. As previously stated, the scope and powers of the cabinet system are left open in the 1968 Constitution and have been defined by the Legislature statutorily. Many mundane responsibilities have been assigned to Governor and Cabinet, to the point that their ability to operate as a policy making body has been severely weakened. This could be reversed simply by inserting a sentence into the Constitution stating that the Governor and Cabinet are to deal only with matters of policy and not the details of administration. Although this sentence would still have to be implemented legislatively, the Legislature would at least have a guidepost to follow.

The Initiative Process. As we have seen, the process by which voters can independently place proposed constitutional amendments on the ballot involves gathering signatures in a majority of the state's congressional districts. The process is seen to be fairly cumbersome. Further, a constitutional prohibition that limits any ballot initiative (other than those dealing with taxes) to a single subject has led in many instances to initiatives being declared unconstitutional by the Florida Supreme Court and removed from consideration. The Constitution Revision Commission is considering the issue of whether to relax the initiative process. Those who favor relaxation claim that voters are alienated from government because it has become too far removed and unresponsive to the electorate. Those who oppose relaxing the initiative process argue that it leads to manipulation by special interests, who can use mass media to get anything on the ballot.

Again, these are important considerations, but from a constitutional perspective, the most significant issue is how changes to the initiative process will affect the balance between branches, the accountability of the overall system, and the ability of Florida to develop a sound system of public administration. Loosening the initiative process would move Florida away from representative government and toward direct democracy. A long tradition in political philosophy argues against increasing democracy beyond certain points. These arguments need to be taken into account along with our new historical circumstances and the special circumstances of Florida. Would greater democracy allow us to instill a heightened sense of common purpose and loyalty among Floridians? Would it empower legislators or the Governor to take a tougher stand on difficult issues?

Tax and Budget Issues. Florida has an antiquated tax structure. The 1968 Constitution prohibits a tax on personal income, and it limits the property tax to 10 mills for any unit of local government. Moreover, the first $25,000 of value is exempted from the property tax, which means that units valued less than $25,000 pay no property taxes at all. In contrast, Florida has a very high sales tax. Only eight other states have sales taxes equal to or above Florida's rate of six percent.

Because people are subject to a sales tax regardless of whether they reside or earn their living in the taxing jurisdiction, this reliance on the sales tax was appropriate when Florida was a rural state dominated by tourism and seasonal residents. There were not many residents, but many people visited, spent money, and hence were subject to the tax. However, in a rapidly growing urban state, heavy reliance on a sales tax inevitably leads to the kinds of revenue-shortfalls Florida has been experiencing periodically since the early 1970s. Sales tax revenues rise only gradually with population growth because taxable expenditures per person are relatively constant regardless of the extent of urbanization. Per capita revenues from a six percent sales tax are about $400 whether the state has one million residents or 20 million. In contrast, costs increase rapidly in growing areas because urban facilities and services are much more expensive than their rural equivalents. Waste water treatment plants cost more than septic tanks, SWAT teams and vice squads cost more than road patrols, and highways with overpasses and traffic signals cost more than two-lane roads with stop signs. With costs thus rising faster than revenues, Florida is unable to pay the bill for growth, at least for growth that requires substantial amounts of services but generates limited taxes.

Generally, tax and budget issues in Florida are taken up narrowly in terms of their fiscal impacts. The issues debated are whether proposed changes to the tax structure will meet current and future needs, and the equity of the proposed changes. From a constitutional perspective, these are not the essential questions. Of more importance is the relationship of the tax structure to the overall governmental system. One of the main problems with Florida's current tax structure is that it leads to confusion and a lack of accountability. Because the sales tax is the state's main source of revenues, money flows into the state government, but because many services are essentially local in nature, such as roads, schools, parks, and libraries, the state government reallocates much of these revenues back to local units. Although this allows for some equalization of opportunity in school districts across urban and rural areas, this advantage is more than off set by the weak connection between taxes and expenditures. Voters are taxed in one place while they receive services elsewhere, and naturally they are alarmed by the growth of state government, the complexity of intergovernmental relations locally, and other phenomenon which they could not possibly understand.

The real need in Florida is not so much for a certain level of taxation as for a tax structure that provides clear and direct connections between taxes and services. This means that governments delivering certain services must be empowered to levy taxes to pay for those services, rather than having to derive funds from another level of government. It also means that the form of taxation should fit its function.

Local Home Rule. Home rule in Florida is in serious need of reform and expansion. Over the past century and a half since Florida became a state, the powers of local government have experienced periods of dramatic expansion and contraction. The 1838 Constitution was very much pro-city. During this period Florida was the only state in the nation in which municipalities could be incorporated without state legislative action. Counties were viewed as extensions of the state and mainly dealt with courts and sheriffs. The 1868 Constitution was also favorable to local government. It required state regulation of local government to be carried out by general law. This meant that individual local governments could not be singled out for special treatment either positive or negative. With respect to home rule, the 1885 constitution reversed this course. The requirement for general laws to regulate local governments was removed, and the state Legislature was vested with authority to control all local government activities. The 1968 Constitution returned to the state's initial home rule orientation, but, as we have seen, its home rule provisions have not had all of their desired effects. In particular, the extension and formation of municipalities has lagged far behind urbanization, and the state has witnessed a proliferation of special purpose districts.

In preparation for the 1997–98 constitution revision process, a gubernatorial commission was established to make recommendations for reforming local government in Florida. The commission included 21 appointees: two by the Speaker of the House, two by the President of the Senate, 13 by the Governor representing local government, and four by the Governor to represent issues relating to local government. The thirteen appointees representing local government were comprised of five representatives of counties, five representatives of cities, two representatives of special districts, and one representative of public schools.

The Constitution Revision Commission is considering a number of reforms of home rule. One is an expansion of the autonomy of general purpose local governments. Cities and counties should be given authority to levy taxes with voter approval and spend their revenues according to local preferences. A second need is for counties and cities to be given authority over the special districts underlying them. As long as special districts remain as creatures of the state Legislature, they will continue

433

to be a source of duplication and conflict at the local level. Third, processes are needed to facilitate annexation, incorporation, and the transfer of services from smaller units of local governments to larger units. As Florida's population continues to grow, its local governments must be kept abreast of urbanization.

CONCLUSION

Floridians are fortunate to have a strong say in the constitution that governs them. But to take advantage of the constitution revision process, they must have a fairly clear picture of their aims and priorities. If their designs become too detailed and complex, as happened in 1977, the whole effort can fail, because when a large and complicated package of proposals is placed before the voters, everyone will find something to dislike. Instead, the Constitution Revision Commission needs to limit its work to fundamental reforms on which most people can easily agree. Highest priority should probably be given to strengthening local governments and the executive branch. A few changes in these areas could help unify the electorate so that many other, more detailed issues could be resolved legislatively.

REFERENCE

1.   deHaven-Smith, Lance (1995). *The Florida voter.* Tallahassee: Florida Institute of Government.

ENDNOTES

1.   For a detailed discussion of Florida's six constitutions, see Allen Morris, *The Florida Handbook,* 1995–96 (Tallahassee: The Peninsular Publishing Company, 1995), pp. 676–680.

2.   To gain insight into the development and workings of the cabinet system over the past twenty-five years since it was modified under the 1968 Constitution, a series of interviews was conducted by Dr. deHaven-Smith with many of Florida's top leaders while he was Director of the Citizens' Commission on Cabinet Reform. These included former Governors, former Cabinet officers, current and former Cabinet Aides, current and former staff in the Governor's Office, academics with special expertise on the Cabinet system, the heads of agencies reporting to the Governor and Cabinet, one of Florida's U.S. Senators and a former Governor, lobbyists who deal frequently with the Cabinet system, the heads of civic groups who regularly appear before the Cabinet, and others. This section is based on these interviews.

3.   Article XI, Florida Constitution.

4. What follows is a list of the amendments. This list was the basis for Figures 16-1 through 16-4.

YEAR	AMENDMENT	FOR	AGAINST	OUTCOME
1969	Bonds for Higher Education	291,112	0,112,795	Pass
1970	Voting Age	501,764	754,282	
1970	Legal Majority at 18	422,450	799,885	
1970	Bonds for Sewerage	816,629	331,250	Pass
1970	Term of Office for House	435,052	675,473	
1970	Article V	503,992	526,328	
1970	Sovereignty Lands`	680,223	429,917	Pass
1970	School Construction Bonds	488,442	650,500	
1971	Corporate Income Tax	841,433	355,023	Pass
1972	Bonds for College	877,346	467,525	Pass
1972	Florida Court Structure	969,741	401,861	Pass
1972	Environmental Bonds	1,256,292	509,679	Pass
1972	Homestead	1,137,735	555,426	Pass
1972	Motor Vehicle License Tax	1,191,118	531,520	Pass
1972	Bonds	1,284,817	474,514	Pass
1972	Initiative Amendment	1,157,648	476,165	Pass
1974	Game & Fish Commission	859,513	366,993	Pass
1974	Tax Assessor Name Change	722,872	534,052	Pass
1974	Pledging Public Credit	658,869	246,305	Pass
1974	Protection of Handicapped	974,892	300,633	Pass
1974	Capital Outlay Projects	864,075	447,571	Pass
1974	Motor Fuel Bonds	547,572	695,379	
1974	Judicial Qualifications Comm	945,869	264,305	Pass
1976	Water Management	735,174	600,066	Pass
1976	Judicial Qualifications Comm	1,514,623	564,441	Pass
1976	Retirement	1,262,413	756,049	Pass
1976	Capitol and Mansion Comm	619,151	1,433,878	
1976	Merit Selection & Retention	1,600,944	527,056	Pass
1976	State Employees	986,727	1,074,822	
1976	Bonds	974,184	1,023,416	
1976	Bonds	949,480	1,099,055	
1976	Administrative Rules	729,400	1,210,001	
1976	Public Disclosure Initiative	1,765,626	461,940	Pass
1978	CRC Basic Document	623,703	1,512,106	
1978	Declaration of Rights	1,002,479	1,326,497	
1978	Legislative	982,847	1,113,394	
1978	Abolition of Cabinet	540,979	2,155,609	
1978	PSC	722,066	2,147,614	
1978	Circuit Court Judges	1,058,574	1,095,736	
1978	Finance and Taxation	779,389	1,368,346	
1978	Education	771,282	1,353,626	
1978	Casino Gambling	687,460	1,720,275	
1980	Homestead Exemption	1,880,729	475,834	Pass
1980	Jurisdiction of Sup. Ct.	940,420	420,266	Pass
1980	Bonds for Housing	826,742	618,694	Pass
1980	Tax Assessment of Agric.	1,003,979	442,386	Pass
1980	Renewable Energy Source	1,042,685	347,766	Pass
1980	Economic Development Tax Exe	916,043	541,630	Pass
1980	Homestead Exemption	1,251,096	289,620	Pass
1980	Abolishing CRC	1,164,824	1,512,682	
1980	Water Facilities St. Bonds	1,826,026	899,906	Pass

1980	Right of Privacy	1,722,987	1,120,302	Pass
1980	Passage of Bills	1,763,624	873,211	Pass
1980	2nd Gax Tax	1,498,801	1,195,483	Pass
1982	Search and Seizure	1,440,523	828,571	Pass
1982	Pretrial Release & Detention	1,412,269	917,092	Pass
1984	Homestead Exemption	2,766,516	734,785	Pass
1984	Disbursement of State funds	2,467,025	919,675	Pass
1984	Legislative speech and debat	1,110,743	2,216,910	
1984	St. Capital Projects Bonds	2,095,916	1,109,900	Pass
1984	Public Education Capital Out	2,553,332	778,114	Pass
1984	Eligibility for County Court	2,529,436	823,219	Pass
1984	Election of Co. Comm.	2,150,510	1,195,654	Pass
1984	Procedures of the JNC	2,720,297	590,960	Pass
1986	Statewide Prosecutor	2,168,701	811,122	Pass
1986	Homestead	1,127,438	2,045,473	
1986	Sup.Ct. Advisory Plans	1,988,841	759,691	Pass
1986	Lottery	2,039,437	1,168,858	Pass
1986	Casino Gambling	1,036,250	2,237,555	
1988	Impeachment of Co. Judges	2,840,296	1,840,751	Pass
1988	Rights of Crime Victims	3,629,963	394,617	Pass
1988	Assessment of highwater rech	2,423,783	1,187,303	Pass
1988	Road & Bridge Const. Bonds	2,141,987	1,602,965	Pass
1988	Tax Exemption	3,415,074	593,913	Pass
1988	Tax & Budget Comm.	2,111,320	1,538,470	Pass
1988	Trial Judge Office Term	1,493,839	2,444,181	
1988	Civil Traffic Hrg. Officers	2,736,373	1,147,126	Pass
1988	Dept. of Veterans Affairs	2,723,848	1,225,915	Pass
1988	Liability Cap on Damages	1,837,041	2,394,932	
1988	English Only	3,457,039	664,861	Pass
1990	Legislative Session	2,615,449	513,970	Pass
1990	Handgun Waiting period	2,840,912	552,248	Pass
1990	Local Expenditures and Reve	2,031,557	1,104,745	Pass
1990	Open Government	2,795,784	392,323	Pass
1992	Tax Exemption	2,908,730	1,752,480	Pass
1992	Bonds	3,089,042	1,461,429	Pass
1992	General Elections	3,369,416	1,337,284	Pass
1992	Access to Public Records	3,883,617	793,229	Pass
1992	Homestead Initiative	2,493,742	2,154,747	Pass
1992	Term Limit Initiative	3,625,500	1,097,127	Pass
1992	Appropriations Act	3,815,541	796,462	Pass
1992	Taxpayer Bill of Rights	4,258,422	472,324	Pass
1992	One-cent Sales Tax	1,886,490	2,824,442	
1992	Tax Exemptions	2,713,189	955,223	Pass
1994	Term of Regular Session	2,713,189	955,223	Pass
1994	State Revenue Collection	2,182,411	1,489,268	Pass
1994	Limited Casino	1,566,451	2,555,492	
1994	Multiple Subject	2,167,305	1,560,635	Pass
1994	Marine Net Fishing	2,876,091	1,135,110	Pass
1996	Tax Limitation	3,372,915	1,497,485	Pass
1996	CRC	2,733,993	1,720,193	Pass
1996	Judiciary	3,436,753	1,153,367	Pass
1996	Sugar Fee for Everglades	2,328,016	2,774,806	
1996	Everglades Abatement	3,397,286	1,594,175	Pass
1996	Everglades Trust Fund	2,825,819	2,108,286	Pass

5. The actual ballot summaries are as follows:

    Constitutional Amendment Article XI, Section 7 (Initiative) Ballot Title: Tax Limitation: Should Two-thirds Vote be Required for New Constitutionally-imposed State Taxes/fees?

    Ballot Summary: Prohibits imposition of new State taxes or fees on or after November 8, 1994 by constitutional amendment unless approved by two-thirds of the voters voting in the election. Defines "new State taxes or fees" as revenue subject to appropriation by State Legislature, which tax or fee is not in effect on November 7, 1994. Applies to proposed State tax and fee amendments on November 8, 1994 ballot and those on later ballots.

    Constitutional Amendment Article VII, Section 9 (Initiative) Ballot Title: Fee on Everglades Sugar Production

    Ballot Summary: Provides that the South Florida Water Management District shall levy an Everglades Sugar Fee of 1¢ per pound on raw sugar grown in the Everglades Agricultural Area to raise funds to be used, consistent with statutory law, for purposes of conservation and protection of natural resources and abatement of water pollution in the Everglades. The fee is imposed for twenty-five years.

    Constitutional Amendment Article II, Section 7 (Initiative)

    Ballot Title: Responsibility for Paying Costs of Water Pollution Abatement in the Everglades

    Ballot Summary: The Constitution currently provides the authority for the abatement of water pollution. This proposal adds a provision to provide that those in the Everglades Agricultural Area who cause water pollution within the Everglades Protection Area or the Everglades Agricultural Area shall be primarily responsible for paying the costs of the abatement of that pollution.

6. Following is the percent supporting each amendment, by county:

	MAKE POLL. PAY	SUGAR FEE	TAX LIMIT
Alachua	69.92	51.97	62.92
Baker	20.19	21.89	70.84
Bay	62.14	29.81	76.20
Bradford	54.56	27.60	74.42
Brevard	68.95	47.07	71.99
Broward	76.44	58.66	66.91
Calhoun	39.00	19.32	67.02
Charlotte	70.20	50.13	70.18
Citrus	69.72	47.84	65.45
Clay	59.92	34.58	81.42
Collier	72.14	54.11	67.95
Columbia	53.84	31.15	71.30
Dade	70.33	42.96	65.15
DeSoto	50.50	33.14	72.32
Dixie	50.45	29.90	66.26
Duval	61.51	32.79	79.09
Escambia	65.61	40.98	74.50
Flagler	74.83	56.91	70.03

Franklin	56.36	30.99	68.31
Gadsden	56.73	36.11	64.20
Gilchrist	54.30	24.69	71.84
Glades	31.66	22.08	74.22
Gulf	50.72	19.72	70.58
Hamilton	40.44	18.88	67.55
Hardee	41.11	23.44	71.21
Hendry	20.26	12.19	79.15
Hernando	69.44	48.82	67.63
Highlands	56.52	37.24	68.51
Hillsborough	69.71	46.10	66.26
Holmes	39.40	15.38	64.08
Indian River	12.09	37.98	73.17
Jackson	47.13	18.08	70.29
Jefferson	52.57	32.29	63.16
Lafayette	31.39	14.37	64.04
Lake	63.03	41.19	72.29
Lee	61.16	40.02	74.26
Leon	72.14	50.27	65.24
Levy	56.24	33.03	71.99
Liberty	37.19	19.71	61.21
Madison	46.30	22.97	65.19
Manatee	71.02	51.52	64.25
Marion	61.35	37.06	71.58
Martin	60.98	44.89	64.56
Monroe	82.58	69.49	73.20
Nassau	61.55	33.66	77.58
Okaloosa	64.57	38.72	77.38
Okeechobee	38.55	24.00	74.30
Orange	68.59	43.91	70.99
Osceola	64.22	39.43	72.73
Palm Beach	68.22	51.22	65.54
Pasco	70.73	46.98	69.11
Pinellas	75.79	52.62	67.70
Polk	56.40	32.89	68.97
Putnam	61.96	33.78	75.19
St. Johns	66.92	39.32	76.78
St. Lucie	75.41	55.66	63.44
Santa Rosa	67.34	44.95	69.55
Sarasota	70.29	44.89	82.36
Seminole	63.13	39.19	72.95
Sumter	58.16	36.84	72.29
Suwanee	42.81	20.85	71.80
Taylor	42.26	24.77	60.66
Union	45.11	24.02	70.70
Volusia	72.87	50.44	70.26
Wakulla	56.14	35.32	67.39
Walton	51.30	26.48	71.06
Washington	38.65	17.92	64.00

PART VI

CONCLUSIONS

THE UNFINISHED BUSINESS OF EXECUTIVE LEADERSHIP AND INSTITUTIONAL REFORM
A DEVELOPING VISION FOR FLORIDA

RICHARD CHACKERIAN AND WILLIAM EARLE KLAY

This book began with the assertion that Florida's government and policies reflect discontinuity emerging from rapid growth and change. Demographic and economic changes since World War II have been enormous. Unfortunately these changes have not been accompanied by changes in the dominant vision that has guided the state throughout the past century. In this chapter we will discuss that vision as well as an alternate vision of the state's future that has been emerging over the past two decades.

The 20th century has been a period in which wealth has largely been obtained through industrialization. In the late 19th and early 20th centuries, Florida's leaders became acutely aware that it lacked many of the requisites for industrial development. It lacked ores and fossil fuels; it is a great distance from the large marketplaces of the North; its people lived in the midst of inhospitable wetlands that spawned malaria and yellow fever; and it had a small population that was both poor and poorly educated. Even agricultural development was hampered by the sandy soils that predominate in the peninsula. Florida did have great expanses of inexpensive land, much of it along beautiful beaches, in the nation's only subtropical peninsula. Beginning in the Bourbon era of the late 19th century, Florida's leaders began to fashion a vision—namely, to sell people on the idea of coming to Florida to spur economic development.

The state set about to foster development in a variety of ways. The first step was to provide land to developers—giving it free to the great railroad builders like Plant and Flagler and selling it cheaply to those who promised to drain the swamps. Hamilton Disston was sold four million acres for one million dollars in 1881 in exchange for promises to drain land. To encourage persons of means to relocate, the constitutional prohibition of income and inheritance taxation was adopted in the 1920's. The income tax prohibition suited a state with a tradition of minimalist government dating back to the Bourbon era of the 1880's. Trying to turn the state's poverty into an advantage, its leaders promoted a constitutional change in the 1940's to assure the "right to work" without paying union dues, thereby assuring prospective employers that wages would likely remain lower than those in more unionized states. Coastal wetlands were rapidly dredged and filled beginning in 1913 with Carl Fisher's creation of Miami Beach, and the filling continued, virtually without restriction, in such areas as Pinellas and Pasco counties, for half a century.

The "development vision" was widely shared by Florida's leaders throughout much of the 20th century. The vision to "sell sun and sand" succeeded in a startling fashion. From a population of slightly more than a half million in 1900, the state grew to nearly 13 million in 1990 and that number may double by the first half of the 21st century! Not surprisingly, doubts began to rise about the adequacy of the state's policies to provide a satisfying life style. With these doubts emerged an alternative to the prevailing vision of virtually unrestricted development and minimal public services. The alternative vision remains emergent but it has several identifiable characteristics which suggest the vision of "stewardship."

A consequence of the development vision, rooted as it was in the Bourbon concept of minimalist government, has been under investment in human resources. Florida traditionally has spent less for education and training than other states and makes less tax effort. More recently, some measures show that spending for public schools approaches the national average, reflecting the emerging vision of stewardship. Most observers agree that success in a highly competitive global economy will depend upon brainpower, yet Florida entered the final decade of the 20th century spending less per pupil on higher education than did any other state in the nation. The continuance of the Bourbon concept of government has placed Florida near the bottom of the states in human capital investment and at the top of states in the incidence of crime, suicide, and other indicators of social disorganization (see Chapter 1).

The development vision brought enormous growth, and the state has innovated in some ways to cope. Naisbitt (1982) could say in 1982 that Florida is a cutting-edge state; that much of what is new and innovative happens first in Florida and later appears in other states. There have been some significant changes. Perhaps the most significant was the 1969 revision of the state constitution. The revision followed the model of traditional administrative reform by reducing the number of government agencies and enhancing the authority of the governor in several ways. The 1968 consolidation of Jacksonville and Duval County and the Metropolitan Dade County "two tier" government adopted in 1957 were

THE UNFINISHED
BUSINESS OF
EXECUTIVE
LEADERSHIP AND
INSTITUTIONAL
REFORM

innovative and probably had a positive effect on the quality of government services.

In the 1970's, Florida was among the nation's leaders in growth management and in the consolidation and de-institutionalization of social services. Florida was also recognized as a leader in such educational policy initiatives as testing of teachers and imposing expanded curriculum requirements for high school graduation. The "sunshine laws" were an important innovation of the Askew administration, although it is not evident that they have resulted in better policy or in greater public confidence in government (see Chapter 1). On principle in a democratic society, they should be regarded as a positive change. Florida has achieved national recognition in the area of information resource management.

It would be a mistake, however, to equate such innovations with the demise of the older guiding vision. Innovation in certain critical areas has been very slow to non-existent. Revenue policy innovation (see Chapter 14) has been particularly difficult with two innovations—the unitary tax and the services tax—quickly reversed. In spite of the adoption of the corporate income tax during the Askew administration, Florida's revenue structure does not keep pace with the growth of the state's economy, and it is unfair because it places a disproportionate burden on the poor. As Grizzle noted (Chapter 9) "This generation's low tax burden will translate into the next generation's lower quality of life."

There has been much discussion of civil service reform but the results, at best, have been mixed. Florida has historically been reluctant to adopt modern human resources management. It was not until the 1940s that Governor Millard Caldwell's leadership finally established the basis for a merit system. Florida's personnel system, however, has never been allowed to reflect anything more than the individualistic values of the old vision. Selection for entry level jobs did come to be based somewhat on merit concepts, but the notion that there could be a true public service, working in the broader interests of the community, has never emerged in Florida. Evidence of this is the fact that funding for training, an investment in the future quality of a public service, has never been more than rudimentary. Virtually no emphasis has been given to executive development and selection, and no one has been very happy with the Senior Management Service or the Selected Exempt Service. The notion that career public servants can be trained to become valued policy advisors to elected officials is alien.

When Florida decided, in the Graham administration, to establish a Selected Exempt Service, all members of that service were removed from the career system and made to work at the pleasure of their appointing executives. Political responsiveness, rather than the development of a career system that can produce top quality executives, is the goal of the system (see Chapter 7). Florida's senior executives now work in a system in which it can be said that "it is every person for himself." This is quite different from senior executive services in the federal government and some other state governments where the senior service is mostly seen as the highest and best extension of the career service. Rather than reflecting communitarian values, Florida's senior service reflects the individualistic values of the earlier vision.

Continuity of leadership is necessary to have successful planned change. In Florida, leadership is discontinuous in all three branches. The Cabinet has provided continuity, but it generally is not a source of innovation (see Chapter 4). The Chief Justice of the State Supreme Court serves only for two years and legislative leaders are similarly limited. Since Florida entered statehood in 1845, custom has almost always limited Senate presidents and speakers of the House to two year terms. One of these powerful "two-year supreme commanders" (see Chapter 5) can accomplish much, but only if the governor and other legislative "commanders" are of like minds. Likewise, a governor can be most effective only when the legislative leadership is either supportive or at the very least acquiescent. Even when one-party Democratic rule prevailed, it was extraordinary difficult to obtain the simultaneous backing of the governor and legislative leaders for policy initiatives.

Numerous examples exist to underscore the importance of likemindedness among the state's powerful, and typically independent, leaders. Constitutional revision in 1968 was the product of state and national supreme court decisions on reapportionment, progressive leadership in the state legislature and the consent of Governor Claude Kirk. The reorganization of human services in the early 1970s was initiated by legislative leaders who received support from Governor Rubin Askew. The governor played a more important part in growth management and in the corporate income tax during the Askew administration, but legislative leadership also played an important role in these policies.

Florida's governors typically reflect the moderately conservative ideology of a public which is suspicious of government intervention and which prizes individual rather than collective effort (see Chapter 3). This political culture, combined with the short terms of the various institutional leaders, creates a low likelihood that there will be powerful and likeminded leadership in the various branches at the same time. The result is non-action. Recently adopted term limits will make all of this worse because they force rotation in office. The important policy innovations in the state's history (i.e., constitutional reform, social services reform, and growth management reform) demonstrate that in Florida an unusual interinstitutional like-mindedness is required for innovative policy adoption. Such like-mindedness is even less likely to occur when there is not a shared vision among the state's leaders. Today the development and stewardship visions compete.

SOME REQUISITES FOR CHANGE: MOVING BEYOND THE PAST

Governments exist, in principle, to deal with the problems citizens cannot deal with individually. Florida's problems are very significant and in many respects getting worse. The crises faced by Florida's governments are, in part, due to the speed with which social and economic change has taken place. They are also due to the fact that, until recently, Florida was a poor state and lacked the resources to respond adequately to public problems. Florida now ranks slightly above the national average in per capita personal income but its revenue system has not kept abreast of the state's economic growth.

The window of moderate resource abundance may be passing because of the enormous costs of social disorganization. The two biggest items driving the state budget in the early 1990's was medical care and prison costs which soaked up most of the tax revenue growth. In the late 1990's economic prosperity has reduced the pressure on government budgets, but the inevitable economic down turn will come and Floridians will once again see the effects of an inadequate tax base. Development, Florida's policy vision, and the encouragement of population growth which is associated with it, shows the early signs of change. Many now realize that the benefits of growth tend to be highly focused and that it is associated with significant public costs (viz., taxes). Growth also multiplies the government decisions that must be made, in some cases exhausting the capacity to decide in a deliberate and considered way. The attempt to control growth through state imposed growth management policies is an important transitional phase to a new vision for Florida which depends less of natural resources and its associated emphasis on population growth.

Florida's Legislature has been a source of important initiatives, but the institutionalized transience of its leaders prevents the Legislature from sustaining a policy vision. In the 1980s a succession of House speakers used advisory committees on the future to help them formulate an anticipatory policy agenda, but that initiative was discontinued after Jon Mills' speakership.

As we discussed in Chapter 4, and demonstrated in the case histories of Chapter 14, executive leadership is a key ingredient to successful policy initiatives in Florida. The Legislature was the source of the important 1968 constitutional revisions. But, legislatures normally are institutionally incapable of providing a new and sustained policy vision. Only strong executive leadership can counter the strong centrifugal political forces in Florida to forge a policy vision more consistent with the changed environment. Vision and legislation unfortunately are not enough. The executive must also have the capacity to implement policies, something that too many assume to be automatic. A major portion of this book is devoted to "Systems of Implementation." In Florida we have suggested, these systems are in disarray. Recent governors have understood that much needs to be done to improve the leadership of government executives and to make the executive branch more innovative and response to public needs. Unfortunately they have used a private sector model to start the process of executive change.

Recent governors have sense that much needs to be done to improve the leadership of government executives and to make the executive branch more innovative and responsive to public needs. Unfortunately they have naively followed a private-sector model of management which has created severe problems. The removal of increasingly larger proportions of state managers from the civil service system has discouraged professionalism in the public service. Simply removing personnel-related constraints while neglecting the development of a high quality work force can lead to a range of consequences many of which are not desirable.

The disciplining factors on discretion in the public service come from legal standards for political neutrality, normative commitments to public service and from cognitive standards of professional practice. Relatedly, when appointments to positions are exempted from civil service protection, they should not be exempted, as is too often the case in Florida, from public service commitment and professional preparation.

In Florida, as is true elsewhere, there are continuing pressures to establish performance criteria for government programs and to tap the power of incentives by rewarding programs and individuals on the basis of performance. Doing so is far more difficult in government than in the private sector. These difficulties were first explored in a series of articles, beginning in 1936, by Nobel Prize winner Herbert Simon (Simon & Ridley 1943). In spite of these difficulties, the emphasis on accountability and incentives should not be discouraged. Advances in computer-based information systems will allow the expansion of performance-based systems. However, the inherent ambiguity and complexity

THE UNFINISHED
BUSINESS OF
EXECUTIVE
LEADERSHIP AND
INSTITUTIONAL
REFORM

of government action, together with the resistance in our culture to rewarding groups of public servants for jobs well done, suggest that neither accountability efforts nor intermittent incentives schemes will yield outstanding service. A culture of public service commitment and a commensurate emphasis on employee development remain the bulwark of administrative improvement.

Change in current attitudes toward a career service will be difficult. Existing attitudes presume that a conflict exists between having a strong career service and having loyalty to elected officials. For elected officials to accomplish policy initiatives, it is essential that public servants be highly responsive to those initiatives. A well functioning democracy needs a responsive public service. When subordinates are not completely dependent on their personal relationship to their superiors, there is a perceived risk of disloyalty. Loyalty—without proven competence in administering programs and a demonstrated commitment to serving the public—is itself risky to elected officials. Loyalty to political leadership did not serve the governor well in 1993 when the Department of Health and Rehabilitative Services[1] computer system made nearly a quarter of a billion dollars in overpayments. Neither a governor nor the immediate staff should devote scarce time and energy to fighting administrative fires.

Another cost of the current system of political appointments for bureau chiefs, division directors, and other executives is that is discourages risk taking. If a major criterion for executive positions is personal support and loyalty, it becomes exceedingly difficult for the state's executives to be critical or to take risks. These qualities are much more possible in an executive branch where professional accomplishment and commitment to public service are the standards by which individuals and careers are judged. Personal loyalty, if carried to the extreme that now exists in Florida, tends to divert energies to bureaucratic politics, that is, to making the boss look good, to expanding one's cadre of personal loyalists, and to seeking the rewards of political success.

The importance of career public servants will be heightened now that term limits have taken effect. We enter an era in which no Senate President of Speaker of the House will have had more than six years of experience in their respective chambers when they assume their posts. More rapid turnover of Cabinet members suggests that turnover in their political appointees will increase. In the agencies under the direct control of the governor, the average tenure of appointed agency heads and their subordinates is already much less than that of the governors who appoint them. In such an environment, the importance of institutional memory will grow. Without such memory, the likelihood of repeating past mistakes increases.

There are no uncomplicated routes to government reform. Professionalism and indeed even the idea of public service commitment have detractors. Bureaucratic personnel systems are vehicles for inflexible, nonresponsive government. Florida has had a centralized, bureaucratic personnel system. The intransigence of this system precipitated the efforts of several administrations to devolve personnel management responsibilities to the agencies. Many of these responsibilities should remain in the agencies. Florida, however, had never had a true career service system—one in which careful attention is given to the identification and training of its most promising members for ever greater responsibilities. Creation of such a system requires the recognition that the long term interests of the community require an investment of resources. There is reason to hope that the emergence of a sense of stewardship will give rise to a true career public service.

In 1993 the National Commission on the State and Local Public Service issued *Hard Truths/Tough Choices: An Agenda for State and Local Reform* (National Commission 1993). A key set of recommendations deals with the need for "stronger executive leadership" (15–20). The essence of these recommendations is that more power should be given to governors by reducing the structural fragmentation. Additional structural reform would likely help to improve Florida's governments. An energized executive branch, however, also requires a professional and committed public service. The governor not only needs power, s/he also needs help (Sherwood & Chackerian 1988).

These recommendations seem to run counter to the current trend toward decentralization. But in fact they are supportive of that trend, especially when seen in an intergovernmental context. The recommendation to increase executive power might be criticized on the ground that it will lead to slower communications, increased organizational complexity, and even to stagnation, slow decision making, inefficiency, and ineffectiveness. These consequences are much less likely if enhanced executive authority is accompanied by changes in intergovernmental relations. Local governments in Florida are highly constrained by the state (Chapter 11, 12, 13, and 16), particularly in fiscal matters. If the state pursues a policy of giving greater discretion to local governments, this could reduce the complexity of the state's role and help stabilize the size of state government. Enhanced local discretion must include more flexibility in how local governments are allowed to raise revenues. State mandates to local governments are deeply resented for a variety of reasons, but particularly because local sources of revenue are tightly controlled by the state.

THE UNFINISHED
BUSINESS OF
EXECUTIVE
LEADERSHIP AND
INSTITUTIONAL
REFORM

Effective decentralization requires that state government depend more on both local governments and the private sector, especially upon not-for-profit organizations. The history of organizational reforms has demonstrated that neither centralization nor decentralization is a panacea. The weaknesses of either model can give rise to pressures to move in the other direction. If the decentralization of state government is accompanied by local fiscal mismanagement, political favoritism, or local intolerance of social diversity, a recentralized government may gain strength. If the current efforts to achieve decentralization are to succeed, the state government must be of exceptional quality. The core state agencies must be staffed by dedicated public servants who know how to create and operate effective systems for planning, information management, and evaluation. Especially, there must be public servants who can manage an extensive system of contracting with service providers and keep that system incorruptibly free from political spoils.

Our vision of Florida's future, then, is one in which policy priorities shift from the short-term development of the physical environment to development of the human resources in our communities and governments. A stronger state executive and more decentralization to local governments also are desperately needed in America's fourth largest state.

REFERENCES

Naisbitt, John (1982). *Megatrends: Ten new directions transforming our lives.* New York: Warner Books.

National Commission on the State and Local Public Service (1994). *Hard truths/tough choices: an agenda for state and local reform.* Albany, NY: State University of New York—Albany, Rockefeller Center.

Sherwood, Frank, & Richard Chackerian (1988). The governor and the transition: getting help and power. *Public Productivity Review, 12* (2).

Simon, H.A., & C.A. Ridley (1943). *Measuring municipal activities: A survey of suggested criteria for appraising administration.* Chicago: International City Manager's Association.

Walker, Jack L. (1971). Innovation in state politics in the American states: A comparative analysis. In Herbert Jacob & Kenneth N. Vines (Eds.), *Politics in the American States: A Comparative Analysis.* Boston: Little, Brown and Company.

CHAPTER

17

INDEX

A

M

R

S

INDEX